江苏省高等学校重点教材

编号2021-2-288

翻译理论与实践教程

主　审　杜争鸣
主　编　陈胜利
副主编　马　宾
编　委　（按姓氏笔画排序）
　　　　于应机　王金华　李震红
　　　　杨　婳　庞学通　孟祥春

苏州大学出版社
Soochow University Press

图书在版编目(CIP)数据

翻译理论与实践教程/陈胜利主编. --苏州:苏州大学出版社, 2024.11. -- ISBN 978-7-5672-5009-3

Ⅰ. H059

中国国家版本馆 CIP 数据核字第 202482YE46 号

书　　名:	翻译理论与实践教程
	FANYI LILUN YU SHIJIAN JIAOCHENG
主　　编:	陈胜利
策划编辑:	汤定军
责任编辑:	汤定军
装帧设计:	吴　钰
出版发行:	苏州大学出版社
社　　址:	苏州市十梓街 1 号　邮编:215006
印　　装:	苏州市古得堡数码印刷有限公司
网　　址:	www.sudapress.com
邮　　箱:	sdcbs@ suda.edu.cn
邮购热线:	0512-67480030
销售热线:	0512-67481020
开　　本:	787 mm×1 092 mm　1/16　印张:19.5　字数:451 千
版　　次:	2024 年 11 月第 1 版
印　　次:	2024 年 11 月第 1 次印刷
书　　号:	ISBN 978-7-5672-5009-3
定　　价:	68.00 元

凡购本社图书发现印装错误,请与本社联系调换。服务热线:0512-67481020

前 言

为什么学习英汉互译?

亲爱的同学,亲爱的读者:

谢谢你们怀着对英汉互译的兴趣翻开这本很可能让你们受益终身的书。在正式开始讨论翻译的具体问题之前,我们首先想强调说明以下几点:

1. 英语和汉语是全世界使用人数最多、使用范围最广的两种语言,在各种情况下把英语或汉语作为母语、第二语言和外国语使用的人数几乎占到了世界人口的一半,而且正在呈几何级数增长。语言与文化方面的观察家们认为,随着时代的进一步发展,尤其是随着中国社会的进一步国际化,英汉两种语言之间的翻译将成为全世界信息网络翻译的主要领域。因此,如果你们掌握了英汉这两种人类使用最多的语言及了解其文化背景,又能在两者之间进行必要的翻译,那么在当代社会你们不会成为落伍者;在国际政治、经济、科学、艺术交流日益频繁,全球主义文化成为时代主旋律的新时代,你们一定能找到自己的用武之地。

2. 从事翻译,需要具备扎实的语言功底,但这绝不意味着只要两种语言功底好就无需学习翻译技能。假如你们真正掌握了两种方言,你们就会知道,把一种方言翻译成另一种方言并非易事:有时候一种方言中的词语很难在另一种方言中找到完全对应的词语。方言之间尚且如此,在中西两种语系不同的语种之间进行翻译其难度可想而知。不同的语言有不同的产生、发展的社会文化背景,人类对世界万物的理解与思维方式不同,因此语言结构体系也有差异,其间的概念与各种形式关系并非整齐划一地个个对应,常常难以对号入座。同时,由于语言在具体的语境中使用时千变万化,无论什么双语词典也都无法解决翻译中所有的具体问题。所以,一个人即使熟练地掌握了两种语言,可以分别在其中任何一种语言体系中纵横自如,但在翻译时仍然可能会不知所措,甚至会突然陷入"失语"的尴尬境地。这是因为双语交叉使用时必然会涉及语言文化现象的相对空缺和相对特殊性,并随时出现二者相互影响、相互干扰的情况。无数双语工作实践经验已经证明,翻译需要专门的训练,扎实的双语功底只是通过训练学好翻译的条件。

3. 语言水平的高低永远是相对的,语言学习也永远没有止境。因此,我们也不能认为只有语言功底十分扎实,语言水平达到尽善尽美的程度才能学习或从事翻译。相反,翻译能力与语言水平的提高具有明显的互动关系。换言之，从事翻译的基础条件是良好的双语功底，但是学习翻译又是进一步打好双语基础的有效途径。在外语教学中，各种教学法随着时代需要的变化也曾经不断花样翻新，但一般都是时髦一时，只能各领风骚数十年甚至只流行几年。相比之下，翻译则历时数百年而毫无衰落迹象，而且在经受了来自"直接法"教学理论的强烈挑战之后，至今仍显示着"方兴未艾"的发展势头。究其原因，关键就在于外语学习与母语和第二语言学习有根本的不同：母语和第二语言是在语言环境中通过感性自然习得的，不需要也不可能借助其他语言参照，而且既不需要也不能体现一个人的文化修养和知识水平；而外语则是在一个人已经度过语言自然习得的阶段后主要依靠理性学习的"另一种语言"，它无法摆脱对母语的参照，而且常常体现着一个人的文化修养和知识水平。正如人不可能两次跨进同一条河流那样，我们在成年后开始学习一种外语，既不可能也不需要重复那种学习母语的自然发展过程。最好的办法就是有意识地借助母语参照，从而根据已经形成的知识，把母语的负面影响变成正面影响，利用翻译比较的手段学好外语。

在英国著名翻译理论家彼得·纽马克（Peter Newmark）看来，翻译在外语学习的各个阶段都具有十分重要的意义：在初级阶段可以节省时间，强化记忆；在中级阶段可以扩大词汇，有助于理解、辨析同义词；在高级阶段可以加强语感和理解，提高跨文化意识。总而言之，翻译是外语学习中培养准确性、简洁性和优雅性的练习，在外语学习的各个方面都具有头等重要的应用价值。我们认为，无论在外语学习的什么阶段，通过翻译比较与翻译实践始终都是一种实用、快捷、高效的方法，可以达到事半功倍的效果。同时，翻译对母语学习也具有很明显的促进作用，它能比写作更快地帮助我们提高母语的表达能力，因为在写作中我们总是倾向于无意识地使用自己已经掌握和熟悉的表达法，而在翻译中我们就经常不得不努力寻找最能表达原文意思和风格的表达法，从而有意识地学习和提高母语水平。在较高级的外语学习阶段，翻译中的语言对比分析促使我们能够在有一种外语作参照的情况下从旁观者的角度重新认识母语，进而摆脱"不识庐山真面目，只缘身在此山中"的混沌状态，把对母语的感性认识提高到理性认知，不仅知其然而且能知其所以然。

4. 有人承认翻译需要技巧，但认为翻译技巧只是文字游戏上的雕虫小技，没有什么大道理可言。这种认识可谓大错特错。其实，翻译对社会来说是一种跨文化交流与文化传播活动，对一个人来说则不仅是语言与文化学习工具和社会交际技能，而且是一种文化鉴赏活动，它能把人培养成一个更全面的文化人。人们对于翻译的需要源于原始社会不同语言群体之间的接触，兴于不同文化社团之间的频繁化接触，盛于民族与民族、国家与国家之间进行的大规模文化交流。今天，随着人类社会进入"信息化"的"全球村"时代，翻译又获得了前所未有的地位和重要意义。在全球主义语境中，它意味着人类信息的共享、新知的传播、文明的互动。因此，翻译工作不仅是一种前景光明的职业，而且是一种崇高的事业。所以，亲爱的同学，我要对你们说：热爱翻译吧！它将使你们的视野更开阔、精神更自由、生活更丰富。

翻译的社会文化含义

翻译是一个十分模糊、伸缩性极大的概念，从一张商品清单的逐词转译，到一首古典诗歌意境的再创造，其间包括了从语言的基本单位转换到不同生活价值观的碰撞和文化类型转变的整个范畴。在这样一个广阔的范畴内，翻译自然可以有多种多样的同义词。所以，一部翻译理论史实际上相当于对"翻译"这个词的多义性的论战。正因为如此，人类翻译活动的历史虽然悠久，但作为一门自成体系的学科，翻译学至今还只是在建构之中。

要客观、全面地认识翻译，就必须取得一种包括语言的科学和语言的艺术本身在内但又不局限于语言本身的广阔视角，即人类不同种族和社会群体的文化在接触、碰撞、交流中互相影响、渗透与互相借鉴、促动的动态视角，即语言、社会、文化三位一体的全透视视角。有了这样一种视角，我们不仅能够更深刻地理解翻译的本质，以高瞻远瞩的跨文化姿态重新审视翻译理论与实践的关系，认清翻译活动中语言与艺术、模仿与创造的辩证关系。

在此，笔者仅从翻译实践方法中切分出三种情况，结合跨文化交际问题说明这种语言、社会、文化交互作用的视角对于解决翻译理论与实践问题的重要性，说明在翻译中每一种用法、理论或实践方法都有其社会文化含义。

一、意译及其文化相对独立性含义

翻译的目的当然是把原语所表达的意思传递给译入语读者，因此一般情况下译者总是追求文字上灵活处理的意译，并把"达意传神"的翻译看作最好的翻译，把在文字上明显受到原语文字影响，不符合译入语习惯的"翻译腔"视为糟糕的翻译。在翻译实践中，如果原语与译入语的形式迥然不同，绝大多数译者自然首先选择译入语文字顺畅通达的意译，而不是读起来生硬拗口的直译。正因为如此，在近代翻译史上，林纾这位实际上不谙外文、利用其古文修养为口述原作内容者代笔的间接转译者被认为是一位翻译大家，而为之口述者却相对来说鲜为人知。这种以意译为导向的翻译态度甚至曾经被文坛上大名鼎鼎的赵景深推到了极端，即所谓"与其信而不顺，不如顺而不信"（鲁迅，1981:343）。对这种极端的观点，虽然鲁迅先生曾经用"乱译万岁"加以讽刺，但他提出的"宁可信而不顺"的所谓"硬译"主张（鲁迅，1981:376-377），却常常被看作另一极端，至今还有一些人不能理解和接受。

实际上，意译的这种显要地位并非完全是由翻译意义这一直接目的决定的，因为在很多情况下直译也同样可以传递意思，甚至可能会产生特殊的修辞效果。"教鱼学泳"与"班门弄斧"相比，意思并不模糊，比喻同样恰当，但在以意译为导向的大潮之中，后者总是受到青睐，这显然不是"得意忘形""达意传神"的表面追求所造成的，必然有更深刻的原因，即民族文化（包括语言文字）传统习俗不为翻译所动所乱，应该保持相对独立性这一藏而不露的含义。遗憾的是，人们一般在把翻译作为一种技艺看待时都显然忽视了这一本质的原因。

对意译的这一社会文化含义，可以有如下更具体的解释：

1. 在用外语译本族语时，放弃外族语文学形象，寻找对应的或近似的本族语文学形象。如果潜意识中认为本族语文化优于外族语文化，则情况更是如此。

2. 在用本族语译外语时放弃本族语文学形象，寻找对应的或近似的外族语文学形象。如果潜意识中认为外族语文化优于本族语文化，则情况更是如此。

3. 在用外语译本族语的过程中，如果遇到外族语文化中有而本族语文化中没有的语言表达形式或文学形象，则站在本族语文化的立场上和价值观的角度对其进行解释。这种解释如果与翻译同步并能融于译文，则被视作灵活的翻译方法。

4. 在用本族语译外族语的过程中，如果遇到外族语文化中没有而本族语文化中有的语言表达形式或文学形象，则站在外族文化的立场上和价值观的角度对其进行解释。这种解释也与用外族语译本族语时一样，最好能成为译文的一部分。

5. 在原语的语言艺术价值不低于甚至高于其语言信息价值时，译入语则从本族语的审美情趣和语言习惯出发，尽可能自由发挥，以期达到与原语艺术水平相当或更高的效果。

6. 把译入语的语言习惯和原语的语言习惯分别看作相对独立的文化的一部分，译入语语言与文化不可分离，如果出现原语文化现象与译入语习惯的矛盾，则应保证译入语语言与文化的统一。

7. 语言和文化一样，其演变是一个漫长的过程，任何一次翻译实践或短期翻译活动都难以影响译入语语言思维习惯。

从跨文化语言交际的角度来看，意译强调的是译入语的文化和价值观体系，相对轻视原语的文化和价值观体系对译入语文化和价值观体系的借鉴作用，忽视不同文化之间的可理解性、可融合性以及相互适应、渗透的历史事实。

二、直译及其文化开放性含义

直译虽然不像意译那样受译者重视，但不仅难以避免，而且也有人身体力行并从理论上为之辩护。前面提到的主张"宁可信而不顺"的鲁迅就是一个突出的代表。他认为，"山背后太阳落下去了"（鲁迅，2005：392）虽然不顺，但比"日落山阴"更能准确地体现原语的主次关系，因此坚持不改为后者。中国已故哲人、美学家、翻译家朱光潜教授也十分重视直译，认为文从字顺的直译就是理想的翻译。

客观地讲，翻译虽是翻译意义，但由于原语的语言形式与意义之间有不可分割的关系，而大致相同的意义可以用不同的形式表达，不同的表达形式又可能造成语气、色彩、强调、联想以及文体和风格上微妙的差异，所以译入语的形态自然或多或少地参照原语。另外，即使那些认为译入语与原语的意义—形式关系自成体系，互不渗透的译者，由于理解原语需要借助其形式，也有可能在翻译时无意中受其影响，从而造成不同程度的直译。

然而，原语形态的无意识影响，译入语的语气、色彩、重点、风格上对原语意义的忠实，也都是造成直译的一部分原因。如果把翻译首先看作跨文化交际的媒体，我们还可以发现隐藏在这些原因后面的文化含义，对此可以做如下具体解释：

1. 原语与译入语的文化可以互相理解，理解的就可谓"达意"，因此译入语不必放弃原语的文学形象和语言表达方式。

2. 原语文化与译入语文化虽有差异，但经过特别的解释后仍可以理解。这种解释不必与译入语融为一体，可以采取加注、附言说明等方式，甚至可以留给读者自己解决。如果译入语读者是受过教育的，那么这种含义就更加明显。

3. 语言思维习惯是文化的一部分，翻译是包括语言思维习惯交流在内的文化交流，或者说文化交流必然伴随着语言思维习惯的相互影响和渗透。因此，不能完全用译入语的思维习惯取代原语的思维习惯，否则翻译的意义或作用就会受到影响。

4. 各民族文化虽有相对独立之处，但都是相互开放的，而且都处于不断变化的状态；变化的主要原因就是外界影响，翻译对于文化的演变实际上起着催化剂的作用。

5. 原语的语言与思维不可分离，在介绍一种外来思想的时候，自然也在同时介绍一种陌生的语言思维习惯。译入语的语言"生硬"的地方往往正是体现外国思维方式之处，体现原语与译入语的区别之处。

6. 译入语文化不是通过翻译完全消化原语文化的特色，不是在其固有的文化价值体系中来安排原语文化现象的位置，而是在其发展可能性中吸收原语文化，从而使自身更加丰富多彩。

在翻译实践中，这些含义也像意译的含义那样深深隐藏在许多表面现象之下，以至于成为人们的一种潜意识，而许多纯粹的直译由于长期使用，已经完全融入译入语，以致时隔一两代后很多人都意识不到其外语直译的本源。这也就是说，它们已经成为译入语文化的一部分。

特别值得注意的是，直译对语言变化的作用绝非仅仅限于词汇，它也完全可以对一种语言的总体结构形成明显的影响。比如，通过从西方大量翻译各种理论书籍，汉语的现代书面语体就发生了很大的变化，形成了重逻辑联系的句法结构，从而使汉语句子大大延长，与传统的汉语书面语和日常口语形成了明显的对照。

三、不译及其社会文化现象可移植性含义

直译与意译经常被简单地看作不同翻译方法甚至具体的翻译技巧，因此围绕这一问题翻译史上一直争论不休。与此相比之下，关于翻译中可能出现多年不译的情况及其与意译的关系问题却没有很多人特别注意。就中国翻译史而言，曾经赴"西天"（印度）取经，并亲自主持了佛经翻译的大唐高僧唐玄奘似乎特别注意不译的种种具体情况。他认为有五种情况可以不译：神秘语、多义词、译入语文化空位词、已经通行的音译词以及特殊而神圣的词语。

由于不译就是翻译的反面，而翻译一般就是翻译意义，所以音译就是一种不译。然而，不译还可以是原文形式完全照搬。对此，我们应该特别注意的是，不译并非不能译，而是与翻译比较之下不译更加适宜。比如，"般若"与"智慧"、"释迦牟尼"与"能仁"、"阿耨菩提"与"大道心众生"虽都有可比之处，但皆以不翻译为宜。在当代，这种以不译为宜的情况也比比皆是。例如，"T恤"不译成"短袖汗衫"，"made in China"不译成"中国制造"，"music TV"不译成"音乐电视"，"CD"不译成"密集盘"，"CPU"不译成"中央处理单元"。

诸如此类的不译,与意译、直译相比,其文化含义最为明显,具体体现为以下几点:

1. 任何一种民族文化现象既是该民族特有的,又是人类所共有的。各民族的文化可以相互移植、融合,从而形成全球主义文化观。

2. 语言与文化一样,都是开放的体系,都具有自由的包容性和重组的可能。

3. 语言与文化现象不译而能被接受,必然另有解释或说明,而这种外在的解释与说明实际上也属于翻译。所以,我认为翻译有"内在"与"外在"之分,内在不译的有外在释义,此处不译的有彼处解释。文化交流中的翻译始终是一个连续的过程。

如果采取跨文化交流的角度,我们可以清楚地看到,由于不译和部分不译的原因,人类历史上很多民族的固有的文化都曾经出现过与外族文化大融合的现象,所有这些文化融合现象都充分说明,文化的交流与语言的接触和交融是同时发生的。

四、翻译的文化含义和翻译理论与实践

综上所述,翻译总是在一定的历史条件下发生和运作的。因此,无论是人们对翻译的一般认识和价值定位,还是翻译者在其翻译中所持的姿态乃至具体的翻译操作方法,都无不受到其所处的历史条件的制约。脱离了历史条件,我们就无法解释翻译中的具体问题,无法对某一翻译活动或一次翻译行为做出客观的评价,也不可能理解或解释翻译者所采用的翻译策略和方法。诚然,翻译确实存在着一个"技巧"问题,但最重要的技巧未必始终是语言转换的技巧,也不纯粹是可以借助灵感自由发挥的天赋才能,而是根据翻译的性质与功能做判断、选择的能力,它与特定翻译实践中运用的具体语言技巧有所不同:翻译实例中的具体技巧始终是灵活的,在不同的情况下运用不同的技巧是为了适合特定的目的,而这种正确判断、选择的能力是指导翻译实践的总体意识,是选择技巧的技巧,是根据翻译目标确定翻译度,即确定内在翻译相对于外在翻译的量的能力。由于翻译的目的必然直接或间接地反映译者本人对翻译文化含义的意识或潜意识,反映他翻译时所采取的文化姿态或立场。因此,把握翻译的文化含义,就是从最高的层次上把握翻译实践的性质,就有可能根据具体的情况做出最明智的抉择。

那么,对翻译的高低优劣究竟应该如何判断呢?我认为可以有以下尺度:

1. 翻译作品中所反映的文化姿态是否符合时代发展的趋势和需要。

2. 这种姿态是否符合译入语读者对象或为之理解、接受,并对读者产生积极的引导、启迪作用。

3. 翻译中所使用的方法或译入语表现形式是否始终适应其文化姿态,是否有自相矛盾之处。

总而言之,对于一个通晓原语与译入语及其所包含的文化内涵的译者来说,如果能够通过技巧的选择始终如一地为其明确的文化姿态或立场服务,而这种姿态或立场又能反映时代潮流,能为读者接受并发挥其预期的社会功能,那么他的译作就是优秀的。

关于本教材所涉及的原文和译文文本,在尊重原作的基础上,笔者对于一些有明显差错的地方进行了修改。

目 录

上编　英汉互译原理要义

第一章　翻译概论与英汉互译原理　/3
　一、翻译的本质与概念　/3
　二、翻译的分类　/5
　三、翻译的基本矛盾　/8
　四、译者的素质　/9
　五、基于英汉语对比的英汉互译原理　/10
　六、英汉互译原理的应用　/12

第二章　静态表达与动态表达互译　/15
　一、翻译原理　/15
　二、核心例句原理分析　/16
　三、翻译练习　/19
　四、练习参考译文　/27
　五、篇章参考译文翻译原理选注　/37

第三章　主语系统与主题系统互译　/39
　一、翻译原理　/39
　二、核心例句原理分析　/42
　三、翻译练习　/44
　四、练习参考译文　/51
　五、篇章参考译文翻译原理选注　/60

第四章　客观视角与主观视角互译　/63
　一、翻译原理　/63
　二、核心例句原理分析　/64
　三、翻译练习　/65

四、课后练习参考译文　/ 70
　　五、篇章参考译文翻译原理选注　/ 74

第五章　形合话语与意合话语互译　/ 77
　　一、翻译原理　/ 77
　　二、核心例句原理分析　/ 78
　　三、翻译练习　/ 79
　　四、英汉互译参考译文　/ 84
　　五、篇章参考译文翻译原理选注　/ 91

第六章　抽象概括与形象具体互译　/ 93
　　一、翻译原理　/ 93
　　二、核心例句原理分析　/ 95
　　三、翻译练习　/ 96
　　四、练习参考译文　/ 102
　　五、篇章参考译文翻译原理选注　/ 108

第七章　指称替代、重复与省略的互译　/ 110
　　一、翻译原理　/ 110
　　二、核心例句原理分析　/ 112
　　三、翻译练习　/ 113
　　四、英汉互译参考译文　/ 117
　　五、篇章参考译文翻译原理选注　/ 122

第八章　正说、反说与问说的互译　/ 123
　　一、翻译原理　/ 123
　　二、核心例句原理分析　/ 124
　　三、翻译练习　/ 126
　　四、练习参考译文　/ 130
　　五、篇章参考译文翻译原理选注　/ 136

下编　英汉互译原理综合应用

第九章　英汉互译原理应用比较　/ 139
　　一、小说　/ 139
　　二、散文　/ 154
　　三、诗歌　/ 183

第十章　英汉互译原理综合实践 ／203

　　一、英汉互译原理在散文中的应用 ／203

　　二、英汉互译原理在小说中的应用 ／217

　　三、英汉互译原理在诗歌中的应用 ／230

　　四、英汉互译原理在应用文中的应用 ／234

附录　第十章参考译文 ／243

主要参考文献 ／297

上编

英汉互译原理要义

第一章 翻译概论与英汉互译原理

一、翻译的本质与概念

对翻译本质的理解与人们对语言性质的理解直接关联,它取决于对不同语言的形式和不同语言形式所包含的不同意义的认识。从语言形式上来看,翻译是不同语言符号形式系统的转换活动,具有一定的机械性和固定性;但从不同语言所包含的不同意义来看,翻译又是对某一文化语境中比较固定的意义在新的不同语境中的阐释和进一步衍生,具有很大的灵活性和可变性。

翻译的复杂性源自自然语言本身所具有的任意性和不同自然语言所承载的不同文化体系及其具体信息的相对独立性和不完全对应性。因此,翻译的本质不仅包括语言形式的转换,而且包括了意义的阐释与变通,而在阐释与变通的过程中译者有很大的主观能动性。在这个意义上,翻译是一种复杂的创造性艺术,而不仅仅是简单的语言实践活动。

"翻译"这一概念有很大的模糊性和伸缩性:一张商品清单的逐词转译是翻译,一首古典诗歌意境在另一种语言中的再创造也是翻译。传统上所说的直译、意译、音译(即不译)都属于翻译的范畴。人们曾对翻译下过很多定义,但是迄今为止关于翻译的本质仍然是一个学术界不断研究、探索的问题。据统计,迄今为止,具有代表性的翻译定义已达160多种。我们常常看到的关于翻译的定义有:

从语言学角度研究翻译,翻译是用一种语言把另一种语言所表达的思想内容准确而完整地重新表达出来的语言活动。

从文化学角度探讨翻译,翻译便是译者将一种语言文字所蕴含的意思用另一种语言文字表述出来的文化活动。

从交际学的角度考察翻译,则翻译又成了一种跨语言、跨社会、跨文化的交际活动。

不言而喻,翻译是一种语言活动;但语言又是文化的载体,语言和文化是不可分离的,表面为语言活动的翻译,其实也是一种文化活动,这就将人们对翻译的认识上升到了文化的视角,扩大了翻译的外延,使人们透过语言看到了其背后更广阔的文化内容,丰富了对翻译的认识;翻译的最终目的是传递信息。因此,翻译的交际观又使人们超越翻译的语言和文化层面,看到了翻译活动中译者与原文及原文作者之间、译者与译文读者之间的互动关系。

作为术语使用的"翻译"有三层含义:翻译研究、翻译产品和翻译行为。翻译研究又可分为理论研究和应用研究、宏观研究、微观研究、描述性研究和规约性研究。翻译产品涉及翻译的方式(归化、异化、杂合化)、种类以及相关评判标准(是作者中心、译者中心、读者中心,还是统筹兼顾、有所偏重?)。翻译行为涉及的因素就更复杂,既有权力、意识形态、文化等外部环境的影响,又有原作者、译者、读者、文本等内部因素的制约。

目前译界对翻译的分歧多源于对翻译行为的定位上。人们从前对翻译行为的定义显然过于狭隘,多把翻译定位在"语言之间的相互转换"。《辞海》对翻译的定义是:"把一种语言文字的意义用另一种语言文字表达出来。"(夏征农,1999:418)该定义既没有涉及译者该怎样表达,也没有涉及译文的读者和翻译过程中的文化因素等。

综上所述,全面考虑翻译的定义,就必须有比较广阔的视野,考虑到语言本身就是文化的一部分,同时只有在特定的语境中才具有明确具体的意义。因此,我们可以说,翻译总体上是把一种语言在其固有语境中所表达的意思用另一种语言在新的语境中重新表达出来的语言转换和文化阐释活动。

这是总体上翻译的定义,但是有时人们常常认为对翻译的定义有必要进行适当的区分:严格意义上的翻译和宽泛意义上的翻译。

严格意义上的翻译仍然属于语言转换,不过它应该是"以原文和原文作者的意图为起点,受译文读者需求、译者翻译目的、译入语文化所制约的语言转换"(王宏,2007)。鉴于此,严格意义上的翻译要以原文为对照,受原文文本限制,如公文、政论、科技、法律等文本的翻译。这类译文既要经得起读,又要经得起对,字面对应准确性最强,常采用直译的翻译方法。

宽泛意义上的翻译则是"以原文为参照,受赞助者、译文读者需求、译者翻译目的、译入语文化所制约的跨文化交际活动"(王宏,2007)。也就是说,此类翻译更多融入的是赞助者、译文读者需求、译者翻译目的和译入语文化的制约。与原文文本相比,这类翻译在内容、长度、文体、语气等方面都可能有相当的变异,如某些文学体裁、对外宣传材料的翻译。它们不拘泥字面上的——对应,而是注重译文的可读性、创造性和艺术性。

就两类翻译而言,严格意义上的翻译属于内向型的文本转换能覆盖大部分文体;宽泛意义上的翻译属于外向型的文化翻译,仅适用于部分文体。

一般认为,语言有三大基本功能:传达功能、表现功能和诉求功能。传达功能主要在于传达讯息,如公文、订货单、科技文献、新闻消息等;表现功能在于表现人类的情感,如文学作品,特别是诗歌;诉求功能主要在于通过语言来影响接受者的思想,如广告。

翻译时,要根据不同的语言功能、不同的文体文本,选择不同的翻译方法:或直译,或基本直译,或"直译+意译",或基本意译,或完全意译。详见表1-1。

表1-1 文体文本与翻译方法

翻译层次		语言功能	常见文体	
字面对应准确性最强(Literalness)	严格要求直译	传达	公文及政治论文	
	基本直译		科技情报、一般学术论文及著作	
	一般要求直译,但必须考虑可读性		新闻报刊	
不求字面对应,但求保证可读性(Readability)		诉求	广告	
	直译与意译兼顾,充分考虑可读性	表现	文学文体	叙事散文 文艺小说
	一般要求意译,力求获得最佳可读性			抒情散文 电影剧本
	基本意译,力求获得最佳可读性与艺术性			诗歌

二、翻译的分类

根据不同的标准,可以对翻译做不同的分类。

(一)根据翻译者翻译时所采取的文化姿态

翻译可以分为归化翻译(naturalized translation)和异化翻译(alienated translation)。

1. 归化翻译就是指把在原语文化语境中自然适宜的成分翻译成在译入语文化语境中自然适宜的成分,使译入语读者能够立即理解。如果遇到了在原语文化语境中难以理解的成分,则应在翻译的同时按照译入语读者的语言习惯、社会行为规范和伦理道德标准对其进行解释,或者对这些成分进行删改。一般所说的"意译"就其文化取向来说属于归化翻译。

2. 异化翻译就是直接按照原语文化语境的适宜性进行翻译,而对其语境可以另外解释,使译入语读者感到不能用自己的语言习惯、社会行为规范和伦理道德标准去理解翻译作品。一般来说,所谓的"直译"就其文化取向来说是一种异化翻译。

应该注意的是,归化翻译与异化翻译只是两种不同的倾向,在同一部译作中,两者可能兼而有之,只是程度不同。

(二)根据翻译作品在译入语文化中所预期发挥的作用

翻译可以分为工具性翻译(instrumental translation)与文献性翻译(documentary translation)。

1. 工具性翻译

工具性翻译指把翻译仅仅作为工具,通过翻译达到与翻译本身并无直接关系的另外的目的。比如,翻译广告是为了推销产品,只要产品畅销,无论如何翻译都是可行的方法。但一般来说,工具性翻译倾向于意译,可以增加或删减原文的内容。

2. 文献性翻译

文献性翻译指把翻译作品本身看作文献,强调其独立存在的价值,因此它比工具性翻译更加注重其语言形式和文学形象对原文的忠实。在文献性翻译中,可以使用直译,也可以使用意译,但在使用意译时一般不随意对原文进行删改。

应该注意的是,有些译作同时具有一定程度的工具性和文献性。

(三) 根据翻译所涉及的语言的形式与意义

翻译可分为语义翻译(semantic translation)与交际翻译(communicative translation)两种。

1. 语义翻译

语义翻译即对语言所直接包含的意义进行翻译,而交际翻译即根据翻译的场合、功能、语境或不同文化价值观进行必要的解释性翻译或变通性翻译。语义翻译在译语语义和句法结构允许的条件下,尽可能准确地再现原作上下文的意义。语义翻译与直译的区别:前者更注重语言意义的组织,而后者则注重语言语法结构。

2. 交际翻译

交际翻译追求译文读者产生的效果尽量等同于原文对原文读者产生的效果。

(四) 根据译者对原文与译文进行比较与观察的角度

翻译可分为文学翻译(literary translation)和语言学翻译(linguistic translation)。

1. 文学翻译

文学翻译是指从文学的角度出发着手翻译,因此强调比较译文相对于原文的审美价值和文学效果,寻求译文与原文之间文学功能的对等。文学翻译理论往往主张在不可能"复制"原文文学表现手法的情况下,译文只能更美而不能逊色,其缺点是不重视语言结构之间的比较与关系问题。

2. 语言学翻译

语言学翻译是指从语言学的角度出发着手翻译,因此强调比较译文与原文的语言结构,寻求原语与译入语之间的系统转换规律,主张把语言学研究的成果用于翻译,同时通过翻译实践促进语言学的进一步深入发展。语言学翻译的缺点是无法解决文化空缺现象问题。

(五) 根据翻译目的语与原语在语言形式上的关系

翻译分为直译(direct/literal translation)与意译(free/liberal translation)。

直译又指字面翻译,直译的语言与原语在形式上关系密切并以其为参照,一般指尽可能保留原语的结构形式上的特点,在译文难以理解时可以另外解释,但翻译过程不能与解释混为一谈。因此,在把语言作为一种文化的前提下,直译属于异化翻译。在特定社会历史条件下,直译法对于促进民族语言吸收外语成分具有一定的推动作用,但是它往往与民族语言传统发生冲突,其使用也常常受到一定的限制。

意译一般不考虑原语的形式结构,就是指撇开原文语言形式翻译其意义,所谓"得意忘形"或"舍形取义——保留内容,舍弃形式",目的是使译文通顺、流畅,无需另外解释。因此,意译是一种归化翻译。

应该注意的是,首先,由于语言的形式与意义不可分割,直译也是为了翻译意思,意译也不能不从理解语言形式出发,因此直译与意译也不能完全割裂开来;其次,直译与意译之分涉及对不同语言结构的认识和解释问题,但由于语言结构同时涉及语法形式结构与语言思维结构或信息结构两个不同的层面,所以究竟什么是直译、什么是意译,人们的看法也可能会有所不同。

(六)根据翻译的媒介

翻译可以分为口译(interpretation / oral translation)、笔译(translation / written translation)、视译(sight translation / interpretation)、同声传译(simultaneous interpretation)、机器翻译(machine translation)、人机协作翻译(computer-aided translation)六种。

1. 口译

口译就是把用一种语言讲的话翻译成另一种语言讲的话。口译也可根据不同情况分为多种:根据讲话人的语言变化与否分为交替翻译(alternative interpretation)与连续翻译(consecutive interpretation)。

(1)交替翻译指交替翻译不同讲话人的不同语言,亦称联络翻译(liaison interpretation)。

(2)连续翻译指把一种固定的语言连续翻译成另一种固定的语言。

2. 笔译

笔译就是指把一种文字的书面材料翻译成另一种文字的书面材料。

3. 视译

视译指阅读一种文字材料的同时将其用另一种语言口头译出。

4. 同声传译

同声传译指在听到一种语言的讲话的同时,将其译为另一种语言,不间断地边听边译。同声传译可以使用专门的设备,也可以用耳语的方式进行。后者称为耳语翻译。

5. 机器翻译

机器翻译指用计算机软件进行翻译。

6. 人机协作翻译

人机协作翻译指人利用计算机做初步翻译,然后对译文进行审阅修订;或由人首先翻译,然后利用计算机对其中可能出现的错误进行修改或提出修改建议供人参考。

此外，还可以根据翻译所涉及的具体学科、专业、行业领域或翻译的场合进行不同的分类。比如，可分为文科、理科、工科等各个学科的翻译，商业、法律、外交、旅游等不同的翻译。不过，翻译本身作为一个相对独立的专业或行业却具有无法避免的跨学科、行业和专业的性质，因此一般不强调对翻译所涉及的具体领域进行细致的划分。虽然在实践中有不少从事翻译的人员的确更擅长于一个或数个专业或行业，在其熟悉的领域从事翻译效率和质量更高，他们也时常不得不接触所不熟悉的新的领域的翻译。实际上，长期从事国际会议的专业翻译人员往往需要接受不同性质的翻译任务，因此常常需要花相当多的时间进行会前准备，熟悉不同专业领域的术语和相关知识。

三、翻译的基本矛盾

为了把握翻译的本质，从而制定正确的翻译原则并用以指导翻译实践，必须对翻译过程中的基本问题和矛盾加以归纳。对此古今中外的思想家、翻译理论家与实践者早已做过很多研究，得出了比较一致的结论。可以简单总结如下。

1. "文"与"质"的矛盾

"文"相对于翻译的语言而言，即翻译作品的文采、文辞、美文的意思；而质则指翻译内容、信息和意义。二者的矛盾实际上也是对老子"美言不信，信言不美"哲学思想的反映。

2. "信、达、雅"之间的矛盾

这是对"文"与"质"的矛盾的进一步发展。其中"达"主要是指顺畅地达到信息传递的目的，具体说来就是要求翻译语言通顺易懂，而"雅"则要求翻译语言通顺易懂的同时还能符合较高的文学语言审美标准。

3. "模仿"与"创造"的矛盾

这是对译者角色定位的问题。"模仿"论认为译者是仆人，作者是主人，因此译者要隐身，让人尽量看不出翻译的痕迹。译文（target text）要"亦步亦趋，人云亦云"，要紧跟原文（source text），不增、不减、不改。"创造"论则认为原文只供参照，作者已经不存在。译者从后台跳至前台，从隐身到显身，对原文可操弄、可增减、可夹带"私货"，彰显译者自己的风格，直至进行艺术创造，与原文"竞争"，一决雌雄。

对以上矛盾进一步思考，还可以引起以下具体问题：

（1）翻译究竟应该主要考虑原文的语言，还是应该主要考虑原文的思想？

（2）译文读上去应该像原文，还是应该像译文？这一矛盾背后隐含的是译文能否独立存在这一更尖锐的问题。

（3）翻译应该表现原作的风格还是译作的风格？是作者的风格还是译者的风格？

（4）翻译应该保留原作的时代语言特征，还是应该跨越时代的变化，体现当代的语言特征？

（5）翻译能否对原作进行增删？

（6）翻译能否改变原作的体裁？比如，诗歌能否翻译成散文？

可见，翻译实践所涉及的矛盾和问题非常复杂，而解决这些矛盾又必然涉及历史、文化、社会习俗、不同语言的性质和语言与思维的关系，并由具体的翻译对象和目的所决定。

我们认为，以上各种矛盾都涉及两种更加深层次的矛盾：一是原语与译语的语言思维习惯的矛盾，二是原语与译语的语言文化历史背景的矛盾。

四、译者的素质

不同翻译的种类对译者素质的要求既有共同之处，又有不同之处。

无论从事任何一种翻译，译者都必须具备如下三种素质。

1. 有一定的语言天赋和扎实的双语基本功，尤其是掌握有关翻译所涉及的词汇、语法。

然而，译者必须同时对语言现象的复杂性及其变化与创新高度敏感，把语言看作不断变化的有生命的事物，而不是一套僵化、机械、一成不变的用词与造句的词法和语法规则。因为任何的语言规则相对于语言运用实际来说都只是权宜的总结，是死板的和滞后的，同时规则也常常是有例外的。译者必须善于根据语言运用的实际情况随时灵活地做出变化甚至创新。

学习语言，要讲语法规则、坚守语言规范，而运用语言则需要灵活，随时打破常规，推陈出新。

2. 理解翻译的性质，掌握基本翻译方法

翻译作为一种技能需要训练，所谓"熟能生巧"，就是说通过大量的翻译实践可以掌握翻译技能。翻译需要实践，需要练习。如何"练"？那是有章可循、有"法"可依的：或增或减，或顺或逆，或分或合，凡此种种，不一而足。至于作为语言活动的翻译，势必涉及不同语言的转换，而每种语言都有其内在的规律。人类语言有其共性，这是我们能够从事翻译的基础；但也有其异性，这是我们需要学习的理由。另外，翻译还是一门艺术。作为艺术的翻译需要将技巧综合运用，以敏锐的感觉和观察选择技巧，灵活发挥，在模仿的基础上创造。

3. 具备有关翻译所涉及领域的广泛知识

比如从事文学翻译，就要有所翻译语言的深厚文学修养；从事某一科技领域的翻译，就必须对这一领域的基本知识比较熟悉。我们常常可能遇到这种情况：由于缺乏有关专业知识，有些语言材料即使其语法十分简单，单词也似乎不难，但我们仍然不能理解，如何翻译当然也就无从谈起了。

4. 有较强的求知欲，敏感、灵活，善于改变思路，另辟蹊径，勇于创新

我们必须承认，人的语言能力和自然、社会知识毕竟是有限的，所以从事翻译的人还必须同时具有强烈的求知欲，对任何新鲜事物怀有好奇心，勇于主动进取和探索，不断学习，通过学习扩大自己的知识面，并通过对已有知识的重新整合灵活地发挥与创造。

五、基于英汉语对比的英汉互译原理

从形式来看,翻译是用一种语言表达另一种语言所表达的意思,所以无论是从语言的角度看,还是从文学的角度看,都有必要认识所翻译的两种语言之间传统思维习惯上的差异。英汉两种语言完全属于不同的语系,其产生、发展的历史都有所不同,因此在传统语言思维习惯方面也有很大差异。英汉互译的原理就是以英汉语言思维对比为基础的语言思维转换行为,因此这种对比分析与研究的结果对翻译实践有着直接的指导意义,可以作为英汉互译的基本原理来理解并加以应用。

英汉语言思维差异体现在语言的各个层次和各个方面,在此我们首先选择其突出的一些方面做一个简单的概括。具体见表1-2。

表1-2 英汉传统语言思维特征主要差异

序号	英语	汉语
1	主语突出(主语系统)(subject-prominent)	主题突出(主题系统)(topic-prominent)
2	语法结构(grammatical structure)	语义结构(semantic structure)
3	自下而上(bottom-up)	自上而下(top-down)
4	从内到外(center-periphery)	从外到内(periphery-center)
5	演绎组织(deductive organization)	归纳组织(inductive organization)
6	一元组织(unitary organization)	二元组织(binary organization)
7	焦点透视(focal perspective)	散点透视(changing perspective)
8	客观视角(objective point of view)	主观视角(subjective point of view)
9	修饰关系(modification)	述谓关系(predication)
10	形合(hypotactic relation)	意合(paratactic relation)
11	以名词为中心(noun-centered)	以动词为中心(verb-centered)
12	抽象概念(abstract generalization)	具体形象(concrete images)
13	静态关系(static relation)	动态关系(dynamic relation)
14	树状/葡萄结构(tree/grape structure)	波状/竹式结构(wave/bamboo structure)
15	末端开放(open end, right branching)	首端开放(open head, left branching)
16	补充(addition)	发展(development)
17	谓语(predicate)	述题(rheme)
18	直接(directness)	间接(indirectness)
19	替代(substitution)	重复/省略(reiteration/omission)
20	低语境(low-context)	高语境(high-context)
21	低音乐性(low musical)	高音乐性(high musical)

实际上，从语音、词法、句法到篇章结构，英汉语之间的种种差异反映在诸多方面，表1-2已经列出的21条仍然未必能够全面、详尽地囊括所有差异；但另一方面，我们也应该意识到，由于语言的共性和在长期发展中语言之间的接触和互相影响的原因，英汉语之间也有一些基本的共同之处。一般来说，英汉语之间的共同之处相对比较容易理解，在翻译中也不涉及很多翻译转换原理与具体的技巧。因此，从英汉互译原理及其与翻译实践技巧的关系这一角度来看，我们应该把重点放在英汉语传统语言思维方式的不同特征方面，切实理解并牢固把握种种差异，用以指导我们的英汉互译实践。

在学习英汉互译原理并将其应用于翻译实践的同时，我们还必须注意三个特殊问题：

第一，对英汉语之间的种种差异有各种各样的说法，但这些说法即使作为"术语"也只是对一般情况或一般倾向的总结概括，我们不应该把这些说法当作僵化的死规定，原因是语言总是处于不断发展变化之中，不同语言的表达方法在这一发展过程中也可以互相借鉴，推陈出新，从而造成特殊的文体修辞效果。因此，在翻译运用中也可能出现"反其道而用之"的情况。比如，我们在原理中强调，英语注重以名词为中心，围绕中心词添加修饰，翻译汉语时应该尽量做动态化处理，常常翻译为主谓或补语结构，但是实际上翻译时也可以将英语的主谓结构反过来翻译成汉语的修饰结构。例如：

The sea was silent, the sky was silent. I was alone with the night and silence. 沉静的大海，沉静的天空，孤独的我伴着黑夜和沉寂。

又如，虽然英语注重抽象、概括，汉语更强调具体、形象，但是实际上任何语言都可以接受抽象概括的或具体形象的表达法，英语中"the salt of the earth"，"a skeleton in the cupboard"，"as cool as a cucumber"都是形象具体的表达法，而翻译为中文后，就必须遵循中文的表达习惯，因此可能反而比较概括、抽象地表达为"社会中坚""家丑""镇定自若"。

第二，上述英汉语言之间的差异有些是具体细节上的，而有些则是总体上的、概括性的，前者往往可以用后者来解释。比如，表1-2中的"语法结构—语义结构""自下而上—自上而下""从内到外—从外到内"的互译转换原则都可以在一定程度上用"主语系统—主题系统"的转换原则概括；"名词中心—动词中心""修饰关系—述谓关系"也可以在一定程度上用"静态关系—动态关系"概括。因此，我们不能将所有差异等同视之，而必须首先理解和把握那些总体上的和概括性的差异，在此基础上更清楚地认识那些更具体、细微的差异，从而做到提纲挈领、纲举目张。根据这一理解，本教程将翻译实践中具有较高层次指导意义的差异作为翻译的基本原理在不同章节中讲解，其他具体的差异则留在课堂上由授课教师处理。

六、英汉互译原理的应用

（一）英译汉

Text A	Text B	翻译原理
If you can't find it here in Hong Kong, it doesn't exist.	天下瑰宝，香港不见，何处可找？	从主语系统（…it…）到主题系统（天下—香港—何处）；从指代（it）到明示（瑰宝）
Money doesn't grow on trees, it grows in our branches.	摇钱不靠树成行，存款增值在我行。/摇钱树上不长钱，我行存款钱生钱。	从主语到主题，从静态到动态（money—摇钱，摇钱树上）；音乐性
Before going on up into the blue hills, Thomas stopped for gasoline at a lonely station.	群山苍翠。加油站孤零零的。入山之前，托马斯在这儿停车加油。	从主语系统（Thomas）到主题系统（群山—加油站—托马斯）；从静态到动态（for gasoline—加油）；形合与意合
He is a round little man with a red face and deep eyes behind a pair of large glasses in a gilt frame polished to shine with dazzling light.	他身材矮胖，脸色红润，眼睛深陷。戴着一副大眼镜，镜架镀金，镜架擦过后闪闪发光，令人眼花缭乱。	从主语系统（he…）到主题系统（他—身材—脸色……镜架……）；从修饰关系到述谓关系；从树状结构到竹状结构
Those privileged to be present at a family festival of the Forsytes have seen that charming and instructive sight—an upper middle-class family in full plumage.	碰到福尔赛家有喜庆的事情，那些有资格去参加的人都看见过那派中上层人家的兴盛气象，不但看了开心，也增长了见识。	主语系统与主题系统（从时间到空间，从空间到时间）；静态与动态
It was only after bitter experiences that David began to understand the complexity of this world.	大卫只是在经历了许多痛苦磨难之后才开始明白，这个世界是多么错综复杂。	从主语（it）到主题（大卫）；名词与动词；静态与动态
The signs of times point to the necessity of the modification of the system of administration.	管理体制需要改革，时代发展的迹象表明了这一点。时代发展的迹象表明，有必要改革管理体制。	名词与动词；末端开放与首端开放
No year passes without evidence of the truth of the statement that the work of government is becoming increasingly difficult.	有人说行政管理变得越来越难做了，这种说法道出了实情，每年都有证据表明确实如此。	静态与动态；末端开放与首端开放；名词与动词；演绎与归纳
Never was such an array of delicious temptations spread before a child.	没有一个孩子曾经见过这么多诱人的好吃的东西展现在他面前。	主观视角与客观视角；抽象与具体

Text A	Text B	翻译原理
This coat won't protect you from the severe cold of Canada.	靠这件大衣你可抵御不了加拿大的严寒。	主观视角与客观视角
To help my self live without fault, I made a list of what I considered the 13 virtues. These virtues are (1) Temperance, (2) Self-control, (3) Silence, (4) Order, (5) Firmness of mind, (6) Savings, (7) Industry, (8) Honesty, (9) Justice, (10) Cleanliness, (11) Calmness, (12) Morality, (13) Humbleness.	为了使自己生活中不犯错误，特列出我认为应该身体力行的13条守则。这些守则是：(1) 节制饮食；(2) 自我克制；(3) 沉默寡言；(4) 有条不紊；(5) 坚定信念；(6) 勤俭节约；(7) 工作勤奋；(8) 忠诚老实；(9) 办事公正；(10) 衣履整洁；(11) 平心静气；(12) 品性高尚；(13) 谦虚恭顺。	名词与动词；静态与动态；主语与主题；音足与形足；重音乐性与轻音乐性
The sky is cloudlessly blue, with the summer sun high in the sky. The grassy slopes of great Vesuvius (维苏威火山) rise to the heavens behind the city, and sunlight shimmers on the waters of the bay a thousand yards from the city walls. Ships from every nation are in port and strange languages can be heard in the streets.	天高云淡，一片湛蓝，夏日高悬天空。山坡上芳草萋萋，高大的维苏威火山拔地而起，耸入天际，衬托着这座城市。粼粼波光映照在海湾的水面上，千码之外就是城墙。各国的船只停泊在港，异邦的语言可闻于街街巷巷。	形合与意合；主语与主题；静态与动态
A very small number of people do not have to work for their incomes. They may be the owners of houses or lands, for example, from which they receive rent; or they may possess shares or deposits with the Post Office or other savings banks, from which they earn interest. They may organize businesses which do not involve them in much work but provide them with a good income.	有一小部分人无须工作就可以获得收入。他们可能拥有房产、地产等，从中收取租金；或许他们有股份或存款存在邮局或其他储蓄行里，从中收取利息。他们可能会管理商务，这不需要他们自己做很多工作，却能给他们提供丰厚的收入。	名词与动词；静态与动态

Text A	Text B	翻译原理
It was the best of times, it was the worst of times, it was the age of wisdom, it was the age of foolishness, it was the epoch of belief, it was the epoch of incredulity, it was the season of Light, it was the season of Darkness, it was the spring of hope, it was the winter of despair, we had everything before us, we had nothing before us, we were all going direct to Heaven, we were all going direct the other way—in short, the period was so far like the present period, that some of its noisiest authorities insisted on its being received, for good or for evil, in the superlative degree of comparison only.	那是好得不能再好的年代；那是糟得不能再糟的年代；那是闪烁着智慧的岁月；那是充斥着愚蠢的岁月；那是信心百倍的时期；那是疑虑重重的时期；那是阳光普照的季节；那是黑夜沉沉的季节；那是充满希望的春天；那是令人绝望的冬日。我们拥有一切，我们一无所有；大家都在升天堂，大家都在下地狱——简而言之，那时候和我们现在非常相似。因此，专门研究那个时代的吵吵嚷嚷的权威们，不论他们是褒还是贬，都认为只能用最极端的字眼来评价它。	音足与形足；重音乐性与轻音乐性；名词与动词；静态与动态

（二）汉译英

Text A	Text B	翻译原理
法古今完人	Onto a full grown man	从动态到静态；从二元结构到一元结构
事情并非凑巧。	It doesn't just happen.	主题与主语；抽象与形象
今天我为母校骄傲，明天母校为我自豪。	Keep alive the good reputation of our university.	一元与二元；抽象概括与形象具体；音乐性
请随便选你喜欢的。	Be free in making your choice.	从动态到静态
中国疆域辽阔,历史悠远。	China has a vast territory and an extremely long history.	从主题（中国疆域……）到主语系统（China …）；从述谓到修饰
你们要梦寐以求登峰造极。	Be a king in your dreams.	从动态到静态
旁观者顿时噤若寒蝉,惴惴不安。	An awed hush fell upon the bystanders.	从主观视角到客观视角
老师走了以后,激烈的争论才结束。	The departure of the teacher brought the heated discussion to an end.	从主观到客观视角；从动态到静态。
苏州大学口笔译中心欢迎您加入我们的行列,帮您提高学术修养,助您发展职业技能,使您以娴熟的双语满怀信心地迎接21世纪的挑战。	The Translation and Interpretation Center (TIC), Soochow University, ready for you to join us, for your academic and professional advancement, in time to meet bilingual needs of the 21st century.	一元与二元；名词与动词；静态与动态；轻音乐性与重音乐性
勤洗手,戴口罩,保持社交距离。	Hands, masks, and space.	从动态到静态

第二章 静态表达与动态表达互译

一、翻译原理

　　语言与思维密切相关，同时必须反映现实。但语言反映现实并不是镜像般地客观反映，而是经过人主观意识过滤的反映。不同民族的语言在对同一个世界进行观察时，因其视角的不同而往往导致很大的差异性。根据现实世界的显著运动和相对静止，我们可以把现实情境和现象切分成静态过程和动态过程两大类。静态过程揭示某一主体属于某一类型，具有某种性质或特征，或处于某一状态；动态过程表明某一主体进行某一动作、发出某一行为或产生某一影响、改变某一客体。

　　语言作为对客观世界的一种人为的反映方式，也有静态和动态的不同表达法。静态的表达法倾向于把事物的运动和变化归结为一个过程或描写为一个状态，而动态的表达法则注重对引起变化或运动过程的行为、动作本身进行描写。英汉语言思维对比研究表明，英语是一种静态表达法较多或倾向于静态表达的语言，而汉语则是一种动态表达法较多或倾向于动态表达的语言。换言之，英语句子的基本意义常常用静态方式表达，而汉语的基本意思则往往用动态方式表达。从词性上来看，静态的表达法主要包括名词、系词、连词、介词、副词及其短语，也有一些行为和动作成分较弱的动词（如系动词、存在动词等）；而动态的表达法主要倾向于使用表示行为、动作、变化的动词。从句子成分上来看，静态的语言表达法主要是主语、宾语及其二者的定语、状语及其独立成分，而动态的表达法主要是谓语和补语。从句式结构上来看，静态的结构往往采用普通的陈述句，而动态的结构则倾向于使用疑问句、反问句。

　　在英译汉中将静态的表达方式转换为汉语的动态表达方式有下列情况：

- 名词静态→动态

Your presence today really honored me.

你今天能够出席让我增色不少。

- 形容词静态→动态（包括短语）

The poor beggar is lame and blind.

那个穷叫花子腿跛着，眼睛也瞎了。

- 介词（介词词组）静态→动态

He has been in the room all day.

他一整天都待在家里。

- 副词静态→动态

The show is already on.

演出已经开始了。

- 独立主格的静态→动态

She came in, book in hand.

她进来了,手里拿着书。

- 存在动词静态→动态

A gentleman is, rather than does.

绅士是生就的,而不是做出来的。

- 弱动态→强动态

If thou would work, I have bread for thee.

如果你愿意劳动,我为你准备了面包。

- 静态句型→动态句型

They must necessarily feel a great pride when they think of this feat.

想到这种成就,他们怎么不感到骄傲呢?

由于汉英互译原理在翻译实践中是可逆的,所以汉译英时就要将转换规则融会贯通反过来应用,根据语言思维习惯把注重动态表达的方式转换为注重静态表达的方式。

二、核心例句原理分析

1. 英语名词（短语）与汉语动态表达法的转换

基本例句	分析说明
A. 英译汉 1. Attention, everyone! 大家注意了! 2. Ticket, please. 请出示车票。 3. Thief! 有贼! 4. Fire! 开火!（开炮!） 5. What a pity! 真令人遗憾!	1. 英语中一个简单的名词,完成了一个动作指令,行使了汉语中动词（短句）的功能。 2. 同上。即使please用作动词,但更重要的动词还是要添加。 3. 一个"贼"字,何等简单!想必情急之下,也容不得你喊"Stop the thief!"吧。 4. 同上,虽然根据不同使用情景也可能是"点火""拿火来"等,但一般离不开动词。 5. "What"转换成"真令人"。

6. There is a knock at the door. 有人敲门。 7. Let's take a rest. 我们休息一下。 8. My pleasure. 别客气。 9. Peace! And no war! 要和平！不要战争！	6. 添加"有人"，是静动转换，也是视角转换。 7. 把英语普通的动词转换成汉语具体的动词，更体现了汉语强调动词意义的倾向。 8. 汉语直接加动词。 9. 简洁严谨。静态的词语传达出了动态的诉求，即"呼唤和平，停止/杜绝战争"。
B. 汉译英 1. 保重。 Take good care of yourself. 2. 她歌唱得好。 She is a good singer. 3. 有人打电话找你。 Someone is calling for you. 4. 美国人酷爱豪华的气派。 The Americans have a passion for grandeur. 5. 你干得不错。 You have done a good job. 6. 保持秩序！（不要乱！） Order!	"care"和"singer"两个单词十分简洁，加一个限定性的词语就传达出了汉语的动态语言的精神，组合运用，具有很强的描述性。 汉语的"打"既具体又有宽泛意义，英文在"calling"后加"for"才能表达"打"和"找"的连动结构。

2. 英语形容词与汉语动态表达法的转换

基本例句	分析说明
A. 英译汉 1. He is drunk, dizzy, and feeling that he is the world. 他喝醉了，头脑晕眩，感觉他就是整个世界。 2. Wet paint! 油漆未干！ 3. Dead end / No passage. 此路不通。	英语中的形容词往往行使汉语中动词的功能，所以在翻译时，它们之间往往要进行相应的转换，如英语说"wet paint"，汉语则说"油漆未干"。
B. 汉译英 1. 别客气。 You are welcome. 2. 你准备好了吗？ Are you ready? 3. 你选什么？ What's your choice?	英语强调选择的结果，以名词"choice"为中心，而汉语则强调选择的过程，以动词"选择"为语义中心。

3. 英语介词（短语）与汉语动态表达法的转换

基本例句	分析说明
A. 英译汉 1. He is in persistent pursuit of knowledge. 他追求知识，孜孜不倦。 2. Up the hill you will see a temple. 爬上山你会看到一座庙。 3. For your information, … 特此通知您，……	英语中的介词也往往行使汉语中动词的功能，所以在翻译时它们之间往往要进行相应的转换，如英语说"Up the hill you will see a temple"，汉语则说"爬上山你会看到一座庙"。
B. 汉译英 1. 看您方便。 At your convenience. 2. 您请先。 After you. 3. 请随便。 Be at home.	从动词到介词短语，实现了由静到动的转换。

4. 英语副词与汉语动态表达法的转换

基本例句	分析说明
A. 英译汉 1. The show is already on. 演出已经开始了。 2. I'll be back. 我还会回来的。 3. Are you up? 你起床了吗？	英语中的副词往往可以行使汉语中动词功能，所以在翻译时它们之间往往要进行相应的转换，如英语说"The show is already on"，汉语则说"演出已经开始了"。
B. 汉译英 1. 闲人莫入。 Business only. 2. 这支队伍士气不高，很快出局了。 The football team was down and out soon. 3. 桌子有条腿掉了。 The table has a leg off.	一动一静，一反一正，相映成趣。

5. 英语独立成分与汉语动态表达法的转换

基本例句	分析说明
A. 英译汉 1. He came in, book in the armpit. 他进来了,胳膊下夹着书。 2. I stood there, silent. 我站在那儿,一言不发。 3. She sat there, still, chin in hand. 她坐在那儿,手托着下巴,一动不动。 4. Winning the game in the end, he felt extremely excited. 最终赢得比赛,他兴奋极了!(比较:在最终赢得比赛时,他感到异常兴奋。) 5. With this understood, you may understand other problems readily. 你如果理解这一点,就很容易理解其他相关问题了。(比较:你如果……)	英语中的独立主格、主语补足语等结构同样也可以行使汉语中动词的功能,所以在翻译时它们之间往往要进行相应的转换。
B. 汉译英 1. 最后他还是死了,手里握着枪。 Finally, he died, gun in hand. 2. 老头嘴里叼着烟斗,说:"你这个年纪的时候,我靠挖煤谋生。" The old man said, pipe in mouth, "When I was of your age, I dug coal for a living." 3. 所有问题都深入讨论过了,他们现在就决定采取行动。 All problems elaborately discussed, they now decided to go into action.	将动词词组或句子转成静态的独立成分。原理同上,逆向运用。

三、翻译练习

◆ 课堂练习 ◆

● 练习1（英译汉）

1. One marvels at the breathless swiftness with which Lu Xun's text "flows" … in a single paragraph.

2. He is a good eater and sleeper, partly because his parents are good workers.

3. An unguided ramble into its recesses in bad weather is apt to engender dissatisfaction with its narrow, tortuous, and miry ways.

4. The father was present at the birth.

5. By reason of his lameness, the boy could not play basketball with his friends.

6. In the event of rain, the sports meet will have to be put off.

7. Officially, he's on holiday; actually, he is in hospital.

8. The grotto was about fifteen feet in depth.

9. This kind of products in our country has been on the increase.

10. The colonel had a firm handclasp and a brilliant smile for everyone.

11. After she was baptized, the Godfather began to teach her the importance of gratitude to God.

12. It was only after bitter experiences that David began to understand the complexity of this world.

13. The signs of times point to the necessity of the modification of the system of administration.

14. No year passes without evidence of the truth of the statement that the work of government is becoming increasingly difficult.

15. I marveled at the relentlessness determination of the rain.

16. Store in a cool dry place away from direct sunlight

17. … what is it, more medicine, more automobile rides, more foolishness to keep me away from my office?

18. One night during a heavy raid Clive told Prue why he would not go back to the army, why he intended to desert. He told her of his childhood, of his illegitimate birth and of his sordid remembrances of childhood in the slums.

19. Carlisle Street runs westward, across a great black bridge, down a hill and up a gain by little shops and meat markets, past single storied houses, until suddenly it stops against a wide green lawn.

- 练习2（汉译英）

1. 努力工作是（获得）成功的唯一捷径。

2. 他在班里学习最迟钝。

3. （转念）再一次想想，他又改变了主意。

4. 孩子们正在玩。

5. 从上海飞到三藩市需要8个小时。

6. 你真的看到UFO出现了？

7. 用计算机软件做翻译当然有可能。

8. 她两年前与那位百万富翁结了婚,结果证明这婚没有结好。

9. 英汉两种语言间的差异,有些现象很难分类。

10. 他们最希望的,就是结束不稳定的局面。

11. 他讲述了伟大与杰出的意义。

12. 商定的那天下起了倾盆大雨。

13. 大多数人意识不到的是,赚多少钱并不等同于有多少收入。

14. 我女儿虽然才7岁,但对数学问题很着迷。

15. 她在不知情的情况下喝下了有毒的汤。

◆ 课后练习 ◆

- **练习1(英译汉)**

1. The discovery of gold in California attracted thousands of immigrants.

2. We know the race is not to the swift, nor the battle to the strong.

3. Father agreed to finance me for a year, and after various delays I came east, permanently, I thought, in the spring of twenty-two.

4. … but their physical resemblance must be a source of perpetual confusion to the gulls that fly overhead.

5. My own house was an eyesore, but it was a small eyesore, and it had been overlooked, so I had a view of the water, a partial view of my neighbor's lawn, and the consoling proximity of millionaires—all of eighty dollars a month.

6. It was sharply different from the West, where an evening was hurried from phase to phase toward its close, in a continually disappointed anticipation or else in sheer nervous dread of the moment itself.

7. Miss Baker and I exchanged a short glance consciously devoid of meaning.

8. Almost before I had grasped her meaning there was the flutter of a dress and the crunch of leather boots, and Tom and Daisy were back at the table.

9. There was always a tapping foot somewhere or the impatient opening and closing of a hand.

10. His eyes glanced momentarily at me, and his lips parted with an abortive attempt at a laugh.

11. After his embarrassment and his unreasoning joy he was consumed with wonder at her presence.

12. We've had gymnastics champions barely out of infancy.

13. When I first saw unemployed men at close quarters, the thing that horrified and amazed me was to find that many of them were ashamed of being unemployed.

14. They were decent young miners and cotton workers gazing at their destiny with the same sort of dumb amazement as an animal in trap.

15. All we do all for the children here is to give them visual, auditory and touchable stimulation with increased frequency, and intensity and duration.

16. Television hasn't been with us all that long, but we are already to forget what the world was like without it.

17. None of the bodies were ever found, although the whole village, full of sympathy, assembled in search.

18. Though they may have the boldest manners and most up-to-date ideas, they share their great grandmothers' humble dependence.

19. When they grew up, they became chasers, runners, jumpers, aimers, throwers and prey killers.

20. America is a country on the move. In unheard of numbers, people of all ages are exercising their way to better health.

21. The early trains were impractical curiosities, and for a long time the railroad company met with troublesome mechanical problems.

22. The most serious problems were the construction of rails able to bear the load, and the development of a safe, effective stopping system.

23. Many visitors came here for the great occasion. There were joyous celebration all over the country, with parades and the ringing of church bells to honor the great achievement.

24. Nrthrop Frye's criticism is richly textured, so dense with insight, and so wide-ranging in its references … The Secular Scripture is in fact the most sophisticated study of popular culture, considered on a world scale, that we have yet had.

- 练习2（汉译英）

1. 使用细菌武器显然是违反国际法的。

2. 他们两个星期不说话了。

3. 看到故乡，他想起了自己的童年生活。

4. 他冷不丁冒出来，吓了我一大跳！

5. 他认识到那样和老板说话是愚蠢的。

6. 阿基米德首先发现固体排水的原理。

7. 威斯敏斯特教堂遐想。

8. 那是我初次与约翰逊会面。

9. 沃尔特·惠特曼访问记。

10. 记一位忠实的朋友。
11. 论具有现代头脑。
12. 她和家人已经有几个星期不说话了。
13. 小女孩已经上了一半楼梯了。
14. 这种鱼便宜,但污染严重,已禁止出售。很多人吃了这种鱼后死于中毒。
15. 他这么做不是为了作秀。
16. 犹豫了一小会儿,他点了点头,算是也向我打了招呼;她向我使了个眼色。
17. 请放心,我一定再来。
18. 请随便选你喜欢的。
19. 他被吸收入党是很自然的一件事。
20. 在这家工厂工作(干活)要起得早。
21. 学外语就要不厌其烦地重复。
22. 为了使自己在生活中不犯错误,特列出我认为应该身体力行的13条守则。这些守则是:(1)节制饮食;(2)自我克制;(3)沉默寡言;(4)有条不紊;(5)坚定信念;(6)勤俭节约;(7)工作勤奋;(8)忠诚老实;(9)办事公正;(10)衣履整洁;(11)平心静气;(12)品性高尚;(13)谦虚恭顺。

● 练习3(英译汉)

(1) Narcissus; or Self-Love (Francis Bacon)

Narcissus is said to have been a young man of wonderful beauty, but intolerably proud, fastidious, and disdainful. Pleased with himself and despising all others, he led a solitary life the woods and hunting grounds; with a few companions he was all in all; followed also wherever he went by a nymph called Echo. Living thus, he came by chance one day to a clear fountain, and (being in the heat of noon) lay down by it; when beholding in the water his own image, he fell into a study and such a rapturous admiration of himself, that he could not be drawn away from gazing at the shadowy picture, but remained rooted to the spot tills sense left him; and at last he was changed into the flower that bears his name; a flower which appears in the early spring, and is sacred to the infernal deities—Pluto, Proserpine, and the Furies.

In this fable are represented the dispositions, and the fortunes too, of those persons who from consciousness either of beauty or some other gift with which nature unaided by any industry of their own has graced them, fall in love as it were with themselves. For with this state of mind there is commonly joined an indisposition to appear much in public or engage in business; because business would expose them many neglects and scorns, by which their minds would be dejected and troubled. Therefore, they commonly live a solitary, private, and shadowed life; with a small circle of chosen companions, all devoted admirers, who assent like an echo to everything they say, and entertain them with mouth-homage; till being by such habits gradually depraved and puffed up, and besotted at last with self-admiration, they fall into such a sloth and listlessness that they grow utterly stupid, and lose all vigour and alacrity. And it was a beautiful thought to choose the flower of spring as an emblem of characters like this: characters which in the opening of their career flourish and talked of, but disappoint in maturity the promise of their youth. The fact too that this flower is sacred to the infernal deities contains an allusion to the same thing. For men of this disposition turn out utterly useless and good for nothing whatever; and anything that yields no fruit, but like the way of a ship in the sea passes and leaves no trace, was by the accidents held sacred to the shades and infernal gods.

(2) What Is an American? (Michel-Guillaume de Crevecoeur)

Michel-Guillaume de Crevecoeur (1735 – 1813) was born in France and came to the American colonies as a military in the French army. He became a naturalized American and settled down to farming. Between 1765 and 1780 he wrote on American life. He returned to France in 1780, came back to America in 1783, and became French consul in New York. In 1790 he went back to France where he lived the rest of his life.

I wish I could be acquainted with the feelings and thought which must agitate the heart and present themselves to the mind of an enlightened Englishman, when he first lands on this continent. He must greatly rejoice, that he lived at a time to see this fair country discovered and settled; he must necessarily feel a share of national pride, when he views the chain of settlements which embellishes these extended shore. When he says to himself, this is the work of my countrymen who, when convulsed by factions, afflicted by a variety of miseries and wants, restless and impatient, took refuge here. They brought along with them their national genius, to which they principally owe what liberty they enjoy, and what substance they possess. Here he sees the industry of his native country, displayed in a new manner, and traces in their works the embryos of all the arts, sciences, and ingenuity which flourish in Europe. Here he beholds fair cities, substantial villages, extensive fields, an immense country filled with decent houses, good roads, orchards, meadows, and bridges, where a hundred years ago all was wild, woody, and uncultivated! ...

After a foreigner from any part of Europe is arrived, and become a citizen; let him devoutly listen to the voice of our great parent, which says to him, "Welcome to my shores, distressed European; bless the hour in which thou didst see my verdant fields, my fair navigable rivers, and my green mountains! —If thou wilt work, I have bread for thee; if thou wilt be honest, sober and industrious, I have greater rewards to confer on thee—ease and independence. I will give thee fields to feed and clothe thee; a comfortable fire-side to sit by, and tell thy children by what means thou hast prospered; and a decent bed to repose on. I shall endow thee, beside, with the immunities of a freeman. If thou wilt carefully educate thy children, teach them gratitude to God, and reverence to that government, that philanthropic government, which has collected here so many men and made them happy, I will also provide for thy progeny: and to every good man this ought to be the most holy, the most powerful, the most earnest wish he can possibly form, as well as the most consolatory prospect when he dies.

Go thou, and work and till; thou shalt prosper, provided thou be just, grateful and industrious."

● 练习4（汉译英）

春 节

农历正月初一是我国汉族以及其他一些少数民族最为隆重的传统节日——春节。自从汉武帝以来，中华民族一直都将春节视为最喜庆的日子。每逢大年初一，孩子们纷纷走上街头放鞭炮，就连大人们也高高兴兴地在爆竹声中辞旧迎新。北宋诗人王安石曾赋诗："爆竹声中一岁除，春风送暖入屠苏。千门万户曈曈日，总把新桃换旧符。"他的诗生动地描绘了人们迎佳节时喜悦的气氛。

其实，春节还未来到，人们就忙碌了起来，各户全家老少齐上阵，粉墙的粉墙，洗被褥的洗被褥，准备"面貌一新迎新年"。有许多家庭还蒸豆沙包以及菜包子，不但自己受用，还招待亲朋好友。每一家都必须"年购"，贮存大量的美味食品在家中，否则一到春节就"惨"了，因为商店在节日期间会店门紧闭，老板及营业员们都回各自家中同亲人们一起过节。

贴年画也是春节必不可少的一种活动。年画的内容非常丰富，有祝福招财的，如画一童子怀里抱着元宝，或者骑在大鲤鱼身上；也有除祸降幅的，如在门板上贴勇士像等。南朝的时候各家各户都在门上贴神荼、郁垒二兄弟的画像，传说他们能降妖伏怪，给人带来吉祥。到了唐朝，人们把自己最崇拜的秦叔宝、尉迟敬德两位大将的画像请到了门上。直至今日，我国的许多地区仍将这两位勇士敬若神明，每逢春节都张贴他们的像以增加吉祥的气氛。有相当一部分地区，特别是在乡村，喜欢把钟馗的画像贴于门首驱邪招福。钟馗一生刚直不阿，专门与恶鬼作对，死后玉皇大帝封他为"斩祟将军"，带领三千神兵天将捕鬼杀怪，在民间享有很高的美誉。

旧岁的最后一天叫"大年三十"，因"除旧岁"而得名"除夕"。除夕之夜，全家人围坐在一起说闲话。在外地工作的亲人赶回来与家人团聚，大伙儿边聊边饮茶，同时还嗑瓜子、吃油炸馓子等小食品。现在的除夕之夜，从晚八时到夜里十二时，各家都以看春节联欢晚会为主要活动，边看边唠家常，其乐融融。在北方，家庭闲聊时还不忘包饺子，除过先吃一部分之外，其余的要留到大年初一吃。当然，春节可不是光吃点饺子就算完啦，好吃的东西多着呢，如糖糕、汤圆、枣馍等。孩子们一见好吃的应有尽有，就拼命地饱口福，吃坏肠胃的可大有人在。有的人家在除夕之夜便给小辈们发压岁钱，有的则等到初一再发。孩子们盼过年，其中有一个目的就是能拿到数目不小的压岁钱，差不多所有的孩子都可以发一笔小财。大年初一天不亮，爆竹声便响成了一片，噼噼啪啪似炒豆一般。父母为孩子们煮好饺子，让他们美美吃一顿。小家伙们吃完一抹嘴,便箭一般冲出去了。小朋友们聚集在大街上点各种各样的"炮",有的叫"冲天响""滚地雷",有的叫"天女散花""红衣骑士",等等,名堂多得很。大人们则走东家访西家地"拜年"。单位的领导此时体现出"与民同乐"的风范,到部属的家里说些"春节快乐""恭喜发财"之类的祝福话语。

拜年的习俗古来有之。传说在很久以前有一种叫"年"的怪兽,每逢腊月三十便冲下山,张着血盆大口寻人吃。惊恐的人们把各种肉食放在门口请它吃,而他们自己闭门躲在家中。第二天人们打开房门,相互祝贺未被"年"吃掉。后来,人们拜年不仅说些祝福的话,还互赠贺年卡,卡片上或印着精美的图画,或写些警言妙句。

人们在欢度春节的时候,也不会忘记已经亡故的亲人。他们会为亡亲敬一盅酒,或燃香祈求上天赐福给阴间的亲人。有的人家会结伴到亡亲的坟地去,在坟头供枣馍、油糕之类的东西。如今提倡火葬,人们则到存放亡亲骨灰的地方祭奠他们,同时给亡亲的长眠之地带去了节日的喜庆气氛。

我国的南方和北方都有"舞狮"贺春节的习俗,在形式及内容上大同小异。在乡下,村与村之间常举行舞狮比赛;在城市里,社区与社区也结阵对垒。一只"狮子"通常由两人舞,一人舞狮头,另一人舞狮身。舞狮头者是关键人物,必须眼明手快、反应敏捷,一般都是由幼童培养起来的。比赛时,两只狮子(通常代表两个团体)在一片锣鼓声中翩翩起舞。张开大口争夺一只巨型绣球。舞狮人身着戏装,上下翻腾,龙腾虎跃,好不雄健!好不威风!充分表现出了中华民族旺盛的生命力和不屈不挠的奋斗精神。舞狮头的人往往要亮出几个危险的高难度动作,如一跃跳到叠架起的桌椅上,赢得观众阵阵的掌声。

一些地区盛行"舞龙"的习俗,这和舞狮一样,也是庆贺新春的重要活动。舞龙需要若干人参与,一人舞龙头,其余人则是"龙身"。巨龙时而昂首阔步,时而张牙舞爪、摇头摆尾,赢得旁观人群的高声喝彩。人们的心随着巨龙翻腾的身体起伏,对舞龙人高超的技艺感到由衷的佩服。最为壮观的是夜间舞龙,巨龙的两只眼睛通常用手电筒充当,显得"目光炯炯"。一道道手电光刺破夜空,使人会联想到巨龙与怪兽搏斗的场景,不由热血沸腾,仿佛自己也加入了与恶势力的酣战之中。

正月十五的元宵节在有的地区被称为"小年",虽说比不得初一和初二那几日气氛隆重,却也热闹非凡。许多店铺以及小商贩们把形形色色的灯笼挂出来展销,其外形有"哪吒闹海""孙悟空""猪八戒""沙僧",也有"猪""猫""狗""兔"等小动物。灯笼内置一蜡烛,在夜间闪闪烁烁,把"猪八戒"们、"狗"们照得通体发亮,煞是好看。在烛光的照耀下,有舞狮的,有舞龙的,有摇旱船和踩高跷的,组成了一幅幅美轮美奂的画面。无论白天还是黑夜,公园里都人山人海,游园的人们边品尝小路边摊点销售的各种小吃,边玩游戏,如抛圈、射击等。孩子们兴奋地在人群中窜来跑去,呼兄喊弟,还不时停下来用压岁钱买一些自己喜欢的小玩意儿。

元宵节"闹灯"是从唐朝传下来的习俗。一入夜,人们纷纷手提灯笼走出家门,一盏盏灯汇集成灯的海洋。古时候都是官府出资将街道装点得焕然一新,到处一片"火树银花"。唐睿宗时,长安的皇宫外庆贺元宵节,曾架起一座高二十丈的灯山,上面镶嵌着五颜六色的彩带以及各种小饰物,还悬挂了五万盏彩灯。百姓们结伴赏灯,观看放焰火和精彩的杂耍表演。到了宋代,民间还添了猜字谜的游戏。出字谜的人把谜语写在细长的纸条上,再将纸条贴在灯笼的下端,猜中的人可领到一些小礼品。明代的元宵节更热闹,戏曲演员们走上街头献艺,给人们带来艺术的享受和欢声笑语。

元宵节的主食是"元宵",或称"汤圆",是一种用糯米做成的带馅球状食物。南北方的元宵基本差不多,有黑芝麻馅的、白糖馅的以及山楂馅的等;南方人还喜欢吃肉馅的元宵。现在的元宵种类丰富,里面裹的馅千变万化,适合于各种口味的食客。

元宵节期间,人们开始了新一轮的"访亲拜友热"。几天过后,热潮消退,人们就彻底收心了,开始专心致志地工作。

四、练习参考译文

◆ 课堂练习 ◆

● 练习1（英译汉）

1. 鲁迅(上文)寥寥数言,一气呵成,如风行水上,让人叹为观止。
2. 他能吃能睡,部分原因在于他父母能干。
3. 若是气候恶劣,又没有向导带路,一个人如果闯进这儿的腹心地带,很可能对它那狭窄、弯曲、泥泞的道路感到不满。
4. 婴儿出生时其父亲在场。
5. 由于跛足,那男孩不能和朋友们一起打篮球。
6. 如果天下雨,运动会将不得不推迟。
7. 官方说,他在度假,实际上他住院了。
8. 这个洞穴深约15英尺。
9. 这种产品在我国一直在增加。
10. 上校和每个人都坚定地握握手,灿烂地笑一笑。
11. 她接受洗礼后,神父便开始教导她对上帝感恩戴德是如何重要。
12. 大卫只是在经历了许多痛苦磨难后才开始理解这个世界有多么错综复杂。
13. 时代迹象表明,有必要改进行政管理体制。
14. 有人说政府工作越来越难做,每年都有证据表明这种说法道出了实情。
15. 雨决意下个不停,毫不留情,对此我感到诧异。
16. 请置于阴凉干燥处,避免阳光照晒。
17. 搞什么名堂?是让我服更多的药,开更多的车,让我更愚蠢,好让我远离办公室,是吗?

18. 一天晚上,在密集的轰炸期间,克莱夫对普露讲明了自己不愿归队、想开小差的原因,讲述了自己童年的往事,讲述了他作为私生子的身世以及一想起来就感到卑贱的贫民窟中的童年生活。

19. 卡莱尔大街往西伸展,越过一座黑色大桥,爬下山岗又爬上去,经过许多小铺和肉市,又经过一些平房,然后突然朝着一大片绿色草地中止了。

● 练习 2（汉译英）

1. Hard work is the only shortcut to success.

2. He is the slowest student in his class.

3. A second thought about it made him change his mind.

4. The children are at play.

5. The flight from Shanghai to San Francisco takes 8 hours.

6. Did you really see the appearance of the UFO?

7. The use of computer software in translation is certainly a possibility.

8. Her marriage with the millionaire two years ago proves to be a failure.

9. Some phenomena in the differences between English and Chinese defy easy classification.

10. What they wanted most was an end of uncertainties.

11. He discussed greatness and excellence.

12. The day agreed upon was pouring rain.

13. What most people don't realize is that wealth isn't the same as income.

14. My daughter, still a little girl of seven, was much absorbed in math questions.

15. She drank the poisonous soup, without any knowledge of it.

◆ 课后练习 ◆

● 练习 1（英译汉）

1. 加利福尼亚发现了金子,吸引了成千上万的移民。

2. 我们知道,身手敏捷不一定就能赢得比赛,力量强大不一定就能赢得战争。

3. 父亲同意资助我一年,但我耽误良多,后来去了东部定居。我记得,是在1922年春天。

4. ……但它们外部特征相似,上面飞过的海鸥因此一直对此迷惑不已。

5. 我自己的房子真是难看,但算不上很难看。人们一直注意不到它。我从房中可以看得到大海、邻家的半块草坪。几个百万富翁就住我附近,这倒叫人欣慰。而这房租不过每月80美元罢了。

6. 东部和西部迥然不同。在西部,黄昏在期望中被驱赶着,步履匆匆,紧张不安,害怕黑夜的到来,但它又总是失望不已。

7. 我和贝克小姐互相匆匆瞥了一眼,眼神空洞,毫无内容。

8. 我甚至还没有领会她话的意思,便听到裙子窸窸窣窣,皮靴咯吱作响,汤姆和戴茜又回到了桌上。

9. 总有人用脚敲打着地板,或者把手一松一合,很不耐烦。

10. 他眼睛看我一下,又马上移开了;他嘴唇张着,想笑,又没笑出来。

11. 他先是尴尬,又是无端高兴,可她来了,让他目瞪口呆。

12. 我们有一些体操冠军,几乎刚刚学会走路没几年。

13. 当我近距离观察失业者的时候,我发现,让我感到恐惧和惊讶的是他们对失业深感羞耻。

14. 他们曾经是年轻又体面的采矿或者棉纺工人,可现在他们面对命运感到麻木而费解,就像落入圈套的困兽一样。

15. 我们所要做的一切,就是要通过视觉、听觉和触觉的手段刺激孩子,同时频率要不断提高,强度不断加大,持续时间不断延长。

16. 人类有电视的历史并不算久远,可人们已经忘了没有电视世界会像什么样子。

17. 尸体一具也没有找到,虽然整个村子的人都很同情,帮着一起找。

18. 虽然有最大胆的行为、最新潮的观点,可他们还是和祖母一样,谦卑地依靠别人。

19. 长大后,他们长于追逐,善于奔跑,强于跳跃,精于瞄准,擅长投掷和捕杀猎物。

20. 美国人永不停歇。大量的人,不分老少,都参加运动,力求更加健康。

21. 早期的火车不太实用,同时引起了人们的好奇心。长期以来,铁路公司面临着棘手的技术问题。

22. 首要问题就是建设一条能承受相当重量的铁路,同时开发安全、有效的停靠系统。

23. 很多游客来这里参加这个盛会。全国到处都有喜气洋洋的庆祝活动,人们游行,教堂钟声响起以纪念这一伟大成就。

24. 诺思罗普·弗莱的批评肌理丰盈、创见良多、涉猎广泛、旁征博引……放眼世界,《世俗圣经》一书堪称当下对大众文化最为精深玄妙的研究。

练习 2(汉译英)

1. The use of bacteriological weapon is a clear violation of international law.
2. They were not on speaking terms for two weeks.
3. The sight of his native place called back his childhood.
4. The suddenness of his appearance gave me a start!
5. He recognized the stupidity of talking like that to his boss.
6. Archimedes first discovered the principle of displacement of water by solid bodies.
7. Thoughts in Westminster Abbey

8. That was my first meeting with Johnson.

9. A Visit to Walt Whitman

10. On a Faithful Friend

11. On Being Modern-Minded

12. But she wasn't on speaking terms with her family for several weeks.

13. The little girl was already halfway up the stairs.

14. This fish which is cheap but heavily contaminated has been forbidden to be sold. Many persons eating this fish died as a result of poison.

15. He didn't do this for show.

16. After an infinitesimal hesitation he included me with a slight nod, and she winked at me again.

17. Be sure that I will certainly come again.

18. Be free to make your favourite choice.

19. Her marriage with the millionaire two years ago is now proved to be a failure.

20. Work in this factory calls for early rise.

21. The study of a foreign language involves tedious repetition.

22. To help myself live without fault, I made a list of what I considered the 13 virtues. These virtues are：（1）Temperance，（2）Self-control，（3）Silence，（4）Order，（5）Firmness of mind，（6）Savings，（7）Industry，（8）Honesty，（9）Justice，（10）Cleanliness，（11）Calmness，（12）Morality，（13）Humbleness.

• 练习3（英译汉）

（1）那喀索斯——论自恋（弗朗西斯·培根）

那喀索斯，人称风度翩翩美少年，惟心性高傲，锱铢必较，蔑视一切，令人不堪。自我陶醉，目无余子，常年出没于林泉猎场，优游岁月，与世人不相往来；有侪侣二三，如鱼得水；行踪所至，仙女跬步不离，芳名厄科。朝夕如此，一日偶至清泉一泓，时值晌午，天气炎热，遂卧躺泉边；俯观水中倒影，始而不觉凝神观照，继而自我恋慕，如痴如狂，谛视自家面貌若隐若现，良久不去；出神入定，有如树木扎根，直至感觉消失；终于变作水仙，名曰那喀索斯；水仙早春开花；遂为冥府诸神之祭品——普路托，普罗塞尔皮娜，复仇三女神。

尔辈自觉造化赋予美貌，或别具天赋，故不假自身勤奋，煞有介事自恋自爱，此辈中人性情命运，寓言之中暴露无遗。如此心境者，每每无意出现于大庭广众，或以营生为务；因营生未免多受冷落鄙夷，怀抱如此心境则沮丧烦恼。故尔辈一生独来独往，与世睽离，黯然无光；交游挑剔，门户狭隘，彼此五体投地，一呼众和，同声相应，口角春风应酬同好；习性相染，久而久之，品性沦丧，趾高气扬，最终沉迷于自我崇拜，坠入懒散萎靡之境地，从而变得绝顶愚蠢，活力锐气丧失殆尽。以春天水仙为同类性格之标志，堪称妙想，事业开创之际一帆风顺，为人称道，风华正茂时豪情满怀，盛年时则俱为泡影。水仙成为冥府诸神之祭品，寓意亦在于斯。如此性情者,终于毫无用处,一无所能;凡事无所结果,犹如沧海行舟,飘然而过,不留痕迹,古人遂奉为阴魂与地狱神明。

(2) 何为美国人?(米·居奎维古尔)

作者简介:米·居奎维古尔(1734—1831)生于法国,随法军进入北美殖民地,取得美国国籍后定居务农。1765—1780年间执笔评论美国人的生活。1780年回法国,1783年又到美国,并成为法国驻纽约领事。1790年回法国安度晚年。

但愿我也像一位初次登上北美大陆的英国开明人士那样,曾经体会到那种使人心潮澎湃、浮想联翩的思想感情。他一定欣喜若狂,庆幸自己有生之年能亲眼看到人们发现这块美丽的国土并在此定居下来。当他看到一座座居所使这漫长的海岸线锦上添花的时候,他怎能不拥有一份民族自豪感呢!他自然会想到,这些杰作都出自我的同胞之手,他们为教派倾轧而震惊,受尽了苦难和贫穷,是在焦躁不安的情况下来这里避难的。他们带来了民族天赋,所以才会享受现在的自由,才会拥有现在的财产。在这里,可以看到故国的勤劳展现出了新的姿态,在其杰作中可以找到那些盛行于欧洲的所有的艺术、科学和创造的萌芽。在这里,他看到了美丽的城镇、富饶的村庄、广阔的田野,看到了一片汗漫无边的国土,其间有典雅的建筑、通达的道路,有果园、草地、桥梁;而这里在100年前还是一片荒蛮,草木丛生,不见农田!……

一个人无论来自欧洲何处,当他到达这里并成为公民以后,就让他虔诚地聆听我们伟大祖国的声音吧。这声音说:"欢迎你登上我的海岸,不幸的欧洲人。铭记这一神圣的时刻吧! 此刻,你看到了我碧绿的田野、美丽的河道和苍翠的群山! 如果你愿意劳动,我为你准备了面包;如果你正直、朴实、勤劳,我要给你更大的报偿——安逸与自主。我将给你土地供你作丰衣足食;给你舒适的壁炉供你取暖,并让你在炉火边告诉你的后代你如何获得成功;我还要给你体面堂皇的床铺供你栖身;还要赐给你一个自由人的特权。如果你愿意精心教育子女,教他们感激上帝、尊重政府,尊重这个使如此之多的人聚集在这里并得到幸福的慈善的政府,我也将供给你的后代。这对任何善良的人来说都应该是他所能怀有的最神圣、最强烈、最殷切的希望,也是人弥留之际最大的慰藉。去吧,去劳动,去耕耘,只要你公正守法、知恩图报、勤奋努力,你必将兴旺、富强。"

● 练习4(汉译英)

The Spring Festival (*Chunjie*)

Chunjie—the first day of the first month in the lunar year marks the most important traditional festival for the Han people as well as for some ethnic groups in China. This tradition of the whole Chinese nation began as early as in Wudi Emperor's Reign of the Han Dynasty. Since then, the day would always see children taking to the streets to fire off firecrackers, and the adults listening to the blasts as they bid farewell to the old times and greet the new year. As regards this there is a poem left to us by a poet of the North Song Dynasty named Wang An-Shi (1021 – 1086), which goes as the following:

Amid the firework crackles, a year is past.
The spring warmth enters Tusu wine in a blast.
As the sun shines upon every house's door,
New couplets appear, and the old seen no more.

This is really a vivid depiction of the joyful atmosphere of the festival celebration.

In fact, even before *Chunjie*, people would get busy for the preparations. In every household, all people would start working, regardless of their age, with some doing the whitewashing, others doing the laundry, so as to "greet the new year with a new look". In many families, steamed *baozi* dough wrap-ups of red bean and vegetables would be prepared, not only for their own consumption but also for treating their relatives and friends. They also have to do the "new-year shopping" to store a good quantity of food in advance, because during the festival the shops would all close, with the owners and their assistants going home to celebrate the festival with their folks.

Posting the New Year Pictures is also a must of the festival activity. The contents of pictures are rich, carrying various messages, some for good wishes and fortune (such as a child carrying gold ingots or riding on the back of a big carp), and others for ridding off evils and for blessings (such as a heroic figure posted on the door). The latter custom comes from the South Dynasty (420 – 589), when people would post the drawings of Shentu and Yulei brothers on their doors because they were believed to have the power of subjugating evil sprits and bringing good luck. Then in the Tang Dynasty (618 – 907), the drawings of the two most worshipped generals Qin Shubao and Wei Chijing were posted instead. Even today, in many districts these two figures were still regarded as sages and their drawings posted to contribute to the propitious atmosphere during the festival. In many parts of the country, particularly in the rural areas, the drawing of Zhong Kui is posted, for he had an upright character and, as a born enemy of the evil spirits, was granted the title of "evil-killer general" by the heavenly ruler of the Jade Emperor after death. He enjoyed a high reputation among the people, for the legend goes that he led three thousand heavenly warriors to catch and kill the evil beings.

The last day of the ending year is called *Danian Sanshi* (literally "the big year's 30th"). It is also named *Chuxi*, for in Chinese it means "the ridding-off (the old) eve". On the evening of this day, family members would all sit together for a conversation on liberal topics. So those who work out would then return for this gathering of their own folks. They would then sit talking over tea and such "odd food" as crack seeds and fried dough chips. Currently, watching the special entertainment TV program of the evening is also a major part of the family activities, which would last from 8 p.m. to midnight through the family talk, adding to the joyful air. In the north, people would not forget wrapping up *jiaozi* as they chat off, and they would not only make enough for the immediate consumption but also for the next day—the first day of the new year.

To be sure, *jiaozi* is not all that is served at the Spring Festival's table. There is too much more: sweet rice cakes, rice dumplings, date-dotted *mantou*, etc. So the children, seeing such gorgeous display of food, find it hard to stop eating, and many would have a stomach trouble because of too much eating.

Yasuiqian, a sum of money as a token for gaining a new year in age, is given to children by their parents. But whether it is given by the new year's eve or the first day of the new year is the family's choice. This also explains why the children are so eagerly looking out for the festival, for the sum of money may not be a small one. Almost all of them may gain "a small fortune".

Even before dawn of the new year's first day, firecrackers would begin to crackle off, sounding like popping corns in a hot pot. The parents serve their children with *jiaozi*, which they have prepared for them to eat to their hearts' content. And the little ones would no sooner finish eating than dash out into the street, for they would gather to fire off all kinds of crackers, with such names as "piercing-the-sky", "sweeping landmines", "the-fairy-spreading flowers", "the cavalier in red coat", etc. There are just too many to mention. In the mean time, the adults go around to *bainian*—paying the new year visits. And the leading figures of organizations would take the opportunity to show their amiability to their employees, as they can now pay visits to them, expressing good wishes for them with such greetings as "Happy New Year", "Good Fortune", etc.

The custom of *bainian* is an ancient one. As the legend goes, there lived a monster named *nian* many many years ago, which would dash down the hill to eat people on the last day of the passing year, with red, wide-open mouth. So the frightened people would place various kinds of meat on the doorway for it to eat, while hiding behind shut doors themselves. Then the next morning, as they open their doors, they would congratulate each other on their good luck of surviving the danger. Later, people would not only just say some good-wishing words but also present each other seasonal greeting cards, with beautiful designs, maxims, or clever sayings.

As people celebrate the Spring Festival, they will not forget their deceased folks. They will pour out a cup of wine for them, or light an incense to pray the god to bless them, for they are believed to live on in another world. Some will also visit their tombs and put some date-dotted *mantou*, fried rice dough cakes at the head of the tombs as sacrifice. Presently, since cremation is called for, people would go to the ash remains depository for the memorial ceremony and bring along with them the joyous air for their folks who are forever at rest.

In both the north and south of China there is the customary lion dance to celebrate the festival, with only minor variation in the form and content. Competitions of lion dance are often held between villages in the rural areas as well as between communities in the cities. A "lion" is usually played by two people, with one playing the head and the other playing the body. The former is regarded as a crucial player, for he must demonstrate extreme agility in action and quickness in perception, which is usually developed in a person from early childhood. In competition, two "lions", with each representing its own party, will fight for a huge ball fringed with tassel (called *xiuqiu*) as they dance to the music of gongs, drums and cymbals. The players dressed in stage costumes will jump up and down in buoyancy. What an action! In it is the full representation of the Chinese people's spirit of fortitudinous strife against the evil. The head player of the lion dance will often run through a series of dangerous stunts, such as jumping onto a chair on a table, so as to win the spectators' applauses.

In some parts of the country there is the custom of "dragon dance" in addition. Like the "lion dance", it is also a major activity of the festival celebration. This dance calls for several participants, with one playing the head and the rest playing "the lion body". So, the huge "lion" will now stride forward with straightened head, now open its mouth and claws, now sway back and forth its head and tail, all for people's acclaims. The spectators' hearts may also go up and down with the action of the "dragon", and they will naturally admire their extraordinary skills shown in the performance.

The "dragon dance" look best during the night, when the huge eyes of the dragon, each plays with a torch inside, give off sky-piercing light, which may lead people to imagine a legendary fight it has had against a monster, making them feel so excited as though they were also involved in the intense war against the evil force.

The Lantern Festival of the 15th day of the new year's first month is called *xiaonian*, literally "the small new year". Though not as solemnly celebrated as the first or second day, it is just as well full of activities. Now many shops and itinerating peddlers would hang out various lanterns to sell. The lanterns bear different designs, such as "Ne Zha on the Sea", "Monkey Sun", "The Pig", and "The Friar Sand". Some may have the image of the pig, cat, dog, rabbit or another pet animal. Inside the lantern there is usually a candle light that keeps flickering during the dark night. The animal and figure designs on the outside show sharp and clear silluettes set off by the light, looking very nice to the spectators.

In the night lit up by candle light, there are various entertainment activities outdoors, such as the dances of the lion and dragon players, land boat rowers and the participants of the stilt parade. All the activities greatly contribute to the superlative scene of delight and beauty.

Regardless of night and day, the public gardens are as crowded as "people mountain and people sea" (*renshan renhai*). The sightseers can enjoy various food specialties on the roadside peddle stands as they play games, such as shooting and throwing loops for prizes. In the mean time, the kids run through the crowd in excitement, calling out for their playmates and buying their favorite small gadgets with their *yasuiqian*.

"Lantern play" on the Lantern Festival is a custom passed down from the Tang Dynasty. On such a day, people will take to the streets as soon as it is dark, with all lanterns coming together to make a Milky Way on land. In the ancient times, the government or its officials would finance for the renovation of the street front to give it a new look. And "the fire trees of silvery flowers" (displays of lanterns and fireworks) were seen everywhere. As recorded of the period of Ruizong Emperor, a high rack of about 70 meters would be constructed outside the royal palace for displaying the lanterns, decorated with colorful ribbons and other things to go with the thousands of colorful bright lanterns. The citizens would go in their own company of each other to appreciate the lantern display, the firework and the wonderful circus performances.

When it was in the Song Dynasty, there appeared the game of word puzzle, in which the person who proposes would write the puzzle on a slip of paper stuck on the lower part of the lantern. Anyone who could hit the answer would get some gift as a prize.

Then the Lantern Festival became even more hilarious in the Ming Dynasty, when opera performers would also put on their arts in the streets to please the people.

The major food item for the Lantern Festival is *yuanxiao*, or *tang-yuan*. It is made of sticky rice, in the form of balls containing fillings. *Yuanxiao* has little variations in the north and south, usually containing such fillings as black sesame, sugar, haw, etc. But in the south people are also fond of meat fillings. Nowadays the contents of *yuanxiao* are getting richer, with a greater variety of fillings to cater for different tastes.

The festival also marks another round of visiting activity. And it is only when this day is past that the enthusiasm of the Spring Festival begin to recede and people will then turn back to concentrate on their work.

【讨论】

通过上文的讲解、注释等,我们已经发现,英语多以名词为中心,汉语多以动词为中心,把英语名词结构翻译成汉语动词结构,符合两种语言的习惯。我们在翻译时应该注意运用这一重要规律,这样我们做翻译就会得心应手。本章只做了一个简单的分析,实际上,把英语名词结构翻译成汉语动词结构,不仅符合汉语习惯,有时还有助于消除歧义,比如英文说"my book",并未说明 my 指的是拥有权还是制作权,如果指的是制作权,中文我们可以有意识地翻译为"我写的书",以便于读者理解。

应该指出,我们不是提倡把英语原文中的名词结构一律译为汉语的动词结构,我们说的是,英语名词结构译为汉语动词结构是一个常见的转换,是一个比较显著的规律。需要指出的是,不能把差异绝对化。例如,英语用抽象名词表达行为或事物的状态和性质的地方,汉语往往倾向于用形容词来表述,如英语的"complexity"可译为"错综复杂的",

"happiness"可译为"幸福美满"。又如,"He recognized the stupidity of talking like that to his boss." 可译为"他意识到,那样和老板说话是愚蠢的。"

英译汉中,有几种汉语常用动词性结构可以用来翻译英语中的名词结构:主谓结构、主谓宾结构、动宾结构、动宾补结构、谓状结构等。这里仅举例说明三种我们常把英语名词译为汉语动词的情况:

(1) 名词+介词短语

这类结构中,介词短语在逻辑上是行为名词的动作对象或动作的发出者,这种结构常常译为汉语的动宾结构或者主谓(宾)结构。例如:

例1. His acceptance into the Party is a quite natural thing. 他被吸收入党是很自然的一件事。

例2. The use of bacteriological weapon is a clear violation of international law. 使用细菌武器显然是违反国际法的。

例3. An unguided ramble into its recesses in bad weather is apt to engender dissatisfaction with its narrow, tortuous, and miry ways. 若是气候恶劣,又没有向导带路,一个人胡闯进腹心地带,很可能对它那狭窄、弯曲、泥泞的道路感到不满。

(2) 介词+名词

这种结构在原文中一般起到时间状语、原因状语、条件状语、让步状语等作用,在翻译时常用相应功能的"介词+动宾"等结构代替。例如:

例4. The father was present at the birth. 婴儿出生时其父亲在场。

例5. By reason of his lameness, the boy could not play basketball with his friends. 由于跛足,那男孩不能和朋友们一起打篮球。

例6. In the event of rain, the sports meet will have to be put off. 如果天下雨,运动会将不得不推迟。

例7. Officially, he's on holiday; actually, he is in hospital. 官方说,他在度假,实际上他住院了。

例8. The grotto was about fifteen feet in depth. 这个洞穴深约15英尺。

例9. Dreadful to me was the coming home in the raw twilight, with nipped fingers and toes, and a heart saddened by the chidings of Bessie, the nurse, and humbled by the consciousness of my physical inferiority to Eliza, John, and Georgiana Reed. 试想,阴冷的薄暮时分回得家来,手脚都冻僵了,还要受到保姆贝蒂的数落,又自觉体格不如伊丽莎他们,心里既难过又惭愧,那情形委实可怕。

(3) (助)动词+名词+介词

这种结构多为固定搭配,其中的(助)动词赋予了名词动词的含义,翻译为汉语常使用动宾、动补等结构。例如:

例10. Too many late nights can do great harm to you. 经常熬夜可能给你造成很大危害。

除上述三种情况外还有许多需要作动词化处理的情况,如在省略句中,比如,"Great nations, if adversaries, cannot draw from each other's strengths." 可译为"如果伟大的国家互相为敌,它们就无法互相汲取长处了。"

五、篇章参考译文翻译原理选注

● 练习3(英译汉)注释

本文是英国著名散文家培根广为流传的散文名篇之一,中文由翻译家杨自伍翻译,两相对照,相映生辉。

1. "Narcissus is said to have been a young man of wonderful beauty, but intolerably proud, fastidious, and disdainful." 这一句英文较长,限定与描述较多,而汉语则有直陈特点。因此,译文干净利落地进行了拆分,简洁明了。而其中的静态的"beauty","proud","fastidious"以及"disdainful"相应地都变成了动作意味强烈的主谓短语或者动词词组"风度翩翩""心性高傲""锱铢必较""蔑视一切"。而译者又在句末加了"令人不堪"四个字,也是妙笔。一来这样具有总结性,且与前面几个词有意义相似之处,另外在汉语中还可起到修正节奏的妙用,形成对仗形式,读来朗朗上口。全句译成"那喀索斯,人称风度翩翩美少年,唯心性高傲,锱铢必较,蔑视一切,令人不堪"十分妥帖自然。

2. "Pleased with himself and despising all others"具有极强的静态描述性,译文中变成了动态的"自我陶醉、目无余子",而"solitary life"也属于静态的表达,译文中成了动态的、更加符合汉语表达习惯的"不与世人往来"。

3. "fell into a study and such a rapturous admiration of himself"的表达核心在于名词"study"与"admiration",译文中相应地变成了动态的"凝神观照"与"如痴如狂",而"fell into"有"坠入,滑入"之意,因此此处译成"不觉"实属妙笔。"remained rooted to the spot"的意义的核心在"rooted",是静态的描述,译文则发挥了汉语动态特征强、语言灵动鲜活的优势,变成了"出神入定,有如树木扎根",意义传达贴切,而且力保原文比喻形象不失。

4. "In this fable are represented the dispositions, and the fortunes too, of those persons who from consciousness either of beauty or some other gift with which nature unaided by any industry of their own has graced them, fall in love as it were with themselves." 一句中,原文属于被动式表达,且有极长的后置定语。汉语变成了主动和直陈式的表达方式,对原文进行了大刀阔斧的拆分,似是信手拈来,译成"尔辈自觉造化赋予美貌,或别具天赋,故不假自身勤奋,煞有介事自恋自爱,此辈中人性情命运,寓言之中暴露无遗"不着斧凿痕迹。其中,静态的"beauty"与"other gift"自然地转换成了动态的"赋予美貌"与"别具天赋",体现了英汉两种语言动静态表达方面的显著差异。

5. 在"Therefore, they commonly live a solitary, private, and shadowed life"一句的

"live a … life"词组结构中,"live"是一个弱化了的动词,其核心在后面的名词。而名词的诸多修饰(前置或后置)就成了意义核心。因此,译文中相应做了调整,"故尔辈一生独来独往,与世睽离,黯然无光"充分体现了汉语的"动态"特点。

6. "fall into such a sloth and listlessness"译成"最终沉迷于自我崇拜,坠入懒散萎靡之境地",也是佳译。"fall"的作用类似于上条注释中的"live",并不是意义的核心。

7. "but like the way of a ship in the sea passes and leaves no trace"一句译文充分发挥了汉语中与英语类似的形象,译成"犹如沧海行舟,飘然而过,不留痕迹",几近完美。

8. 从总体上看,原文逻辑谨严,句式较为复杂,用词古朴庄重,文采斐然,是英国早期论说文的典型特征。而译文句句相扣、层次分明,用词介乎文白之间,对应了原文之古朴庄重,十分得体。从总体韵律看,原文朗朗上口又不失谨严法度,译文则对仗工整且长短有致,读来跌宕起伏、铿锵有力。合而观之,该译文实属佳品。

第三章 主语系统与主题系统互译

一、翻译原理

从语法和语义结构的不同特征或倾向性来看,世界上的语言有些比较注重句法结构及其形式上的主语,有些则比较注重语义结构及其话语上的主题。主语与主题既可以一致,也可以不一致,作主语的不一定总是主题,作主题的有时候也不是主语。英汉对比之下,英语是比较重视主语的语言,而汉语则是比较重视主题的语言。这种差异往往直接造成这两种语言在语序上的不同,比如:

A1. It is a large room.

A2. This room is large.

B1. 这个房间很大。

B2. 它(这)是个大房间。

在这四句话中,A1 比 A2 更符合英语常规思维习惯,而 B1 比 B2 更符合汉语常规思维习惯。这正是由于两种语言对主语与主题的注重程度不同而造成的:英语注重主语的习惯导致了句子 A1 中使用虚化的"it"在形式上作主语,而实际上是话语主题的"房间"被安排在句子的末尾;汉语注重主题的习惯造成句子 B1 中把主题词"房间"直接置于句首。在英语中,"it"是主语而不是主题,在汉语中,"房间"既是主语又是主题。

由上例可以看出,主语与主题虽然一般都出现在句子的开始,但二者并不是等同的概念。这一点,从下句中更能明显地看出来:

A3. 翻译,我很喜欢。

B3. Translation, I like very much.

在上例中,汉语中"翻译"是明确的主题,英语中宾语前置(主题化),"I"是主语。

实际上,英语的主语与汉语主题系统结构之间有很大差异,二者的组织方式和所能容纳的对象范围完全不同,具体如下:

1. 英语的主语一般情况下不省略,而汉语只要从语境中可以推知就可以省略。

＊下雨了。

It is raining.

＊现在12点了。

It is 12 o'clock.

2. 英语的主语系统结构最常见的组织单位是三元的"主＋谓语动词＋宾语(或补语)",系动词"(to) be"不能省略,而汉语的主题系统结构最基本的组织单位是二元的"主题＋述题",除判断句使用判断动词"是"外可以不使用任何系动词。比如:

＊The sky is cloudlessly blue.

天高云淡,一片湛蓝。

＊He is a round little man.

他身材矮胖。

3. 英语的主语只能是名词、代词、名词性短语(包括动名词和不定式短语),而汉语的主题则基本上不受词性的限制。比如:

＊It is very kind of you to help me.(代词作形式主语)

你能帮我真是好心。(句子主题)

＊Tact must be used in requesting permission.(名词作主语)

征求同意,应注意方式方法。(动宾结构作主题)

＊There is no stranger here.(名词作主语)

这里没有外人。(指示词作主题)

＊This is something worth serious consideration.(代词作主语)

这件事值得认真考虑。(名词词组作主题)

＊You are not yet an experienced driver.(代词作主语)

开车你还没经验。(动宾结构作主题)

4. 英语的主语作为句法分析的概念只能统管一个句子,一个新的句子必须有新的主语,而汉语的主题作为一个话语分析的概念可以统管一段话语,主题一致或可以推知时就可以省略,需要时又随时添加。比如:

＊He has a daughter who works in the suburb. She has been called for by telephone and will be here in the afternoon.

他有个女儿,在郊区工作,已经打电话去了,下午就能赶到。

＊*Winesburg, Ohio* has the stature of a modern classic. It is at once beautiful and tragic, realistic and poetic.

《俄亥俄,温斯堡》是一部现代经典小说集,既优美又悲壮,既现实又超脱。

＊She had such a kindly, smiling, tender, gentle, generous heart of her own.

她心底厚道,为人乐观,性情温柔,待人和蔼,气量又大。

5. 英语的主语作为句法分析概念不涉及语义层次的安排,而汉语的主题作为话语概念涉及层次安排,即从上到下、从大到小、从整体到局部、从外到内安排主题。

* The leaves of this tree look very beautiful.

这棵树叶子的颜色很美丽。

* The roof of his house is very special, with the white-washed walls in traditional Anhui style.

他家房子屋顶很特别,白色的粉墙是传统徽派风格。

* Before going on up into the hills, Thomas stopped for gasoline at a lonely station.

入山之前,托马斯在这儿停车加油。

* Periodically I go back to a churchyard cemetery on the side of an Appalachian hill in northern Virginia to call on family elders.

每隔一段时间,我都要回北弗吉尼亚一趟,回到阿巴拉契亚山一座小山丘的山坡上,在那儿的教堂公墓里参拜家族中的先辈。

6. 英语一般不以时间、地点、条件、环境等成分作主语,而汉语则可以用时间、地点词作主题或默认的主题。虽然在语法概念上这类成分是否主题仍有争议,但汉语倾向于将其置于句首,而英语则更倾向于将其置于句尾。

* I'm on duty today, and will be off work tomorrow.

今天我值班,明天休息。

* This is a place of beautiful scenery, situated between water and hills.

这里很好,依山傍水,景色宜人。

7. 英语的主语有较强的客观性倾向,因此很多情况下直接从事物本身出发,引起被动句或形式主语;而汉语的主题有较强的主观性倾向,所以与英语相比被动句较少,没有形式主语(参见第三章)。

* It is believed that the troops had already crossed the river.

人们认为部队已经过了河。

* It didn't occur to me that you would object.

我没有想到你会反对。

由于上述差异,英汉互译不能仅以句子为单位进行语法结构转换,还要以话语为单位进行语义结构的转换。具体地讲,英译汉时常常需要从不同的英语结构成分中总结、提取主题,往往把被修饰的中心词作为主题,把修饰成分作为述题,根据汉语主题意义重新安排语序,并通过语义关系将不同的成分连接起来;而汉译英时则需要适当选择主语,通过合理的语法结构和形式变化将不同的句法成分连接起来。根据这个原理,在英汉互译实践中,常常也有必要根据两种语言思维的特点对语序及标点符号进行调整,只有这样才能摆脱原文形式上的束缚,使译文在意义忠实于原文的同时,读上去更加自然、顺畅。

二、核心例句原理分析

核心例句	原理分析
A. 英译汉 1. It is absurd talking like that. 那样说是很荒唐的。 2. It is a fine day, isn't it? 今天天气不错,是吧? 3. It is now clear to everybody that translation needs special training. 翻译需要专门训练,这一点大家现在都很清楚了。 4. It's now 9 o'clock. It's time to begin our class. 现在9点了,该上课了。 5. This is a decision he must make for himself. 这个决定他得自己做。 6. This is something hard to imagine. 这种事情难以想象。 7. This is a book everybody wants to read. 这本书每个人都想读。 8. He that never climbed never fell. 永远不攀登,就永远不会摔跤。 9. —Who is it? —It's me. —谁?—是我。 10. You are talking delightful nonsense. 你满口胡言,倒让人开心。 11. He is a fool that thinks not that another thinks. 和别人想得不一样就是傻子。 12. He that once deceives is ever suspected. 骗人一次,招疑一世。	1. 形式"it"主语略去不译,使用"那样说"作主题。 2. 点明"it"所指,即天气,符合汉语习惯。 3. 略去形式主语不译,以"that"引导的真实主语作主题,译文自然流畅。 4. 两句合并成一句,构成汉语"主题+述题"二元结构。 5. 选择"这个决定"作主题,比起"这是个他必须自己做的决定"更像汉语。 6. 选择"这种事情"作主题,"难以想象"作述题,完成了从主语系统到主题系统的转换。 7. 选择"这种书"作主题,"每个人都想读"作述题。 8. 由"he"引起的英语主从复合句译成以"永远不攀登"为主题的无主句。 9. 译文中"it"略去不译,译出汉语口语的味道。 10. 原文中的"delightful"不宜直译成定语,处理成述题"倒让人开心",不仅达意,而且没有任何翻译腔。 11. 英语主从复合句译成汉语二元架构的简单句,简单明了。 12. 汉语译文主题和述题对仗工整,且押韵,朗朗上口,哲理性很强。

核心例句	原理分析
B. 汉译英 1. 学英语很难。 It is difficult to learn English. 2. 为钱结婚等于出卖自由。 He that marries for wealth sells his liberty. 3. 今年的蚕花,光景是好收成。 His family would probably have a fine crop of silkworms this year. 4. 得到母亲去世的消息,我很悲痛。 I was deeply grieved to learn of mother's death. 5. 做针线就专心做针线! If you are knitting, then put your heart in it. 6. 老通宝恨洋鬼子不是没有理由的。 It was not without reason that old Tongbao hated the foreign devils. 7. (由于)能源危机日益严重,因此需要采取规模上与之相应的应急计划。 The growing crisis in energy calls for a crash program of just this magnitude. 8. 我当时不得不应付的困难几乎是无法描述的。 It was almost impossible to describe the difficulties I had then to cope with. 9. 人们更愿意畅所欲言,这是最值得注意的。 The most noticeable is that people are more willing to speak their minds. 10. 用传统的观点来看,是难以看到根本区别的。 It is difficult to see the essential difference in the light of traditional grammar. 11. 你(们)选翻译课是很明智的。/ 你们选翻译课,这很明智。 It is very wise for you to take the course of translation.	1. 选用"it"作主语,使句型颇为地道。 2. 无主句译成有主句,符合英文句法。 3. 原文是典型的"主题+述题"结构,译文依据上下文确定"His family"为主语,译文流畅自然。 4. 原文主题和述题转换成含动词不定式的英语简单句。 5. 原文是主题"做针线"+述题"就做针线",属无主句。主题和述题之间暗含条件关系。译成英文中采用条件复合句,使逻辑关系外化。 6. 原文语气较强,译文中应使用"it"引导的强调句。 7. 原文主谓结构转换成偏正结构,译成以"The growing crisis in energy"为主语的英语简单句,表达简短有力。 8. 英语句子向右扩展,汉语句子向左扩展,此句原文的主题"我当时不得不应付的困难"较长,不宜直接译成英语的主语,形式主语"it"是最佳选择。 9. 原文是汉语中典型的"主题+述题"结构,译文把原文述题部分要交代的意思放在主语部分,后半句包含表语从句,通过调整语序和使用从句增强了英译文表达的地道性。一般说来,汉语无主句较多,而英语句子必须要有主语。 10/11. 第10句和第11句的翻译属于一种情况,都是将"主题+述题"汉语无主句转换成由形式主语"it"引导的常用英语句型,同时前后两部分位置颠倒,使表达符合英语习惯,摆脱了翻译腔。

三、翻译练习

◆ 课堂练习 ◆

• 练习1（英译汉）

1. It was with difficulty that I could bring myself to admit the identity of the man being before me with the companion of my boyhood.

2. He got his haberdashery at Charvet's, but his suits, his shoes and his hats in London.

3. You don't grow the grain you eat and you don't make the clothes you wear.

4. The girl was used to this kind of dialogue for breakfirst and more of it for dinner.

5. It is a truth universally acknowledged that a single man in possession of a good fortune must be in want of a wife.

6. He enjoyed a lucrative practice, which enabled him to maintain and educate a family with all the advantages which money can give in this country.

7. The Forsytes were resentful of something, not individually, but as a family …

8. The history of a tree from the time starts in the forest until the boards which it yields are used, would form an interesting and, in many instances, an exciting story.

9. This is an article for the reader to think of when he or she is warm in bed, a little before he goes to sleep, the clothes at his ear, and the wind moaning in some distant crevice.

10. During one of his periods of consciousness Clive told Prue that he had risked his life to save a strange woman, because he knew at last that he did have faith in himself and his country.

11. Doctor Eduardo Plarr stood in the small port on the Parana, among the rails and yellow cranes, watching where a horizontal plume of smoke stretched over the Chaco. It lay between the red bars of sunset like a stripe on a national flag.

12. He little imagined how my heart warmed towards him when I beheld his black eyes withdraw so suspiciously under their brows, as I rode up, and when his fingers sheltered themselves, with a jealous resolution, still further in his waistcoat, as I announced my name.

13. … My holiday afternoons were spent in ramble about the surrounding country. I made myself familiar with all its places famous in history or fable. I knew every spot where a murder or robbery had been committed, or a ghost seen. I visited the neighboring villages, and added greatly to my stock of knowledge, by noting their habits and customs, and conversing with their sages and great men …

14. The more we can enjoy what we have, the happier we are. It's easy to overlook the pleasure we get from loving and being loved, the company of friends, the freedom to live where we please, even good health.

15. Lu finished the rest of the journey quickly. He caught up with the rear guard before dark.

- **练习 2（汉译英）**

1. 弄得不好,就会前功尽弃。

2. 这个问题他认为已经不存在了。

3. 智慧的体现就是自相矛盾,这是人生对人生观开的玩笑。

4. 他是个讨饭的,身材矮小,面色苍黄,衣衫褴褛,瘸腿,满脸胡子。

5. 她心底厚道,为人乐观,性情温柔,待人和蔼,气量又大。

6. 群山苍翠,加油站孤零零的。入山之前,托马斯在这儿停车加油。

7. 她是哈丁顿一位富裕医生的女儿,有才华,又迷人,但有点脾气。

8. 难怪那个老妇人从商店里偷东西那么容易,人们发现她女儿就在里面工作。

9. 是什么东西发出这样的哭声？是邻居的婴儿吗？／不是。是他们的猫。

10. 他们在谈到新政时感到自豪,这是可以理解的。

11. 我们还要积极吸引跨国公司来华投资,特别是鼓励他们投资研究开发和参与国有企业的改组、改造。

12. 著作权属于公民的,公民死亡后,其作品的使用权和获得的报酬权在本法规定的保护期内,依照继承法的规定转移。

13. 近代史开始时,世界拥有的每一项重大成就已为历史发端期的人们所知晓。

14. 中国疆域辽阔,历史悠远,各地自然和人文环境不尽相同。

15. 今天布什总统正好来访,我认为这是很有意义的。

16. 我便从此整天站在柜台里,专管我的职务。虽然没有什么失职,但总觉得有些单调、有些无聊。掌柜是一幅凶脸孔,主顾也没有好脾气,叫人活泼不得；只有孔乙己到店,才可以笑几声,所以至今还记得。

17. 岛上绿树葱茏,果林成荫,一丛接一丛的橄榄树、柠檬树和松树覆盖全岛,环境凉爽宜人。一到春天,这遍岛花果成片开放,香气袭人。

18. 警察在场时,如果任何人犯了或被指控犯了非逮捕罪,拒绝警察的要求提供姓名或住所,或者提供警察有理由认为是虚假的姓名和住所,警察可予以拘捕以便查明他的姓名和住所。

19. 魏良辅等人所创的"新声"起初只限于清唱,却吸引了不少文人墨客。他们热情高涨,争相把新的昆山腔运用于传奇形式,使清唱的"新声"发展成为舞台上演唱的戏曲剧种。

20. 新开业的高技术公司可以获得风险资本融资,这对美国高技术产业收入的大幅度增长和竞争力的提高,以及对加利福尼亚州硅谷和其他高技术密集区所取得的经济发展和就业水平的增长,都起了重要的作用。

◆ 课后练习 ◆

• 练习 1（英译汉）

1. That is a NATO matter and any comment on it should appropriately come from NATO.

2. Jordan can not politely turn down the invitation to an Arab foreign ministers' conference.

3. The year 1983 began—and ended—with an unusual oil crises: fears that the price of crude oil would not go up but down.

4. He shook his head and his eyes were wide, then narrowed in indignation.

5. The prisoners were permitted to receive Red Cross food parcels and write censored letters.

6. He crashed down on a protesting chair.

7. With the fear of largely imaginary plots against his leadership, his self-confidence seemed totally to desert him.

8. Not to educate the children is to condemn them to repetitious ignorance.

9. His failure to observe the safety regulations resulted in an accident to the machinery.

10. The isolation of rural areas because of distance and the lack of transport facilities is compounded by the paucity of the information media.

11. His period in office was marked by a steep rise in Iran's oil revenues and the beginning of a social-political crisis brought on by wide-scale misuse of the $22 billion a year earnings from oil.

12. Her boyfriend has returned home from Long Isand and he told her of the house where he was boarded, and lodged, a red-titled bungalow, on a little hill, overlooking the blue sea, with a large, shady garden behind it.

13. All my subjects will leave no stone unturned to carry out every will, every avaricious desire and even every whim of mine, even though they were all beyond the possible.

14. On several occasions I watched him paint fluffy little chicks and vivid cormorants with their heads in clear green water.

15. I do not pretend that the conversation I have recorded can be regarded as verbatim reports. I never kept notes of what was said on this or the other occasion, but I have a good memory for what concerns me, and though I have put this conversation in my own words they faithfully represent, I believe, what was said.

16. Those privileged to be present at a family festival of the Forsytes have seen that charming and instructive sight—an upper middle-class family in full plumage.

17. Without being a novel in the usual sense of the word, the connected stories have the full range and emotional impact of a novel.

18. Rocket research has confirmed a strange fact which had already been suspected there is a "high temperature belt" in the atmosphere with its center roughly thirty miles above the ground.

● 练习 2（汉译英）

1. 加利福尼亚南部阳光充足,气候宜人,是拍摄影片的理想场所。

2. 他又矮又胖,面色红润,戴着一副大眼镜,镜框镀金,擦得光亮照人。

3. 阅读罗素的作品给我带来了数不清的快乐时光,在这方面除了索尔斯坦·维布伦,任何其他当代的科学作家都不能与他相比。

4. 我外祖父务农,于年终几个月内且兼业裁缝。

5. 这些问题问得好,要回答就要好好动一下脑筋。

6. 这种房屋结构简单,对于想建造私人房屋的人们特别有吸引力。

7. 北京的名胜古迹,北京的妙处,我应该说是了解的;其他老北京当然也了解。

8. 经国吾弟:咫尺之隔,竟成天涯之遥。

9. 孙中山先生首创之中国国民党,历尽艰辛,无数先烈前仆后继,终于推翻帝制,建立中华民国。

10. 我看到的面孔有些热情焕发,充满光彩;有些则呆滞麻木或阴森吓人;另一些面孔喜怒无常,缺乏诚意;没有一张面孔显示出一个理性灵魂所具有的静穆的威严。

11. 哲学是受它的方法制约的,哲学的发展是决定于逻辑方法的发展的。这在东方和西方的哲学史中都可以找到大量的例证。

12. 生活的经验固然会叫人忘记许多事情。但是有许多记忆经过了多少时间的磨洗也不会消失。

13. 这样的情形,老先生有几十年的经验了,当然不会去注意。

14. 我从北地向东南旅行,绕道拜访了我的家乡,就到 S 城。

15. 根据《汽车金融公司管理办法》(以下简称《办法》)及有关行政法规制定本细则。

16. 由我市学者编写的《吴文化读本》出版了,无论是从普及吴文化的知识,还是从宣传苏州、构筑苏州文化新优势的角度来看,这都是一件值得庆贺的事。

17. 中国政府为解决香港问题所采取的立场、方针、政策是坚定不移的。

18. "一个国家,两种制度",我们已经讲了很多次了,全国人民代表大会已经通过了这个政策。

19. 要相信香港的中国人能治理好香港。

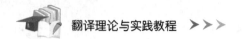

练习 3（英译汉）

（1）

Sleep at a late hour in the morning is not half so peasant as the more timely one. It is sometimes, however, excusable, especially to a watchful or overworked head; neither can we deny the seducing merits of the other doze—the pleasing wifulness of nestling in a new posture, when you know you ought to be up, like the rest of the house. But then you cut up the day, and your sleep the next night.

In the course of the day few people think of sleeping, except after dinner; and then it is often rather a hovering and nodding on the borders of sleep than sleep itself. This is a privilege allowable, we think, to none but the old, or the sickly, or the very tired and cre-worn, and it should be well understood before it is exercised in company. To escape into slumber from an argument; or to take it as an affair of course, only between you and your biliary duct; or to assent with involuntary nods to all that you have just been disputing is not so well; much less, to sit nodding and tottering beside a lady; or to be in danger of dropping your head into the fruit-plate or your host's face; or of waking up, and saying "Just so" to the bark of a dog; or "Yes, Madam," to the black at your elbow.

Care-worn people, however, might refresh themselves oftener with day-sleep than they do; if their bodily state is such as to dispose them to it. It is a mistake to suppose that all care is wakeful. People sometimes sleep, as well as wake, by reason of their sorrow. The difference seems to depend upon the nature of their temperament; though in the most excessive cases, sleep is perhaps Nature's never-failing relief, as swooning is upon the rack. A person with jaundice in his blood shall lie down and go to sleep at noonday, when another of a different complexion shall find his eyes as unclosable as a statue's, though he has had no sleep for nights together. Without meaning to lessen the dignity of suffering, which has quite enough to do with its waking hours, it is this that may often account for the profound sleeps enjoyed the night before hazardous battles, executions, and other demands upon an over-excited spirit.

（2）Speech by Former British Prime Minister Edward Heath at Welcoming Banquet, 25 May, 1974

Respected Mr. Vice-Premier,

My Distinguished Chinese Hosts and Friends,

It is a great pleasure to be here in Peking and to have this occasion for thanking the Government and the people of China for all the kindness and hospitality which they have shown me.

It was a keen disappointment when I had to postpone the visit which I had intended to pay to China in January.

I was all the more delighted when, as a result of the initiative of your government, it proved possible to reinstate the visit so quickly.

This visit gives me the opportunity which I have long sought, to see for myself the achievements of the Chinese people.

I have of course read of these achievements and many visitors to your country have told me about them—in particular Sir Alec Douglas-Home who came here as British Foreign Secretary in 1972, and before him, Sir Anthony Royle.

I also welcomed the opportunity of discussions with Ji Pengfei, Foreign Minister, when we welcomed him on his visit to London in June 1973.

There has been no doubt in my mind of the progress which you have achieved.

Now I shall be able to see it for myself and I know that this will be a most rewarding experience.

We in Britain have a social and political system which differs in many respects from your own.

It is the result of different experiences and a different tradition.

● **练习 4（汉译英）**

（1）看护

孤傲清高的庄教授，终于耐不住寂寞，不觉忿忿然了。他是名牌大学的名教授，到国外讲学时生了病都未曾受到这般的冷落，高级知识分子名义上享受高级干部的待遇，可他这个"高知"怎么能跟对面床上的"高干"相比呢？人家床边老有处长、科长之类的干部伺候着，间或还有一两位漂亮的女人来慰问一番。床头柜和窗台上堆满了高级食品，有六个小伙子分成三班昼夜二十四小时守护着他。医生、护士查病房也是先看那位财大势大的所谓王经理，后看他这个不是毫无名气的化学系教授，如果检查经理的病情用半个小时，检查他最多用十分钟。他的床边总是冷冷清清，儿子在几千公里以外搞他的导弹，女儿在国外上学，只有老伴每天挤公共汽车给他送点饭来，为他灌上一暖瓶热水。系里更是指望不上，半个月能派人来探望他一次就很不错了。人一落到这步境地最没有用的就是学问、名气和臭架子。庄教授偏偏放不下他的身份，每天冲墙躺着，对王经理床边的一切不闻不问不看。鬼知道这位是什么经理？现在"公司"遍地有，成千上万的大单位可以叫"公司"，一两个人也可以戳起一块"公司"的招牌……

这一天王经理突然病势恶化，医生通知准备后事。他床边围着的人就更多了，连气宇轩昂的刘副经理也来了，他不愿假惺惺地用些没用的空话安慰一个快死的人。先沉默了一会儿，然后说了几句很实在的话，询问经理有什么要求，还有什么不放心的事情，他对垂死者提出的所有问题都满口答应。该说的话都说完了，便起身告辞，着手去安排经理的后事。看护王经理的人呼啦都站起身，撇下病人，争先恐后地去搀扶刘副经理，有的头前开门，有的跟在身边赔笑，前呼后拥，甚是威风。刘副经理勃然大怒：

"我又不死，你们扶着我干什么？"

庄教授破例转过脸来，见孤零零的王经理奄奄待毙，两滴泪珠横着落在枕头上，他庆幸自己是"高知"，不是"高干"。知识和钢笔到死也不会背叛他……

（2）《骆驼祥子》选段之一

这么大的人，拉上那么美的车，他自己的车，弓子软得颤悠颤悠的，连车把都微微地动弹；车厢是那么亮，垫子是那么白，喇叭是那么响；跑得不快怎能对得起自己呢，怎能对得起那辆车呢？这一点不是虚荣心，而似乎是一种责任，非快跑、飞跑，不足以充分发挥自己的力量与车的优美。那辆车也真是可爱，拉过了半年来的，仿佛处处都有了知觉与感情，祥子一扭腰、一蹲腿，或一直脊背，它都就马上应和着，给祥子以最顺心的帮助，他与它之间没有一点隔膜别扭的地方。赶到遇上地平人少的地方，祥子可以用一只手拢着把，微微轻响的皮轮像阵利飕的小风似的催着他跑，飞快而平稳。拉到了地点，祥子的衣裤都拧得出汗来，哗哗的，像刚从水盆里捞出来的。他感到疲乏，可是很痛快的，值得骄傲的，一种疲乏，如同骑着名马跑了几十里那样。假若胆壮不就是大意，祥子在放胆跑的时候可并不大意。不快跑若是对不起人，快跑而碰伤了车便是对不起自己。车是他的命，他知道怎样小心。

（3）《骆驼祥子》选段之二

北平的洋车夫有许多派：年轻力壮，腿脚灵利的，讲究更漂亮的车，拉"整天儿"，爱什么时候出车与收车都有自由；拉出车来，在固定的"车口"或宅门一放，专等坐快车的主儿；弄好了，也许一下子弄个一块两块的；碰巧了，也许白耗一天，连"车份儿"也没着落，但也不在乎。这一派哥儿们的希望大概有两个：或是拉包车；或是自己买上辆车，自己的车，再去拉包月或散座就没太大关系了，反正车是自己的。

比这一派岁数稍大的，或因身体的关系而跑得稍差点劲的，或因家庭的关系而不敢白耗一天的，大概多数拉八成新的车；人与车都相当漂亮，所以在要价的时候也还能保持住相当的尊严。这派的车夫，也许拉"整天"，也许拉"半天"。在后者的情形下，因为还有相当的精气神，所以无论是冬天还是夏天总是"拉晚儿"。夜间，当然比白天需要更多的留神与本事；钱自然也多挣一些。

年纪在四十以上、二十以下的，恐怕就不易在前两派里有个地位了。他们的车破，又不敢"拉晚儿"，所以只能早早地出车，希望能从清晨转到午后三四点钟，拉出"车份儿"和自己的嚼谷。他们的车破，跑得慢，所以得多走路，少要钱。到瓜市、果市、菜市，去拉货物，都是他们；钱少，可是无须快跑呢。

在这里，二十岁以下的——有的从十一二岁就干这行儿——很少能到二十岁以后改变成漂亮的车夫的，因为在幼年受了伤，很难健壮起来。他们也许拉一辈子洋车，而一辈子连拉车也没出过风头。那四十以上的人，有的是已拉了十年八年的车，筋肉的衰损使他们甘居人后，他们渐渐知道早晚一个跟头会死在马路上。他们的拉车姿势，讲价时的随机应变，走路的抄近绕远，都足以使他们想起过去的光荣，而用鼻翅儿扇着那些后起之辈。可是这点光荣丝毫不能减少将来的黑暗，他们自己也因此在擦着汗的时节常常微叹。不过，与他们比较，另一些四十岁上下的车夫，他们似乎还没有苦到了家。这一些是以前绝没想到自己能与洋车发生关系,而到了生和死的界限已经不甚分明,才抄起车把来的。被撤差的巡警或校役,把本钱吃光的小贩,或是失业的工匠,到了卖无可卖、当无可当的时候,咬着牙,含着泪,上了这条死亡之路。这些人,生命最鲜壮的时期已经被卖掉,现在再把窝窝头变成的血汗滴在马路上。没有力气,没有经验,没有朋友,就是在同行中也得不到好气儿。他们拉最破的车,皮带不定一天泄多少次气;一边拉着人,还得一边儿央求人家原谅,虽然十五个大铜子儿已经算是笔甜买卖。

四、练习参考译文

◆ 课堂练习 ◆

• **练习1(英译汉)**

1. 我好不容易才使自己相信,面前这位面色苍白的人和我童年时代的伙伴确系一人。
2. 普通的服饰买自夏费商店,可衣服鞋帽总要在伦敦买。
3. 你吃的粮食不是你自己种的,你穿的衣服也不是你自己做的。
4. 这类话不仅早餐有,午餐也有,这姑娘早就习惯了。
5. 有钱的单身汉总要娶位太太,这是一条举世公认的真理。
6. 他的业务很赚钱,够养家庭,够养子女了,所有在国内钱能换来的好处都齐了。
7. 有种事情是福尔赛家人全都痛恨的,不仅他们各个人痛恨,而且作为一个富尔赛家人,就必然要痛恨……
8. 一棵树,从它在森林中生长起直到被制成木板使用为止,这段历史会构成一个饶有趣味的故事,在很多情况下这个故事十分激动人心。
9. 这篇文章是让读者暖暖和和躺在床上品赏的——这时候他或者她即将入睡,衣服放在耳边,风声在远方一个什么缝隙里呼啸。
10. 克莱夫还能间歇性地恢复知觉,其间他告诉普露他冒着生命危险去救一个陌生女人,原因就在于他最终已经明白,他对自己、对自己的国家是有信心的。
11. 在阿根廷巴拉那一座小小的码头,周围铁轨纵横交错,黄色的起重机随处可见,爱德华多·普拉尔医生伫立在其间久久地观望:一缕浓烟横着扩散开来,笼罩在查科城的上空,悬浮在落日时分的红霞之间,有如一面国旗上印着的条纹。
12. 在我骑着马走上前去时,看见他的黑眼睛缩在眉毛下猜忌地瞅着我。而在我通报自己的姓名时,他把手指更深地藏到背心袋里,完全是一副不信任的神气。刹那间,我对他产生了亲切之感,而他根本未觉察到。
13. a)……无数假日下午尽兴消磨在郊垧的漫游之中。那里在历史或传说中是有名的地方，我无不十分熟悉。我知道那里的每一处杀人越货之所与鬼魂出现之地。我继而访问了许多邻村，观察其地的风俗习惯，并与当地的圣贤与伟人交谈，因而极大增加了我的原有见闻……

b)……每逢假日下午，我总到附近乡村去漫游。有些地方是有神话传说的，我都亲加勘察，把它们摸熟了。什么地方发生过盗案或者凶杀案的，什么地方有过鬼魂出现的，我都知道。邻近各村我常去观光，当地的耆老硕德我总去踵门求教，因此我的智识也大为增加。

14. 我们越能乐在其中，就越能幸福。施人以爱，被人所爱，友人相伴，对住所的选择随心所欲，乃至身体健康，这一切所带来的快乐都易为人们所忽略。

15. 这以后的路，卢进勇走得特别快。天黑的时候，他追上了后卫部队。

● 练习2（汉译英）

1. If things are not handled properly, all our efforts would be spent in vain.

2. He doesn't believe the problem exists any longer.

3. Wisdom appears in contradiction to itself, which is a trick life plays on philosophy of life.

4. He is a little yellow, ragged, lame, unshaven beggar.

5. She had such a kindly, smiling, tender, gentle, generous heart of her own.

6. Before going on up into the blue hills, Thomas stopped for gasoline at a lonely station.

7. She was an intelligent, attractive and somewhat temperamental daughter of a well-to-do doctor in Haddington.

8. It is no wonder that the old woman could steal from the shop so easily, since it is found out that her daughter was working there.

9. What is it that makes such a cry? Is it the neighbor's infant? / No. It is the neighbor's cat.

10. They spoke with understandable pride of the new policy.

11. Vigorous efforts should be made to draw investment from transnational corporations, whose investment in research and development and participation in the reorganization and technological upgrading of state-owned enterprises should be especially encouraged.

12. Where the copyright in a work belongs to a citizen, the right of exploitation and the right to remuneration in respect of the work shall, after his death, during the term of protection provided for in this Law, be transferred in accordance with the provisions of the Law of Succession.

13. Almost everything which really matters and which the world possessed at the commencement of the modern age was already known to man at the dawn of history.

14. China has a vast territory and an extremely long history with the natural and cultural environment differing from region to region.

15. The visit by President Bush coincides with this day, and his visit is highly meaningful.

16. Thenceforward I stood all day behind the counter, fully engaged with my duties. Although I gave satisfaction at this work, I found it monotonous and futile. Our employer was a fierce-looking individual, and the customers were a morose lot, so that it was impossible to be gay. Only when Kung I-chi came to the tavern could I laugh a little. That is why I still remember him.

17. Covered by groves of olive, lemon and pine trees, the island is cool, green and shady, and, in the spring is a fragrant mass of blossoms.

18. When any person in the presence of a police officer commits or is accused of committing a non-seizable offence and refuses on the demand of a police officer to give his name or residence or gives a name or residence which the officer has reason to believe to be false, he may be arrested by that police officer in order that his name or residence may be ascertained.

19. At first, the New Aria created by Wei and others was confined to opera singing without makeup and acting, which attracted numerous literary figures who were enthusiastic about applying Kunshan Singing Style to legendary stories. Gradually, it developed into a staged form of opera.

20. The availability of venture capital financing to young, high technology companies has been a primary contributor to the dramatic revenue growth enjoyed by, and the increased competitiveness of, America's high technology industry and to the economic expansion and increased employment levels experienced in California's Silicon Valley and other areas of high technology concentration.

◆ 课后练习 ◆

● 练习1（英译汉）

1. 这是北约组织的问题，任何有关意见都应该由北约组织来发表，这才是适宜的。

2. 约旦若拒绝接受阿拉伯外长会议的邀请，它在礼貌上也是说不过去的。

3. 1983年新年伊始，就存在着一种异乎寻常的石油危机：人们担心原油价格下降，而不是上涨。这一年结束时情况依然如故。

4. 他摇了摇头，双目睁得圆圆的，接着又眯成了一条线，脸上露出了愤怒的神色。

5. 允许俘虏接受红十字会的包裹，也允许他们写信，不过信要经过检查。

6. 他猛然坐到一张椅子上，椅子被压得吱吱作响，像是在抗议。

7. 由于害怕有人阴谋推翻他的领导地位，他似乎完全丧失了自信，但所谓的阴谋在很大程度上是他假想出来的。

8. 如果不对儿童进行教育的话，那就是要使他们一再陷入愚昧状态。

9. 他没有遵守安全规则，导致机器出了故障。

10. 因为距离远，交通工具缺乏，农村社会与外界隔绝，这种隔绝又由于信息媒介匮乏而变得更加严重。

11. 他执政期间有两个特点：一是伊朗的石油收入猛增；二是由于大规模滥用每年220亿美元的石油收益而开始造成一种社会政治危机。

12. 她的男友刚从长岛回来，跟她谈起了供他吃住的那幢房子。那是一幢坐落在小山上的红瓦平房，俯视着蓝色的大海，房后还有一个绿树成荫的大花园。

13. 我的意欲，我的贪欲，乃至每一个幻想，都可竭尽全体臣民的力量去实现，即使是无法实现的。

14. 我曾多次见他画小鸡，毛茸茸，很可爱；也见过他画的鱼鹰，水是绿的，钻进水里，很生动。

15. 书中的谈话，我并不要假充是逐字逐句的记载。在这或其他的场合下，人家的谈话我从不记录下来。可是，与我有关的事我记得很清楚。所以，虽则是我写的，敢说能忠实地反映他们的谈话。

16. 碰到福尔赛家有喜庆的事情，那些有资格去参加的人都见过那派中上层人家的兴盛气象，不但看了开心，也增长了见识。

17. 作品虽然并非一般意义上的"长篇小说"，但其中故事篇篇相关，不乏长篇小说所具有的广阔视野和感人魅力。

18. 人们早就怀疑，大气层中有一个"高温带"，其中心在距地面约30英里的高空。利用火箭进行研究后，这一奇异的事实得到了证实。

● 练习2（汉译英）

1. The constant sunshine and mild climate of southern California made it and ideal site for shooting motion pictures.

2. He is a round little man, with a red face and a pair of large glasses in a gilt frame polished with dazzling light.

3. I owe innumerable happy hours to the reading of Russell's works, something which I cannot say of any other contemporary scientific writer, with the exception of Thorstein Veblen.

4. My mother's father was a farmer who also practiced tailoring during the off months of the year.

5. They are good questions, because they called for thought-provoking answers.

6. The simplicity of construction makes the houses especially attractive to people who want to build their own houses.

7. Like all other long-timers of Beijing, I'm supposed to be very familiar with its scenic spots and historical sites, nay, its superb attractions.

8. Dear brother Ching-Kuo: It is never expected that the short distance between us should be keeping us poles apart.

9. After going through untold hardships during which countless revolutionaries unflinchingly laid down their lives, the Kuopingtang founded by Dr. Sun Yat-sen finally overthrew the monarchy and established the republic.

10. I see faces, keen and bright; others dull or dangerous; others, unsteady, insincere—none that have the calm authority of a reasonable soul.

11. That philosophy is conditioned by its method, and that the development of philosophy is dependent upon the development of the logical method, are facts which find abundant illustrations in the history of philosophy.

12. Lots of things are apt to fade from memory as one's life experiences accumulate. But some memories will withstand the wear and tear of time.

13. The old man had been thoroughly familiar with this transformation for decades, so he paid no attention now.

14. During my travels from the North to the Southeast I made a detour to my home, then to City S.

15. These Rules are formulated in accordance with the Measures for Administration of Auto Financing Companies (hereinafter referred to a "the Measures") and other relevant administrative regulations.

16. As regards the publication of *Reading the Wu Culture*, which is now in press, I would say that it is something deserving my congratulation to the contributing scholars in our city, whose achievements are significant in all terms: in popularizing knowledge of Suzhou culture, building a better image of the city, and constructing its new advantageous stronghold.

17. The Chinese Government is firm in its position, principles and policies on Hong Kong.

18. We have discussed the policy of "one country, two systems" more than once. It has been adopted by the National People's Congress.

19. We should have faith in the Chinese of Hong Kong, who are quite capable of administering their own affairs.

● 练习3（英译汉）

（1）

早上睡到很晚的时辰，还不及早睡早起一半的愉快。有时候或许可以原谅，特别是当人夜不能寐或过分劳累的时候；此外，不可否认，睡懒觉自有它的诱人之处——明明知道自己应该像家里其他人那样起床，却偏偏要换上一个姿势，再懒洋洋"迷糊那么一会儿"。不过，这么一来，你就把白天切碎，而你这一睡，当晚也难以成眠。

翌日之中，很少有人想到睡觉，除非在午饭以后——那时候，人往往逍遥打一个盹儿，在睡乡的边缘上徘徊一阵儿,但算不上真正的睡眠。而且,我们认为,只有老人、病人或者疲劳不堪、忧思苦虑的人,才能得到允许享受这种特权。否则,与人辩驳之际颓然入睡,或因胆汁旺盛而闷闷不乐即自顾自进入黑甜之乡,或者对于对方才争论之事并非出于本意地频频点头,一律加以首肯,都是不太恰当的事。尤其是,某位夫人坐在身旁,自己却尽在那里打瞌睡,身子不住地摇摇晃晃,一不小心,不是一头栽进面前的果盘里,就是撞到主人的脸上;再不然,一声狗叫,悚然惊醒,连忙表示:"对,对!"或者胳膊肘旁的黑人女仆殷勤回答:"是,夫人!"——这些都不太妙。

　　人在忧虑之中往往不能成眠,其实他们大可以通过白天的睡眠来恢复一下精神,只要他们的身体状况许可他们这么做的话。认为忧愁一定不能睡觉,是一种误解。忧患有时促人清醒,有时催人入眠。这种差别似乎由于人的气质不同而产生。不过,在一些最极端的场合下,睡眠或许是造物主赐给人的一种永远不变的慰藉,正如人到了拷问台上就要晕倒。一个血液中有了黄疸病已到中午倒头便能入睡;相反,具有另外一种气质的人,哪怕一连几夜未眠,却仍像一座雕像似的,苦于不能合眼。笔者无意抹杀受苦受难的庄严性,因为人在清醒的时候所遭到的苦难已经足够叫他烦恼,然而这也正好说明了人处在凶险鏖战或死刑判决的前夜,以及其他迫使精神过度兴奋的状态之中,为什么还能够酣然沉睡。

（2）英国前首相希思在欢迎宴会上的讲话（1974年5月25日）

- **译文 1**

尊敬的副总理先生：
尊贵的中国主人和朋友们：

　　我感到十分愉快,能够来到北京,并且有此机会向中国政府和中国人民表示感谢,感谢他们给予我的盛情款待。

　　我本来打算在今年1月访问中国,后来不得不推迟,这曾使我深感失望。

　　由于贵国政府的提议,这次访问才得以这样快地重新实现,这使我感到格外高兴。

　　这次访问使我有机会亲眼看一看中国人民所取得的成就,这是我长期向往的。

　　当然,我曾经读过关于这些成就的材料;许多访问过贵国的人,特别是1972年以英国外交大臣身份来华访问的亚历克·道格拉斯-霍姆爵士以及在他之前的安东尼·罗伊尔爵士也向我介绍过这些成就。

　　1973年6月,我们欢迎姬鹏飞外长访问伦敦的时候,我也很高兴能有机会同他进行会谈。

　　你们已经取得了进步,对此我毫不怀疑。

　　现在我将亲眼看到这些进步,而且我知道这是一次非常有益的经历。

　　我们英国的社会政治制度在许多方面都与你们的不同。这是不同经历和传统造成的。

- **译文 2**

尊敬的副总理先生：
尊贵的中国主人和朋友们：

　　我十分高兴能来到北京并有此机会感谢中国政府和中国人民给予我的盛情款待。

　　我曾深感失望地被迫推迟了原定于1月的访华计划。

使我感到格外高兴的是,由于贵国政府的提议,这次访问又能这样快地重新实现。

这次访问给了我寻求已久的机会,即亲眼看一看中国人民所取得的成就。

当然,我曾经读过关于这些成就的材料;许多访问过贵国的人也向我介绍过。其中特别值得一提的是1972年以英国外交大臣身份来华访问的亚历克·道格拉斯-霍姆爵士以及在他之前的安东尼·罗伊尔爵士。

我也很高兴曾有机会与姬鹏飞外长进行过会谈,那是1973年6月我们欢迎他访问伦敦的时候。

对你们已经取得的进步,我毫不怀疑。

现在我将亲眼看到这些进步了,我知道种体验将对我非常有益。

我们英国的社会政治制度在许多方面都与你们的有所不同。这是因为我们有不同的经历和传统。

● 练习4(汉译英)

(1) **Hospital Nursing**

Prof. Zhuang has always been aloof and proud, but even such a person as him is now feeling angry, because the loneliness is really too much for him to bear. As a well-known professor in an equally well-known prestigious university in China, he has never been treated with such neglect, not even when he was ill in bed in a foreign country on a lecture visit. It is said that intellectuals enjoy the same treatment of high-rank cadres, but how could he—certainly ranked among the intellectuals—match with the high-rank cadre lying on the sickbed opposite him? All the time, that one has by his bed cadres like division directors and section heads to care for him. In addition, there are even smart young ladies coming to see him and give him some heart-warming words. On his bed stand and window-still are piles of De Lux foodstuff. There are about half a dozen young men on three shifts taking care of him around the clock. Doctors and nurses who come for checks will also first check that guy, that is Manager Wang, who is lacking neither money nor power, and then come to himself—although as a professor of Chemistry he himself is no less well-known. Besides, if Manager Wang's checkup is to take half an hour, his will probably take no more than a quarter. At his bedside is always a cheerless, deserted air, with his son thousands of miles away on the missile project, and his daughter abroad at school. There is only his other half to come each day to bring him a meal and fill his thermos bottle. As for his department, there is even less that he can count on, for it could at best send someone to visit him every other week. For anyone who has fallen into such a situation, what is of least use is nothing else but learning, reputation and putting on airs. However, Prof. Zhuang is just such a person who will not give in regarding his image. So every day he just lies facing the wall, not paying the least attention to whatever is going on at Manager Wang's bedside. God knows what sort of manager this one is! For this is an age of companies everywhere. As organizations of thousands of people may be called a company, one or two persons may hold up a company sign as well.

Then day comes when Manager Wang's conditions suddenly get worse, and the doctor announces that his funeral affairs should be arranged. Naturally, more people have gathered around his bedside, including even Mr. Liu, the always self-assuming vice manager. Instead of lying with some meaningless sweet words to comfort a dying man, Mr. Liu first kept silent for a little while, and then said something very factual, such as asking if he has any demands to make, or if there is anything that he still worries about. To whatever demand the dying man has made, the vice manager gives a satisfactory answer without any hesitation. After all is said, Mr. Liu gets up to take his leave, for he has to arrange the funeral. Then, suddenly, those people attending Manager Wang all rise at once, leaving the patient behind, to win their chance to help Mr. Liu on his way, some go to the front to open the door, others walk on his side, all smiling to please him. Such a crowd! And what a scene! Mr. Liu flies off his handle and shouts:

"It is not me who is dying! What is the point of helping me?"

As an exception, Prof. Zhuang turns over, and sees that Manager Wang lies there all by himself, waiting for his last moment, two lines of tears from his face trickling down to the pillow … The professor feels it fortunate that he himself is an "intellectual", not a "high official", and that his pen will never betray him, not even on his last day.

(2) An Excerpt of *Camel Xiangzi*

How could a man so tall, pulling such a gorgeous rickshaw, his own rickshaw too, with such gently resounding springs and shafts that barely wavered, such a gleaming body, such a white cushion, such a sonorous horn, face himself if he did not run hard? How could he face his rickshaw? This was not false pride. It seemed to be a kind of duty. He couldn't show off his strength and exhibit the excellence of his rickshaw to full capacity if he didn't fly. That rickshaw was really endearing. It seemed to understand everything and have feelings after he had pulled it for six months. It responded promptly when he turned or squatted or straightened up and gave him the most compatible kind of assistance. There was not the slightest separation or disharmony between them. When he came to a flat stretch with little traffic, Hsing Tzu might hold the shafts with only one hand and fly along safely with the whisper of the rubber tires urging him on like a damp cool breeze. You could wring the sweat out of his clothes when he got to his destination. It was just as if they had come out of the washtub. He felt exhausted, but it was a happy, honorable exhaustion, like that following a long ride on a famous horse. If you are bold, it does not follow that you are careless. When Hsiang Tzu ran boldly, he was certainly not careless. Not to run hard would make him feel he had failed his passenger. To run hard and wreck the rickshaw would make him feel he had failed himself.

The rickshaw was his life; he knew how to be careful with it. With caution and boldness combined he gained more self-confidence as he went along. He was convinced that both he and the rickshaw were made of iron.

(3) **An Excerpt of** *Camel Xiangzi*

The rickshaw men in Peking form several groups. Those who are young and strong and springy of leg rent good-looking rickshaws and work all day. They take their rickshaws out when they feel like it and quit when they feel like it. They begin their day by going to wait at rickshaw stands or the residences of the wealthy. They specialize in waiting for a customer who wants a fast trip, they might get a dollar or two just like that if it's a good job. Having struck it rich they might take the rest of the day off. It doesn't matter to them—if they haven't made a deal on how much rent they'll have to pay to the rickshaw agency. The members of this band of brothers generally have two hopes: either to be hired full time, or buy a rickshaw. In the latter case it doesn't make much difference if they work for a family full time or get their fares in the streets; the rickshaw is their own.

Compare the first group to all those who are older, or to all those who, due to their physical condition, are lacking in vigor when they run, or to all those who, because of their families, do not dare waste one day. Most of these men pull almost new rickshaws. Man and rickshaw look equally good so these men can maintain the proper dignity when the time comes to ask for the fare. The men in this group work either all day or on the late afternoon and evening shift. Those who work late, from four P.M. to dawn, do so because they have the stamina for it. They don't care if it is winter or summer. Of course it takes a lot more attentiveness and skill to work at night than in the daytime; naturally you earn somewhat more money.

It is not easy for those who are over forty and under twenty to find a place in these two groups. Their rickshaws are rickety and they dare not work the late shift. All they can do is start out very early, hoping they can earn the rickshaw rental and their expenses for one day between dawn and three or four in the afternoon. Their rickshaws are rickety and they run very slowly. They work long hours on the road and come out short on fares. They are the ones who haul goods at the melon market, fruit market, and vegetable market. They don't make much but there's no need to run fast either.

Very few of those under twenty—and some start work at eleven or twelve—become handsome rickshaw men when older. It is very difficult for them to grow up healthy and strong because of the deprivations they suffer as children. They may pull a rickshaw all their lives but pulling a rickshaw never gets them anywhere. Some of those over forty have been pulling rickshaws for only eight or ten years. They begin to slow down as their muscles deteriorate. Eventually they realize that they'll take a tumble and die in the street sooner or later. Their methods, charging all that the traffic will bear and making short trips look like long ones, are quite enough to bring their past glory to mind and make them snort with contempt at the younger generation. But past glory can scarcely diminish the gloom of the future and for the reason they often sigh a little when they mop their brows. When compared to others among their contemporaries, however, they don't seem to have suffered much. They never expected to have anything to do with pulling rickshaws. But when faced with a choice between living and dying, they'd had to grab the shafts of a rickshaw. They were fired clerks or dismissed policemen, small-time merchants who had lost their capital, or workmen who had lost their jobs. When the time came, when they had nothing left to sell or pawn, they gritted their teeth, held back their tears, and set out on this death-bound road. Their best years are already gone and now the poor food they eat becomes the blood and sweat that drips on the pavement. They have no strength, no experience, and no friends. Even among their coworkers they are alone. They pull the most broken-down rickshaws. There's no telling how many flats they get in a day. They'll get a fare and then beg for "understanding and pardon". Fifteen cents is a large fee but they want a tip, too.

五、篇章参考译文翻译原理选注

- 练习3（英译汉）注释

（1）

① "Sleep at a late hour in the morning is not half so peasant as the more timely one. It is sometimes, however, excusable, especially to a watchful or overworked head."以"sleep"为主语，属主语突出的句型，难以直译，故译文以"早上睡到很晚的时辰"作为起点，符合汉语常用时间作话题的习惯，与后半句构成二元结构，流畅自然。

② "This is a privilege allowable, we think, to none but the old, or the sickly, or the very tired and care-worn, and …"译为"而且，我们认为，只有老人、病人或者疲劳不堪、忧思苦虑的人，才能允许享受这种特权……"。

由于英语句子往往在中间有插入成分，具有思维缜密、逻辑性强的特点，汉译时不可照搬这种结构。故将插入语"we think"调到开头充当主句进行翻译，避免了译文的欧化。英语中物称主语"this"的位置在译文被人称主语"老人、病人或者疲劳不堪、忧思苦虑的人"所代替，既是话题，又是人称主语，增强了译文的可读性和流畅度。

③ "It is a mistake to suppose that all care is wakeful"译为"认为忧愁一定不能睡觉，是一种误解"。形式主语"it"略去不译，调整原文词序，这样得到的译文符合"主题＋述题"的模式。

④ Without meaning to lessen the dignity of suffering, which has quite enough to do with its waking hours, it is this that may often account for the profound sleeps enjoyed the night before hazardous battles, executions, and other demands upon an over-excited spirit.

笔者无意抹杀受苦受难的庄严性，因为人在清醒的时候所遭到的苦难已经足够叫他烦恼，然而这也正好说明了人处在凶险鏖战或死刑判决的前夜，以及其他迫使精神过度兴奋的状态之中为什么还能够酣然沉睡。

英语原文是包含两个从句的主从复合句，两个物称主语分别是"which"和"it"，译成汉语时，添加人称主语"笔者"和"人"，使译文符合汉语多用人称主语的特点。

（2）

① 第一句原文是由形式主语"it"引导的常见英语句型，两种译文都按汉语习惯做了变通，改用"我"作主语。

② 第二句与第一句类似，物称主语"it"被人称主语"我"所代替。两种译文语序不同，第一种译文与原文语序出入较大，但符合语序安排与事物发生先后一致，且符合中文"主题+述题"的句式，句末出现的"失望"与下句句末的"高兴"构成对比，先抑后扬，十分流畅。第二种译文则稍显生硬突兀，没有第一种译文来得舒缓自然。

● **练习4（汉译英）注释**

《骆驼祥子》选段一

① 《骆驼祥子》的作者老舍多以城市人民生活为题材，爱憎分明，有强烈的正义感。老舍能纯熟地驾驭语言，运用北京话表现人物、描写事件，具有浓郁的地方色彩和强烈的生活气息。老舍笔下的人物性格鲜明，细节真实，再加之语言讽刺幽默、诙谐轻松，作品深受人民喜爱。

② "那辆车也真是可爱，拉过了半年来的，仿佛处处都有了知觉与感情，祥子一扭腰、一蹲腿，或一直脊背，它都就马上应和着，给祥子以最顺心的帮助，他与它之间没有一点隔膜别扭的地方"的主题是"那辆车"，后面的内容围绕这个主题铺陈开来，靠语义"粘合"在一句话中，英译文没有复制原文的架构，而是根据原文这句话所表达的四层意思，分成四句话分别予以交代，意思明确，结构井然。

《骆驼祥子》选段二

① "北平的洋车夫有许多派……但也不在乎"的主题系统较为复杂，具有多层次性特征。如首句以"北平的洋车夫"为主题，冒号后面各句的主题分别是：年轻力壮，腿脚灵利的→拉出车→来弄好了→碰巧了。各个主题相互联系，虽然有的句子没有主语，但每句都呈"主题+述题"结构。全段一气呵成，凸现汉语语篇的整体感。英译时首先不仅要根据语义调整标点、进行断句，还要使每一句具有主语，分别重构成合乎英语语法规则的主语系统。相应地，英译文中各句都有了主语，除"The rickshaw men in Peking"外，总共用了12个代词。这显示了英语主语一般不可省略的规律。

② 在"在后者的情形下,因为还有相当的精气神,所以无论冬天、夏天总是'拉晚儿'。夜间,当然比白天需要更多的留神与本事;钱自然也多挣一些"中,从"在后者的情形下"开始到段落结束这两句,分别以"在后者的情形下"和"夜间"作主题,娓娓道来,却省略了主语,这是汉语的常态。英译时分别补上"the men in this group","those","they","it"和"you"作主语,使之符合英语语法。

③ 在翻译"年纪在四十以上、二十以下的,恐怕就不易在前两派里有个地位了"时,根据英语习惯,译成以形式主语"it"引导的句型。

④ 中文最后一句英译时需要加上主语,同时"皮带不定一天泄多少次气"译成"There's no telling how many flats they get in a day"显得非常地道,丰富了句法变化。

第四章 客观视角与主观视角互译

一、翻译原理

中国的传统思维把主体自身作为宇宙的中心,认为"万物皆备于我"。这种思维认为人认识了自身,也就认识了自然界和万物的根本规律,用主体的修养代替对客体的认识。古人往往不以自然为认识对象,而是把自然人性化或者把人自然化,"天人合一",主客体不分,不在认识自然的基础上反思,而是从主体出发,在直观经验的基础上直接返回到主体本身。因此,传统思维有着浓厚的主体意向。人们注重直觉意象而非逻辑推理,注重求善而非求真。意向性思维使主体介入客体,客体融入主体,"物便是我,我便是物","物我一体","山性即我性","山情即我情",由此使客体主观化、自然人格化,达到情景交融、情感与理性合一。主体意向与本体认知合一,突出了主体能动性,使思维受制于情感,以情感代替理性。

西方传统思维以自然为认知对象,认为只有认识自然,才能把握自然,只有探索自然,才能征服自然,因而主客两分,天人对立,划分内心世界与外部自然界,区分自我意识与认识对象,将自然作为自身之外的对象来研究。西方哲学创立了本体论而持尊重客观的态度。理性主义把主体作为"旁观者",对客体尤其是本质世界进行探究。这种思维倾向必然摆脱主体意识而通向客体意识。西方注重科学的思维传统,明确区分主体与客体,排除主观因素,强调客观性,使客体客观化,物我两分,以客观和冷静的态度对待客观世界。

这两种思维差异在各自的语言上表现为:汉语往往以人作为句子的出发点,描述客观事物时也往往是从人的视角着手,而不是从客观事物本身;汉语无主句也往往可以添加人作主语;被动句相对较少。而英语句子物作主语的非常多,在描述主体与客体关系、互动的时候往往从客体着手;形式主语句、"there be"句型和被动句相对较多。因此,从宏观上看,汉语句子往往主观性比较强,而英语句子则表现出更明显的客观性。

二、核心例句原理分析

核心例句	原理分析
A. 英译汉 1. An apple a day keeps the doctor away. 一天一苹果,医生不烦我。 2. Where does the missing key go? 谁的钥匙? 3. My leg is killing me. 我腿疼得要命。 4. An idea came to me. 我想到了一个主意。 5. What became of him later? 后来他怎样了? 6. It is impossible for me to finish it today. 我今天不可能完成(这个)。 7. My bitterness knows no bounds. 我痛苦得没完没了。 8. That sounds interesting. 听上去很有意思。 9. It smells fishy. 令人怀疑。 10. Where there is a will, there is a way. 有志者,事竟成。 11. What happed to him? 他怎么了?	1. 汉语多以主体为描述或者话语的出发点,而英语多以客体(对象)为话语的出发点。因此,"apple"在这里是主语,强调了它的益处或者中心性。 2. 用"where"而不是"who",完全客观化。 3. 直译就是"我的腿要我的命",意译就要主观化。 4. "主意"到了我这里,因此突出了主意本身。 5. 事情当先,纯粹客观。 6. 英文主语用"it",汉语还是"我"。 7. "痛苦"是客观的,"我"是主观的。 8. 英语没有省略什么,汉语省略了主题。 9. 原理同上。 10. "there is"是客观的。 11. 同例5。
B. 汉译英 1. 走进苏州 The Gateway to Suzhou 2. 站在山顶可以看见大海的风景。 The hilltop commands a good view of the seaside. 3. 我觉得这书读起来很有意思。 The book reads interesting. 4. 我不知道他到底遭了什么殃。 I just wonder what befell him. 5. (我)脚踩在地毯上,一点声音也没有。 The carpet killed the sound of my footsteps. 6. 你有没有过就是想揍人的念头? Does it ever occur to you that you just want to punch somebody? 7. 我内心有一种深深的负罪感。 A strong sense of guilt overwhelmed me. 8. 刹那间,我热泪盈眶。 Tears came into my eyes immediately.	1. 汉语"走进苏州"其实省略了主体"人"或者"大家",而英语则转换了视角,变成客观"The Gateway to Suzhou"。 2. 英语"hilltop"直接作主语。 3. 英语从"book"本身出发,汉语以我为本。 4. 后半句原理同上。 5. 英语"carpet"作主语,汉语必须改变。 6. 英语"it"当先,汉语主语仍是"你"。 7/8. 视角转变,物称转人称。

三、翻译练习

◆ 课堂练习 ◆

- 练习1（英译汉）

1. Evening found him in London.
2. I just wonder what befell him.
3. I usually have two books going at the same time.
4. Passage to India
5. Across China
6. And, incidentally, it is a chronic complaint of wives that their husbands do not notice new dresses, new hats, and changes in household arrangements.
7. A given event will be "seen" in several different ways by as many witnesses.
8. As the weeks went by, Swain's visits grew more frequent.
9. It roused something in me.
10. The image of that woman gradually faded away from my mind.
11. By the third criterion, the great literatures of the Orient spring to mind.
12. As to the general moral principles of marriage, there is perhaps a fairly wide measure of agreement, in spite of the wide disagreement as to the consequences to be drawn from them.
13. Nowadays, there is a heated debate going on about the search for the best government model which can both lead Turkey to the European Union and which can play its cards wisely in case of a US attack on Iraq.
14. Since I've been bumming around with nothing much to do, it suddenly dawned upon me that I've never seen the movie so I decided to look for it.
15. The history of Xi'an has seen the rise and fall of 13 dynasties, and made tremendous contributions to the Chinese civilization and even to the civilization of the oriental world.

- 练习2（汉译英）

1. 我只会想到一个名字，那就是莎士比亚。
2. 我想到的是在北京婚姻登记处登记结婚时的有意思的情景。
3. 我现在意识到书本知识我早忘光了。
4. 我一时想不起来了。

5. 他怎么了?

6. 他后来怎么样了?

7. 雨天没完没了。

8. 医生们对这一复杂的病症大为不解。

9. 这个故事本没什么寓意。

10. 我再一次表达了道歉的意思。

11. 她嘴角流露出了某种表情,让人感到温暖。

12. 我看到她被强烈的情感控制着。

13. 我可理解不了他的大作的本质。

14. 联想2026年会怎么样?

15. 在练塘,政府给投资者以希望,人民给投资者以信心。

◆ 课后练习 ◆

● 练习1(英译汉)

1. The shock that followed this declaration found voice in a sustained "Ah-h-h!" as the door of the coupe swung open.

2. It never occurred to me that one man could start to play with the faith of fifty million people—with the single mindedness of a burglar blowing a safe.

3. Possibly it had occurred to him that the colossal significance of that light had now vanished for ever.

4. As I went over to say good-bye, I saw the expression of bewilderment had come back into Gatesby's face, as though a faint doubt had occurred to him as to the quality of his present happiness.

5. His parents were shiftless and unsuccessful farm people—his imagination had never really accepted them as his parents at all.

6. A tour to Tibet will certainly delight you.

7. Before darkness consumed her, Jaonne heard the little girl say: "He cut my leg off and now I have to take yours. After all, you are his daughter!"

8. Frequently gaps in our knowledge are found that have to be filled in.

9. The abnormal behaviors of rats before an earthquake bewildered the rat watchers.

10. My memory failed me at the moment and I'll come back to it when it comes to me.

11. Mark my words, kids: solutions will not come to you nor helpers will knock your door, unless you yourself try to find the way out. This is the way of the world.

12. There's something unutterable in her heart.

13. Some tasty ways to keep the doctor away may still be unknown to you.

14. Depression came back to him after the holiday was over.

15. Something inherent to the occasion had affected them all.

16. At Steventon Rectory there can have been little fear of isolation from the momentous events in Europe and in America.

17. There was comfort in finding his estate rather more, and his debts much less, than he had feared.

18. Somehow, out path took us toward the park, across the foot bridge high above the rolling water.

19. Tobacco and smoking were the subject of 413 broadcast news stories during the year.

● **练习2（汉译英）**

1. 旁观者顿时噤若寒蝉,惴惴不安。

2. 我通常同时读两本书。

3. 近观你就会看清这个古老博物馆的真正面貌。

4. 凭直觉,我感到不应该走进那幢房子。

5. 人们对充满世界的颜色和运动都习以为常了。

6. 如果我没有记错,我想我去年在纽约见过你。

7. 我万一有个三长两短,别告诉我父母。

8. 我现在觉得我似乎在哪里见过她,要么是看过她的照片。

9. 我对相对论迷惑不解,别再拿这种问题来烦扰我了。

10. 他看到了我们,蓝色的眼睛里立刻有了一丝希望。

11. 你穿这件大衣不能抵御哈尔滨的寒冷。

12. 沿着这条路你可以到达市中心。

13. 滥用药物,人会产生依赖性。

14. 三十七年前,我到过这个村子,那时的样子我已经记不起来了。

15. 我骨子里有一种反叛精神。无论什么时候,不管什么人告诉我如何如何,我总是背道而驰。

16. 对厨房进行革新,这是一种病毒,而中年持家者就是其牺牲品。

17. 我感到尴尬的是还要向女儿道歉。

18. 到徐州见着父亲,看见满院狼藉的东西,又想起祖母,不禁簌簌地流下眼泪。

19. 一周锻炼三次以上,你的健康会受益无穷。

20. 那段时间的报纸价格很贵,各家只得相互传阅着看。

● 练习 3（英译汉）

（1） **An Excerpt from *Vanity Fair***

When the great crash came—the announcement of ruin, and the departure from Russell Square, and the declaration that all was over between her and George—all over between her and love, her and happiness, her and faith in the world—a brutal letter from John Osborne told her in few curt lines that her father's conduct had been of such a nature that all engagements between the families were at an end—when the final award came, it did not shock her so much as her parents, as her mother rather expected (for John Sedley himself was entirely prostrate in the ruins of his own affairs and shattered honor). Amelia took the news very palely and calmly. It was only the confirmation of the dark presages which had long gone before. It was the mere reading of sentence—of the crime she long ago been guilty—the crime of loving wrongly, too violently, against reason. She told no more of her thoughts now than she had before. She seemed scarcely more unhappy now when convinced all hope was over, than before she felt but dared not confess that it was gone. So she changed from the large house to the small one without any mark of difference, remained in her little room for the most part, pined silently, and died away day by day. I do not mean to say that all females are so. My dear Miss Bullock, I do not think your heart would break in this way. You are a strong-minded young woman, with proper principles. I do not venture to say that mine would, it has suffered, and, it must be confessed, survived. But there are some souls thus gently constituted, thus frail, delicate, and tender.

（2） **An Excerpt from *The Great Gatesby***

I suppose he'd had the name ready for a long time, even then. His parents were shiftless and unsuccessful farm people—his imagination had never really accepted them as his parents at all. The truth was that Jay Gatsby of West Egg, Long Island, sprang from his Platonic conception of himself …

For over a year he had been beating his way along the south shore of Lake Superior as a clam-digger and a salmon-fisher or in any other capacity that brought him food and bed. His brown, hardening body lived naturally through the half-fierce, half-lazy work of the bracing days. He knew women early, and since they spoiled him he became contemptuous of them, of young virgins because they are ignorant, of the others because they were hysterical about things which in his overwhelming self-absorption he took for granted.

But his heart was in a constant, turbulent riot. The most grotesque and fantastic conceits haunted him in bed at night. A universe of ineffable gaudiness spun itself out in his brain while the clock ticked on the washstand and the moon soaked with wet light his tangled clothes up on the floor. Each night he added to the pattern of his fancies until drowsiness closed down upon some vivid scene with an oblivious embrace. For a while these reveries provided an outlet for his imagination; they were a satisfactory hint of the unreality of reality, a promise that the rock of the world was founded securely on a fairy's wing.

An instinct toward his future glory had led him, some months before, to the small Lutheran College of St. Olaf in southern Minnesota.

● 练习4（汉译英）

当我读童话《雏菊》的时候,我确乎被一种细腻感伤的东西打动了。不知为何,我耳畔响起了20世纪80年代曾流行一时的一首歌曲,那熟悉的旋律就如涟漪荡漾过来。"没有花香,没有树高,我是一棵无人知道的小草。从不寂寞,从不烦恼,你看我的伙伴遍及天涯海角。"歌的名字是《小草》,它与文中的雏菊有着相同的性格,可它们的命运却大不相同。

文中的小雏菊长在栅栏旁,靠近沟渠,长在一丛最亮丽的青草中。它柔弱不堪,地位卑微,或许一生都不会引人注意。静静地,它绿了;静静地,它开了;同样是静静地,它枯萎了,归于遗忘。它从不抱怨自己出身贫寒,命运不济。相反,它很开心,开心得像天上高飞的云雀。它对自己的现状感到满足:它享受着周围郁金香与牡丹等那些高傲的花儿的绚烂多姿。它认为上帝给予它的恩赐已经很是丰厚了:阳光照耀着它,云雀也来光顾它。它追求平静的生活,而平静的生活于它并不是虚无缥缈的梦。

但安宁并不长久。雏菊看到那些曾让自己黯然失色的郁金香被锋利的刀割了去,这让它战栗不已:这就是高傲的代价。更为残酷的是,开心的云雀被关到了笼中,只能仰望着蔚蓝色的天空,渴望着外面的自由。小雏菊连同它生在其中的那丛草被拔了起来,放到了鸟笼中作为云雀的草坪。即使是现在,雏菊也没有为自己的命运感到伤心,因为它毕竟能和云雀在一起。

然而,云雀因为缺水与渴望自由,它的心碎了,而雏菊也不能伸展自己的叶子。它们一同消逝了,带着翅膀上与叶子上的青梦。

不管怎样,我们常常被那些纤细微小而不是雄伟宏大的东西所打动。小雏菊最能唤醒我们沉睡的良心与感官。在我们每个毛孔都流淌着傲慢与偏见、贪婪与残酷的时候,它能让我们清醒。

因此,切莫忘了雏菊告诉我们的:伟大的总想做渺小的,而渺小的却总做伟大的。

四、课后练习参考译文

◆ 课堂练习 ◆

● 练习1（英译汉）

1. 他在傍晚时分才到伦敦。
2. 我不知道他到底遭了什么殃。
3. 我通常同时读两本书。
4. 印度之行
5. 走遍中国
6. 顺便插一句，妻子们总是在抱怨说她们的丈夫注意不到她们的新衣帽和家具位置的变化。
7. 有多少目击者，对一件事情就会有多少观察方式。
8. 随着时间的流逝，斯万来得越来越勤了。
9. 我触景生情。
10. 我逐渐忘记了那个女人的形象。
11. 按照第三条标准来衡量，人们马上会想到东方各国的伟大文学……
12. 对于婚姻的普遍道德原则，人们的意见基本相同，尽管人们对于这些原则所产生的后果众说纷纭。
13. 目前，围绕寻求最佳政府体制，从而能领导土耳其加入欧盟并在美国攻打伊拉克时明智出牌这个问题，人们正在进行一场热烈的辩论。
14. 我一直懒散地闲荡，无所事事，突然想到自己还从来没有看过这部电影，于是决定找到它看看。
15. 西安在历史上见证了13个王朝的兴衰起落，对中国乃至世界东方的文明做出了巨大的贡献。

● 练习2（汉译英）

1. Only one name suggested itself to me: Shakespeare.
2. What came to my mind was the interesting scene that took place at the Beijing Marriage Bureau Office as we registered our marriage.
3. I realize now that most of the book learning has slipped my mind.
4. My memory failed me at that moment.

5. What happed to him?

6. What became of him later?

7. The rainy days see no end.

8. The complicated case puzzled all the doctors.

9. There is no moral to this story.

10. Again a sort of apology arose to my lips.

11. A warmth flowed from her.

12. I saw that turbulent emotions possessed her.

13. The nature of his composition is really above me.

14. What will 2026 hold for Lenovo?

15. Here in Liantang the investors find hope in the government and confidence in the local people.

◆ 课后练习 ◆

● 练习1（英译汉）

1. 门旋开了，他大吃一经，连续发出"啊啊"声。

2. 他从没有想到一个人可以玩弄五千万人的信任。

3. 或许他已经想过，灯光所蕴含的巨大意义已经消失殆尽了。

4. 当我过去说再见的时候，我看到盖茨比的脸上又有了迷惑不解的表情，似乎他对当前的幸福质量有了一丝怀疑。

5. 他父母是农民，操劳不止，穷困潦倒。他想象中从未真正把他们认作父母。

6. 到西藏旅行一次你肯定会很高兴的。

7. 在黑夜吞噬她之前，乔尼听到那个小女孩说："他（乔尼的父亲）把我的腿锯掉了，我现在也要来锯你的腿！因为，你是他的女儿！"

8. 我们会经常发现我们知识有空白之处，还需要填补。

9. 观察老鼠的人看到地震前老鼠的行为反常，感到大惑不解。

10. 我一时记不起来了，等我想起来再说。

11. 孩子，记住我的话，除非自己去寻找出路，否则你不会随便碰到解决问题的方法的，也不会有人找上门来帮你。

12. 她心里有些东西难以表达。

13. 你或许还不知道，有些吃法让你吃得香，还能保你不用看病。

14. 暑假结束，他情绪又低沉了。

15. 他们全都受到这次集会的特殊气氛的影响。

16. 斯蒂文顿教区的人们并不担心自己被隔绝于欧洲和美洲的重大事件之外。

17. 当他发现并非他以前所担心的那样,而是他的财产多于债务时,他感到很欣慰。

18. 我们不知不觉地朝公园走去。公园就在人行桥那边,桥下很深的地方,汹涌的河水流。

19. 那一年里,广播新闻报道提及烟草和烟草工业413次。

- 练习2(汉译英)

1. An awed hush fell upon the bystanders.

2. I usually have two books going at the same time.

3. A closer look will present you a true picture of the time-honored museum.

4. My intuition told me that I should not enter that house.

5. The panorama of color and action which fills the world is taken for granted.

6. If my memory serves me well, I think I saw you in New York last year.

7. If anything should occur to me, just keep it from my parents.

8. It occurred to me now that I had seen her, or a picture of her, somewhere before.

9. The issue of relativity already baffled me, so don't bother me with that sort of stuff.

10. When he saw us a damp gleam of hope sprang into his light blue eyes.

11. This coat will not prevent you from the cold of Harbin.

12. This road will lead you to the center of the town.

13. Abuse of the drug can lead to dependence.

14. The image of the village I visited 37 years ago has faded away from my memory.

15. There is a rebel deep in my soul. Anytime anybody tells me the trend is such and such, I go in the opposite direction.

16. Kitchen renovation is a virus that preys upon the middle-aged homeowner.

17. It embarrassed me a lot to apologize to my daughter.

18. When I met father in Xuzhou, the sight of the disorderly mess in our courtyard and the thought of grandma started tears trickling down my cheeks.

19. Doing physical exercises three times or more a week will bring enormous benefits to your health.

20. Newspapers were expensive in those days and tended to be shared between households.

- 练习3(英译汉)

(1)《名利场》节选

大祸临头了,父亲宣告破产,全家搬出勒塞尔广场,埃米丽亚知道自己和乔治的关系断了,她和爱情、和幸福已经无缘,对于这世界也失去了信念。正在这时,约翰·奥斯本寄给她一封措辞恶毒的信,里面短短几行,说是他父亲行为恶劣到这步田地,两家之间的婚约当然应该取消。最后判决下来的时候,她并不怎么惊骇,倒是她爹妈料不到的——我该说是她妈妈意料不到的,因为约翰塞特里那时候事业失败,名誉扫地,自己都弄得精疲力尽了。艾米丽亚收到信的时候,颜色苍白,样子倒很镇静。那一阵子她早已有过许多不吉利的预兆,如今不过坐实一下。最后的判决虽然现在刚批下来,她的罪过是老早就犯下的了。总之,她不该爱错了人,不该爱得那么热烈,不该让情感淹没了理智。她还像原来一样,把一切都藏在心里不说。从前她虽然知道事情不妙,却不肯承认,现在索性断绝了念头,倒也不见得比以前更痛苦。她从大房子搬到小房子,根本没有觉得有什么差别。大多时候她都闷在自己的小房间里默默地伤心,一天天地憔悴下去。我并不是说所有的女人都像埃米丽亚这样。亲爱的勃洛葛小姐,我想你就不像她那么容易心碎。你是个性格刚强的女孩子,有一套正确的见解。我呢,也不敢说像她那样容易心碎。说句老实话,虽然我经历过一番伤心事,过后也就慢慢地忘怀了。不过话又说回来,有些人天生一副温柔的心肠,的确比别人更娇嫩,更脆弱,更禁不起风浪。

(2)《了不起的盖茨比》节选

我想这个名字他老早就想好了。他的父母在农场做工,没有歇息,穷困潦倒。在他的想象中,他压根儿就没有把他们认作父母。他自己的柏拉图式的理念中突然跳出了长岛西卵的吉·盖茨比这么个名字,这才是事实……

有一年多的时间,他在苏比利尔湖南岸找到了一条生路,要么拾贝,要么打三文鱼,或者搞其他行当,赖以填饱肚子,有个栖身之所。他皮肤棕色,体格健壮。凉爽宜人的日子,他外出做活,时紧时松,过得很自然。他很早就和女人们发生了关系。可女人们把他惯坏了,他因此又瞧不起女人们:年轻的处女他认为无知,而其他的女人对一些事情吹毛求疵,而他由于强烈的自我陶醉却认为这些事情是理所当然的。

但是他总是心潮激荡,永不止息。夜里,躺在床上时,他脑海萦绕着最为伟大而虚幻的自负情绪。当闹钟在脸盘架上滴答不停,湿湿的月光浸泡着他堆在地板上的衣服的时候,他脑海中幻想出一个宇宙,俗丽而又难以描摹。每天晚上他都给他幻想的图案添上一两笔,直到睡意袭来,幻想停留在一些生动的情景上,使他忘记了一切,昏然入睡。有一段时间,白日梦为他的想象提供了空间;这些白日梦提示他,眼前的现实也不真实——这种提示让他满意;这些白日梦又向他许诺说世界的基石就建在仙子的翅膀上,安然无恙。

几个月前,他被追求未来荣耀的本能引导着,进了明尼苏达州南部路德教会办的小圣奥拉夫学院。

● 练习 4(汉译英)

Something subtle and sentimental touched me when I read the fairy *The Daisy*. Somehow, the familiar melody of a song popular in the early 1980s rippled in upon my ears. "Without the fragrance of flowers, or the height of trees, I am an unknown grass. Never lonely, nor worried I am, cause I have companions in every corner." The song is called "The Little Grass", and the grass in it resembles the daisy in character, but differ in destiny.

The little daisy in this piece grows nearby the paling, by the ditch and in the midst of the most beautiful grass. Humble and vulnerable, it may go unnoticed the whole life. Silently it is green, silently in bloom, and silently withers and slips into oblivion. It never complains about its humble origin and bad luck. On the contrary, it is merry, merry as the happy lark high up in the sky, and contented with its situation: the splendor of other proud flowers like tulips and peonies is its enjoyment. It thinks it is generously gifted by God: the sun shines on it, and the lark visits it. A tranquil life is its clear aspiration, rather than its vague fantasy.

But the tranquility doesn't last long. The little daisy trembles to see that some tulips who eclipse itself are cut with a sharp knife—this is the price of pride. What is more cruel is that the happy lark is caged, looking up at the blue sky, and yearning for liberty. The little daisy, together with a patch of grass amidst which it grows, is yanked out and put into the cage to serve as the bird's turf. Even now, the little daisy doesn't feel sad about its fate. It can be together with the lark, after all.

However, the want of water and freedom tears the bird's heart apart. Then the little daisy can't unfold its leaves. They both perished, with tender dreams on their wings and leaves.

Anyway, we tend to be touched by something small rather than big. And the little daisy can best awaken our dormant conscience and senses, and make us sober up when very pore of ours trickles down with pride and prejudice, greed and cruelty.

So don't forget what the little daisy conveys to us: the great always want to be little, and vice versa.

五、篇章参考译文翻译原理选注

• 练习3（英译汉）注释

（1）

1. "When the great crash came—the announcement of ruin, and the departure from Russell Square, and the declaration that all was over between her and George—all over between her and love, her and happiness, her and faith in the world—a brutal letter from John Osborne told her in few curt lines that her father's conduct had been of such a nature that all engagements between the families were at an end—when the final award came, it did not shock her so much as her parents, as her mother rather expected (for John Sedley himself was entirely prostrate in the ruins of his own affairs and shattered honor)."一句层次繁多，纵横交错，在语法结构上算是一句，但就意义而言，却是一个较大的语义群。译者首先大刀阔斧地进行信息拆分重组，使其更符合汉语的表达习惯。

2. 原文第一句以一些可观的对象为叙述起点,如"the great crash came",而这一"大祸"又同时包含了两个客观的对象:"the departure from Russell Square"和"the declaration that",而其下又含有各自的内容或层次。"departure"是一个对象,而译文中却换成了更为符合汉语表达习惯的主体中心"全家搬出勒塞尔广场";同时,该词还体现了两种语言动静态表达方面的差异(请参见本书第二章)。

3. "a letter from John Osborne told her … that …"中,话语叙述的起点是"信",译文中话语叙述的起点是"人",具体说就是"写信者":"约翰·奥斯本寄给她一封措辞恶毒的信",然后再叙述信的内容,十分自然。

4. "her father's conduct had been of such a nature that all engagements between the families were at an end"中,父亲的行为是叙述的对象,是一典型的"客体中心",而译文中对象直接变成了"主体",即对人的行为的描述转而变成了从行为方面描述作为"主体"的人:"他父亲行为恶劣到这步田地,两家之间的婚约当然应该取消",转换十分自然,不露半点痕迹。

5. 原文中的"award"属于反语,本义是"奖赏",作者把惩罚说成奖赏,有嘲讽意味,但主要目的是加重语气与表达效果,译文中没有顺其道而行之,而是采用意义还原的办法,同时为了传达效果,直接加重了该词的语气,译成"惩罚"顺理成章。

6. "But there are some souls thus gently constituted, thus frail, and delicate, and tender."这一句中"But"一词译成了"不过话又说回来",符合汉语表达,彰显译者的汉语功夫。而"frail, and delicate, and tender"译成"更娇嫩,更脆弱,更禁不起风波"更属难得之佳译。

(2)

1. his imagination had never really accepted them as his parents at all:在他的想象中,他压根儿就没有把他们认作父母。

2. "The truth was that Jay Gatsby of West Egg, Long Island, sprang from his Platonic conception of himself."的出发点是"事实";译文"他自己的柏拉图式的理念中突然跳出了长岛西卵的吉·盖茨比这么个名字,这才是事实"中,"事实"成了解释总结性的东西。

3. "His brown, hardening body lived naturally through the half-fierce, half-lazy work of the bracing days."的描述对象是"身体",译文中进行了主体与客体的转换,自然而然地转向了"以人为中心",因此变成了"他皮肤棕色,体格健壮。凉爽宜人的日子,他外出做活,时紧时松,过得很自然"。而译者对语句进行的拆分也十分见功力。

4. 同样"But his heart was in a constant, turbulent riot"一句转换成了以人为中心的而不是以物为中心的表达方式。"但是他总是心潮激荡,永不止息"更符合汉语表达习惯。

5. "The most grotesque and fantastic conceits haunted him in bed at night."以"自负情绪"为叙述起点,译文"夜里,躺在床上时,他脑海萦绕着最为伟大而虚幻的自负情绪"中,"他"成了主语与描述起点,"自负情绪"成了他脑海中的产生物,失去了叙述起点的位置。

6. "A universe of ineffable gaudiness spun itself out in his brain while the clock ticked on the washstand and the moon soaked with wet light his tangled clothes up on the floor."和译文主客体描述起点的转换同注释5。

7. "An instinct toward his future glory had led him, some months before, to the small Lutheran College of St. Olaf in southern Minnesota."一句是主动式表达,而译文选择了被动式表达,显示了他的"不由自主"或"无可奈何",别有深意。同时,原句的主语与话语叙述起点都是"本能",而译文中的叙述起点成了"他"。腾挪转换之间,似是不经意而为之,实则要么出于对两种语言的精准把握,转换得心应手,要么是把握了整体与大局,在细节上处处着意,否则定是欧化句式与拗口的表达。

- **练习4（汉译英）注释**

1. "当我读童话《雏菊》的时候,我确乎被一种细腻感伤的东西打动了"的主语与话语逻辑起点是"我",英文译成"Something subtle and sentimental touched me when I read the fairy *The Daisy*."显然转向了以"细腻感伤的东西"为逻辑与话语起点。

2. "不知为何,我耳畔响起了20世纪80年代曾流行一时的一首歌曲,那熟悉的旋律就如涟漪荡漾过来"的英译文也同样发生了话语叙述起点的变化,具体说,即从"我"转向了"一首歌的旋律"。译成"Somehow, the familiar melody of a song popular in the early 1980s rippled in upon my ears."简洁而不失味道。

3. 从"它追求平静的生活,而平静的生活于它并不是虚无缥缈的梦"与英译文"A tranquil life is its clear aspiration, rather than its vague fantasy."对照来看,我们不难发现两种语言的主观描述视角与客观描述视角的大致倾向。值得指出的是,英语中的抽象名词如该句中的"aspiration"等,大多至少含有两层含义:一层表示性质、状态、特征、过程等的抽象存在(如"aspiration"之抽象的"渴望,追求"之意);另一层则表示具体化的某事物(如"aspiration"之具体的"渴望/追求的东西"之意)。关于形象具体与抽象概括的阐释与翻译,请参见本书第六章。

4. "然而,云雀因为缺水与渴望自由,它的心碎了"是直陈式的,中心是"云雀";英译文"However, the want of water and freedom tears the bird's heart apart"则更强调了心碎的原因,因此"the want of water and freedom"也就相应提到了句首叙述起点的位置。

5. "在我们每个毛孔都流淌着傲慢与偏见、贪婪与残酷的时候,它能让我们清醒"与英文"And (the daisy can) make us sober up when very pore of ours trickles down with pride and prejudice, greed and cruelty."同样也不着痕迹地进行了主客观视角的转换。

第五章 形合话语与意合话语互译

一、翻译原理

在语言结构的组合关系上,英语倾向于形合(依附形式——词语的曲折变化、词缀、关联性词语)的组合关系,而汉语则倾向于意合(仰仗意义——内在逻辑)的组合关系。英语的形合有广义与狭义之分,广义的形合包括一切借助形式或形态手段完成句法组合的方式,如语法词类标记、构词或组词标记、语法范畴标记(如性、数、时态、语态等);狭义的形合只包括词汇手段。汉语的意合则无所谓广义与狭义之分,各个语言成分只要语义相关、符合逻辑,就可以构成意合。英语广义的形合与汉语的意合倾向从一个方面可以反映出这两种语言的另外一些不同特征,即前者注重外在的语法结构,是具有较高客观组织规律的语言,而后者强调内在的语义结构,是具有较高主观组织意识的语言(参见第三章、第四章)。比如:

(1)中国队打败美国队。

(2)中国队大胜美国队。

(3)四川人不怕辣,江西人辣不怕,湖南人怕不辣。

例(1)与例(2)表面结构一致,所用的动词本意正好相反,但意义完全相同,翻译为英语都可以是"The Chinese (team) has beaten the American by a great margin.",这是因为中国人理解这两句的意义时并不依靠句法结构,而是根据自然语序通过主观分析将例(1)中的"败"理解为"使……败",而在理解例(2)时则不理解为"使……胜"。用英语表达同样的意思无论用动词"beat","defeat"还是"win",都有严格的语法形式,即主动语态现在完成时的方式,英语的意思通过"has beaten"和"by"这种广义上的形合使意义明确。

例(3)中的谓语部分(述题部分)的三个汉字的顺序可以随意颠倒,但并不会引起任何理解上的问题。按照英语思维习惯,无论如何翻译,都最好添加一定的关联词语使其间关系明确、意义清楚。

If it is said Sichuan people do not fear what is peppery, then we can say that peppery food is never a fear to Jiangxi people. And as for Hunan people, they just fear that the food is not peppery enough.

虽然中文只有18个汉字,但英文翻译变成了41个单词,其中添加的主要是出于形合需要的关联词语和语法结构性词语。

根据这个原理,英译汉时往往需要省略不必要的语法结构词和关联词,使中文更加简洁,而汉译英时则常常有必要添加这类词语,使英文更加符合英语造句作文的基本规范。

二、核心例句原理分析

基本例句	分析说明
A. 英译汉 1. If winter comes, can spring be far behind? 冬天来了,春天还会远吗? 2. Until all is over, ambition never dies. 不到黄河心不死。 3. Smart as a rule, but this time as a fool. 聪明一世,糊涂一时。 4. Carrion crows bewail the dead sheep, and then eat them. 乌鸦吃死羊,先要哭一场。 5. Daughters and dead fish are no keeping wares. 女大不可留,鱼死不能放。 6. Dying is as natural as living. 生死皆自然。/ 生也自然,死也自然。 7. Every man is a fool or a physician at forty. 年到四十不懂保健就是傻瓜。 8. The sports meet has been put off until next week because of the heavy rain. 下大雨,运动会推迟到下星期。 9. The book is due tomorrow, so I have to rush through it tonight. 这本书明天到期,我今晚得赶快看完。	1. "if"为英语形合标记,中文注重意合,因此传统的归化性翻译均不译。 2. "until"与"if"本质相同,在形式上是连接性词语,但翻译中文时只考虑意义,也做归化性意合处理。 3. 英文通过形合手段"as … as"将句子连成一个一元化的整体,中文以二元相对的形式将一元化的整体一分为二。 4. "and"这一形合手段消失。 5. 中文翻译一分为二,通过意义类比自然衔接。 6. 同3。 7. "or"翻译意义,不翻译形式,实现了从形合到意合的自然转换。 8. 中文"下大雨"与后面的意思依靠读者(听话人)主动参与理解,而英文则用形合手法表明。 9. "so"在汉语中不译也能理解,反而自然简洁。
B. 汉译英 1. 不怕慢,只怕站。 It is better to move slowly than just to mark time. 2. 施恩勿记,受恩勿忘。 If you confer a benefit, never remember it; if you receive one, remember it always. 3. 道高一尺,魔高一丈。 Where God has his church, the devil will have his chapel.	1. 中文两部分之间根据意合原则不用任何连接词也很清楚。英文则用形式说清楚。 2. 英文添加"if"和"it"。 3. "where","his","it"都可以看成形式连接性词语,中文没有必要。

基本例句	分析说明
4. 种瓜得瓜,种豆得豆。 As you sow, so you reap. 5. 物极必反。 Once a certain limit is reached, a change in the opposite direction is inevitable. (Extremes meet.) 6. 人不犯我,我不犯人。 We will not attact unless we are attacted.	4. "as","so"都是形合手段,必须采用,除此之外还添加主语。 5. 英文为了形式关系的外在表现不惜烦琐,否则是不完整的病句。相比之下汉语相对简单。 6. 英文添加"unless"实现语法连接。

三、翻译练习

◆ 课堂练习 ◆

● 练习1（英译汉）

1. He that serves God for money will serve the devil for better wages.

2. The man who saves when young will have more to spend when he is old.

3. If you leap into a well, Providence is not bound to fetch you out.

4. If you are too fortunate, you will not know yourself; if you are too unfortunate, nobody will know you.

5. In time of prosperity, friends will be plenty; in time of adversity, not one amongst twenty.

6. Prue was of an upper middle-class family and Clive was from the slums.

7. *This Above All* is a story of great emotional conflict between a girl who knew and loved the England of hunting, cricket, and afternoon tea, and a man who knew and hated the England of slums, mines, starvation, and disease.

8. Home on rest leave, after the disaster of Dunkirk, Clive Briggs went first to Leaford and then to Gosley, both resort towns on the coast of England.

9. As I walked along the sand, I was captivated by the warm breeze, the sound of the ocean, and the light glinting off the water.

10. Then came the twilight colors of sea and heaven, the wine pink width of water merging into lawns of aquamarines, the sky a tender palette of pink and blue.

11. The harbor looked most beautiful in its semi-circle of hills and half-lights. The color of a pearl gray and a fairy texture, soft, melting halftones. Nothing brittle of garish.

● 练习 2（汉译英）

1. 留得青山在，不怕没柴烧。
2. 子曰："人无远虑，必有近忧。"
3. 我赤裸裸地来到这世界，转眼间也将赤裸裸地回去。
4. 否极泰来。
5. 上梁不正下梁歪。
6. 酒醉智昏。
7. 燕子去了，有再来的时候；杨柳枯了，有再青的时候；桃花谢了，有再开的时候。
8. 她，是个美人儿，在街上，绝大多数男人会看上一眼。
9. 1995年，我出生在北京，是老三，上面有两个姐姐。后来，又生了个弟弟，爸爸这才决定不生老五了，有老四继承香火就行了。
10. 一条浩浩荡荡的长江大河，有时流过很宽阔的境界，平原无际，一泻万里。
11. 兵者，国之大事，死生之地，存亡之道，不可不察也。
12. 阿Q没有家，住在未庄的土谷祠里；也没有固定的职业，只给人家做短工，割麦便割麦，舂米便舂米，撑船便撑船。
13. 四铭太太正在斜日光中背着北窗和她八岁的女儿秀儿糊纸锭，忽听得又重又缓的布鞋底声响，知道四铭进来了，并不去看他，只是糊纸锭。

◆ 课后练习 ◆

● 练习 1（英译汉）

1. What our enemy has started we must finish.
2. What about calling him right away?
3. Even chaff tastes sweet as honey when one is hungry, whereas honey doesn't taste sweet at all when one is full.
4. It is a common property of any matter that is expanded when it is heated and it contracts when cooled.
5. When in Rome, do as the Romans do.
6. Here are many wonderful stories to tell about the places I visited and the people I met.
7. Gathering my mantle about me and sheltering my hands in my muff, I did not feel the cold, though it froze keenly; as was attested by a sheet of ice covering the causeway, where a little brooklet, now congealed, has overflowed after a rapid thaw some days since.
8. Down from here, the river becomes wide and calm. If you take a light skiff down the stream, you will drink in the beauty along the river.

练习 2（汉译英）

1. 他帮着我，我帮着他。
2. 言语不多，道理深。
3. 亡羊补牢，犹未为晚。
4. 这里气候温和，四季分明，雨量充沛，日照充足，适合多种农作物生长栽培。
5. 开汤审评，清香四溢，滋味鲜醇，回味甘甜，余香犹存，经常泡饮，明目清心，止渴益神，减肥健美，堪称茶中佳品。
6. 只许州官放火，不许百姓点灯。
7. 素有天堂之称的苏州，物华天宝，人杰地灵，先民们在这里创造了悠久的历史文化，这就是我们通常所说的吴文化。
8. 在世纪之交新的历史条件下，江泽民总书记提出了"三个代表"重要思想，其中一条是强调中国共产党要始终代表中国先进文化的前进方向。先进文化是符合人类发展的方向，体现社会生产力发展的要求，代表大多数社会成员的根本利益，反映时代发展潮流的文化，是人类文明进步的结晶、社会前进的精神动力。
9. 愿此书在今后能成为青少年认识苏州的教科书，成为普通读者了解苏州的导引，更成为外国友人探寻苏州的一座文化桥梁。
10. 李力：男，现年二十五岁，毕业于北京大学中文系。二十岁开始发表作品，已发表小说二十余篇。该同志有一定的组织领导能力，拟提升为文艺科科长。

练习 3（英译汉）

From These Weary Bones I Cry（Excerpt）

I began to dream of flying, to rid myself of the dead. I dreamt of sprouting great feathered wings from my shoulder blades and taking flight into the sea-colored sky to join the city pigeons. I spiraled up from the endless string of yesterdays, from dark plantation soil salted with sweat and tears and red blood. And I left behind the dead of today, the murdered children on city sidewalks, the infant whose umbilical cord remains wrapped around her neck, the sad, blank eyes of those who have seen their dreams crumbled into dust by poverty's iron heel. That was the most terrible part of it, I think, not the memory of long-ago death or even the blood of today. But that great emptiness of the ago abandoned. The death of a dream lingered much longer, I thought, than the death of living flesh, and I discovered my barrio was a graveyard of dreams.（Whatever happens, Langston Hughes wonders distantly, and his eyes are filled with sorrow.）

I wanted to be an artist, Orland-of-the-Roof told me. He had no home and so lived on top of others, on black-tarred tenement rooftops, sweating and stinking in the summer heat and turning so cold in the bitter gales of winter that his toes became purple and mottled and too swollen to fit into his thin-soled second hand shoes. My papi laughed at me and my ma just shook her head, but I said why not? I can be great like da Vinci or the other man—whass his name?—Pablo Picasso, maybe. A real artist in museums and everything, and years later people will say my name Orlando like I was some kinda magic nigga, you know? A legend.

What happened, I asked him, scratching a mosquito bite on my leg.

He shrugged once, shoulders thin and sharp through the worn cloth of his shirt. His face was lined even though he was young, not old enough to be my father hardly, and the skin on his arms where veins should have crossed like thin blue rivers was thick and black and scarred, a gross travesty of human flesh. Who knows, he said, shaking his head back and forth. His eyes were black and bottomless, and I shivered despite the muggy heat of the August day. Who knows? A million things and more. I stared, later on, into our stained, spotted mirror and tried to imagine my own face with eyes that black and void. I tried to imagine the sudden cold that must come from having one's dreams snatched from wanting hands, the vast hopelessness that must then spread, like ripples on water.

And so I dreamt of flying. I could not, of course, stay to watch my eyes lose their light, and so I sprouted magnificent wings that no one else seemed to see. I flew from moans of the dying and blood-blackened snow, from the lash of the whip on smooth black shoulders and the hunger that gnawed at my stomach like a feral animal. I flew from the bullet-broken, white-boned skeleton that haunted me years after my cousin's death, long-fingered and empty-eyed, flew from the gentle swing of the bark-colored boy that hangs from the southern tree. I flew from the blue-lipped child beneath the oil-stained newspaper, from the sink of charred young flesh and the screams of the still burning. And I flew to escape my own world, that ravisher of dreams, my father's fist and my mother's blood, months of sleeping on cold hard floorboards and a winter wind that licked through the city shelter to steal the breath from my throat. My wings caressed the air.

I think I know what carries the caged bird through its lifelong imprisonment behind bars, what keeps it from beating its wings frantically until the bars of its cage are laced with blood. It is its dream of something more, of vast blue skies it has never seen or only half-remembers, of sweet-smelling air and great wild free that stretches out to the very ends of the earth. It is the same dream that caused black-skinned field hands to still sometimes in their toil despite sorrow-stained slave and unmarked graves, the same dream that allowed the red-skinned man to hope even after blood-black snow and stolen lands.

• 练习4(汉译英)

(1) 中国园林

走进中国园林,你会被它特有的东方情调所吸引:在一种清幽宁静的氛围中漫步,会发现这里与西方建筑相比,小巧细腻、曲折含蓄而充满静谧;与大自然的风光相比,更具人性的追求,一石一木都有着文化的意味。中国园林之美,在于它熔文化与艺术于一炉。北方的皇家园林,往往既有小桥流水、曲径通幽的园林胜景,又有气势宏伟的宫殿式建筑群,充分表现了皇家气派,现存者尤以北京的颐和园为最。私家园林中江南一带的留园、拙政园、网师园等凭借天然的山水、植被优势,展现有别于北方园林的意趣;这些园林多属官吏、富商和文人所有,与私人的住宅连在一起,既有住房、厅堂、书房,又有许多亭、廊、榭、阁、山水、植被组成的园林胜景,往往形体不大,却着力于模拟自然山水的神态。在城市中再造山林,其表现特征就是诗情画意,所追求的是避去世俗烦嚣,在自然风景中怡然自得。这些不同类型的园林,呈现出一种安定、自足而幸福的生活状态,可以说是一种生活的艺术,又从某些方面反映了古代中国人的人生观、宇宙观,以及不同阶层的生活方式、价值取向、审美趣味等。

(2) 《孙子兵法传世典藏本》前言

《孙子兵法》是世界公认最古老的军事理论著作,中华民族传统文化遗产中的璀璨瑰宝。其作者孙武,字长卿,尊称孙子、孙武子、吴孙子。孙武出生在中国春秋时代的齐国,故里乐安(今中国山东省惠民县)。青年时期,因避齐国内乱而出奔吴国,相传隐居在吴国都城姑苏郊外(今中国江苏省苏州市穹隆山),潜心撰著兵法。公元前512年,经吴国大臣伍子胥举荐,孙子将孙子兵法十三编晋献给吴王阖闾。经与吴王问对及吴宫教战,吴王知孙子能用兵,卒以为将。孙武为将后,与伍子胥共同辅佐吴国,经国治军,西破强楚,北威齐晋,南服越人,显名诸侯。孙子功成身退,终老吴地。

两千五百年来,孙子被尊为"武圣""兵学鼻祖"。《孙子兵法》言简意赅,精博深邃,极富哲理,古今中外,推崇备至,被尊为"兵经""兵学圣典"。中国古代杰出的西汉史学家司马迁在《史记》中指出:"世俗所称师旅皆道孙子十三篇。"

《孙子兵法》的对外传播,始于公元8世纪的中国唐朝初期,日本学者吉备真备于公元735年携兵法返回日本。公元1772年,法国神父约瑟夫·阿米欧首译《孙子兵法》法文本在巴黎出版发行。公元1860年,《孙子兵法》俄文本在俄国面世。公元1905年,英国卡尔思罗普将《孙子兵法》译为英文本,在日本东京出版。公元1910年,英国汉学家贾尔斯在伦敦出版《孙子兵法》英文本。同年,布鲁诺·纳瓦拉翻译的《孙子兵法》德文本在柏林出版。据不完全统计,迄今为止,世界各国已有《孙子兵法》三十余种文字的译本。

《孙子兵法》问世后广为流传,简牍、锦书到刊刻、影印,蔚为壮观。《孙子兵法》的版本虽然繁多,但主要分为两大传本系统,即《武经》本系统和《十家注》系统,而这两大本系统都是以《曹注本》为底本进行校勘而流传于世。

自20世纪以来,随着白话文运动在中国的兴起,《孙子兵法》白话译本便应运而生。

鉴于以上诸多原因,为了便于《孙子兵法》在中外传播,我们特将《孙子兵法》传世本、白话本、英译本的代表作编成《孙子兵法传世典藏本》出版发行,以供人们在探究《孙子兵法》真谛时,在寻根溯源、判定真伪是非时,在人们检阅、比勘、诠释和研究以及文化鉴赏时,提供珍贵的资料。

《孙子兵法》虽然诞生在中国,它却是全世界人民的共同财富。《孙子兵法传世典藏本》,将由中国联合国教科文组织全国委员会作为《孙子兵法》传世本、白话本、英译本的代表作,呈交给联合国教科文组织,以志永存。

(3) 苏州情缘(现代诗歌)

来了,来了,又来了,寒山寺
古运河之水源于北京
杨柳依依,黄昏的枫桥,钟声缭绕
苏州迎来了美丽的夜晚
故乡啊,故乡啊,我的故乡——苏州
来了,来了,又来了,美丽的水乡
古运河之水流向杭州
梧桐树荫　人们享受着绿意
如梭的船家　你奔向何方
拥抱苏州温柔的夜色
来了,来了,又来了,北寺塔
滔滔的运河之水　诉说着历史
如今的繁花仍留着隋唐的遗迹
河中月色等待着
苏州静谧夜色中的你和我

四、英汉互译参考译文

◆ 课堂练习 ◆

• 练习1(英译汉)

1. 能为钱侍奉上帝,那么只要钱多就能给魔鬼卖力。
2. 年轻节约用,年老不受穷。
3. 自己要作孽,老天不来救。
4. 运气太好不知己,运气太坏无人理。

5. 人走运朋友盈门,人倒霉鬼也不愿登门。/ 贫居闹市无人问,富在深山有远亲。

6. 普露出身于中产阶级上层家庭,克莱夫却来自贫民窟。

7.《这是头等大事》讲述了一个充满感情冲突的故事:年轻的姑娘乐于英国的狩猎、曲棍球、晚茶,而男主人公却对英国的贫民窟、矿井、饥荒、病痛深恶痛绝。

8. 敦刻尔克大劫难过去了,克莱夫·布利格斯放假回家,先后去了利夫德和戈斯里这两个英国海滨度假城。

9. 沿着沙滩漫步,海风拂面,海上波涛阵阵,波光粼粼,令人迷醉。

10. 暮霭沉沉,海天一色,红浪翻涌,碧波横流,天空红蓝相映、五彩生辉。

11. 只见海港环抱于半圆形小山丛中,煞是好看,朦朦胧胧,一片银灰,宛若仙境,它浓淡交融,光影柔和,清雅绝俗。

● 练习 2(汉译英)

1. As long as the green mountains are here, one should not worry about firewood.

2. The Master said, "He who will not worry about what is far off will soon find something worse than worry close at hand."

3. I have come to this world stark naked, and in the twinkling of an eye, I am to go back as stark naked as ever.

4. When misfortunes reach the limit, good fortune is at hand.

5. If the upper beam is not straight, the lower ones will go aslant. / When those above behave unworthily, those below will do the same.

6. When wine is in, wit is out.

7. If swallows go away, they will come back again. If willows wither, they will turn green again. If peach blossoms fade, they will flower again.

8. She is so strikingly beautiful that men stare at her whenever she goes out.

9. I was born in Beijing in 1955. I already had two elder sisters and after me a brother was born. Then my father decided that was enough.

10. A mighty long river sometimes flow through a broad section with plains lying boundless on either side, its waters rolling on non-stop for thousands upon thousands of miles.

11. The art of war is of vital importance to the state. It is matter of life and death, a road either to safety or to ruin. Hence it is a subject of inquiry which can on account be neglected.

12. Ah Q had no family but lived in the Tutelary God's Temple at Weizhuang. He had no regular work either, being simply an odd-job man for others: when there was wheat to be cut he would cut it; when there was rice to be hulled he would hull it; when there was a boat to be punted he would punt it.

13. With her back to the north window in the slanting sunlight, Ssu-ming's wife with her eight-year-old daughter, Hsiu-erh, was pasting paper money for the dead when she heard the

slow, heavy foot-steps of someone in cloth shoes and knew her husband was back. Paying no attention, she simply went on pasting paper money.

◆ 课后练习 ◆

● 练习1（英译汉）

1. 既然敌人已经登台,我们就必须收场。/既然敌人已经开始,我们就必须奉陪到底。
2. 马上给他打个电话,你觉得如何?
3. 饿了吃糠甜加蜜,饱了吃蜜也不甜。
4. 热胀冷缩是所有物质的共性。
5. 入乡随俗。
6. 我访问了一些地方,遇到了不少人,要谈起来,奇妙的事儿可多着哩!
7. 我把斗篷裹紧,把双手藏在皮手筒里,我并不觉得冷,虽然天气冷得彻骨;这可以由小路上结的一层冰来证明。现在已经又结了冰的一条山涧,在几天前迅速解冻的时候水曾漫到这条小路上来过。
8. 自此而下,江面宽阔,水流平缓,一叶轻舟,顺流而下,沿江美景,饱览无遗。

● 练习2（汉译英）

1. As he helps me, I also help him.
2. The few words carry profound philosophy.
3. It is not too late to mend the fold even after some sheep have been lost.
4. It enjoys a temperate climate with well-marked seasons and has plenty of rainfall and sunshine, favorable for growing crops.
5. After you infuse it, the tea is full of delicate fragrance, if you taste it carefully, the flavor is mellow with a sweet and lasting fragrance. To drink of ten can not only quench your thirst, benefit your mind but also make you slim, strong and handsome and clear your eyesight. So it is regarded as the best quality tea among all kinds of teas.
6. While the magistrates were allowed to burn down houses, the common people were forbidden even to light lamps.
7. Historically known as a paradise on earth, Suzhou is a blessed land of inspiration with abundant produce, natural environment and talented personages. The ancestors of Suzhou people created a splendid culture of a long history, which is what we usually refer to as the Wu culture.
8. As proposed by former President Jiang Zemin at the turn of the century, one of the "three represents" to be emphasized is that the Chinese Communist Party should represent the

direction of the advanced Chinese culture, which should conform to the direction of the development of mankind, meet the needs of the development of productivity, take behalf of the interest of the majority of the society and represent the tide of the contemporary cultural development. Such an advanced culture is the pith of human civilization and a driving force for social progress in essence.

9. I wish this book will become a course book for the youth to learn about Suzhou, and a guidebook for all other readers, and function as a bridge for international friends, who can then cross it and explore the city as they wish.

10. Li Li, male, presently 25 years old, graduate from the Chinese Department of Beijing University, who began to publish creative works at the age of 20 and by now has about two dozen pieces published, who has demonstrated considerable ability of a leader and organizer, is hereby proposed for the position of the section director of affairs in literature and art.

● 练习3（英译汉）

就是这些无奈的倦骨头让我哭泣（节选）

我开始梦想着飞行,这样就可以让自己摆脱死人。我梦想自己肩膀上长出了巨大的羽毛翅膀,飞向那海色的天空,和城市的鸽子飞到一起。我盘旋上升,飞离无穷无尽的昨日的缠绕,飞离那昏暗的种植园的土地,那被汗水、泪水和红色的血浸染的土地。这样我也就把那些今天的死者留在身后,那些在城市的马路边上被害的儿童,那个脖子上还缠绕着脐带的幼婴,那些眼看着贫困的铁蹄把他们的梦想踏碎成灰土人的悲伤、渺茫的眼睛。那是最令人悲伤的了,我想是的,并不是早已过去的久远的往事,甚至也不是今天的鲜血,而是那被抛弃的以往旷无边际的空虚。我感到,死者的梦要遗留得更加长久,比活人的肉体死后留得更长久。我发现,我所在的少数民族居住区是一片梦想的坟地（无论发生什么事情,兰斯顿·休斯还在远方纳闷,他的眼睛充满了哀伤）。

我想当个艺术家,屋顶奥兰德这样对我说。他没有家,所以就住在别人家的上面,住在出租房上黑色沥青的屋顶,夏天不停地流汗,发散着汗臭味,在冬天的狂风中又那么冷,脚指头冻成了紫色,斑斑点点,肿得穿不上他那二手薄底鞋子。我老爹笑我,我老妈只是摇头,可是我回答说为什么不行呢！我也可以像达·芬奇或别的人物那样伟大——是什么名字来着——巴勃罗·毕加索,也许吧。当一个真正的博物馆艺术家,无所不能,很多年以后人们说到我的名字奥兰德时会感到我似乎是个具有魔力的黑人。你说呢？当一个传奇式人物。

然后呢？我问他道,一边抓抓我腿上蚊子叮过的地方。

他肩膀耸了一下。他的肩膀瘦小,尖尖的瘦骨从穿破的旧衬衣里露了出来。他的脸上带着皱纹,可他还很年轻,不应该显得像我父亲那般年纪,他双臂皮肤上的血管本来应该像蓝色的河水,却显得深重、发黑而且带着疤痕,成了人肉体勾勒的滑稽画。谁知道呢？他说着说着不断前后点着头。他的眼睛是黑色的,深不见底。尽管八月天气闷热,我还是禁不住瑟瑟发抖。谁知道呢？还有一百万桩以上的事。

后来，我盯着我们那带着锈斑、麻麻点点的镜子，想要想象我自己要是有那双黑色而深陷的双眼会是什么样子。我想要想象出自己的梦想突然被那些贪婪的双手剥夺时的那种突如其来的冷战，想象那种随后在心里扩散开的无边的绝望感，就像是水上的涟漪。

所以我才梦想着飞行。当然，我不能待在那儿看着自己的眼睛失去光亮。于是我突然长出了一双大翅膀，一双别人似乎都看不见的大翅膀。我飞走了，离开了临死者的呻吟，离开了那血迹染黑的白雪，再也听不见那抽打在那些光滑的黑肩膀上的皮鞭声，感觉不到那种像野兽一样撕咬着我的肚子的饥饿感。我飞离了那枪弹打破的白色骷髅，就是自从我的堂弟死后一直在我眼前出现的那个骷髅，它久久徘徊在我眼前不愿离开，眼窝空空的。我飞走后再也看不到那挂在南方那棵树上，肤色就像树皮一样的男孩在那里缓缓地晃动，再也看不到那油渍斑斑的报纸下覆盖着的那个嘴唇紫青的小孩，再也看不到那年轻黑色的肉体沉入大海，听不到那还在发烧的孩子的哭叫声。同时，我飞走后也就逃离了我自己的那个世界，那个剥夺梦想的世界，逃离了父亲的拳头和母亲的血，不再连续几个月睡在冰冷、坚硬的地板上，让冬天的风穿过城市的那个安身之处，悄悄从我的喉咙夺走我的呼吸。我的双翅轻抚着空气。

我想我知道是什么东西让关在笼子里的鸟儿在禁闭中能一直生活下去，又是什么东西让它疯狂地拍打翅膀，直到笼子的格条上染上了鲜血。这就是它对更多的事情的梦想，对那种它从来没有看到过或只能记得模模糊糊的浩瀚蓝天的梦想，对那种馥郁的空气和伸向地球最边远处的巨大野树的梦想。也就是这样一种梦想让田里那些肤色黝黑的劳动者一如既往地做着苦工，尽管那些奴隶处处有心酸，那些墓碑连名字都没有标出。就是这样一种梦想让那红皮肤的人在看到白雪被人血染黑，土地被强取豪夺以后还能怀抱着希望。

● 练习 4（汉译英）

（1） The Chinese Garden

Walking into a Chinese garden, one cannot help but be enchanted by its unique oriental flavor; and walking in such an atmosphere of tranquility and peace, one will discover something unlikely to be found in Western architecture, which is delicate and refined, complex and contained in its quietude. In contrast with natural scenery, the beauty of Chinese gardens lies in their combining cultural and art into one. In northern imperial gardens, natural scenes with bridges, creeks and winding paths are interspersed with magnificent palatial architectural groups, fully exemplifying the royal dignity, the most typical of those still existing being the Summer Palace in Beijing. In contrast, private gardens south of the Yangtze River, such as the Lingering Garden, the Humble Administrator's Garden and Master-of-Nets Garden, play upon their hills, rivers and naturally rich vegetation and achieve a charm not to be found in northern gardens. These gardens typically belong to government officials, merchants and scholars, serving as part of their private residence, combining living quarters, reception halls and studies with a fascinating array of pavilions, corridors, terrace houses, hills, creeks and vegetation, not large in size but intent on capturing the feeling of natural scenery. The objective of re-creating hills and forests in the city is to show the poetic charm of nature, to draw people away from the maddening crowds, and to seek contentment and peace in nature. These gardens of different nature exemplify a life of stability, contentment and ease, an art of living so to speak. In a sense they reflect the ancient Chinese view of life, of the universe, and the lifestyles of different strata of society and their respective approaches to life, and aesthetic tastes.

(2) **Preface to *A Treasure Book of the Art of War***

The Art of War is internationally recognized as the earliest theoretical work on military strategy and a sparkling gem in the treasure of the Chinese cultural heritage. The author is commonly known by the name of Sun Wu, though other names such as Sunzi (Suntzu), Sun Wuzi and Sun Changqing are also used at times when appropriate according to traditional Chinese appellation system. He was born in the ancient Qi State during the Spring-Autumn Period in Chinese history. His home place was Le'an, what is now known as Huimin County of Shandong Province. In his youth, the Qi State was for a period in chaos and to evade the situation he left home for the Wu State, where according to commonly accepted conjecture he settled town in seclusion in the Qionglong Mountain outside the ancient town of what is now Suzhou City of Jiangsu Province. Then he buried himself in writing *The Art of War*. In 512 BC, with the recommendation of Wu Zixu, a minister of the Wu State, Sun presented his 13 collections of bamboo slip writing to Helu, the king of the state, who had a personal interview with him and then let him conduct a trial drilling in the palace. Convinced of his qualification as a commander in warfare, Helu appointed him the chief general. Since then, Sun began working together with Wu Zixu to help strengthen the state through government and military administration, and eventually helped it to develop into such a great military power as to defeat the strong army of Chu in the west, form a threat to the great Qi and Jin in the north, and subjugate Yue in the south. These feats won great reputation to Sunzi among the lords. Just at the peak of his success, Sun retired from the government, and then lived the rest of his life in the Wu territory.

Over 2,500 years, Sun Zi has been acclaimed as "the martial saint" and "the originator of military strategy". His work, *The Art of War*, featuring precision in concise language, profundity and breadth of meaning, and a sound philosophy in itself, has always been recommended to the utmost everywhere in the world ever since it was known, respected as "the classic script of strategics" and "the holy book on warfare". The historian Sima Qian of the Han Dynasty remarked in his Shiji (Records of the Grand Historian): "When it comes to the way of military commanding and maneuvering in the general sense used by the world, the commonly referred work is Sun's thirteen collections of bamboo slip writing."

The spreading of *The Art of War* to foreign land began in the early period of the Tang Dynasty (in the 8th century BC), when a Japanese scholar named Shinbi Yoshibi returned to his homeland from China with a copy in the year 735 BC. Then in 1772 AD, Jean Joseph Marie Amoit, a French priest of the time had his first French translation of the work published in Paris. In 1860, the Russian translation was published in Russia. In 1905, the English version translated by E. F. Calthrop was first published in Tokyo, Japan. And then in 1910, the English sinologist L. Giles brought out a second English version in London. In the same year, Bruno Navarra's German version was seen in print in Berlin. Since these early endeavors to publicize the work, succeeding translations have continued to come out. As a result, and according to statistics by no way considered as complete, Sun's work now appears in at least 30 languages of the world.

Ever since it came into being, *The Art of War* has been spread far and wide in various forms of reproduction, including those of the early bamboo writing slips, brocade, and the modern xeroxed copies. However, in spite of its spectacular variety in form, the reproductions largely fall into two categories: one reproduced on the basis of Wujing (or *The Strategics Script*) version and the other on Shijia Zhu (or *Ten Exegestists'*) version. Both of these are rooted in Caozhuben version (or *Cao's Annotated Version*).

Since Baihuawen Movement in the early twentieth century (the Vernacular Movement in 1917 – 1919), the plain common vernacular of Baihua based on Beijing dialect of course has come into use for reproducing *The Art of War*.

In view of the above diversity in the work's reproduction, and with the purpose to facilitate its further publicity at home and abroad, we have decided to publish a new compilation to include the most influential classic Chinese versions, the contemporary vernacular language version and a representative new English version under the title of *A Treasure Book of the Art of War*, in the hope that it will serve as a valuable source of reference to our readers in their attempts to find the genuine truth of the work, trace its original thought and clear up possible confusions in its understanding, or when they come to study it in their academic research in terms of traditional Chinese comparative philology, annotations, exegesis and cultural appreciation.

Although Sun Zi's *The Art of War* originated in China, it is nevertheless a common heritage of humanity. Therefore, this compilation, as a representative collection of the different versions, is meant to be presented by the Chinese National Commission for UNESCO to the United Nations for collection.

(3) **Suzhou, the Land of My Heart (A Modern Poem)**

I'm coming, coming, once again to the Chilly Hill Temple,
To the Grand Canal flowing down from Beijing.

Here are the tender willows, the Maple Bridge at dusk and the resounding bell,
With which Suzhou greets another evening.
Here, and just here, lies my beloved land, land of my heart.
I'm coming, coming, once again to the beautiful water city,
To the Grand Canal flowing to the city of Hangzhou.
Here in the shade of phoenix trees, life is happy in the green,
The dwelling boats passing apace, and moving about,
To embrace the tender night of the lovely city.
I'm coming, coming, once again to the North Temple Pagoda,
By the torrential water of the Grand Canal relating a long story.
In today's prosperity are also remains of the Sui-Tang Dynasties,
Here the moonlight on the water is waiting
For you and me to enjoy the sweet, serene evening.

五、篇章参考译文翻译原理选注

● 练习3（英译汉）注释

1. "I began to dream of flying … tears and red blood"中使用介词作为形合手段。除了最常用的"of"外还使用了三个"from"，但在中文翻译中这些形合方式全都变成了以动词成分为主的意合方式，既是从形合到意合的转换，又是由静到动的转换，这样的转换造成的效果使中文读上去一气呵成。

2. 译文第一段倒数第二句"我感到，死者的梦要遗留得更加长久，比活人的肉体死后留得更长久"是对原文中"… than …"进行分析处理的结果，而根据的原理就是从形合到意合的转换规律。否则就是一个读上去显得啰唆的长句。原文"I discovered my barrio …"之前用"and"作为形合手段连接两个分句，而译为中文时自然删除连接词，并且在形式上重新开始一个句子。句号的使用并没有使语气中断，因为中文是依靠主题意义的关联衔接的。这说明形合与意合的不同倾向与主题与主语的差异有很大关系。

3. 原文中的几个"and"和"so"在译文中都转换成了意合方式，显示这种词语的省略和转换在英译汉中是一个普遍现象。

4. 第四段除了连接词"and"转换为意合方式以外，最值得注意的是句首"I asked him, scratching a mosquito bite on my leg"的翻译："我问他道，一边抓抓我腿上蚊子叮过的地方"。英语"ing"的语法结构形式被语义化为"一边"，其实也可以理解为从形合到意合的转变。

5. 原文第五段中"of"和"from"多次使用，翻译都在主题一致原则下直接以动态性的谓语成分处理，集中体现了英译汉由静到动的普遍规律。

6. 最后一段原文中的"dream of …"和"dream that …"有不同的处理：前者因为强调的缘故译为"的梦想"，而后者则根据由形合到意合的原则处理。前者是由于特殊需要而保留了形式，这一点也很值得注意。

- 练习4（汉译英）注释

这首由日语翻译而来的中文现代诗歌没有介词，各行和各个不同语段之间的关系完全由读者自己体会，而这对于习惯意合思维方式的中国人来说并不难，但译为英文如果不以形合手法表明的话读者就可能不容易理解。此诗几乎每行都有这种由中文意合到英文意合方式的转换，应该特别注意。

第六章 抽象概括与形象具体互译

一、翻译原理

英汉对比研究表明,传统的英语思维常用比较抽象概括的概念表达具体形象的事物,比较重视抽象思维的运用,具有较强的抽象性。而汉语思维则更习惯于运用形象的方法表达抽象的概念,不太重视纯粹意义的抽象思维,具有较强的形象性和具体性。比如:

英语	汉语
1. cross	1. 十字架
2. wall clock	2. 挂钟
3. desk clock	3. 座钟
4. train	4. 火车
5. nibble	5. 蚕食
6. at the apex of one's power	6. 如日中天
7. have a complete picture in one's mind	7. 胸有成竹
8. with irresistible force	8. 势如破竹
9. paper clip	9. 回形针
10. knickers	10. 灯笼裤
11. dummy; comforter	11. 橡皮嘴

英汉语之间这种思维习惯上的差异根源在于两个国家文化背景不同,语言产生、发展和演变的土壤也不同。中国文化的重要特征之一是"尚象";西方文化的重要特征之一是"尚思"。中国文化"尚象"的传统形成了中国人偏重形象的思维方式,西方文化"尚思"的传统形成了西方人偏重抽象的思维方式。

英汉文字的演变和发展的历史就是东西方形象思维和抽象思维的最好佐证。中国文字是由整体象形文字发展而来的会意文字,有书画共源的特点,其起源的形象当是原始图画,经后世演化,逐渐由图画形式改为线条即成为象形文字,凸现简单的物象,有较强的直观性,如"日""月""人""雨"等。另外,由汉字组成的词语直观性也很强,如"娃娃头"

(pageboy style)、"硬币"(coin)等,形象鲜明生动,而相应的英文大多只说明功能。可以说,汉字的产生和发展是中国人形象思维的结果。西方文字也是由图形演变而来,其字母的形成和发展和汉语的象形文字有很多相似之处,只是由于西方文化的"尚思"传统,主体抽象思维抽走了具体物象的形象,逐渐形成了概括某一类物象的概念符号,不像汉字那么直观形象。因此,西方文字的演变与发展跟抽象思维方式有着密切的联系。

上例所示英汉语言思维差异实际上不仅反映在词语层面,而且延伸到语言的所有层面。比如:

1. 这里的风景多美呀!
What beautiful scenery here!
2. 真好玩!
How funny!(What a fun!)
3. 世界风云
World Affairs Review
4. 没有得到情报就说明发展情况令人满意。
The absence of intelligence is an indication of satisfactory developments.

其中,不仅"absence","intelligence","indication"和"developments"四个意义比较抽象的单词分别翻译为"没有""情报""表明""情况",而且分别添加了"得到""就""令人"等字词,从而使语言表现得更加具体。

由于上述原因,抽象表达法在英语里使用得相当普遍,尤其在社会科学论著、官方文章、报刊评论、法律文书、商业信件等文体中。在英译汉中,我们必须对大量的抽象概括表达方式进行形象化和具体化处理,把一些具有抽象概括意味的名词译为较为形象具体的动词、形容词,或使用较为具体的名词,从而使汉语译文富有色彩和魅力;在汉译英中则时时需要反其道而行之,对十分具体、形象的表达法尽量予以概括和提炼,使英语显得简练、地道。

当然,我们侧重说英语民族擅长用抽象概念表达具体的事物,比较重视抽象能力的运用;而汉语民族更习惯于运用形象的方法表达抽象的概念,不太重视纯粹意义上的抽象思维。但这绝不意味着英语民族不会形象思维,不使用形象的语言。事实上,为了表达的需要,在英译汉的过程中,我们也常常将英语中的形象表达做抽象化处理,如"pull the wire"(背后操纵)、"hit the right nail on the head"(正中要害)、"as cool as a cucumber"(镇定自如)、"a perfect Apollo"(一位标准美男子)、"Homer sometimes nods"(智者千虑,必有一失)、"The pen is mightier than the sword"(文胜过武)、"What is learned in the cradle is carried to the grave"(少时所学,到老不忘)。

二、核心例句原理分析

核心例句	原理分析
A. 英译汉 1. Our parents always expect progress of us in school and question its absence. 我们的父母总是期望我们在学校有进步,如果我们没有做到,他们就会问为什么。 2. One of the characteristics of the Chinese language is the predominance of the verb. 汉语的特点之一是常用动词。 3. The appearance of the book on the market caused a sensation. 这本书一上市就轰动。 4. Careful comparison of two ways of life will show the superiority of the former over the latter. 如果你仔细比较这两种生活方式,你将会发现前者比后者优越。 5. The newspaper claims to be the mirror of public opinions. 该报宣称忠实反映了公众的意见。 6. We have made some achievements, and we must guard against complacency. 我们取得了一些成就,但要防止自满情绪。 7. These problems defy easy classification. 这些问题难以归类。 8. No wonder the sight of it should send the memories of quite a number of the old generations back 36 years ago. 难怪老一辈子的许多人见了(这件东西),就会回想起36年前的往事。 9. The adoption of this new device will greatly cut down the percentage of defective products. 采用这种新装置可大大地降低废品率。 10. The thought of returning filled him with fear. 一想到还要返回,他就心有余悸。	1. 抽象名词"absence"既起强调概念的作用,又可简化句子,否则该句则需写成"Our parents always expect us to make progress in school and if we fail to do so, they will ask why."。相比之下,英文味道骤减。 2. "characteristics","predominance"都由抽象到形象。 3. "appearance"形象化为"上市"。 4. 抽象名词"comparison"既起强调概念的作用,又可简化句子,否则该句则需写成"If you compare two ways of life carefully, you will find the former is superior to the latter."。相比之下,此句多出两个人称主语"you",句子又由原来的单句变成了复句。 6. 抽象名词"complacency"译成了"自满情绪"。范畴词"情绪"的添加使译文更加具体形象。 7/8. 第7句和第8句既是由动到静,又是具体形象化的处理。 9. 抽象名词"adoption"译为汉语动词"采用",取代"to adopt this new device"。 10. "fear"译为"心有余悸"。

核心例句	原理分析
B. 汉译英 1. 简是做理查德妻子的合适人选吗? Is Jane a possibility as a wife for Richard? 2. 山上的那间大屋是我企望得到的东西。 The big house on the hill is my ambition. (= the object desired). 3. 你最想得到的是什么东西? What's your greatest desire (= something longed for)? 4. 地球绕轴自转,引起昼夜的变化。 The rotation of the earth on its own axis causes the change from day to night. 5. 这不是一支真枪,却是一件极好的仿制品。 This is not a real gun, but it is a good imitation (= a thing that imitates something else). 6. 情人眼里出西施。 Beauty lies in lovers' eyes. 7. 老师走了以后,激烈的争论才告结束。 The departure of the teacher brought the heated discussion to an end. 8. 昙花一现。 A wonder lasts but nine days. 9. 竹报平安。 All is at peace. 10. 她是母亲的好帮手。 She is a great help to her mother.	1. 汉语具体名词"合适人选"译为英语抽象名词"possibility",取代"a suitable person"。 2/3. 对抽象性名词"ambition","desire"要具体理解,译为"想得到的东西"等。 4. 抽象名词"rotation"使概念突出,句子简化;若不用抽象名词"rotation",不仅句子成为复合句,而且读者也不易立即掌握主要概念,如写成"The earth rotates on its own axis, which causes the change from day to night."。 5. 原理同上。 6. 汉语具体名词"西施"泛化为英语抽象名词"beauty"。 7. 抽象名词"departure"既起强调概念的作用,又可简化句子,否则该句则需写成"After the teacher had left, the heated discussion then ended."。 8. "昙花"的形象抽象为"wonder"。 9. 不翻译"竹"的形象。 10. 汉语具体名词"好帮手"译为英语抽象名词短语"a great help"。

三、翻译练习

◆ 课堂练习 ◆

• 练习1(英译汉)

1. We are deeply convinced of the correctness of his police and firmly determined to pursue it.

2. The blockade was a success.

3. It is a pleasure to meet you.

4. Physical training is an absolute necessity to university students.

5. There have been but few arrivals at this watering-place.

6. The actress was quite a phenomenon in show business circle.

7. As he is a perfect stranger in the city, I hope you will give him the necessary help.

8. So we drove between the green of the park and the stony lifeless elegance of hotels and apartment buildings.

9. In that moment, feeling Mother's back racked with emotion, I understood for the first time her vulnerability.

10. The administration was free from corruption.

11. Her jealousy is the cause of her failure.

12. We have made some achievements, and we must guard against complacency.

13. At this very moment, through the wonder of telecommunications, the whole world is seeing and hearing what we say.

14. She was slender, and apparently scarcely past girlhood: an admirable form, and the most exquisite little face that I have ever seen had the pleasure of beholding; small features, very fair.

15. "Oh, certainly, sir: I'll just fetch a little sewing, and then I'll sit as long as you please."

● 练习2（汉译英）

1. 你对此事沉默不语，我感到迷惑不解。

2. 他毫无表情，因此我怀疑他是否听着。

3. 她苍白的脸色清楚地表明了她那时的情绪。

4. 我甚至极力压低嗓门，尽量不让我的语调带有丝毫暗示或咄咄逼人的口吻。

5. 对此，请允许我以陪同我访问的代表团和我本人的名义向你们表示诚挚的谢意，并向你们传达我们人民的兄弟般的友好情谊。

6. 当蔚蓝的天空和碧绿的原野之间出现了一望无际的大海时，女学生的脚步停下了，她望着海。

7. 国家要加大对中西部地区的支持力度。

8. 中国的现代化建设离不开与世界各国的经济合作与贸易往来。

9. 他感到一股爱国热情在胸中激荡。

10. 作为第一步，联合国可以在该领土上成立一个确有成效的管理机构。

11. 我正在阅读有关此剧本的主要批评文章。

12. 她眼中的迫切神情说明她急不可待。

13. 例如，在抗战初起时，许多人有一种毫无根据的乐观倾向，他们把日本估计过低，甚至以为日本不能打到山西。

14. 不入虎穴,焉得虎子。

15. 信后又添几句道:"塞翁失马,安知非福,使三年前结婚,则此番吾家破费不赀矣……"

16. 只可惜这些事实虽然有趣,演讲时用不着它们,该另抱佛脚。

17. 老太太道:"家里没有个女主人总不行的。我要劝柔嘉别去做事了。她一个月会赚多少钱!管管家事,这几个钱从柴米油盐上全省下来了。"

18. 西湖如镜面,千峰凝翠,洞壑幽深,风光绮丽。

19. 老师是桃花沟的李白、齐白石、钱锺书;老师是桃花沟的杨振宁、钱学森、华罗庚;老师是桃花沟的陶行知、马卡连科……

20. 我们力求使这本刊物充满着浪漫的人文精神、深邃的哲思和妙趣横生的智慧,同时也希望它高而不孤、博而不杂、温柔敦厚、真率可喜,在你我之间联结温馨的友情。设想我们长夜相对、促膝谈心,它会是几畔的一杯清茗。当你好整以暇、细细品味,齿颊间悠远的清芬会令你回味无穷。若你为俗务所苦,只能在匆匆之间浅吸,亦会觉到有暗香缓缓拂过心头。

◆ 课后练习 ◆

● 练习1(英译汉)

1. Exertion already had chipped about 20 pounds off him.

2. Sickness had robbed her of her confidence that she could carry the load.

3. Starvation was a remote threat to them.

4. There is a crying need for a new remedy.

5. The whole devastating experience sharpened my appreciation of the world around me.

6. This fact explains the preference for computers in the world today.

7. Although the civil war was officially over, the hostility and tension between blacks and whites and North and South persisted.

8. Jefferson saw one possible solution.

9. What about its (radar) uses in peace?

10. Many black women have stood out in revolt against social inequalities.

11. There was a wide emptiness over road and pavement.

12. The project has been considerably speeded up.

13. A successful scientist applies persistent and logical thought to the observations he makes.

14. The power is strong enough to shatter complacency.

15. On profit distribution, this is all I have got to say.

16. Both sides are willing to hold face-to-face talks in order to ease tension in the Middle East.

17. From the evaporation of water, people know that liquids can turn into gases under certain condition.

18. We are eager to benefit from your curiosity.

19. Our son has been a disappointment (= someone disappointing) to us.

20. My dad has three dependents (= a person who depends on another for material support): my mother, my sister and I.

21. His skill at games made him the admiration (= a person that causes such feelings) of his friends.

22. For a whole hour we made our preparation and at last everything that we needed was ready.

23. Many people of the town sought out George Willard; they told him of their lives, of their compulsions, of their failure.

● 练习2（汉译英）

1. 我在想为什么许多人对出国如此热衷。
2. 爱情不分贵贱。
3. 电动机发明之后,电力才开始造福人类。
4. 摩天大楼极大地消耗甚至浪费电力。
5. 冬季您若怕冷的话,可以到没有酷暑和严冬的"春城"昆明。
6. 华侨离乡背井,远居国外。因此,他们在感情上越来越向往祖国。
7. 1994年要迈出决定性步伐,即出台几项改革政策,把中国进一步推向市场经济。
8. 有了儿子,又要工作,又要做家务就不能卿卿我我了。
9. 她脸色苍白,眼圈发黑,看得出她一夜没睡好。
10. 我一见了妹妹,一心都在她身上,又是喜欢,又是伤心,竟忘记了老祖宗。
11. 由于长江不断改道,在这里形成了众多的湖泊。
12. 过去实行"闭关自守"政策,结果搞得"民穷财困"。
13. 这些格言强调的是无私,劝导人们要在物质和精神两方面去关心朋友。
14. 在不到一百年的时间里,上海就变成了外国人在中国进行冒险、寻求浪漫生活的地方。
15. 我们中国人崇尚教育,爱好学习。
16. 在经济发展中,我们要控制人口,节约资源,保护环境,并把它们放到重要位置上。
17. 这本短小精悍的书一问世立即受到人们,特别是大学生的青睐,并多次再版。无须解释人们为什么这么喜爱这本书,因为只要稍加浏览,就可以看到书里收集的格言反映了文明社会中对于友谊的看法。

18. 前不久,一个外国人告诉我他在一家超市碰到的一件令他十分尴尬的事。
19. 总之,就全国范围来说,我们一定能够逐步顺利解决沿海同内地贫富差距的问题。
20. 收入分配关系还没有理顺。
21. 大力发展教育和科技事业。
22. 基础研究在一些前沿领域取得可喜的进展。
23. 积极推进住房体制改革。
24. 要加快建设城市贫困居民的最低生活保障制度。

• 练习3(英译汉)

On Conversation (Extracted)
Samuel Johnson

None of the desires dictated by vanity is more general, or less blamable, than that of being distinguished for the arts of conversation. Other accomplishments may be possessed without opportunity of exerting them, or wanted without danger that the defect can often be remarked; but as no man can live, otherwise than in an hermitage, without hourly pleasure or vexation, from the fondness or neglect of those about him, the faculty of giving pleasure is of continual use. Few are more frequently envied than those who have the power of forcing attention wherever they come, whose entrance is considered as a promise of felicity, and whose departure is lamented, like the recess of the sun from northern climates, as a privation of all that enlivens fancy, or inspirits gaiety.

It is apparent that to excellence in this valuable art some peculiar qualifications are necessary; for every one's experience will inform him, that the pleasure which men are able to give in conversation, holds no stated proportion to their knowledge or their virtue. Many find their way to the tables and the parties of those who never consider them as of the least importance in any other place; we have all, at one time or other, been content to love those whom we could not esteem, and been persuaded to try the dangerous experiment of admitting him for a companion, whom we knew to be too ignorant for a counsellor, and too treacherous for a friend.

I question whether some abatement of character is not necessary to general acceptance. Few spend their time with much satisfaction under the eye of uncontestable superiority; and therefore, among those whose presence is courted at assemblies of jollity, there are seldom found men eminently distinguished for powers or acquisitions. The wit whose vivacity condemns slower tongues to silence, the scholar whose knowledge allows no man to fancy that he instructs him, the critic who suffers no fallacy to pass undetected, and the reasoner who condemns the idle to thought and the negligent to attention, are generally praised and feared, reverenced and avoided.

- 练习4（汉译英）

（1）甘当书痴（柯灵）

说到书，我很动感情。因为它给我带来温暖，我对它满怀感激。

书是我的恩师。贫穷剥夺了我童年的幸福，把我关在学校大门的外面，是书本敞开它宽厚的胸脯，接纳了我，给我以慷慨的哺育。没有书，就没有我的今天——也许我早就委身于沟壑。

书是我的良友。它给我一把金钥匙，引导我打开浅短的视线、愚昧的头脑、闭塞的心灵。它从不吝惜我帮助。

书是我青春期的恋人、中年的知己、暮年的伴侣。有了它，我就不再寂寞，不再怕人情冷暖、世态炎凉。它使我成为精神世界的富翁。我真的是"不可一日无此君"。当我忙完了，累极了；当我愤怒时、苦恼时，我就想亲近它，因为这是一种绝妙的安抚。

我真愿意成为十足的"书迷"和"书痴"，可惜还不够条件。

不知道谁是监狱的始作俑者。剥夺自由，诚然是人世最酷虐的刑法，但如果允许囚人有读书的权利，那还不算是自由的彻底丧失。我对此有惨痛的经验。

对书的焚毁和禁锢是最大的愚昧、十足的野蛮、可怕的历史倒退。

当然书本里也有败类、瘟疫之神、死亡天使，当与世人共弃之。

作家把自己写的书送给亲友、献与读者，是最大的愉快。如果他的书引起共鸣，得到赞美，那就是对他最好的酬谢。

在宁静的环境、悠闲的心情中静静地读书，是人生中最有味的享受。在"四人帮"覆亡的前夜，我曾经避开海洋般的冷漠与白眼，每天到龙华公园读书，是拥有自己独立苍茫的世界。这是我一个终身难忘的经历。书本是太阳、空气、雨露。我不能设想，没有书的世界是什么样的世界。

（2）终生遗憾（木木）

八十年代，有一姑娘号召：1.70米以下男人均为"残废"。于是全国未婚女青年纷纷揭竿而起。

我细细量过九十九次自己标高，实属"终生残废"系列。

但那时年少，血旺气盛，誓与凡俗抗争到底，于是连哄带骗将一净高1.74米女孩拐回家做起了太太，这一壮举颇为"残疾人"扬了一段眉、吐了半口气。

将太太置回家中后我才意识到我的悲哀。这一愤世之举不仅未了我"终生残废"而又平添了"终生遗憾"，我从未享受过将男人坚定有力的胳膊窝勾着太太姣美柔滑的后脖子上街遛弯的幸福。

这一幸福对我来说不仅意味着双脚要离开这生我养我的土地，而且神圣的肚脐亦将昭之于众。

现在,每每出门,高扬的手臂牢牢地挂在太太肩头,其状如猴子紧紧扒着电杆,任凭太太在马路上将我拖来拖去……

痛苦的我常常痛苦地想,如果能重活一回,我再也不与世俗去抗争,因为与世俗抗争是要付出代价的。

四、练习参考译文

◆ 课堂练习 ◆

● 练习1(英译汉)

1. 他们深信这一政策是正确的,并有坚定的决心继续奉行这一政策。
2. 封锁很成功。
3. 遇到你真是高兴。
4. 参加体育锻炼对大学生来说是绝对必要的。
5. 来这个浴场的人很少。
6. 这位女演员堪称是演艺界的杰出人才。
7. 因为他对这个城市完全陌生,我希望你能给他必要的帮助。
8. 我们驱车前行,一边是青翠的公园,另一边则是十分呆板、毫无生气的豪华旅馆和公寓建筑。
9. 妈妈非常激动,我感到她的背在颤抖。就在那一刻,我第一次明白妈妈也有脆弱的一面。
10. 这届政府没有腐败现象。
11. 她的嫉妒心理是她失败的根源。
12. 我们取得了一些成就,但要防止自满情绪。
13. 此时此刻,通过奇妙的电讯传播工具,全世界都在观看和收听我们的讲话。
14. 她苗条,显然还没有过青春期。挺好看的体态,还有一张我生平从未见过的绝妙的小脸蛋。五官纤丽,非常漂亮。
16. 啊,当然可以,先生!我就去拿点针线活来,然后你要我坐多久,我就可以坐多久。

● 练习2(汉译英)

1. Your silence on this matter puzzled me.
2. The vacancy of his expression made me doubt if he was listening.
3. The pallor of her face indicated clearly how she was feeling at the moment.

4. I even tried to keep the tone of my voice low, trying to rob it of any suggestion or overtone of aggressiveness.

5. Allow me on behalf of the delegation that accompanies me and in my own name, to sincerely thank you for this and convey to you the message of friendship and fraternity of our people.

6. And there, below the serene blue sky and beyond the vivid green of the fields, was a vast expanse of ocean stretching to the horizon. The girl halted and gazed at the sea.

7. The state will increase its support for the central and western parts.

8. China's modernization is inseparable from her economic cooperation and trade ties with other nations.

9. He felt the patriot rise within his breast.

10. The first step might be to bring about an efficacious United Nations presence in the Territory.

11. I'm reading all the chief criticisms (= a review or other articles expressing such judgment and evaluation) of the play.

12. The eagerness of her eye betrayed her impatience.

13. For instance, at the outset of the war many people were groundlessly optimistic, underestimating Japan and even believing that the Japanese could not get as far as Shanxi.

14. Nothing venture, nothing gain.

15. The postscript read: "This may be a blessing in disguise. If you had married three years earlier, this would have cost us a large sum of money …"

16. Such a pity that while these items of information were all very interesting, they could not be used in the lecture. He would have to read something else.

17. Mrs. Fang said, "It's no food for a household to be without a mistress. I will persuade Jou-chia not to go out and work. How much can she earn in a month? If she looked after the house, she'd be able to save those few dollars from the four necessities of life."

18. The West Lake is like a mirror, embellished all around with green hills and deep caves of enchanting beauty.

19. In the eyes of the villagers, he (the teacher) was no less than a great man of letters, a great artist, a great scientist as well as a great educator.

20. In trying to fill the journal with romantic humanism, profound philosophical thought and sparkling wit, we hope that it will be your refined yet not aloof, erudite yet not confusing, tender, honest, frank and pleasant friend. It is like a fragrant cup of tea that will leave you a delicate aftertaste when you leisurely savor it, or a warm, quiet fragrance in your heart with only a quick sip.

◆ 课后练习 ◆

• 练习1（英译汉）

1. 经过连日辛劳,他已经瘦了大约20磅。
2. 她疾病缠身,丧失了挑起这副重担的信心。
3. 他们一时不必担心饿死。
4. 现在急需想出新法子来补救。
5. 经过这场灾难,我觉得人生更有乐趣了。
6. 这个事实说明了当今世界计算机得到优先采用的原因。
7. 虽然内战已正式结束了,但是黑人与白人之间、北方与南方之间的敌对状态和紧张局面依然存在。
8. 杰斐逊找到了一个可行的解决办法。
9. 和平时期它（雷达）有哪些用途?
10. 许多黑人妇女已经站出来反对种种不平等的社会现象。
11. 公路上和人行道上一派空旷景象。
12. 工程进度大大加快了。
13. 凡是有成就的科学家总是对观察到的结果进行持续不断和合乎逻辑的思考。
14. 这种力量大得足以打破自满情绪。
15. 在利润分配问题上,我要说的就是这些。
16. 双方都愿意举行面对面会谈以缓和中东的紧张局势。
17. 从水的蒸发现象,人们得知液体在一定条件下能转变为气体。
18. 我们殷切希望从你们的探索精神中获益。
19. 我们的儿子成了令我们失望的人。
20. 爸爸需要养活三口人:妈妈、姐姐和我。
21. 他的运动技巧使他成为友人称羡的人。
22. 我们用了一个小时的时间准备所需的物品,最后一切都准备妥当了。
23. 小城里很多人都来找乔治,向他讲述他们自己的故事,讲述他们心里难以遏止的欲望和冲动,讲述他们想做而又未能做成的事情。

• 练习2（汉译英）

1. I have always wondered at the passion many people have of going abroad.
2. Love lives in cottages as well as in courts.
3. Electricity power became the servant of man only after the motor was invented.
4. Skyscrapers become lavish consumers, and wasters of electric power.

5. If you dislike the cold in winter, you can visit Kunming, the "Spring City" which is spared temperature extremes.

6. Absence and distance make the overseas Chinese heart increasingly fond the motherland.

7. The decisive moves in 1994 to bring China closer to a market economy involve some reform policies.

8. A son, a job and housekeeping forced romance out.

9. She was pale, and there were dark signs of sleeplessness beneath her eyes.

10. I was so carried away by the mixture of joy and sorrow at sight of my little cousin—I forgot our Old Ancestress.

11. The constant change of the course of the Yangtze River has contributed to a great deal of lakes in this area.

12. The pursuit of the policy of self-seclusion resulted in the destitution of its people and exhaustion of its financial resources.

13. The maxims stress selflessness and concern for the material and spiritual welfare of the friends.

14. In less than a hundred years, Shanghai became a place for foreigners to seek adventure and romance in China.

15. The Chinese show a high respect for learning and a love of knowledge.

16. Great importance must be attached to population control, the conservation of resources and environmental protection in economic growth.

17. This short work enjoyed an immediate acceptance, especially among college students, and was reprinted many times. Its popularity needs no explanation, for a brief perusal of the questions shows that they embody the notions of civilized friendship.

18. Not long ago, a foreign visitor told me of his embarrassment in a supermarket.

19. In short, taking the country as a whole, I am confident that we can gradually bridge the gap between coastal and inland areas.

20. The distribution of income needs to be straightened out.

21. Vigorously develop education and science and technology.

22. Gratifying progress was made in some frontiers.

23. We must press ahead with the reform of housing.

24. We should accelerate the establishment of a minimum standard of living for impoverished urban residents.

- 练习 3（英译汉）

论谈话的艺术（节选）

塞缪尔·约翰逊

虚荣心使人生出种种愿望，其中最普通，或者最少受非议的，莫过于希望能以谈话艺术博得他人刮目相看。人或许会有其他才艺却没有机会施展；即使没有，也不必担心这一缺陷会经常被人发现。但是，除非归隐山林，人只要活在世界上，就难免会因四周亲友的时亲时疏，有时得意，有时气恼，所以予人快乐的本领也就始终会有用武之地。有些人不论到哪里都能成为众人瞩目的中心，一进门就仿佛欢乐也同时降临，但是一旦离去，大家又会惋惜不已，仿佛北方严寒天气里太阳突然消隐，仿佛想象失去了灵感，欢乐失去了源泉，少有其他人能像他们那样经常受到大家的艳羡。

显而易见，若要谙练这一宝贵艺术的精妙，必须具备某些特殊条件。我们的经验告诉我们，有人虽能通过谈话给人快乐，但是给人快乐的多寡与其道德学问并无相应的比例关系。许多人，若是换在其他场合，你绝不会认为他们有什么重要，但是他们会成为你家餐桌或者聚会的座上嘉宾。有些人，你虽无法尊敬，却常常情不自禁地喜欢。有些人，你明知他们不学无术，不足以成为良师，而且狡黠多变，亦不足以成为益友，却依然愿意冒险一试，将他们引为伴侣。

我十分怀疑，如果没有一点个性的涵养，是否还能左右逢源，受人欢迎。很少有人乐于在咄咄逼人的傲慢目光下度过他们的时间。因此，凡被争相邀请出席欢乐聚会的人，鲜见有钱有势的显贵人士。诙谐幽默者，如果妙语连珠，迫使拙于言辞的人羞于启口；饱学之士，如果高深莫测，令人难以从中受到教益；批评家，如果对于每个错误都不轻易放过；善于思辨者，如果迫使懒于思考的人不得不思考，迫使漫不经心的人不得不集中注意力。那么，十之八九，虽会受到称颂赞扬，却令人感到畏惧，虽会受到崇敬，却令人退避三舍。

- 练习 4（汉译英）

（1）Eulogizing Books（Ke Ling）

Books are my sweethearts in my youth, my bosom friends in my middle age, and my companions in my declining years. Accompanied by books, I never feel lonely, nor fear social snobbery or fickleness of the world. They have made a rich man of me in the inner world. I cannot do without them even for a single day. When I feel tired out after finishing my work, or when I am in a bad mood, I'll try to get close to books for comfort—the best way for me to find spiritual consolation.

Oh, if only I were a confirmed bibliomaniac or bookworm! But unfortunately, I'm still not fully qualified for one yet!

I don't know who was the despicable originator of the prison. Deprivation of freedom is the most savage punishment on earth for sure, but, as I've learned from my own personal bitter experience, if prisoners are permitted the right to read they should not be regarded as totally devoid of freedom.

Burning or banning books is the height of folly and barbarity, signifying a most horrible retrogression in history.

Of course there is also some rubbish among books to be avoided like the plague or death by all.

It is the greatest pleasure for a writer to present to his friends gift copies of a book authored by himself or to have it offered to the reading public. And he will feel richly rewarded if his book arouses public interest and earns wide acclaim.

It is the greatest joy of life for one to spend his leisure time reading in quiet surroundings. On the eve of the fall of the "Gang of Four", I used to go to Longhua Park every day for a reading session, seeking shelter from a sea of frosty looks and hostile stares in a world of my own. That will forever remain and unforgettable experience of my life.

Books are sunlight and air, rain and dew. I can't imagine what would become of the world without books.

(2) **Lifetime Regret (Mu Mu)**

In the 1980s, one young lady issued a public pronouncement dismissing all men under the height of 1.70 metres as "handicapped". It was met with an avalanche of responses from virtually all unmarried women in the nation.

After making perennial efforts to measure my exact height, I reached the inescapable conclusion that I was permanently handicapped. Back in those days, I was a callow young chap vastly capable of daring and fool-hardiness, and determined to wrestle with this prejudice against men's lack of height. So by hook or by crook, I married a girl who was 1.74 metres in height. Such an astonishing tour de force thus achieved greatly bolstered the morale and esteem of those of us who were "handicapped".

But only after the girl was enticed into matrimony did I begin to feel my self-inflicted anguish. This over-reaction of mine not only failed to put an end to my "permanent handicap", but also gave me lifetime regret. I was deprived of the earthly pleasure of walking with my wife in the street with my strong arm around her delicate neck because it meant that my feet would be lifted from the land that had nurtured me, and worse still, my sacred belly-button would be put on public display.

What happens now is that whenever we go out together, with my outstretched arms tightly clinging to my wife's shoulder, I am pretty much like a monkey hanging on to a wire pole, allowing her to drag me along the street …

In excruciating agony, I often ponder this: if I could live my life once again, I would never try to achieve the elimination of prejudices of any kind for the simple reason that there is a price to pay.

五、篇章参考译文翻译原理选注

● 练习3（英译汉）注释

1. "… without hourly pleasure or vexation, from the fondness or neglect of those about him, the faculty of giving pleasure is of continual use" 译文将抽象名词"pleasure"、"vexation"、"fondness"、"neglect"、"faculty"、"use"全都具体化为"得意""气恼""时亲时疏""本领""用武之地"，因而读起来自然流畅。

2. "like the recess of the sun from northern climates, as a privation of all that enlivens fancy, or inspirits gaiety"（仿佛北方严寒天气里太阳突然消隐，仿佛想象失去了灵感，欢乐失去了源泉）译文将抽象名词"recess"，"privation"全都译成动词，使其具体化为"消隐失去"。英汉语言的具体和抽象之别、静态和动态之别一目了然。

3. 整个第三段，作者约翰逊向我们展示了他作为杰出散文家的一面：谈锋四溢，文笔优美。段中使用了大量的抽象名词和名词短语（也有个别副词和动词），如"acceptance"，"under the eye of uncontestable superiority"，"whose presence"，"men eminently distinguished for powers or acquisitions"，"vivacity"，"slower tongues to silence"，"the idle to thought and the negligent to attention"，"generally"，"avoid"。汉译时，译者根据汉语的特点，大量使用四字短语，使之具体形象：左右逢源、受人欢迎，咄咄逼人的傲慢目光，出席，有钱有势的显贵人士，妙语连珠，拙于言辞的人羞于启口，懒于思考的人不得不思考，漫不经心的人不得不集中注意力，十之八九，退避三舍。

● 练习4（汉译英）注释

（1）

① "……它给我一把金钥匙，引导我打开浅短的视线、愚昧的头脑、闭塞的心灵"一句中，译者翻译时用了两个动作名词"broadening"和"ridding"。其实，"愚昧的头脑、闭塞的心灵"汉语里可视为"同义重复"，英译时只要译出一个"意象"就行了。试比较：They provide me with a key to the door out of ignorance and into a new horizon。

类似的经典句子如"沉鱼落雁之容,闭月羞花之貌"，一般情况下，译为"Her beauty would outshine the moon"就可以了。

② "……它从不吝惜我帮助"中物称主语"它" + 有灵动词"吝惜"，在汉语里叫"拟人"修辞手法，在英语里是一种常态表达法。译文"They spare no efforts to help me"可谓"神形兼备"。

③ 译文"……当我忙完了,累极了;当我愤怒时、苦恼时,我就想亲近它,因为这是一种绝妙的安抚"非常工整,无懈可击:When I feel tired out after finishing my work, or when I am in a bad mood, I'll try to get close to books for comfort—the best way for me to find spiritual consolation。如果我们换个思维,多用抽象的名词来译,结果会如何呢?试比较:To my indignation, dismay or tiredness after work, they are a kind of panacea。

《傲慢与偏见》的开始句是"有钱的单身汉总要娶位太太,这是一条举世公认的真理",而原文是"It is a truth universally acknowledged, that a single man in possession of a good fortune, must be in want of a wife"。在这里抽象名词"possession","want"是英语里的妙用。

(2)

① "揭竿而起"这一生动形象的短语被译为"avalanche of responses",一动一静,相映成趣。

② "……但那时年少,血旺气盛,誓与凡俗抗争到底"一句中形象表达"血旺气盛","凡俗"被抽象成英语的"daring and fool-hardiness","(wrestle with this) prejudice"。

③ "连哄带骗",动感十足的汉语表达,译成英语为"by hook or by crook",名词化了。

④ "愤世之举"静化为"over-reaction"。

⑤ "……而且神圣的肚脐亦将昭之于众"一句中"昭之于众"译为"(put) on public display",使用带有名词的介词短语,弱化了汉语的动感,表达更富有英文味。

第七章 指称替代、重复与省略的互译

一、翻译原理

对事物的指称及其在连贯话语中的替代、重复和省略是任何语言中都存在的普遍现象,但不同语言对这些现象的表现方式和侧重点、倾向性或某一特别现象的使用频率则有一定的差异。英汉语言思维对比研究表明,由于深刻的历史原因和语言的总体差异,英语与汉语对事物与概念的指称、替代和重复有各自的传统习惯。英语作为一种有曲折变化的语言,注重语法形式结构所表现的各种静态组合关系(如各种修饰、限定成分),通过语言形式本身表明所指事物之间联系,对语境的依赖性相对较低。这种情况直接造成的结果是:英语在话语衔接手段上大量使用替代和替换性词语指示话语中已经出现或将要出现的事物与概念,代词和各种关系词用来指称上下文中提到的事物是一种比较普遍的现象,因此使用十分频繁,而重复与完全省略的现象则相对较少。与英语相比,汉语由于没有英语那样的曲折变化,不注重语法形式分析,句子单位不像英语那样明确、清楚,在很多情况下无论是使用句号还是使用逗号都不会造成理解上的问题,对其理解比英语更需要依赖语境和话语的主题意义,因此与英语相比则较少使用替代和替换性词语指示语言中已经出现的事物和概念,代词和关系词使用不如英语那样频繁,而重复与省略的频率则明显高于英语。汉语只要语境明确,从上下文中可以推知,所指事物往往就可以省略;如果省略可能造成理解上或修辞上的问题,汉语则往往宁可使用重复手段,而不是替代或替换手段。

从语言构成的成分来看,替代、省略和重复主要涉及三种具体情况,即名词性、动词性和小句的替代、重复和省略。

(一) 名词

例1 我爱花,所以也爱养花。
I love flowers and hence have taken to growing them.

例2 There are three main groups of oils: animal, vegetable and mineral.
油主要分为三大类:动物油、植物油、矿物油。

例3 事情并非凑巧(事出有因)。

It doesn't just happen.

在例1中,中文重复"花",而英文则用代词替代。例2英文省略"oil",中文则重复"油"。例3中文的"事情""事"由代词"it"替代。

(二) 动词

例1 I will do anything you want me to.

你要我做什么,我就做什么。

例2 Go thou, and work, and till.

去吧,去劳动,去耕耘。

例3 He studies English, French and Japanese. And so do I.

他学英语、法语和日语,我也学。

例1中英文第二次省略动词"do",而中文则重复"做"。例2英文使用连词,省略汉语中习惯使用的动词。例3英文用"And so do I"替换前面已经出现的动宾结构,中文则重复。

(三) 其他词语

例1 In a motor a current is sent through both the armature and the field.

在电动机里,电流既通过电枢也通过磁场来输送。(重复使用"通过","通过"在汉语里也是介词)

例2 While stars and nebulae look like specks or small patches of light, they are really enormous bodies.

星星和星云看起来只是斑斑点点,或是小小的片片光亮,但确实是一个个巨大的天体。

例3 经过大扫除后,教室里一切整整齐齐,看上去干干净净。

After the general cleaning, all things in the classroom are in good order and look clean.

例4 They are used in computers as switches that simply turn on and off.

它们在计算机中起开关作用,只是开开关关而已。(试比较:它们在计算机中起开关作用,只是开和关而已)

(四) 小句

例1 We gossip about them and vice versa. (… and they gossip about us)

我们谈论他们的是非,他们也谈论我们的是非。

例2 是知难行易还是知易行难,我常常很疑惑。

I often wonder if it is harder to know a thing than to make it or the otherwise.

例1英文用"vice versa"替代一句话,而中文则不使用替代。例2英文用"the otherwise"替代相反的情况,而中文则明示相反情况。

总之,英汉互译中的指代、重复与省略的情况有着比较明显的差异,而造成这种差异的性质与两种语言思维的不同性质有密切的关系。比如,在上述例子中,差异的原因主要涉及英语的静态、意合的性质和汉语的动态、形合的性质。要更深入地理解这一点,还可以参阅第三章、第七章。

二、核心例句原理分析

核心例句	原理分析
A. 英译汉 1. They went, shutting the door, and locking it behind them. 他们走了,关了门,随手上了锁。 2. As I begin, I thank President Clinton for his service to our nation. 首先,我要感谢克林顿总统为我国做出的贡献。 3. Laura pretended to pay attention, but rarely heard him. 劳拉装出认真在意的样子,但压根没在听他说。 4. Reading maketh a full man; conference a ready man … 读书使人充实,讨论使人机智。 5. There are three main groups of oils: animal, vegetable and mineral. 油主要分为三大类:动物油,植物油,矿物油。 6. No tears in the writer, no tears in the reader. 作者不含着泪写,读者就不会含着泪读。 7. The walls were soft fawn color with blush of pink in it. 墙呈柔和的黄褐色,略带粉红。 8. Other automobile corporations also made Detroit their headquarters. 其他汽车公司也把总部设在底特律。	1. 英语中使用两个代词,汉语则不用代词。 2. 英语使用"his",汉语不用"他的"。 3. 英语使用代词"him",汉语则添加了"说"。 4. 英语中"maketh"使用一次,汉语则翻译两次"使",不省略。 5. 英语不重复"oil",汉语则出现三次。 6. 英语不用动词,也不重读。汉语用动词而且重复。这是从静态到动态的转换。 7. 英语使用代词"it",汉语不用代词。 8. 英语根据需要添加"their",汉语则不需要"他们的"。
B. 汉译英 1. 我们说,长征是历史记录上的第一次,长征是宣言书,长征是宣传队,长征是播种机。 We answer that the Long March is the first of its kind in the annals of history, that it is a manifesto, a propaganda force, a seeding machine.	1. "长征"在汉语中连续重复,在英语中"the Long March"则没有必要重复。 2. 汉语中"解放思想"重复出现,英语使用"it"替代。 3. 中文省略"想"的宾语,英文使用"it",语法上不省略。

核心例句	原理分析
2. 新时期的解放思想,关键就是在这个问题上的思想解放。 To emancipate the mind in the new period, the key lies in doing it on this question. 3. 唉,我现在想想,那时真是太聪明了。 Oh, when I come to think of it, I can see how smartly I was in those days! 4. 翻译不仅需要理解语言,而且需要理解语言背后的文化。 Translation calls for understanding both the language and the culture behind it.	4. "理解"在汉语中重复出现,英语中使用替代方法。

三、翻译练习

◆ 课堂练习 ◆

● 练习1(英译汉)

1. I am honored and humbled to stand here, where so many of America's leaders have come before me, and so many will follow.

2. We are not the story's author, who fills time an eternity with his purpose. Yet his purpose is achieved in our duty, and our duty is fulfilled in service to one another.

3. There are two basic ways to see growth: one as a product, the other a process.

4. … all these are examples of people who have measurable results to show for their efforts.

5. In order to grow, to travel new roads, people need to have a willingness to take risks, to confront the unknown, and to accept the possibility that they may "fail" at first.

6. These feelings of insecurity and self-doubt are both unavoidable and necessary if we are to change and grow.

7. The breeze streaming through the open car window made Laura's long blond hair dance as she pulled up at her friend Sara Tello's house.

8. As the truck stopped, she saw the scowling, muscled man with the mustache.

9. One rare evening out, when my mother had successfully coaxed my usually asocial father to join us for a night in the town …

10. His eyes swept the dance floor, the other diners, and the members of the band.

11. It was indeed the first, last, and only dance that I ever had with my father.

12. To the ordinary man, one kind of oil may be as important as another. But when the politician or the engineer refers to oil, he almost always means mineral oil, the oil that drives tanks, aeroplanes and warships, moter-cars and diesel locomotives.

● 练习2（汉译英）

1. 饿了吃糠甜如蜜，饱了吃蜜也不甜。

2. 有喜有忧，有笑有泪，有花有实，有香有色，既须劳动，又长见识，这就是养花的乐趣。

3. 我讲三个问题：经济问题、国际形势问题、中美关系问题。

4. 自周秦以来，中国是一个封建社会，其政治是封建的政治，其经济是封建的经济。

5. 新的政治力量，新的经济力量，新的文化力量，都是中国的革命力量，它们是反对旧政治、旧经济、旧文化的。

6. 这种新民主主义的文化是科学的。它是反对一切封建思想和迷信思想，主张实事求是，主张客观真理，主张理论和实践一致的。

7. 我知道父亲爱我，而且爱得很深，但他就是不知道如何表达他的爱。

8. 我心中暗笑他的迂：他们只认得钱，托他们只是白托。

9. 我来北京后，他写了一封信给我，信中说……

10. 邓小平理论坚持社会主义理论和实践的基本成果，抓住"什么是社会主义、怎样建设社会主义"这个根本问题，深刻地揭示社会主义的本质，把对社会主义的认识提高到新的科学水平。

11. 新时期的解放思想，关键就是在这个问题上的思想解放。

12. 马克思列宁主义、毛泽东思想一定不能丢，丢了就丧失根本。

13. 同时一定要以我国改革开放和现代化建设的实际问题，以我们正在做的事情为中心，着眼于马克思主义理论的运用，着眼于对实际问题的理论思考，着眼于新的实践和新的发展。

14. 现在许多大轮船烧油而不烧煤。

15. 汽车不是亨利·福特发明的，但他是用机器大量生产汽车的第一人，从而使普通老百姓也能拥有汽车。

16. 1914年，底特律的产业工人的基本工资是每周11美元，而福特却宣布他给工人每天支付5美元。

◆ 课后练习 ◆

● 练习 1（英译汉）

1. Most men and women sink into a timid despair if they feel themselves unloved.

2. As Russell later stated in an interview, "I should deal with sexual morality exactly as I would with everthing else."

3. Those who face life with a feeling of security are much happier than those who face it with a feeling of insecurity, at any rate so long as their sense of security does not lead them to disaster.

4. As the best law is founded upon reason, so are the best manners.

5. One principal point of this art is to suit our behaviour to the three several degrees of men; our superiors, our equals, and those below us.

6. Most people complain about fortune, few of nature; and the kinder they think the latter has been to them, the more they murmur at what they call the injustice of the former.

7. I got to know Prof. Carcassonne better and better through my work. He was in his early forties, one of the youngest professors at the university. He remained single and lived with his mother in Carcassonne, a scenic city near Toulouse.

8. If you keep reading simple English stories at a natural speed without referring to the dictionary, as you did with Chinese when you were a child, you will soon get a good sense of English.

9. There are three types of airsteam reaction engines: the ramjet, the turbojet and turboprop.

10. The engineer must have acknowledge not only of what these properties are and mean, but also of how they are determined.

11. Refrigerators and air-conditioning units must obey not only the first law (energy conservation) but the second law as well.

12. You have seen how water expands when it is heated and contracts when it is cooled.

13. One's thoughts must directed to the future, and to things about which there is something to be done. This is not always easy; one's own past is a gradually increasing weight. It is easy to think to oneself that one's emotions used to be more vivid than they are, and one's mind more keen. If this is true, it should be forgotten, and if it is forgotten, it will probably not be true.

● 练习2（汉译英）

1. 为了推动中美关系的发展，中国需要进一步了解美国，美国也需要进一步了解中国。

2. 中国人民珍惜同各国人民的友谊与合作，也珍惜自己经过长期奋斗而得来的独立自主权利。

3. 实践证明，我们协调经济发展与环境保护两者之间关系的做法是行之有效的。

4. 我们总要相信，全世界也好，我们中国也好，多数人是好人。

5. 这就是要倾听人民群众的意见，要联系人民群众，而不要脱离人民群众的道理。

6. 你没有搞好，我是不满意的，得罪了你就得罪了你。

7. 相互了解是发展国与国之间关系的前提。唯有相互了解，才能增进信任、加强合作。

8. 每个国家、每个民族都有自己的历史文化传统，都有自己的长处和优势。

9. 它是通过各种学科、各种学派的相互砥砺、相互渗透而发展的，也是通过同世界各国的相互交流、相互学习而进步的。

10. 任何机器如果不适当加以润滑就不能长期运作。

11. 慢慢地因工作上的联系，和卡尔卡松教授熟识起来。在克莱蒙文科大学的教授中，他算是最年轻的，大约四十一二岁，还没有结婚，他只有一个母亲，住在卡尔卡松城。该城靠近图卢兹，是个风景区。

12. 燕子去了，有再来的时候；杨柳枯了，有再青的时候；桃花谢了，有再开的时候。但是，聪明的，你告诉我，我们的日子为什么一去不复返呢？——是有人偷了他们吧：那是谁？又藏在何处呢？是他们自己逃走了吧：现在又到了哪里呢？

13. 李约翰教授是昆虫学博士。李约翰博士的专门研究是蝴蝶，因为李约翰博士是美国留学生，所以他研究有素的蝴蝶都是合众国蝴蝶、加拿大蝴蝶，以及南美洲蝴蝶。

14. 那年冬天，祖母死了，父亲的差事也交卸了，正是祸不单行的日子，我从北京到徐州，打算跟着父亲奔丧回家。到徐州见着父亲，看见满院狼藉的东西，又想起祖母，不禁簌簌地流下眼泪。父亲说："事已至此，不必难过，好在天无绝人之路！"

● 练习3（英译汉）

Suzhou gardens take in many bridges as they take in the beautiful landscape of mountains and waters.

However, this taking in is not copying, but superlative recreation.

In Suzhou gardens are so many beautiful forms of bridges, displaying all possibilities of changes. There are bridges of the polygonal arches, triple arches, single arch, pointed-top arch, semicircle arche, pavilion type, even-step type, treading type, no-water-under type, corridor type, etc. Every bridge has its own particular posture and its own overlook. Some are so low as if floating on the water, while others are as high as castles. Some bridges use very huge stone plates in their construction, while others employ finely carved stone pieces. Whatever shape they assume or whatever style they are in, they all change their shapes in the reflection on water …

The bridge is like a tourist guide, for when you follow her you can enjoy a better show of the continuously changing display of the scenes. She is the key phrase in a poem, and as you reflect upon it you will be inspired. She is also like a philosopher who leads you beyond in your understanding. She resembles a fairy, for when you bid farewell to the garden, it will get into your dreams at night.

No. The truth is that bridges are just bridges. Nevertheless, they lead you into the paradise.

● 练习4（汉译英）

（1）中国政府历来关心和重视老龄事业。多年来，国家大力弘扬中华民族敬老养老的文化传统，采取切实、有效的措施，积极探索适合中国国情的老龄事业发展模式。特别是近年来，中国政府全面贯彻落实科学发展观，积极应对人口老龄化挑战，把发展老龄事业作为经济社会统筹发展和构建社会主义和谐社会的重要内容，综合运用经济、法律和行政手段，不断推动老龄事业发展。

（2）在苏州水城里，随便到哪几条小巷走一圈，都像走进了一个桥的博览会，五步一架，十步一跨，谁也记不清一路上经过了多少座桥。有心看桥的游客更是难以挪动步子，那大大小小的桥似乎成了厚厚薄薄的书，它的文化气息很浓，让人玩味不已。走上一座桥，兴致盎然地欣赏水巷景色，只见近处有桥，远处也有桥，望断水也望不断桥。本来上桥就是为了下桥，可是多情的客人上了桥就不肯下桥，总希望在桥上多盘桓一会儿，就像赴一个迟到的约会，约的人虽然已经走了，留下的惆怅却悄悄地被周围的景色消融了。

四、英汉互译参考译文

◆ 课堂练习 ◆

● 练习1（英译汉）

1. 站在这里，我很荣幸，也感到受宠若惊。许多美国领导人走在我前面，也会有很多领导人从这里继续前进。

2. 我们不是这段历史的作者，是杰斐逊作者本人的伟大理想穿越时空，并通过我们每天的努力变为现实,在相互服务中履行着各自的职责。

3. 对于成长,有两种基本看法:一是当作结果来看;二是当作过程来看。

4. ……这些都是能表明人们的努力取得了可衡量成果的例子。

5. 为了成长起来,为了走新路,人们需要有敢于冒险、勇于面对未知事物和经得起一开始可能遭到"失败"的精神。

6. 如果我们要改变自己、要成长,这些不安全感和自我怀疑的态度都是难免的、必然的。

7. 当劳拉·库塞拉把车停在好友萨拉·特略的家门口时,习习微风穿过开着的车窗,令劳拉金色的长发更显飘逸。

8. 货车停下后,劳拉看见那个肌肉发达,留着一撮胡子的怒气冲冲的男人。

9. 那时一个少有的夜晚,母亲终于说服我那通常是很孤僻的父亲和我们一起到市中心逛逛……

10. 他的眼睛扫过舞池,扫过其他的就餐者,扫过乐队的成员。

11. 那的确是我和父亲跳过的第一支舞,也是最后一支舞,一生仅有的一支舞。

12. 对于一般人来说,这种油或那种油可能都是重要的。但是当政治家或工程师谈到油的时候,他所指的几乎总是矿物油。这种油可以用来开坦克、开飞机、开军舰、开汽车、开柴油机。

- 练习2(汉译英)

1. Husks will taste like honey when you are hungry, and vice versa.

2. Joy and sorrow, laughter and tears, flowers and fruit, fragrance and color, manual labour and increased knowledge—all these make up the enjoyment of flower cultivation.

3. I am going to speak on three issues: the economy, the international situation and the relation between China and the US.

4. From the Zhou and Qin Dynasties onwards, Chinese society was feudal, as were its politics and its economy.

5. These new political, economic and cultural forces are all revolutionary forces which are opposed to the old politics, the old economy and the old culture.

6. New democratic culture is scientific. Opposed as it is to all feudal and superstitious idea, it stands for seeking truth from facts, for objective truth and for the unity of theory and practice.

7. I knew that he loved me and that his love was deep. He just didn't know how to express it.

8. I sniggered at father for being so impractical, for it was utterly useless to entrust me to those attendants, who cared for nothing but money.

9. After I arrived in Beijing, he wrote me a letter, in which he says …

10. Deng Xiaoping Theory, upholding the basic achievements of the theory and practice of scientific socialism, has grappled with the fundamental question of what socialism is and how to build it and incisively expounded the essence of socialism, raising our understanding of socialism to a new scientific level. (改译: Deng Xiaoping Theory, upholding the basic achievements of the theory and practice of scientific socialism, has grappled with the fundamental question of what socialism is and how to build it and incisively expounded its essence, raising our understanding of it to a new scientific level.)

11. To emancipate the mind in the new period, the key lies in doing it on this question.

12. We must never discard Marxism-Leninism and Mao Zedong Thought. If we did, we would lose our foundation.

13. Meanwhile, centering on the practical problems in the reform, opening up and the modernization drive and on the things we are doing, we must emphasize the application of the Marxism Theory, the theoretical study of practical problems, and new practice and development.

14. Many big ships now burn oil instead of coal.

15. Henry Ford did not invent the automobile, but he was the first man to mass-produce it, and this made it available to the ordinary man.

16. In 1914, when the basic wage for an individual worker in Detroit was $11 a week, Ford announced that he could pay his workers $5 a day.

◆ 课后练习 ◆

● 练习1（英译汉）

1. 大多数男女感到没人爱时都陷入怯懦而绝望的处境。

2. 罗素在一次接受采访时说:"我必须研究性道德,正如我也研究别的事情一样。"

3. 人带着安全感面对生活会比没有安全感快乐得多,只要安全感不带来灾难就会如此。

4. 最好的法律是建立在理智之上的,同样最好的举止行为也是建立在理智之上的。

5. 礼貌艺术的一大要素是,以适当的举止行为对待三种不同层次的人,即高于我们层次的、与我们同一层次的和低于我们层次的人。

6. 很多人抱怨命运,却很少有人抱怨自然;人们越是认为自然对他们仁爱有加,便越是嘀咕命运对他们的所谓不公。

7. 慢慢地因工作上的联系,我和卡尔卡松教授熟识起来。在克莱蒙文科大学的教授中,他算是最年轻的,大约四十一二岁,还没有结婚,他只有一个母亲,主宰卡尔卡松城,该城靠近图卢兹,是个风景区。

8. 如果你能一直坚持以自然的速度阅读简单的故事而不查词典,就像你小时候读中文故事那样,你很快就会获得英语语感。

9. 气流作用的发动机有三种:冲压式喷气发动机、涡轮喷气发动机和涡轮螺旋桨发动机。

10. 工程师不仅必须具备有关性能及其含义方面的知识,而且还必须具备测定性能方面的知识。

11. 电冰箱和空调装置不仅应遵循第一定律(能量守恒),而且应遵循第二定律。

12. 你已经明白水受热时如何膨胀、冷却时又如何收缩。

13. 一个人应当考虑未来,考虑那些可以有所作为的事情。要做到这一点是不大容易的;人过去的经历就是一个越来越沉重的包袱。人很容易自以为自己过去感情比现在丰富、思想比现在敏锐。要是事情果真如此,那就应该已经记不得了;但如果真的已经记不得了,那么事情很可能并非如此。

- 练习 2 (汉译英)

1. To promote the development of China-US relations, China needs to know the United States better and vice versa.

2. The Chinese people cherish its friendship and cooperation with other peoples, as well as their right to independence they have won through protracted struggles.

3. The practice has proved that our coordination of economic development and environmental protection is effective.

4. We must believe that in China, as everywhere else in the world, the majority of the people are good.

5. This principle means that we should listen attentively to the views of the masses, keep in close touch with them and not become alienated from them.

6. You have done a poor job and I am not satisfied, and if you feel offended, so be it.

7. Mutual understanding is the basis for state-to-state relations. Without it, it would be important for countries to build trust and promote cooperation with each other.

8. Every country or nation has its own historical and cultural traditions, strong points and advantages.

9. It has enriched itself through the contention and infiltration of various disciplines and schools of thought, and also through the mutual exchanges and learning between China and other countries.

10. No machine would work for long if it were not properly lubricated.

11. I got to know Prof. Carcassonne better and better through my work. He was in his early forties, one of the youngest professors at the university. He remained single and lived with his mother in Carcassonne, a scenic city near Toulouse.

12. If swallows go away, they will come back again. If willows wither, they will turn green again. If peach blossoms fade, they will flower again. But, tell me, you the wise, why should our days go by never to return? Perhaps they have been stolen by someone. But who could it be and where could he hide them? Perhaps they have just run away by themselves. But where could they be at the present moment?

13. Prof. Li Yuehan (John Li) was an entomologist. His specialty was butterflies, and, because he had studied in the United States, his research was restricted to the butterflies of that country, as well as Canada and South America.

14. In that winter, my grandma died and my father lost his job. I left Beijing for Xuzhou to join him in hastening home to attend my grandma's funeral. When I met him in Xuzhou, the sight of the disorderly mess in our courtyard and the thought of my grandma started tears tricling down my cheeks, he said, "Now that things have come to such a mass, it's no use crying. Fortunately, Heaven always leaves one way out."

● 练习 3（英译汉）

苏州园林在把明山秀水搬进来的同时，把偌多的桥也稍带进来了。

不是照搬，那是绝妙的创作。

苏州园林里的桥形式多样，造型美观，极尽灵巧变化之能事。多边形拱桥、三孔拱桥、单孔拱桥、尖拱桥、半圆拱桥、亭桥、平桥、踏步桥、旱桥、廊桥，每座桥有每座桥的姿态，每座桥有每座桥的风貌。有的是平直小桥，桥几乎与水齐平，自然质朴而富有野趣。有带屋顶的廊桥，两旁红栏碧槛，掩映生姿，倒映水中，犹如彩虹，水波荡漾，桥影欲飞。有的高大如驼峰高耸，气势雄伟。有的玲珑典雅，古意盎然。有的是巨石覆盖砌叠，宛如混沌中凿琢的千古磐石，散发出原始的浑厚朴拙。全是不朽的精致艺术。有的桥为青石板铺就，桥与路平，素朴小巧，散步桥上，步履安详而舒坦。

她是导游，跟着她走，你会移步换景；她是诗眼，轻抚片刻，你会诗兴顿生；她是哲人，两眸相对，你会凝思悠远；她是精灵，告别园林，她会潜入你的梦境。

不，她只是桥，跟着她，你才能走入天堂的意境。

● 练习 4

（1）The Chinese government has always cared for and paid attention to undertakings for the aged. For years, the state has made great efforts to promote the cultural tradition of the Chinese nation that elderly people are respected and provided for; and taken effective measures to explore a development mode of undertakings for them that suits China's conditions. Especially in recent years, the government has implemented the outlook of scientific development in an all-round way and positively meets the challenge posed by the ageing of the population. It has considered undertakings for the aged an important part of balanced social and economic development as well as of the building of a harmonious society, and has adopted economic, legal and administrative measures to constantly promote the development of undertakings for the aged.

(2) Everywhere you go in Suzhou's alleys, you will find as if you are in an expo of bridges, which are situated so close to one another that you will soon forget how many you have already crossed on your way. As for those with a definite purpose to see them, it is even hard to move on. All these bridges make a large book of strong, lasting cultural taste. Standing on the top of one bridge and viewing the water alley scenes, you will find more nearby or at a distance. Even if you lose sight of the water, you may still see a bridge. Though the bridge serves as a passage across the water, the visitor would however linger on it and become reluctant to cross.

五、篇章参考译文翻译原理选注

• 练习3（英译汉）注释

1. 中文不翻译英文代词"they"，否则就是画蛇添足。
2. "However, this taking in"在中文中略去不译，原因在于主题并没有变化。
3. 英文里大量使用代词取代"bridge"或"bridges"，而译成中文则添加"桥"也不嫌重复，如果省略也可以，但反而有些不符合习惯。下面译文也有多处反映。从整篇中英文分别使用的"桥"和代词统计来看，中文中的重复和英文中的替代是一个普遍现象。

• 练习4（汉译英）注释

（1）原文中"老龄"和"事业"出现多次重复，英文译文尽量使用替代或替换的方法，避免重复，这是使英文更加归化的需要。

（2）原文中出现的"桥"在短短一个段落中竟有13处，而翻译成英文后"bridge"只出现了5次。

第八章 正说、反说与问说的互译

一、翻译原理

不同民族思维习惯和文化的差异造成了语言表达方式的不同。在一种语言中的正面表达，翻译到了另一种语言中可能会反过来说。这就造成了正说与反说的互译现象。在英汉语言互译中这种现象俯拾即是。例如，将呼喊中的"Freeze!"译为"不许动!"，"Order!"译为"不要乱!"；警示语"Wet paint!"译为"油漆未干!"；招贴语"Staff only"译为"非公莫入"。广义上的正反译不仅限于肯定与否定之分，也包括其他问题，如将"Least said, soonest mended"译为"多说反而坏事"就是利用反义词构成正说与反说的互译。不过，正说与反说的互译大多数是通过肯定和否定的互换完成的。因此，本书只分析肯定与否定这一具有规律性、典型性的问题，而不牵涉正说与反说的其他问题。本章涉及的另一个问题是问说，即反问句和陈述句的转换翻译。例如，汉语诗句"谁不忆江南?"被译为英语"Yangtze Delda, an ever-lasting impression of all people"这是典型的问说与正说的互译。问说与正说的互译问题可以看作反说与正说互译问题的一个变体。

英语不像汉语一样喜欢反问和否定的说法，更偏重直接的肯定表达，因此造成英语的正说和汉语的反说或问说的互译趋势，这一特点从上述例句中便可略知一二。这种现象可能有三大原因：一是汉语可以表示否定意义的非否定词汇匮乏和英语可以表示否定意义的非否定词汇富足；二是英语的求静性与汉语的求动性的影响；三是变换角度，采用现成说法，获得理想的翻译效果。

汉语中的否定词语常用的有"不""没""无""未"。诸如"否""非""免""勿""毋""莫"等词只是在文言文中常见，现在使用频率并不高。汉语中含有否定意义的非否定词也微乎其微，如"少""难""欠"等。然而英语中可以用来表示否定意义的非否定词（短语）相对来说要多得多，如"hardly"，"scarcely"，"seldom"，"barely"，"few"，"little"，"fail"，"without"，"beyond"，"until"，"unless"，"lest"，"ignorant"，"refrain"，"refuse"，"neglect"，"absence"，"instead of"，"other than"，"except"，"rather than"。这就在一定程度上造成了英语的正说和汉语的反说或问说的互译趋势。

英汉语言本身的特点差异也是一个不容忽视的因素。英语倾向于多用名词,因而叙述呈静态(static);汉语倾向于多用动词,因而叙述呈动态(dynamic)。有时汉语中用否定、反面的说法或反问来表达英语中的肯定说法以增加动态效果,使表达更有力量。例如,将"keep upright"译为"切勿倒置",以及上文提到的"Order"被译成了"不要乱"。

不同民族的人们也许使用的语言不尽相同,但他们生活在同一个地球上,会有类似的生活体验。因此,在翻译过程中会变换角度,寻找类似的现成的说法,这时也会形成英汉语言中正说与反说及问说的互译现象。例如,将"此路不通"译为"dead end",将"urban clearway"译为"市区通道,不准停车"。这种现象在处理成语或谚语的翻译时尤为突出,下文会有大量实例。

二、核心例句原理分析

核心例句	原理分析
A. 英译汉 1. Business only. 闲人莫入。 2. Silence! 不要吵! 3. A secret makes a woman woman. 女人没有秘密没有女人味。 4. If you can't find it here in Hong Kong, it doesn't exist. 天下瑰宝,香港不见,更在何方? 5. I took it for granted, all the times, that it would last somehow. 我从不怀疑,到底不改,这缘分没有完了。 6. He who has a mind to beat his dog will easily find a stick. 欲加之罪,何患无辞? 7. The explanation is pretty thin. 这种解释,理由很不充分。 8. I think that his offer can be rejected safely. 我认为,可以拒绝他的建议而万无一失。 9. They had been in the capital for three days, but had remained in seclusion. 他们来到首都已经三天了,却一直没有露面。 10. He seemed to be at a loss for the precise word to complete his thought. 他似乎想不出恰当的字眼把他的思想充分表达出来。	1. 正说转反说,使用现成说法,以求风格一致,增强动态效果。 2. 同上。 3. "有"和"没有"如掌心掌背,正说转反说,汉语注重否定,双重否定在语法上仍属否定,但比肯定效果更强。 4. 正说转问说,反问更能增强效果。 5. "took for granted"就是不怀疑。正说转反说,变换说法,更符合目标语言的习惯和韵味。 6. 原理同上。 7. 以否定方式翻译"pretty thin"。正说转反说,由汉语、英语的词汇特征所决定:英语可表达否定意义的非否定词汇富足,而汉语则缺乏此类词汇。 8. 同上。 9. 同上。 10. 同上。

核心例句	原理分析
B. 汉译英 1. 请勿动手! Hands off! 2. 请勿靠近! Keep away! 3. 谁不忆江南? Yangtze Delda, an ever-lasting impression of all people. 4. 如梭的船家,你奔向何方? The dwelling boats, passing apace, moving about. 5. 外表靠不住/人不可貌相。 Appearance is deceptive. 6. 我待人毫无保留。 I have a completely open mind. 7. 这个方案他们可以接受而又不失体面。 This is a plan they could accept with dignity. 8. 我觉得无拘无束,就不知不觉地说起话来。 I felt so much at ease that I found myself speaking. 9. 她说话干脆果断,完全没有哼哼哈哈的腔调。 She has an decisive manner of speaking, happily free from umms and ers. 10. 这是个无理的要求。 This is a bogus demand.	1. 反说转正说:其一是词汇问题;其二使用现成说法,达到简洁、达意的理想效果。 2. 同上。 3. 问说转正说,英语更喜欢直来直去,汉语较委婉,同时更强调问说所承载的动态力量。 4. 同上。 5. 反说转正说,使用现成说法,简洁、达意。 6. 反说转正说,由汉语、英语的词汇特征所决定:英语可表达否定意义的非否定词汇富足,而汉语则缺乏此类词汇。 7. 反说转正说,英语更喜欢直来直去,汉语较委婉。 8. 反说转正说,由汉语、英语的词汇特征所决定。 9/10. 原理同上。

值得说明的是,虽然有英语的正说和汉语的反说或问说的互译趋势,但由于语言本身具有灵活性,并不排除相反的可能,即存在英语的反说与汉语的正说的互译现象。例如:

(1) Good wine needs no bush.

酒好客自来。

(2) Never put off what you can do today until tomorrow.

今日事,今日毕。

(3) We never know the worth of water till the well is dry.

井干方知水宝贵。

(4) Those who cannot remember the past are condemned to repeat it.

忘记过去必定会重蹈覆辙。

因此,在翻译过程中应当灵活应用,切莫机械照搬这一原理。

三、翻译练习

◆ 课堂练习 ◆

• 练习 1（英译汉）

1. Faults are thick where love is thin.
2. For me, however, it was a night of wakefulness.
3. My memory fails me at this moment.
4. This guy is far from being honest.
5. He is ignorant of Chinese classical music.
6. It is beyond my power to finish this task within a week.
7. Opportunity knocks but once.
8. Good winner, good loser.
9. All's fish that comes to his net.
10. Always prepare for a rainy day.
11. He said the census, the first since 1981, has now been scheduled for July 17, a far less auspicious day than July 18 for the island's estimated 20 million people.
12. People thought for many years that we would breed ourselves out of existence.
13. The stamp, issued in honor of one of the country's premier Buddhist societies, was dated 2544 BC, for "before Christ", instead of BE, for "Buddhist era", which would have signified the year of 2001 according to the Buddhist calendar.
14. But some foods seem to have a timeless taste appeal and an enduring ability to leap on to clothing—red wine and coffee figured prominently on both the 1991 and 2001 lists.
15. The man walked uncomfortably through the modern high-speed train, stumbling over people sitting in the corridors, as he searched in vain for a working WC.
16. I really doubt we have no way out.

• 练习 2（汉译英）

1. 天下没有不散的筵席。
2. 这计划尚未落实。
3. 我弄不懂这个意思。
4. 我不知从哪里得到的。

5. 使用按键,勿用力过猛。

6. 我们克服亚洲金融危机和世界经济波动对我国的不利影响……

7. 必须清醒地看到,我们工作中还有不少困难和问题。

8. 收入分配关系尚未理顺。

9. 有些地方治安状况不好。

10. 当他……怎能不感到一份民族骄傲感呢?

11. 喜欢在夏天滑雪吗?在沙漠里?迪拜变不可能为可能,弄来了400多吨冰雪以吸引旅游者光临这个海湾阿拉伯酋长国。

12. 数百年来,鬼魂目击事件一直连续不断。就在3年前我们每周还能收到两个鬼魂目击事件的报告。

13. 对蝉来说,12年是不妙的周期,那样的话周期是2、3、6和12年的天敌都有机会捕食它们。

14. 泰国政府的一位高级官员说,位于热带的泰国打算推出最新的节能招数,要求职员不要穿着套装。

15. 它性能极佳。不过要是你喝酒太多,要它辨认你的声音可能不太容易。

16. 齐景公问政于孔子,孔子对曰:"君君,臣臣,父父,子子。"公曰,"善哉!信君不君,臣不臣,父不父,子不子,虽有粟,吾得而食诸?"

◆ 课后练习 ◆

● 练习1(英译汉)

1. Better be the head of an ass than the tail of a horse.

2. I have read your articles, I expected to meet an older man.

3. I found myself at a loss for words of consolation.

4. Among the blind the one-eyed man is king.

5. Many men, many minds.

6. Familiarity breeds contempt.

7. Fire and water may be good servants, but bad masters.

8. The horse refused the brook.

9. Murder will out.

10. He just refrained from retorting her.

11. A lot of companies are not interested—they say it's a minority market and not commercially viable, but it's a big minority.

12. Amazon said Germans were the least romantic, with 69 percent saying Valentine's Day was unimportant, compared to 54 percent of Britons and 46 percent of French.

13. Dr. Colin Gill said rather than complain, women should encourage men to pop out for a swift half.

14. The last thing we want is the entire workforce taking an announced sickie on the day of a big match.

15. That's a tidy sum for most people in recession-wrecked Japan but a far cry from the wads of cash handed across jewelry-store counters during the heady "bubble economy" days of the 1980s.

16. This may well be a blessing in disguise.

● 练习2（汉译英）

1. 我们必须自觉地把思想认识从那些不合时宜的观念、做法和体制的束缚中解放出来。

2. 好事不出门。

3. 与其诅咒黑暗，不如点上蜡烛。

5. 小洞不补,大洞吃苦。

6. 事实不容否认。

7. 要想人不知,除非己莫为。

8. 欲速则不达。

9. 多亏他们的努力,现在我们家乡几乎没有人不知道保护环境的重要性。

10. 馆娃宫殿今何在,遗比几更改,年年岁岁旧情思,响屧廊声飘向有谁知。

11. 许多真正的小提琴大师都是男性,这也许意味着当人在天赋的引领下走向卓越的境界时,性别的影响力就大大减弱了。

12. 挪威在两性平等方面跨出了史无前例的一步：政府宣布将强令所有公司保证妇女在董事会成员中所占比例不低于40%。

13. 据民意测验专家估计,由于希拉克和若斯潘所主张的政策并无明显差别,不参加第一轮投票的选民将达到空前的数目。

14. 不仅如此,这还是对那些见人就以为可能是流氓的人的一种讽刺。

15. 我们不要钱,我们只是想让他们别再在广告中提到猫,这给许多人尤其是孩子造成了关于猫的不良印象。

16. 子曰:"衣敝缊袍,与衣狐貉者立,而不耻者,其由也与? 不忮不求,何有不臧?"子路终身诵之。子曰:"是道也,何足以臧?"

● 练习3（英译汉）

Sunday Before the War (Abridged)

It rained in the morning, but the afternoon was clear and glorious and shining, with all the distances revealed far into the heart of Wales and to the high ridges of the Welsh mountains.

The cottages of that valley are not gathered into villages, but two or three together or lonely among their fruit-trees on the hillside; and the cottagers, who are always courteous and friendly, said a word or two as one went by, but just what they would have said on any other day and without any question about the war. Indeed, they seemed to know, or to wish to know, as little about that as the earth itself, which beautiful there at any time, seemed that afternoon to wear an extreme and pathetic beauty. The country, more than any other in England, has the secret of peace. It is not wild, though it looks into the wildness of Wales; but all its cultivation, its orchards and hopyards and fields of golden wheat seem to have the beauty of time upon them, as if men there had long lived happily upon the earth with no desire for change nor fear of decay. It is not the sad beauty of a past cut off from the present, but a mellowness that the present inherits from the past; and in the mellowness all the hillside seems a garden to the spacious farmhouses and little cottages; each led up to by its own narrow, flowery lane. There the meadows are all lawns with the lustrous green of spring even in August, and often over-shadowed by old fruit-trees—cherry, or apple, or pear; and on Sunday after the rain there was an April glory and freshness added to the quiet of the later summer.

Nowhere and never in the world can there have been a deeper peace; and the bells from the little red church down by the river seemed to be the music of it, as the song of birds is the music of spring. There one saw how beautiful the life of man can be, and how men by the innocent labours of many generations can give to the earth a beauty it has never known in its wildness. And all this peace, one knew, was threatened; and the threat came into one's mind as if it were a soundless message from over the great eastward plain; and with it the beauty seemed unsubstantial and strange, as if it were sinking away into the past, as if it were only a memory of childhood.

……

So the next morning one saw a reservist in his uniform saying goodbye to his wife and children at his cottage-gate and then walking up the hill that leads out of the valley with a cheerful smile still on his face. There was the first open sign of trouble, a very little one, and he made the least of it; and, after all, this valley is very far from any possible war, and its harvest and its vintage of perry and cider will surely be gathered in peace.

● 练习4（汉译英）

从百草园到三味书屋（节选）

冬天的百草园比较无味；雪一下，可就两样了。拍雪人（将自己的全形印在雪上）和塑雪罗汉需要人们鉴赏，这是荒园，人迹罕至，所以不相宜，只好来捕鸟。薄薄的雪，是不行的；总须积雪盖了地面一两天，鸟雀们久已无处觅食的时候才好。扫开一块雪，露出地面，用一枝短棒支起一面大的竹筛来，下面撒些秕谷，棒上系一条长绳，人远远地牵着，看鸟雀下来啄食,走到竹筛底下的时候,将绳子一拉,便罩住了。但所得的是麻雀居多,也有白颊的"张飞鸟",性子很躁,养不过夜的。

这是闰土的父亲所传授的方法,我却不大能用。明明见它们进去了,拉了绳,跑去一看,却什么都没有,费了半天力,捉住的不过三四只。闰土的父亲是小半天便能捕获几十只,装在叉袋里叫着撞着。我曾经问他得失的缘由,他只静静地笑道:你性子急,来不及等它走到中间去。

我不知道为什么家里人要将我送进私塾里去了,而且还是全城中称为最严厉的私塾。也许是因为拔何首乌毁了泥墙罢,也许是因为将砖头抛到间壁的梁家去了吧,也许是因为站在石井栏上跳下来了罢……都无从知道。总而言之:我将不能常到百草园了。Ade,我的蟋蟀们!Ade,我的覆盆子们和木莲们!……

出门向东,不上半里,走过一道石桥,便是我的先生的家了。从一扇黑油的竹门进去,第三间是书房。中间挂着一块扁道:三味书屋;扁下面是一幅画,画着一只很肥大的梅花鹿伏在古树下。没有孔子的牌位,我们便对着那扁和鹿行礼。第一次算是拜孔子,第二次算是拜先生。

第二次行礼时,先生便和蔼地在一旁答礼。他是一个高而瘦的老人,须发都花白了,还戴着大眼镜。我对他很恭敬,因为我早听到,他是本城中极方正、质朴、博学的人。

不知从哪里听来的,东方朔也很渊博,他认识一种虫,名曰"怪哉",冤气所化,用酒一浇,就消释了。我很想详细地知道这故事,但阿长是不知道的,因为她毕竟不渊博。现在得到机会了,可以问先生。

"先生,'怪哉'这虫,是怎么一回事?……"我上了生书,将要退下来的时候,赶忙问。

"不知道!"他似乎很不高兴,脸上还有怒色了。

我才知道做学生是不应该问这些事的,只要读书,因为他是渊博的宿儒,绝不至于不知道,所谓不知道者,乃是不愿意说。年纪比我大的人,往往如此,我遇见过好几回了。

四、练习参考译文

◆ 课堂练习 ◆

● 练习1(英译汉)

1. 一朝情义淡,样样不顺眼。
2. 而我却度过了一个不眠之夜。
3. 我一时想不起来。
4. 这个家伙很不老实。

5. 他对中国古典音乐一无所知。

6. 我不能在一周之内完成这项工作。

7. 机不可遇,时不再来。

8. 胜不骄,败不馁。

9. 来者不拒。

10. 未雨绸缪。

11. 他说,这次同时也是1981年以来的首次人口普查,现已改期至7月17日,这天对这个岛国的大约两千万居民来说远远不如18日吉利。

12. 长期以来的观念是人类会无节制地繁衍直至灭亡。

13. 这张邮票为纪念该国一个重要佛教组织而发行,其上的日期印成了"公元前2544年"(2544 BC),而不是"佛历2544年"(2544 BE),后者按佛教历法表示公元2001年。

14. 不过有些食品似乎拥有永远的魅力以及经久不衰的蹦到衣服上的能力——红酒和咖啡在1991年和2001年的排行榜上都占据着显著的位置。

15. 这个人磕磕绊绊地越过坐在走道中的人,艰难地穿过这列现代化的高速列车,却终于没能找到一个能用的厕所。

16. 我就不信,我们真的就没有出路了?

● 练习 2(汉译英)

1. All good things must come to end.

2. The project is as yet all in the air.

3. The meaning evades me.

4. I forget where I got it.

5. Avoid operating the keys roughly.

6. We overcame the adverse effects the Asian financial crisis and world economic fluctuations had on China.

7. We must be clearly aware that there are still quite a few difficulties and problems in our work.

8. Things have yet to be straightened out in the matter of income distribution.

9. Public order is poor in some places.

10. He must necessarily feel a national pride, when he …

11. Fancy skiing in summer? In the desert? Dubai is defying the odds by bringing in more than 400 tons of snow and ice to lure visitors to the Gulf Arab emirate.

12. Ghost sightings have remained consistent for centuries. Until three years ago we'd receive reports of two new ghosts every week.

13. For the cicadas, 12 years is bad because predators on 2-, 3-, 6-, and 12-year cycles would eat them.

14. Tropical Thailand is to ask workers to stop wearing suits as part of the country's latest bid to conserve energy, a senior government official said.

15. It works perfectly, but might have trouble recognizing your voice after one takes too many pints.

16. Duck Ching of Chi asked Master K'ung about the government. Master K'ung replied saying, "Let the prince be a prince, the minister a minister, the father a father, and the son a son." The Duke said, "How true! For indeed when the prince is not a prince, the minister not a minister, the father not a father, the son not a son, one may have a dish of millet in front of one and yet not know if one will live to eat it."

◆ 课后练习 ◆

● 练习1（英译汉）

1. 宁为鸡口，勿为牛后。

2. 我读过你的文章，没想到你这么年轻。

3. 我简直想不出安慰的话来。

4. 山中无虎猴称王。

5. 人多心不齐。

6. 亲不敬，熟生蔑。

7. 水火是忠仆，用之不慎成灾主。

8. 马突然停步不肯跳过小溪。

9. 纸包不住火。

10. 他只是克制住不反驳她。

11. 许多公司不感兴趣——他们认为这是个少数市场，从商业角度看不可行，其实这个少数市场并不小。

12. 亚马逊说德国人最不浪漫，他们中的69%认为情人节无足轻重，而在英国和法国这一比例分别是54%和46%。

13. 科林·基尔博士说，妇女不但不该抱怨，反而应当鼓励男人们出去短时间地喝上一两杯。

14. 我们最不希望发生的事情就是整支劳动大军在有重要比赛的日子集体去休所谓的病假。

15. 在经济不景气的日本，这对大多数人来说是个可观的数目，但与80年代歌舞升平的"泡沫经济"时期交到珠宝店柜台的大把钞票相比实在不算什么。

16. 这也许是"塞翁失马，焉知非福"。

● 练习 2（汉译英）

1. We must conscientiously free our minds from the shackles of the outdated notions, practices and systems.

2. Good news goes on crutches.

3. Better to light one little candle than to curse the darkness.

4. Where there is smoke, there is fire.

5. A stitch in time saves nine.

6. Facts are facts.

7. What is done by night appears by day.

8. Haste makes waste.

9. Owing to their efforts, now few people in my hometown are ignorant of the importance of environmental protection.

10. The ancient Guan-Wa Palace is now lost,

And its traces never the same all times.

But all times, the affection is not forgot.

With the wood-sole shoes' steps still echoing about.

11. Many of the masters of the violin are men, perhaps indicating that gender is far less important as the inner muse takes over on the road to excellence.

12. Norway struck an unprecedented blow for sexual equality when the government said it would force companies to guarantee that at least 40 percent of board members are women.

13. Pollsters reckon a record number of voters, turned off by a lack of clear policy distinctions between Chirac and Jospin, will stay away from polling stations in the first round of voting.

14. Even more than that, it's a bit of sarcasm aimed at the people who just look at people and think they might be hooligans.

15. We want no money, just for them to stop referring to cats in their ads, as it gives a negative perception of cats to many people, especially children.

16. The master said, "Wearing a shabby hemp-quilted gown, yet capable of standing unabashed with those who wore fox and badge." That would apply quite well to Yu, would it not?

Who harmed none, was foe to none,

Did nothing that was not right.

Afterwards Tzulu (Yu) kept on continually chanting those lines to himself. The master said, "Come now, the wisdom contained in them is not worth treasuring to that extent."

- **练习3（英译汉）**

战前星期天（节选）

早晨下了雨，午后放晴，阳光明媚，逶迤伸展到远处威尔士腹地以及威尔士山脉巍峨群峰的景致，全部呈现在眼前。谷地的农舍并不集成村落，而是三两簇聚，要不就孤零零的，掩埋在山腰的果树丛中。农舍的住户从来彬彬有礼，态度友善，见人走过，会说上一两句话，然而也只是任何寻常日子的家常话，全不问打仗的事。看来，对于战争，他们知之甚少，也不想了解更多，漠然宛若他们脚下的大地。这儿的土地常年秀美，而在这天下午更是披上了一种极度的凄婉动人的美。这片乡野，比起英格兰的任何乡野，更得和平的奥秘。虽说面对威尔士荒原，这片乡野并非蛮荒，倒是以其耕作的成绩，以其果园、啤酒花藤栽培场和金黄色的麦田，显示出日月流逝留下的美，仿佛这儿的人常年以来一直在土地上幸福度日，既不期盼变更，也不畏惧衰亡。这不是一种与现今隔绝的往昔的悲凉美，而是现今继承自往昔的一种醇美。就在这一片醇美之中，四周的山坡似乎成了宽敞农宅和玲珑家舍的家园，每座都由各自花色烂漫的小径引至门前。这儿的牧场全是精心整理的草地，即使在八月仍是一片春日的葱郁；不少地方更有栽培经年的樱桃、苹果、梨树等果树掩映。这在雨后的星期天，除了残夏特有的恬静，田乡还透出一种四月的辉耀和新生气息。

世间任何地方在任何时候都不可能领略比这儿更为深沉的和平。从山下河畔那座红砖小教堂传出的钟声，像是和平的主题音乐，正如啁啾鸟语是春天的音乐一样。在这儿，你看到了人类生活有多么美好，人类又如何以迭代的诚实劳动给土地带来一种土地在蛮荒时代从未领略到的美。然而，你也意识到，这儿的和平景象正遭到威胁。这威胁如同穿越向东延伸的大平原传来的无声讯息，随之，田野之美顿时变得虚空而诡奇，似乎正融入往昔而渐渐消失，渺远宛若童年的回忆。

…………

于是，翌日早晨，人们看见一名预备役士兵穿上制服，在农舍门口告别妻孥，爬山出谷去了，脸上仍挂着欣喜的笑容。那时出现麻烦的第一个征兆，一点蛛丝马迹而已，当事人更是尽量不事声张。归根到底，这片谷地远在可能燃起的战火之外，这儿的一应作物以及用于今年酿酒的梨子和苹果都将在和平环境中收摘归仓。

- **练习4（汉译英）**

In winter the garden was relatively dull; as soon as it snowed, though, that was a different story. Imprinting a snowman (by pressing your body on the snow) or building snow Buddhas required appreciative audiences; and since this was a deserted garden where visitors seldom came, such games were out of place here. I was therefore reduced to catching birds. A light fall of snow would not do; the ground had to be covered for one or two days, so that the birds had gone hungry for some time. You swept a patch clear of snow, propped up a big bamboo sieve on a short stick, sprinkled some rice husks beneath it, then tied a long string to the stick and retired to a distance to hold it, waiting for birds to come. When they hopped under the sieve, you tugged the string and trapped them. Most of those caught were sparrows, but there were white-throated wagtails too, so wild that they died less than a day of captivity.

It was Runtu's father who taught me this method, but I was not adept at it. Birds hopped under my sieve all right, yet when I pulled the string and ran over to look there was usually nothing there, and after long efforts I caught merely three or four. Runtu's father in only half the time could catch dozens which, stowed in his bag, would cheep and jostle each other. I asked him once the reason for my failure. With a quiet smile he said:

"You're too impatient. You don't wait for them to get to the middle."

I don't know why my family decided to send me to school, or why they chose the school reputed to be the strictest in the town. Perhaps it was because I had spoiled the mud wall by uprooting milkwort, perhaps because I had thrown bricks into the Liangs' courtyard next door, perhaps because I had climbed the well coping to jump off it … There is no means of knowing. At all events, this meant an end to my frequent visits to Hundred-Plant Garden. Adieu, my crickets! Adieu, my raspberries and climbing figs!

A few hundred yards east of our house, across a stone bridge, was where my teacher lived. You went in through a black-lacquered bamboo gate, and the third room was the classroom. On the central wall hung the inscription Three-Flavour Study, and under this was a painting of a portly fallow deer lying beneath an old tree. In the absence of a tablet to Confucius, we bowed before the inscription and the deer. The first time for Confucius, the second time for our teacher.

When we bowed the second time, our teacher bowed graciously back from the side of the room. A thin, tall old man with a grizzled beard, he wore large spectacles. And I had the greatest respect for him, having heard that he was the most upright, honourable and erudite man in our town.

I forget where it was that I heard that Dongfang Shuo was another erudite scholar who knew of an insect called guai-zai, the incarnation of some unjustly slain man's ghost, which would vanish if you doused it with wine. I longed to learn the details of the story, but Mama Chang could not enlighten me, for she after all was not an erudite scholar. Now my chance had come. I could ask my teacher.

"What is this insect guai-zai, sir?" I asked hastily at the end of a new lesson, just before I was dismissed.

"I don't know." He seemed not at all pleased. Indeed, he looked rather angry.

Then I realized that students should not ask questions like this, but concentrate on studying. Being such a learned scholar, of course he must know the answer. When he said he did not know, it meant he would not tell me. Grownups often behaved like this, as I knew from many past experiences.

五、篇章参考译文翻译原理选注

● 练习 3（英译汉）注释

1. 将"or"翻译成"要不",体现了汉语喜欢用否定表达的特点,主要由汉语、英语词汇特点决定。

2. 将"without any question of"翻译为"全不问",是由于英语中像"without"这样的可以用来表达否定意义的非否定词或短语非常多。

3. 将"little"翻译为"也不想(了解)更多",正说转反说,原因同上。

4. 将"often over-shadowed by old fruit-trees"翻译成"不少地方更有……果树掩映",汉语又一次转换说法,体现不同的思维与表达习惯。

5. 将"made the least of it"翻译成"尽量不事声张",正说转反说,除了词汇原因,汉语中用否定表达还增加了动态效果。

● 练习 4（汉译英）注释

1. 将"无味"翻译成"dull",反说转正说。英语中像"dull"这样的可以用来表达否定意义的非否定词或短语非常多。

2. 将"不相宜"翻译成"out of place",反说转正说,原因同上。

3. 将"无处觅食"翻译为"gone hungry",反说转正说,变换角度,简洁明了。如果英语同样用否定表达来译未免太啰唆:"(the birds) could not find food anywhere"。

4. 将"不过"翻译为"merely",也是出于词汇原因。

5. 句中的"不能常到百草园了"被译为"this meant an end to my frequent visit to Hundred-Plant Garden",汉语中的动态词"不能(到)"翻译成英语中便成了"an end to"这一静态意味十足的词组。

6. 将"出门向东,不上半里"中的否定词省略,直接翻译成"A few hundred yards east of our house",体现了汉语喜欢用否定表达的特点。

7. 将"没有"翻译成"in the absence of",体现了英语中用来表达否定意义的非否定词或短语非常多。

8. "不知"翻译成"I forget",也是出于词汇原因。

9. 将"绝不至于不知道"翻译为"must know the answer",反说转正说,变换思维角度,简洁明了地达到表达效果。(需要说明的是,双重否定在句法上仍属否定)

下编

英汉互译原理综合应用

第九章 英汉互译原理应用比较

一、小 说

1. *Pride and Prejudice* by Jane Austen (Excerpt from Chapter 1)

The Original

IT is a truth universally acknowledged that a single man in possession of a good fortune must be in want of a wife.

However little known the feelings or views of such a man may be on his first entering a neighbourhood, this truth is so well fixed in the minds of the surrounding families, that he is considered as the rightful property of some one or other of their daughters.

"My dear, Mr. Bennet," said his lady to him one day, "have you heard that Netherfield Park is let at last?"

Mr. Bennet replied that he had not.

"But it is," returned she; "for Mrs. Long has just been here, and she told me all about it."

Mr. Bennet made no answer.

"Do not you want to know who has taken it?" cried his wife impatiently.

"You want to tell me, and I have no objection to hearing it."

This was invitation enough.

"Why, my dear, you must know, Mrs. Long says that Netherfield is taken by a young man of large fortune from the north of England; that he came down on Monday in a chaise and four to see the place, and was so much delighted with it that he agreed with Mr. Morris immediately; that he is to take possession before Michaelmas, and some of his servants are to be in the house by the end of next week."

"What is his name?"

"Bingley."

"Is he married or single?"

"Oh! single, my dear, to be sure! A single man of large fortune; four or five thousand a year. What a fine thing for our girls!"

"How so? How can it affect them?"

"My dear, Mr. Bennet," replied his wife, "how can you be so tiresome! You must know that I am thinking of his marrying one of them."

"Is that his design in settling here?"

"Design! Nonsense, how can you talk so! But it is very likely that he may fall in love with one of them, and therefore you must visit him as soon as he comes."

"I see no occasion for that. You and the girls may go, or you may send them by themselves, which perhaps will be still better; for, as you are as handsome as any of them, Mr. Bingley might like you the best of the party."

简·奥斯汀《傲慢与偏见》(第1章节选)译文比读

• 译文1 （王科一 译）

凡是有钱的单身汉,总想娶位太太,这已经成了一条举世公认的真理。

这样的单身汉,每逢新搬到一个地方,四邻八舍虽然完全不了解他的性情如何、见解如何,可是,既然这样的一条真理早已在人们心目中根深蒂固,因此人们总是把他看作自己某一个女儿理所应得的一笔财产。

有一天班纳特太太对她的丈夫说:"我的好老爷,尼日斐花园终于租出去了,你听说过没有?"

班纳特先生回答道,他没有听说过。

"的确租出去了,"她说,"朗格太太刚刚上这儿来过,她把这件事的底细一五一十地告诉了我。"

班纳特先生没有理睬她。

"你难道不想知道是谁租去的吗?"太太不耐烦地嚷起来了。

"既是你要说给我听,我听听也无妨。"

这句话足够鼓励她讲下去了。

"哦!亲爱的,你得知道,郎格太太说,租尼日斐花园的是个阔少爷,他是英格兰北部的人;听说他星期一那天乘着一辆驷马大轿车来看房子,看得非常中意,当场就和莫理斯先生谈妥了;他要在'米迦勒节'以前搬进来,打算下个周末先叫几个佣人来住。"

"这个人叫什么名字?"

"彬格莱。"

"有太太的呢,还是个单身汉?"

"噢!是个单身汉,亲爱的,确确实实是个单身汉!一个有钱的单身汉;每年有四五千镑的收入。真是女儿们的福气!"

"这怎么说?关女儿们什么事?"

"我的好老爷,"太太回答道,"你怎么这样叫人讨厌!告诉你吧,我正在盘算,他要是挑中我们一个女儿做老婆,可多好!"

"他住到这儿来,就是为了这个打算吗?"

"打算!胡扯,这是哪儿的话!不过,他倒作兴看中我们的某一个女儿呢。他一搬来,你就得去拜访拜访他。"

"我不用去。你带着女儿们去就得啦,要不你干脆打发她们自己去,那或许倒更好些,因为你跟女儿们比起来,她们哪一个都不能胜过你的美貌,你去了,彬格莱先生倒可能挑中你呢?"

- **译文 2（孙致礼 译）**

有钱的单身汉总要娶位太太,这是一条举世公认的真理。

这条真理还真够深入人心的,每逢这样的单身汉新搬到一个地方,四邻八舍的人家尽管对他的性情和见识一无所知,却把他视为自己某一个女儿的合法财产。

"亲爱的贝内特先生,"一天,贝内特太太对丈夫说道,"你有没有听说内瑟菲尔德庄园终于租出去了?"

贝内特先生回答道,没有听说。

"的确租出去了,"太太说道。"朗太太刚刚来过,她把这事一五一十地全告诉我了。"

贝内特先生没有搭话。

"难道你不想知道是谁租去的吗?"太太不耐烦地嚷道。

"既然你想告诉我,我听听也无妨。"

这句话足以逗引太太讲下去了。

"哦,亲爱的,你应该知道,朗太太说,内瑟菲尔德让英格兰北部的一个阔少爷租去了;他星期一那天乘坐一辆驷马马车来看房子,看得非常中意,当下就和莫里斯先生讲妥了;他打算赶在米迦勒节以前搬进新居,下周末以前打发几个佣人先住进来。"

"他姓什么?"

"宾利。"

"成亲了还是单身?"

"哦!单身,亲爱的,千真万确!一个有钱的单身汉,每年有四五千镑的收入。真是女儿们的好福气!"

"这怎么说?跟女儿们有什么关系?"

"亲爱的贝内特先生,"太太答道,"你怎么这么令人讨厌!告诉你吧,我正在思谋他娶她们中的一个做太太呢。"

"他搬到这里就是为了这个打算?"

"打算!胡扯,你怎么能这么说话!他兴许会看中她们中的哪一个,因此,他一来你就得拜访他。"

"我看没有那个必要。你带着女儿们去就行啦,要不你索性打发她们自己去,这样或许更好些,因为你的姿色并不亚于她们中的任何一个,你一去,宾利先生倒作兴看中你呢。"

- 译文 3 (方华文 译)

单身汉如果手中有一笔可观的钱财,势必需要讨房妻室,这已成为举世公认的真理。

这样的单身汉,每逢乔迁新居,左邻右舍对他的感受和观点虽一无所知,但是,既然以上的真理早已在人们的心中根深蒂固,所以邻居仍总是将其视为自己某一个女儿应该得到的一份财产。

一日,贝内特太太对她的丈夫说:"亲爱的,尼瑟费德别墅终于租出去了,你听说过没有?"

贝内特先生说自己没有听说有这档子事。

"这是千真万确的,"她继续侃侃而谈,"朗太太刚刚上这儿来过,把事情原原本本都告诉了我。"

贝内特先生没有搭理她。

"你难道不想知道是谁把别墅租了去吗?"贝太太耐不住性子,大声嚷嚷起来。

"既然你打定主意要讲给我听,我也只好洗耳恭听了。"

有了这样一句话,对贝内特太太来说就足够了。

"嗬,亲爱的,你要知道,朗太太说租尼瑟费德别墅的是英格兰北部的一个阔少爷,家里有的是钱;听说星期一那天,他乘坐一辆驷马大车来看过地方,对房子十分满意,当场就和莫里斯先生拍板成交了;他打算在米迦勒结账节之前搬进来,下个周末便派几位仆人来收拾。"

"这人叫什么名字?"

"他叫宾利。"

"是个单身汉,还是有妻室的人?"

"哈!是单身,亲爱的,这可是千真万确的!他是个家底非常殷实的单身男子,每年有四五千镑的进项。咱们的女儿要交好运啦!"

"你净东拉西扯!这与她们有什么关系?"

"我亲爱的老爷,"贝太太说道,"你怎么这样不开窍!实话告诉你吧,我在盘算着怎样嫁一个女儿给他做太太呢。"

"他搬到这儿来,就为这个目的?"

"要说这是他的目的,那纯粹是不着边际地瞎猜!不过,说不定他真的会爱上咱们的某个女儿呢。所以,他一搬来,你就到他府上拜访。"

"我到他府上算应的哪门子景。你让女儿们自己去得了。要不然你和他们一道去,这样做更好些,因为论姿色你比她们哪个都不差,宾利先生或许会选中你呢。"

- 译文 4 (杜争鸣 译)

有条真理举世公认:男人单身又有一大笔钱财就一定想娶妻。

无论人们对这样一个男人的性情或见解如何缺乏了解,但他一进左邻右舍的圈子,周围的人家都会因为这条真理在脑子里已经深深扎根而把他看成自己哪个女儿应得的财产。

"我亲爱的先生啊,"贝内特先生的太太有一天对他说,"你听说了吗?奈瑟菲尔德的别墅终于租出去了!"

贝内特先生说他还没听到。

"可这是真的,"他太太回应道。"因为朗太太刚才还在这里,是她把这事原原本本告诉我了。"

贝内特先生没有回话。

"难道你不想知道是谁租了别墅吗?"他太太声音高起来,显得不耐烦。

"你想说给我听,我也不是不愿听。"

他这样说就让太太够起劲了。

"听着,亲爱的,你要知道,朗太太说租了别墅的是一个年轻人,家底殷实,来自英格兰北部;还说他过来的时候是星期一,乘着驷马大车,专门来看地方,看了以后非常满意,当时就答应了莫里斯先生。说是要在米迦勒结账节前就搬过来,家里一些佣人下个周末就要来了。"

"他名字叫什么?"

"宾利。"

"结婚了还是单身?"

"哦!是单身,亲爱的,这是肯定的!单身一人,家产可多啦,一年就有四五千镑。这对我们的女儿来说可不是小意思啦!"

"怎么这么说呢?这对她们有啥啦?"

"贝内特先生,我亲爱的,"他妻子回答道,"你怎么这么缠人啊!你不会不知道我是在想让他娶我们一个女儿。"

"他在这里住下来的企图就是这个吗?"

"企图!说废话。你怎么这么说呢!说真的,他很有可能爱上我们哪个女儿。所以,他一来你就必须去拜访。"

"我看这不合适。你和女儿们倒是可以去,或者你就亲自把女儿送过去吧,这样也许更好;既然你的姿色比起她们中哪个也不差,宾利先生倒是可能在你们里面最喜欢你呢。"

2. *Jane Eyre* by Charlotte Bronte (Excerpt from Chapter 11)

The Original

The chamber looked such a bright little place to me as the sun shone in between the gay blue chintz window curtains, showing papered walls and a carpeted floor, so unlike the bare planks and stained plaster of Lowood, that my spirits rose at the view. Externals have a great effect on the young. I thought that a fairer era of life was beginning for me, one that was to have its flowers and pleasures, as well as its thorns and toils. My faculties, roused by the change of scene, the new field offered to hope, seemed all astir. I cannot precisely define what they expected, but it was something pleasant: not perhaps that day or that day month, but at an indefinite future period.

I rose; I dressed myself with care: obliged to be plain—for I had no article of attire that was not made with extreme simplicity—I was still by nature solicitous to be neat. It was not my habit to be disregardful of appearance, or careless of the impression I made; on the contrary, I ever wished to look as well as I could, and to please as much as my want of beauty would permit. I sometimes regretted that I was not handsomer: I sometimes wished to have rosy cheeks, a straight nose, and a small cherry mouth: I desired to be tall, stately, and finely developed in figure; I felt it a misfortune that I was so little, so pale, and had features so irregular and so marked. And why had I these aspirations and these regrets? It would be difficult to say: I could not then distinctly say it to myself; yet I had a reason, and a logical, natural reason too. However, when I had brushed my hair very smooth, and put on my black frock—which, Quaker-like as it was, at least had the merit of fitting to a nicety—and adjusted my clean white tucker, I thought I should do respectably enough to appear before Mrs Fairfax; and that my new pupil would not at least recoil from me with antipathy. Having opened my chamber window, and seen that I had left all things straight and neat on the toilet-table, I ventured forth.

Traversing the long and matted gallery, I descended the slippery steps of oak; then I gained the hall: I halted there a minute; I looked at some pictures on the walls (one, I remember, represented a grim man in a cuirass, and one a lady with powdered hair and a pearl necklace), at a bronze lamp pendant from the ceiling, at a great clock whose case was of oak curiously carved, and ebon black with time and rubbing. Everything appeared very stately and imposing to me: but then I was so little accustomed to the grandeur hall-door, which was half of glass, stood open; I stepped over the threshold. it was a fine autumn morning; the early sun shone serenely on embrowned groves and still green fields; advancing on to the lawn, I looked up and surveyed the front of the mansion. It was three stories high, of proportions not vast, though considerable; a gentleman's manor-house, not a nobleman's seat: battlements round the top gave it a picturesque look. Its gray front stood out well from the background of a rookery, whose cawing tenants were now on the wing. They flew over the lawn and grounds to alight in a great meadow, from which these were separated by a sunk fence, and where an array of mighty old thorn trees, strong, knotty, and broad as oaks, at once explained the etymology of the mansion's designation. Farther off were hills: not so lofty as those round Lowood, nor so craggy, nor so like barriers of separation from the living world; but yet quiet and lonely hills enough, and seeming to embrace Thornfield with a seclusion I had not expected to find existent so near the stirring locality of Millcote. A little hamlet, whose roofs were blent with trees, straggled up the side of one of these hills: the church of the district stood nearer Thornfield; its old tower-top looked over a knoll between the house and gates.

夏洛蒂·勃朗特《简·爱》(选自第11章)译文比读

● 译文1 （李霁野 译）

太阳从鲜艳的蓝印花布的窗幔间照射进来时,显出纸糊的墙和铺地毯的地板,和罗沃德的光板同褪色的粉墙很是不同,使得这房子在我看来是一个很愉快的小地方:一看它我的精神就振作起来了。外表对于年轻人很有影响;我想一个美好的生活时代为我开始了——一个既有荆棘和劳苦,也有鲜花和欢乐的时代。我的才智被这种情景变迁、这种令人心怀希望的新地方所刺激,似乎全活动起来了。我的才智究竟希望得到什么东西,我无法准确说明,不过是一种令人愉快的东西:并不就在那一天或那一月,却在一个不明确的未来的时期。

我起来了;我细心替自己穿着:虽然不得不朴素——因为我没有一件衣服不是做得非常简朴的——我却天生的满心想要整洁。不修边幅或不留心给人的印象如何,并不是我的习惯;反之,我总愿尽力显得好看一点,愿尽力在我不美的限度之内讨人喜欢。我有时惋惜我没有更漂亮一些;我有时愿意有玫瑰的面颊、直梁的鼻子和一张樱桃小嘴;我渴望有美好的高身材;我觉得我这样小,这样苍白,这样五官引人注目的不端正,是一种不幸。为什么我有这些愿望和惋惜呢? 要说明是困难的:那时候我连对自己也说不明白;然而我也有一个理由,而且是一个合乎逻辑的、自然的理由。不论怎样,当我把头发梳得很平,穿上我的黑衣裙——这虽然像教友派一样朴素,至少有一种非常合身的好处——并戴好干净的白颈饰的时候,我想我总可体面地到费尔法克斯太太前露面,我的新学生至少也不会厌恶地避开我了吧。我打开房间的窗户。看梳妆台上一切都放得整齐干净了,我就大胆走出去了。

我穿过了铺席的长走廊,下了那光滑的橡木楼梯;于是我到了过厅,在那里站了一会儿,我看着墙上的画(我记得有一张画着穿护身甲的严肃男子,一张画着戴宝石项链、敷发粉的贵妇),看着从天花板悬下的黄铜灯,看着一座大钟,钟架是用雕得石怪的橡木,和因为时间与摩擦而发了黑的乌木做成的。一切东西在我看来都庄严堂皇;不过那时候我对富丽堂皇的东西的见识是很少的。一半装玻璃的过厅门是开着的,我走出门限。是天气晴朗的秋晨;朝阳在变褐的树丛和仍然发青的田地上恬静地照耀着;我向前走到草坪上面,向上细看看这宅子的前边。这宅子有三层高,占地面积不算庞大,不过也可观:是一所绅士住宅,并不是一个贵族府第;绕在顶上的雉堞使得它富有画意。宅子的灰色前沿从乌鸦巢的背景中显出来,巢中住的呱呱叫着的乌鸦正在飞翔;它们飞过草坪和园地,要在一个大草场上落下,草场那里有一段塌了的篱笆和这边隔开,并有一排结实有节粗得像橡树一样的老荆棘,这即刻就说明这宅子命名的来源了。再向前去就是小山:没有绕着罗沃德的山那样高,也没有那样险峻,也并不是那样的隔离人生的屏障;然而这山已经是够安静孤寂的了,而且用来包围着桑恩费尔德的那一种世外气象,我也没有料想到会在这样靠近米尔科特的热闹地方找到。房顶和树掺杂着的小权落,散布在山的一边;这地方的教堂更靠近桑恩费尔德:教堂的旧塔顶,俯瞰着房屋与大门之间的土阜。

● 译文2（祝庆英 译）

　　太阳从鲜艳的蓝色印花窗帘缝隙间照进来，照亮了糊着墙纸的四壁和铺着地毯的地方，这跟劳渥德的光秃秃的木板和沾污的灰泥墙完全不同。这个房间看上去是个如此明亮的小地方，我一看见它就精神振奋起来。外表对于青年人是有强烈的影响的。我想，对我来说，生活中一个比较美好的时期正在开始，一个有着荆棘和劳苦，同时也有鲜花的欢乐的时期。由于场景有了变动，由于有希望出现一个新天地，我的官能被唤醒，似乎完全都活跃起来。我不能确切地说明它们在期待什么，不过那总是一种愉快的东西：也许不只是在那一天或者那一个月，而是在一个不明确的未来时期。

　　我起身了，细心地穿着衣服；不得不穿得朴素——因为我没有一件衣服不是做到极其简单的——可是我却天生酷爱清洁。不修边幅，不管自己给人家留下什么印象，这些都不是我的习惯；相反，我一直希望：尽可能使自己显得好看些，在缺少美貌所许可的范围内尽可能使自己讨人喜欢。我有时候惋惜自己没长得再漂亮一点；有时候希望有红彤彤的脸蛋、挺直的鼻子和樱桃般的小嘴；希望自己长得高、庄严、身材丰满；我觉得自己长得那么矮小、那么苍白，五官长得那么不端正、那么特征显著，真是一种不幸。为什么我会有这些渴望、这些惋惜呢？那是很难说的；当时我就没法对自己说清楚；不过，我有个理由，而且是个合乎逻辑的、自然的理由。不管怎样，我还是把头发梳得很平整，穿上黑上衣——这看来虽然像贵格会教徒，但至少有非常合身的好处——把干净的白色领饰整整好，我想我总可以够体面地去见菲尔费克斯太太，我的新学生至少不会厌恶地躲开我吧。我把这卧室的窗户打开，注意让梳妆台上我所有的东西都放得整整齐齐，就鼓起勇气去了。

　　我穿过铺着地席的长过道，走下滑溜溜的橡木梯级，来到大厅，在那儿停了一会儿，看墙上的几幅画（我记得有一幅画是一个穿胸甲的严峻的男子，还有一幅画是一位敷发粉、戴珍珠项链的贵妇人），看看天花板上垂下来的一盏青铜灯，再看看一只大钟。钟壳是用雕着古怪花纹的橡木跟因为年久和摩擦而发黑的乌木做成的。对我来说，一切都显得雄伟和庄严，可是当时我对富丽堂皇也太不习惯了。大厅的门有一半镶着玻璃，正开着，我跨过门槛。那是秋天的一个早晨，天气很好，朝阳宁静地照耀着已经发黄的树丛和还是一片绿色的田地。我走到草坪上，抬起头来，观察一下这个宅子的正面。它有三层高，体积虽然可观，但还算不上宏大；是绅士的住宅，而不是贵族的府第；顶上的一圈雉蝶墙给它增添了画意。宅子的灰色正面明显地突出在白嘴鸦巢的背景上。白嘴鸦巢里的哇哇叫的居民这会儿正在飞翔。它们飞过草坪和庭园，要去停落在一个大牧场上。一道坍塌的篱笆把牧场和这边隔开。那边有一排高大的老荆棘，粗壮多节，大得像橡树，一下子就说明了这宅子命名的由来。再过去是小山，山不像劳渥德周围的那么高，那么巉峻嶙峋，也不那么像把人世隔开的屏障；不过，这些小山也已经够幽静、够寂寞的了，它们似乎用一种隐遁气氛把桑菲尔德包围起来，在离米尔考特这个热闹地区那么近的地方竟会有这种隐遁气氛存在，却是我没有料到的。一个小村落零零落落落花流水地散开在一座小山的山坡上，房顶和树夹杂在一起。区教堂就在桑菲尔德附近，钟楼的旧顶俯视着房子和大门之间的一个土墩。

● **译文3（黄源深 译）**

阳光从蓝色鲜艳的印花布窗帘缝隙中射进来,照出了糊着墙纸的四壁和铺着地毯的地板,与罗沃德光秃秃的楼板和痕迹斑驳的灰泥全然不同。相形之下,这房间显得小巧而明亮,眼前的情景使我精神为之一振。外在的东西对年轻人往往有很大影响,我于是想到自己生涯中更为光明的时代开始了,这个时代将会有花朵和欢愉,也会有荆棘和艰辛。由于这改变了的环境,这充满希望的新天地,我的各种官能都复活了,变得异常活跃。但它们究竟期望着什么,我一时也说不清楚,反正是某种令人愉快的东西,也许那东西不是降临在这一天,或是这个月,而是在不确定的未来。

我起身了,小心穿戴了一番,无奈只能简朴——因为我没有一件服饰不是缝制得极其朴实的——但渴求整洁依然是我的天性。习惯上我并不无视外表,不注意自己留下的印象。相反,我一向希望自己的外观尽可能标致些,并希望在我平庸的外貌所允许的情况下得到别人的好感。有时候,我为自己没有长得漂亮些而感到遗憾,有时巴不得自己有红润的双颊、挺直的鼻梁和樱桃般的小口。我希望自己修长、端庄、身材匀称。我觉得很不幸,长得这么小、这么苍白,五官那么不端正而又那么显眼。为什么我有这些心愿却又有这些遗憾?这很难说清楚,当时我自己虽然说不上来,但我有一个理由,一个合乎逻辑的、自然的理由。然而,当我把头发梳得溜光,穿上那件黑色的外衣——虽然看上去确实像贵格会教派的人,但至少非常合身——换上了干净洁白的领布时,我想我可以够体面地去见费尔法克斯太太了,我的新学生至少不会因为厌恶而从我面前退缩。我打开了房间的窗户,并注意到已把梳妆台上的东西收拾得整整齐齐,便大着胆子走出门去了。

我走过铺着地席的长廊,走下打滑的橡树楼梯,来到了大厅。我站了一会儿,看着墙上的几幅画(记得其中一幅画的是一个穿着护胸铁甲、十分威严的男子,另一幅是一个头发上搽了粉和戴着珍珠项链的贵妇),看着从天花板上垂下来的青铜灯;看着一个大钟,钟壳是由雕刻得稀奇古怪的橡木做的,因为年长月久和不断地擦拭,变得乌黑发亮了。对我来说一切都显得那样庄严肃穆、富丽堂皇。那时我不大习惯于这种豪华。一扇镶着玻璃的大厅门敞开着,我越过了门槛。这是一个晴朗的秋天早晨,朝阳宁静地照耀着透出黄褐色的树丛和依然绿油油的田野。我往前来到了草坪上,抬头细看这大厦的正面。这是幢三层楼屋宇,虽然有相当规模,但按比例并不觉得宏大,是一座绅士的住宅,而不是贵族的府第。围绕着顶端的城垛,使整座建筑显得很别致。灰色的正面正好被后面一个白嘴鸦的巢穴映衬着,显得很凸出,它的居住者正在边房呱呱叫个不停,飞越草坪和庭园,落到一块大草地上。一道矮篱把草地和庭园分开。草地上长着一排排巨大的老荆棘树丛,强劲多节,大如橡树,一下子说明屋宇名称字源意义的由来。更远的地方是小山。不像罗沃德四周的山那么高耸,那么峻峭,也不像它们那么是一道与世隔绝的屏障。但这些山十分幽静,拥抱着桑菲尔德,给它带来了一种我不曾料到在闹闹嚷嚷的米尔科特地区会有的清静。一个小村庄零零落落地分布在一座小山的一侧,屋顶与树木融为一体。地区教堂坐落在桑菲尔德附近,它古老的钟楼俯视着房子与大门之间的土墩。

3. *This Above All* (précis of the novel) by Eric Knight

The Original

Critique: *This Above All* is a story of great emotional conflict between a girl who knew and loved the England of hunting, cricket, and afternoon tea, and a man who knew and hated the England of slums, mines, starvation, and disease. The author attempted to show what war can mean to a civilian as well as to a front-line soldier.

The Story:

Home on rest leave, after the disaster of Dunkirk, Clive Briggs went first to Leaford and then to Gosley, both resort towns on the coast of England. At a band concert in Gosley he met Prudence Cathaway, who was stationed nearby with women's army corps. Prue was of an upper middle-class family and Clive was from the slums, but they were attracted to each other and became lovers the second time they were together.

Prue told him of her family. Her grandfather had been a general in the last war and felt unwanted and useless in this one; her father was a doctor, a famous brain specialist. She told him of her aunt Iris, who wanted only to get to America and who pretended that she wanted her children to be safe when it was really for herself she feared. Iris' brother was in America, buying steel for the British government. Prue also told Clive that she had broken her engagement to a conscientious objector, and because she was ashamed for him she had joined the W. A. A. F.

Clive seemed reluctant to talk about himself, other than to say he had been born in the slums. In fact, it was many days before Prue knew he was in the army and had been in the rear-guard action at Dunkirk.

When they found that Prue could get a leave which would give them ten days together, they went to Leaford. Most of the time they were quite happy but each time Prue mentioned the War Clive became angry and sullen and seemed to get pleasure from taunting her about her family. Sometimes they quarreled without knowing the reason and were reconciled only because of their desire for each other.

During the last five days of their stay, Clive's friend Monty joined them. Monty was also slum-born. It was Monty who told Prue of Clive's heroism at Dunkirk. Monty's story puzzled Prue more than ever. She could understand even less why Clive was so bitter.

While they were at Leaford, air raids became frequent. One night during a heavy raid Clive told Prue why he would not go back to the army, why he intended to desert. He told her of his childhood, of his illegitimate birth and of his sordid remembrances of childhood in the slums. He asked her if a country that ignored its poor were worth fighting for. England was still fighting a gentleman's war, he said, and the leaders were asking the slum boys to win the war and then go back to the mines and the factories and the mills from which they had come. He was through. Prue tried to tell him that he must go back to save himself. She said it was his pride that had brought him up from the filth, and his pride and that of the others like him would change all the conditions of which he had told her. He would not listen to her.

At the end of the leave Prue returned to her camp. Clive, true to his word, did not go back to the army at the end of his furlough. He wandered along the coast while trying to decide what he really wanted to do. Once he went into a church and talked with the pastor, but he scoffed when the minister told him that we fight because we have faith in our ability to build a better life than we have had. He accused the minister and all the churches of betraying Christ and His teachings because the rich who support the church must not be told of their sin in neglecting their fellow men. Before he left the church the minister told him that realism and reasoning like his had brought was hunger and cruelty, and that only faith could restore human dignity and freedom throughout the world.

At last Clive tired of running away; there was no place for him to go. Finally he decided to give himself up, to let the army decide for him whether he was wrong, for he was too exhausted to decide his problem for himself. Perhaps Prue and the minister had been right; perhaps faith in himself meant faith in his country and the willingness to die for it.

On the train to London, Clive suddenly remembered something Prue had said, a remark which had no meaning at the time. Now he knew she was going to have a baby. He felt that he could not give himself up before he saw Prue and asked her to marry him. He managed to evade the military police in London and call Prue. They arranged to meet at the station in London and to marry as soon as possible. Clive knew at last that he loved Prue, and he was determined that his child would never know the hurt an illegitimate child must always feel.

While he was waiting for Prue's train, a bomb fell on a nearby building. As he tried to help rescue a woman trapped in the basement of the building, the wall collapsed on him. He regained consciousness with Prue sitting beside him in a hospital room. Monty and her father had helped her find him. Prue's father was honest with her. He had tried to save Clive's life with an emergency operation, but part of the brain tissue was gone and there was no hope that Clive would live. During one of his periods of consciousness Clive told Prue that he had risked his life to save a strange woman, because he knew at last that he did have faith in himself and his country.

Clive died in the night during a heavy bombing raid. Afterward Prue walked along the streets of London and saw the volunteer firemen and the Cockney policemen performing their duties among the wreckage, and she knew why Clive had died. Feeling the child stir within her, she hoped that by sacrifices like Clive's child and all children might have the chance to live in a good and free world.

埃里克·奈特《至关重要》(《这是头等大事》)译文比读

- **译文1:《至关重要》(王萱 译)**

短评:

《至关重要》描写了一对青年男女激烈的情感冲突。那个姑娘所知所爱的英国是游猎、板球和午茶的国度,而小伙子所知所恨的英国则只有贫民窟、矿山、饥饿和疾病。作者力图表现的是,战争对于百姓、对于前线士兵,都意味着什么。

概要:

敦刻尔克大撤退后,克莱夫休假回家,他先到里佛,然后去戈斯雷,这两处都是英国沿海的风景胜地。在戈斯雷的一场音乐会上,他遇到驻扎在附近女子军团的普鲁登斯·凯瑟韦。普鲁出身于中上层的家庭,而克莱夫则来自贫民窟,但是二人互相爱慕,第二次见面,就成了恋人。

普鲁向克莱夫讲述自己的家庭。她的祖父在第一次世界大战中曾是将军,但在这次战争中感到自己毫无用处;他的父亲是医生,是位著名的脑科专家。普鲁说,她的姑姑伊丽丝一心想去美国,她借口为了孩子平安无事,但实际上全是为她自己考虑。伊丽丝的弟弟在美国,为大英帝国采办钢铁。普鲁还告诉克莱夫,她已经同一名根据信仰拒绝服兵役的人解除了婚约,并因为为他感到羞耻而参加了妇女空军辅助兵团。

克莱夫似乎不愿多谈自己的事,只说他出生在贫民窟里。实际上,很多天后,普鲁才知道,他在部队里服役,敦刻尔克撤退时,他在后卫部队中。

他们得知普鲁可以有一段假期,两人能有十天时间在一起,便一同去了里佛。大多数时间里两人都很愉快,但是每当普鲁谈起战争,克莱夫就怒气冲冲,郁郁寡欢,似乎要以奚落她的家庭来获得开心。有时他们莫明其妙地吵了起来,仅仅出于彼此相互需要对方才言归于好。

两人在一起的最后五天里,克莱夫的朋友蒙蒂来了。蒙蒂也出生在贫民窟里,是他把克莱夫在敦刻尔克的英勇事迹告诉了普鲁的。蒙蒂的话使普鲁更加迷惑不解,她更不能理解为什么克莱夫如此痛苦。

他们在里佛时,空袭越来越频繁。一天夜里,在一声猛烈的空袭中,克莱夫告诉普鲁,为什么他不愿意返回部队,为什么他打算开小差。他向她讲述了自己的童年,讲到他是个私生子,讲到他在贫民窟里悲惨的少年时代。他问普鲁是否值得为一个对自己的穷人不管不顾的国家而战。他说,英国打的还是一场老爷先生们的战争,领导者让贫民窟的孩子们把仗打赢,然后再回到他们原来的工厂和矿山去。他厌倦了这一切。普鲁力劝克莱夫回部队去,拯救自己。她说,他的自尊心使他从贫民窟的肮脏中走出来;他的自尊,以及像他一样的人们的自尊,将会改变他所说的一切。克莱夫听不进去。

假期结束,普鲁回营了。克莱夫说到做到,休假期满时没有返回部队。他沿着海岸漫无目标地走着,一边考虑着自己究竟想做些什么。一次,他走进教堂,同牧师攀谈起来。牧师告诉他,我们打仗是因为自信有能力建设一种前所未有的美好生活。但是克莱夫对此嗤之以鼻。他谴责牧师和一切教堂都背叛了基督和基督的圣训,因为任何人都不告诉供养着教堂的那些富人们他们对同胞置之不理的罪过。离开教堂前,牧师告诉他,是他这种现实主义和推理方法带来了战争、饥饿和残暴,而只有信念才能在全世界恢复人的尊严与自由。

最后,克莱夫走投无路,厌倦了逃亡生活。他终于决定自首,让军队来替他判断自己是否有错,因为他已筋疲力尽,无法解决自己的问题。或许,普鲁和那位神父是对的;或许,对自己抱有信心就意味着对祖国怀有信心,意味着愿意为国牺牲。

在开往伦敦的列车上,克莱夫突然想起普鲁说过一句话;当时他没有理解她的意思。现在他明白,她怀孕了。他感到,在见到普鲁、向她求婚之前,他不能自首。在伦敦,他想方设法避开宪兵,给普鲁打了电话。他们约定在伦敦火车站会面,尽快结婚。克莱夫终于明白自己深深爱着普鲁。他决心永远不让孩子知道私生子所受的伤害。

当克莱夫等候普鲁的火车时,一颗炸弹落在附近一座大楼上。他正在试图抢救一位困在大楼底部的妇女,墙塌了,压在他身上。他苏醒过来的时候,躺在医院里,普鲁坐在他身边。蒙蒂和普鲁的父亲曾帮助她找到了克莱夫。普鲁的父亲很坦率地对女儿说,他曾用急救手术挽救克莱夫的生命,但是他已经损失了一部分脑组织,因此他不会有希望活下来。在他神志清醒的一段时间里,克莱夫告诉普鲁,他冒着生命危险去救一个素不相识的妇女,是因为他最终明白了,他还是对自己、对国家怀着坚定的信念。

夜间,在一次猛烈的空袭中,克莱夫死去了。事后,普鲁走在伦敦的街道上,看到志愿消防队员和伦敦东区的警察们在废墟中尽着自己的职责,这时她便明白克莱夫是为什么死的。她感到胎儿在她体内蠕动,她希望,像克莱夫那样做出牺牲,便能使他的孩子,以及所有的孩子们,都能有机会生活在一个美好而自由的世界里。

- **译文 2:《这是头等大事》(杜争鸣 译)**

评介:《这是头等大事》讲述了一个充满感情冲突的故事:年轻的姑娘乐于英国的狩猎、曲棍球、晚茶,而男主人公却对英国的贫民窟、矿井、饥荒、病痛深恶痛绝。作者旨在表现战争对普通市民、对前线士兵来说究竟意味着什么。

故事:敦刻尔克大劫难过去了,克莱夫·布利格斯放假回家,先后去了利夫德和戈斯里这两个英国海滨度假城。在戈斯里听音乐会时他结识了附近女子兵团里的普露·卡瑟威。普露出身于中产阶级上层家庭,克莱夫却来自贫民窟,但两人情投意合,才见面两次就觉得难舍难分。

普露对克莱夫讲了自己的出身:她祖父在第一次大战中当过将军,而在这次战争中却感到自己成了无人问津的废人;父亲做医生,是一位颇有名气的脑神经专家。她说她姑妈艾丽斯一心想到美国,表面上是担心孩子们的安全,实际上只是自己害怕。艾丽斯的兄弟住在美国,一直在为英国政府购买钢材。普露还告诉克莱夫说自己曾与人订婚,但由于对方借故宗教良心拒服兵役,就解除了和他的婚约。正是由于为他感到羞耻普露才参加了女子兵团。

克莱夫似乎不愿谈论自己,只说自己是在贫民窟里出生的。他们认识很多天以后普露才了解到,他原来也是军人,而且参加过敦刻尔克大撤退的掩护战斗。

当他们得知普露可以请到假,两人能在一起待十天时,就去了利夫德城。在那里,他们绝大部分时间都过得很愉快,只是普露一提起战争克莱夫就变得脾气暴躁,愤懑不乐,似乎把奚落普露的家庭当成了唯一的乐事。有时候两人吵架的原因简直莫名其妙,最后平息下来也只是由于各自都对对方有欲望。

在他们待在一起的最后五天里,克莱夫的朋友蒙迪也和他们聚到了一起。蒙迪也是贫民窟出身,他对普露讲述了克莱夫在敦刻尔克的英勇行为,可这却使普露更加迷惑不解,她就是不明白克莱夫为什么会这样尖刻。

就在他们还在利夫德城的时候,空袭已经频繁了起来。一天晚上,在密集的轰炸期间,克莱夫对普露讲明了自己不愿归队、想开小差的原因,讲述了自己童年的往事,讲述了他作为私生子的身世以及一想起来就感到卑贱的贫民窟中的童年生活。他问普露:如果一个国家对自己的穷人视而不见,那还值得去为它打仗吗?他说,英国现在打的是绅士的仗,战争领袖们要贫民窟的小伙子们打赢这场战争,然后再回到矿井、工厂和作坊里去干活,哪儿来哪儿去。他自己已经打完了。普露竭力劝他回部队去,说只有这样才能保全自己,说他有他的自豪,正是这种自豪使他从贫民窟的污泥浊水中长大成人,还说他的自豪感,加上所有像他这样的人的自豪感,可以改变他所说的那种生活状况。但是,克莱夫对普露的这番话就是听不进去。

普露假满回营,克莱夫则恪守其言,没有按期归队。他在海岸上游荡着,同时考虑着自己究竟要干些什么。有一天,他走进一所教堂跟神父谈了一次话,可是当神父告诉他英国之所以要打下去,就是因为他们深信自己有能力创造比以前更加美好的生活时,他却对此嗤之以鼻,指责这位神父和英国所有的教堂都背叛了基督耶稣和他的箴言,因为他们不讲那些资助教堂的富人们无视自己同胞的罪过。在他离开教堂前,神父说正是他这种现实思想和思考问题的方法导致了战争、饥饿和残酷的行为,唯有信仰能够在全世界恢复人类的尊严和自由。

最后,克莱夫终于不想再这样东躲西藏地混下去了;他也没有地方可去,于是决定主动自首,让军队对他做裁决。他自己已经身心疲惫,说不清自己究竟是怎么了。也许普露和神父是对的;也许自己的信念就应该是对国家的信念,就意味着情愿为国家牺牲。

在开往伦敦的火车上,克莱夫突然想起普露曾说过一件事,当时并不觉得那话有什么意义,现在却明白了——她原来已有身孕,于是觉得不能马上就去自首,得先见到普露向她求婚。他想方设法地躲过伦敦的军事警察给普露打通了电话,和她约定在伦敦车站见面并尽快结婚。克莱夫终于确信自己是爱普露的,他下决心不让自己的孩子再去体验那种私生子时时刻刻都能体会到的伤害。

他正等着普露乘坐的那列火车,一颗炸弹落到了附近的一幢楼房上。就在他竭力帮忙去营救被困在楼房底层的一位妇女时,一堵墙倒塌,把他压在下面。他在医院的病房里苏醒过来时,看到普露就坐在自己身边。是蒙迪和她的父亲帮助她找到克莱夫的。普露的父亲对女儿不忌讳地吐露真情:他已实施紧急手术尽量挽救克莱夫的生命,但是由于部分脑组织损伤,看来克莱夫的性命难保。克莱夫还能间歇性地恢复知觉,其间他告诉普露他冒着生命危险去救一个陌生女人,原因就在于他最终已经明白,他对自己、对自己的国家是有信心的。

克莱夫死在一个空袭轰炸异常猛烈的夜晚。空袭过后,普露走在伦敦的街道上,看到志愿消防员和东区的警察正在救火、维持治安,她明白了克莱夫是为什么死的。此时,她感到腹中的胎儿正在蠕动,希望像克莱夫这样的牺牲可以使他的孩子以及所有的孩子们有机会生活在一个自由、美好的世界里。

4. *Tess of the D'Urbervilles* by Thomas Hardy (Excerpt from Chapter 2)

The Original

This fertile and sheltered tract of Country, in which the fields are never brown and the springs never dry, is bounded on the south by the bold chalk ridge that embraces the prominences of Hambledon Hill, Bulbarrow, Nettlecombe-Tout, Dogbury, High Stoy, and Bubb Down. The traveler from the coast, who, after plodding northward for a score of miles over calcareous downs and corn-lands, suddenly reaches the verge of one of these escarpments, is surprised and delighted to behold, extended like a map beneath him, country differing absolutely from that which he has passed through. Behind him the hills are open, the sun blazes down upon fields so large as to give an unenclosed character to the landscape, the lanes are white, the hedges low and plashed, the atmosphere colorless. Here, in the valley, the world seems to be constructed upon a smaller and more delicate scale; the fields are mere paddocks, so reduced that from this height hedgerows appear a network of dark green threads overspreading the paler green of the grass. The atmosphere beneath is languorous, and is so tinged with azure that what artists call the middle distance partakes also of that hue, while the horizon beyond is of the deepest ultramarine. Arable lands are few and limited; with but slight exceptions the prospect is a broad rich mass of grass and trees, mantling minor hills and dales within the major. Such is the Vale of Blackmoor.

托马斯·哈代《德伯家的苔丝》(《苔丝》)(选自第2章)译文比读

译文1:《德伯家的苔丝》(张谷若 译)

这一片土壤肥沃、山峦屏障的乡野地方,田地永远不黄,泉水永远不干,被一道包括着汉敦山、野牛冢、奈岗堵、达格堡、亥司陶和勃布砀这些高岗的陡峭的白垩质山岭在南面环抱着。一个从海边上来的旅客,往北很费劲地走了几十里地的石灰质丘阜和庄稼地以后,一下到了这些峻岭之一的山脊上面,看见了一片原野,像地图一样平铺在下面,和刚才所走过的决然不同,他不由得又惊又喜。他身后,山是旷敞的,太阳明晃晃地所照耀着的那些地,都非常广阔,让那片景物显得好像没有围篱界断似的,篱路是白的,树篱是低矮的,并且编在一起,大气是没有颜色的。但是在这个山谷里,世界好像是在更细小、更精致的规模上建造起来的。那儿的地都只是一些小小的草场,显得非常小,因此从这个高岗上看来,那儿那些纵横的树篱好像是一张用深绿色的线织成的网,展铺在浅绿色的草地上。山下的大气都懒洋洋的,并且染上了那样一片天蓝色,因而连这片景物上艺术家叫作中景的那一部分也都染上了那种颜色,而远处的天边则是一片最深的海蓝色。长庄稼的地块数不多,面积有限。全部景物,除了很小的例外,是大山抱小山,大谷套小谷,而在那些小山和小谷上盖着一片绵连、茂盛的草和树。布蕾谷就是这种样子。

● 译文2:《苔丝》(吴迪 译)

在这片土地肥沃、群山遮掩的乡间地带,田野永不枯黄,泉水永不干涸,它的南面邻接着险峻的石灰岩山岭,这山岭环绕着汉勃勒顿山、公牛冢、荨麻谷、多格堡、高斯陀以及巴勃荡等高地。从海滨地区来的游客,向北艰难地走了几英里路的石砂质丘陵和谷类庄稼地之后,突然来到这种峻岭的边缘,向下鸟瞰,惊喜地发现一片原野像地图一样平铺在脚下,与刚才所路过的截然不同。他的身后是莽莽重山,灿烂的阳光倾泻在看起来广袤无垠的原野上。一条条小径呈现白色,一排排低矮的小树编成的篱笆,空气清澈。在这儿的峡谷间,世界仿佛是在更纤小、更精制的规模上建构起来的;田野仅仅是浓缩了的放牧的围场,从这儿的高处看下去,栽成树篱的一排排灌木好像是由绿线编织的网,铺在淡绿色的草地上。下方倦怠的大气染上了一片蔚蓝,就连艺术家称作中景的部分也带有那种色彩,而远处的地平线上却呈现出最深沉的蓝色。可耕的土地数量不多,面积有限。除了很少的一部分之处,整个景色就是辽阔的草地和茂密的树林,大山抱着小山,深谷套着浅谷,这就是布莱克摩山谷。

二、散 文

1. Introduction to Bertrand Russell's Autobiograpy

The Original

What I Have Lived for

Three passions, simple but overwhelmingly strong, have governed my life: the longing for love, the search for knowledge, and unbearable pity for the suffering of mankind. These passions, like great winds, have blown me hither and thither, in a wayward course over a deep ocean of anguish, reaching to the very verge of despair.

I have sought love, first, because it brings ecstasy—ecstasy so great that I would often have sacrificed all the rest of my life for a few hours for this joy. I have sought it, next, because it relieves loneliness—that terrible loneliness in which one shivering consciousness looks over the rim of the world into the cold unfathomable lifeless abyss. I have sought it, finally, because in the union of love I have seen, in a mystic miniature, the prefiguring vision of the heaven that saints and poets have imagined. This is what I sought, and though it might seem too good for human life, this is what—at last—I have found.

With equal passion I have sought knowledge. I have wished to understand the hearts of men. I have wished to know why the stars shine ... A little of this, but not much, I have achieved.

Love and knowledge, so far as they were possible, led upward toward the heavens. But always pity brought me back to earth. Echoes of cries of pain reverberate in my heart. Children in famine, victims tortured by oppressors, helpless old people a hated burden to their sons, and the whole world of loneliness, poverty, and pain make a mockery of what human life should be. I long to alleviate the evil, but I cannot, and I too suffer.

This has been my life. I have found it worth living, and would gladly live it again if the chance were offered me.

罗素自传导言译文比读

- **译文1：我一生的追求（杜争鸣 译）**

三种激情，简单而又无比强烈的激情——支配了我一生：对爱的渴望，对知识的追求，以及对人类的苦难不堪忍受的怜悯之情。这三种激情，有如飓风，把我刮到了天南海北，使我命途多舛，经历了痛苦的深海，也到过极度绝望的边缘。

我曾追求爱，首先是因为它能使人陶醉——使人深深地陶醉，以至于我愿牺牲全部余生来换取片刻的这种欢快。我曾追求爱，其次是因为它能排遣孤独——在这种孤独中，人的意识战战兢兢，看破滚滚红尘，俯视着那冰冷的、深不可测的、死气沉沉的地狱。我曾寻求它，最终是因为在爱的结合中我看到了一幅神秘的缩影，展示了圣贤和诗人想象中所预先构建的天堂景象。这就是我所追求的，尽管它可能显得太美好而非芸芸众生所能企及，但是我最终还是得到了它。

我曾以同样的激情追求知识。我曾希望理解人心，我曾希望了解星辰何以光芒照耀，我也曾尽力领悟那种得以使数字支配万物流变的毕达哥拉斯之幂的力量。对此我稍有所得，但收获并不很多。

爱情与知识，尽其可能引人向上升入天堂，但是怜悯之情总是把我带回到大地。痛哭的回声震荡在我心中：孩子们在挨饿，受害者在遭受压迫者的折磨，无依无靠的老人成了他们子女们可憎的负担，整个人世间充满了孤独、贫困和痛苦，这都在嘲弄着人类生活的理想。我渴望能消灾灭难，却无能为力，反而身受其害。

这就是我的一生。我觉得此生值得度过，而且如果给我机会我也愿欣然重度此生。

- **译文2：我的人生追求（方舟子 译）**

有三种简单然而无比强烈的激情左右了我的一生：对爱的渴望、对知识的探索和对人类苦难的难以忍受的怜悯。这些激情像飓风，无处不在、反复无常地吹拂着我，吹过深重的苦海，濒于绝境。

我寻找爱，首先是因为它使人心醉神迷，这种陶醉是如此的美妙，使我愿意牺牲所有的余生去换取几个小时这样的欣喜。我寻找爱,还因为它解除孤独,在可怕的孤独中,一个颤抖的灵魂从世界的边缘看到冰冷、无底、死寂的深渊。最后,我寻找爱,还因为在爱的交融中,我看到了圣贤和诗人们想象出的天堂的情景。这就是我所寻找的,而且,虽然对人生来说似乎过于美妙,这也是我终于找到了的。

以同样的激情我探索知识。我希望能够理解人类的心灵。我希望能够知道群星为何闪烁。我试图领悟毕达哥拉斯所景仰的数字力量,它支配着此消彼涨。仅在一定的程度上,我达到了此目的。

爱和知识,只要有可能,通向天堂。但是怜悯总把我带回尘世。痛苦呼喊的回声回荡在我的内心。忍饥挨饿的孩子,惨遭压迫者摧残的受害者,被儿女们视为可憎的负担的无助的老人,连同这整个充满了孤独、贫穷和痛苦的世界,使人类所应有的生活成了笑柄。我渴望能够减少邪恶,但是我无能为力,而且我自己也在忍受折磨。

这就是我的一生。我发现它值得一过。如果再给我一次机会,我会很高兴地再活一次。

- **译文3:我为何而生(傅雷 译)**

三种情感,虽朴实却无比强烈地主宰着我的生命:对爱情的渴望,对知识的求索,以及对人类所遭受苦难的不可遏制的同情。这些激情似飓风,肆意地使我飘忽不定的心灵掠过茫茫苦海,又坠落到绝望的边缘。

我追寻爱,首先因为爱能使我神魂颠倒——这种体验如此强烈,我甚至愿意以余生换取哪怕片刻的销魂。我追寻爱,因为它可排解孤独——处在这可畏的孤独之中,一个颤抖的灵魂掠过世界的边缘,能够窥视冷酷荒寂的万丈深渊。最后,我追寻爱,还因为在爱的交融中,圣贤和诗人们想象的天国的景象,像神秘的袖珍画像一样,映入眼帘.这就是我所寻找的,尽管它对人生来讲可能太完美,但至少是我亲眼所见。

我以同样的激情追求知识。我希冀能够了解人类的内心世界。我希望能够知道群星为何闪烁。我试图领悟毕达哥拉斯所景仰的数字的永恒力量,它统掌乾坤。在这方面我略有成就,但还不够.

爱和知识是最有可能引领我升入天国,但怜悯之心总是把我拉回人世。我的心中回荡着人类痛苦的呼喊。嗷嗷待哺的儿童,惨遭蹂躏的受难者,被儿女视为累赘的孤苦无助的老人,以及满世界的孤独、贫困和痛苦都是对人类理想生活的嘲弄。我期望减少邪恶,但力不从心,我自己也备受其害。

这就是我的人生。但我觉得颇有价值,如果再有机会,我将欣然重活一次。

- **译文4:我为什么而活(译名未知)**

三种单纯然而极其强烈的激情支配着我的一生,那就是对于爱情的渴望,对于知识的寻求,以及对于人类苦难痛彻肺腑的怜悯。这些激情犹如狂风,把我拖到绝望边缘、深深的苦海上东抛西掷,使我的生活没有定向。

我追求爱情,首先因为它叫我销魂,爱情令人销魂的魅力使我常常乐意为了几小时这样的快乐而牺牲生活中的其他一切。我追求爱情,又因为它减轻孤独感——那种一个颤抖的灵魂望着世界边缘之外冰冷而无生命的无底深渊时所感到的可怕的孤独。

我追求爱情,还因为爱的结合使我在一种神秘的缩影中提前看到了圣者和诗人曾经想象过的天堂。这就是我所追求的,尽管人的生活似乎还不配享有它,但它毕竟是我终于找到的东西。

我以同样的热情追求知识。我想理解人类的心灵。我想了解星辰为何灿烂。我还试图弄懂毕达哥拉斯学说的力量,是这种力量使我在无常之上高居主宰地位。我在这方面略有成就,但不多。

爱情和知识只要存在,总是向上导往天堂。但是,怜悯又总是把我带回人间。痛苦的呼喊在我心中反响、回荡。孩子们受饥荒煎熬,无辜者被压迫者折磨,孤弱无助的老人在自己的儿子眼中变成可恶的累赘,以及世上触目皆是的孤独、贫困和痛苦——这些都是对人类应该过的生活的嘲弄。我渴望能减少罪恶,可我做不到,于是我也感到痛苦。

这就是我的一生。我觉得这一生是值得活的。如果真有可能再给我一次机会,我将欣然重活一次。

- **译文 5:我为何而活?（Quyu 译）**

有三种简单然而无比强烈的激情左右了我的一生:对爱的渴望、对知识的探索和对人类苦难的难以忍受的怜悯。这些激情像飓风,反复地吹拂过深重的苦海,濒于绝境。

我寻找爱,首先是因为它使人心醉神迷——这种陶醉是如此的美妙,使我愿意牺牲所有的余生去换取几个小时这样的欣喜。我寻找爱,还因为它解除孤独——在可怕的孤独中,一个颤抖的灵魂从世界的边缘看到冰冷、无底、死寂的深渊。最后,我寻找爱,还因为在爱的交融中,神秘而又具体入微地,我看到了圣贤和诗人们想象出的天堂的情景。这就是我所寻找的,而且,虽然对人生来说似乎过于美妙,这也是我终于找到了的。

以同样的激情我探索知识。我希望能够理解人类的心灵。我希望能够知道群星为何闪烁。我试图领悟毕达哥拉斯所景仰的数字力量,它支配着此消彼长。仅在一定的程度上,我达到了此目的。

爱和知识,只要有可能,通向着天堂。但是怜悯总把我带回尘世。痛苦呼喊的回声回荡在我的内心。忍饥挨饿的孩子,惨遭压迫者摧残的受害者,被儿女们视为可憎的负担的痛苦无助的老人,使人类所应有的生活成了笑柄。我渴望能够减少邪恶,但是我无能为力,而且我自己也在忍受折磨。

这就是我的一生。我发现它值得一过。如果再给我一次机会,我会很高高兴地再活一次。

- **译文 6:我为什么而活着（胡作玄、赵慧琪 译）**

对爱情的渴望,对知识的追求,对人类苦难不可遏制的同情心,这三种纯洁但无比强烈的激情支配着我一生。这三种激情,就像飓风一样,在深深的苦海上,肆意地把我吹来吹去,吹到濒临绝望的边缘。

我寻求爱情,首先因为爱情给我带来狂喜,它如此强烈以致我经常愿意为了几个小时欢愉而牺牲生命中的其他一切。我寻求爱情,其次是因为在爱情的结合中,我看到圣徒和诗人们所想象的天堂景象的神秘缩影。这就是我所寻求的,虽然它对人生似乎过于美好,然而最终我还是得到了它。

我以同样的热情寻求知识,我希望了解人的心灵。我希望知道星星为什么闪闪发光,我试图理解毕达哥拉斯的思想威力,即数字支配着万物流转。这方面我获得了一些成就,然而并不多。

爱情和知识,极其可能地把我引上天堂,但是同情心总把我带回尘世。痛苦的呼号的回声在我心中回荡,饥饿的儿童,被压迫者折磨的受害者,被儿女视为可恶的老人以及充满孤寂、贫穷和痛苦的整个世界,都是对人类应有生活的嘲讽。我渴望减轻这些不幸,但是我无能为力,而且我自己也深受其害。

这就是我的一生,我觉得它值得活。如果有机会的话,我还乐意再活一次。

2. "Of Study" by Francis Bacon

The Original

Studies serve for delight, for ornament, and for ability. Their chief use for delight, is in privateness and retiring; for ornament, is in discourse; and for ability, is in the judgment, and disposition of business. For expert men can execute, and perhaps judge of particulars, one by one; but the general counsels, and the plots and marshalling of affairs, come best, from those that are learned. To spend too much time in studies is sloth; to use them too much for ornament, is affectation; to make judgment wholly by their rules, is the humor of a scholar. They perfect nature, and are perfected by experience: for natural abilities are like natural plants, that need proyning, by study; and studies themselves, do give forth directions too much at large, except they be bounded in by experience. Crafty men contemn studies, simple men admire them, and wise men use them; for they teach not their own use; but that is a wisdom without them, and above them, won by observation. Read not to contradict and confute; nor to believe and take for granted; nor to find talk and discourse; but to weigh and consider. Some books are to be tasted, others to be swallowed, and some few to be chewed and digested; that is, some books are to be read only in parts; others to be read, but not curiously; and some few to be read wholly, and with diligence and attention. Some books also may be read by deputy, and extracts made of them bothers; but that would be only in the less important arguments, and the meaner sort of books, else distilled books are like common distilled waters, flashy things.

Reading maketh a full man; conference a ready man; and writing an exact man. And therefore, if a man write little, he had need have a great memory; if he confer little, he had need have a present wit: and if he read little, he had need have much cunning, to seem to know, that he doth not. Histories make men wise; poets witty; the mathematics subtitle; natural philosophy deep; moral grave; logic and rhetoric able to contend. Abeunt studia in mores. Nay, there is no stand or impediment in the wit, but may be wrought out by fit studies; like as diseases of the body, may have appropriate exercises. Bowling is good for the stone and reins; shooting for the lungs and breast; gentle walking for the stomach; riding for the head; and the like. So if a man's wit be wandering, let him study the mathematics; for in demonstrations, if his wit be called away never so little, he must begin again. If his wit be not apt to distinguish or find differences, let him study the Schoolmen; for they are cymini sectors. If he be not apt to beat over matters, and to call up one thing to prove and illustrate another, let him study the lawyers' cases. So every defect of the mind, may have a special receipt.

弗朗西斯·培根《论读书》译文比读

- **译文 1（王佐良 译）**

读书足以怡情，足以傅彩，足以长才。其怡情也，最见于独处幽居之时；其博彩也，最见于高谈阔论之中；其长才也，最见于处世判事之际。练达之士虽能分别处理细事或一一判别枝节，然纵观统筹、全局策划，则舍好学深思者莫属。读书费时过多易惰，文采藻饰太盛则矫，全凭条文断事乃学究故态。读书补天然之不足，经验又补读书之不足，盖天生才干犹如自然花草，读书然后知如何修剪移接；而书中所示，如不以经验范之，则又大而无当。有一技之长者鄙读书，无知者慕读书，唯明智之士用读书，然书并不以用处告人，用书之智不在书中，而在书外，全凭观察得之。读书时不可存心诘难作者，不可尽信书上所言，亦不可只为寻章摘句，而应推敲细思。书有可浅尝者，有可吞食者，少数则须咀嚼消化。换言之，有只需读其部分者，有只需大体涉猎者，少数则须全读，读时须全神贯注，孜孜不倦。书亦可请人代读，取其所作摘要，但只限题材较次或价值不高者，否则书经提炼犹如水经蒸馏，淡而无味矣。读书使人充实，讨论使人机智，笔记使人准确。因此不常作笔记者须记忆力特强，不常讨论者须天生聪颖，不常读书者须欺世有术，始能无知而显有知。读史使人明智，读诗使人灵秀，数学使人周密，科学使人深刻，伦理学使人庄重，逻辑修辞之学使人善辩：凡有所学，皆成性格。人之才智但有滞碍，无不可读适当之书使之顺畅，一如身体百病，皆可借相宜之运动除之。滚球利睾肾，射箭利胸肺，慢步利肠胃，骑术利头脑，诸如此类。如智力不集中，可令读数学，盖演题须全神贯注，稍有分散即须重演；如不能辨异，可令读经院哲学，盖是辈皆吹毛求疵之人；如不善求同，不善以一物阐证另一物，可令读律师之案卷。如此头脑中凡有缺陷，皆有特药可医。

- **译文 2（王楫 译）**

读书可以怡情养性，可以撷拾文采，可以增长才干。在幽居独处时，最能体现其怡情养性的作用；在友朋交谈中，最能体现其撷拾文采的作用；在处世论事之际，最能体现其增长才干的作用。阅历丰富的人虽能逐一判断或处理具体问题，但出谋划策，统筹全局，唯有博学之士最能胜任。读书费时过多则懒散；过于追求文采显得矫揉造作；全凭书中条条框框论事，未免书生气过重。须知读书固可补天然之不足，而经验又补读书之不足。因为天生才干犹如天然花木，须靠读书修枝剪叶。而书本知识如不以经验相制约，其教导也难免过于笼统。有实际才干的人鄙薄书本；头脑简单的人羡慕书本；只有聪明人才会运用书本。因为书籍本身并不教人如何运用，运用之道，乃在书外，且高于书本，唯有通过观察才能学到手。读书有时不可存心与作者辩难，不可以轻信盲从，也不可寻章摘句，作为谈助，而须权衡与琢磨。有的书浅尝即可，有的书可以狼吞虎咽，少数书籍则须咀嚼消化。换言之，有些书只需阅读一部分，另一些读时可不求甚解，但少数则须通读，且须勤勉而专心。有些书也可以请人代读，然后读其所作摘要；但只限于题材比较次要以及比较寻常的书。否则书经提炼犹如水经蒸馏，成为淡而无味的东西。读书使人充实，讨论使人机敏，作笔记使人精确。不常作笔记的人须有很强的记忆力，不常讨论的人须有急智，不常读书的人则须十分乖巧，方能不知而佯作知之。读历史使人明智，读诗使人机灵，数学使人周密，自然科学使人深刻，伦理学使人庄重，逻辑与修辞使人能言善辩。专心致学者，性格也受陶冶。心智方面的种种障碍，无不可读适当的书加以排除，正如身体百病，皆可以适当的运动治疗。滚球利睾肾，射箭利胸肺，慢步利肠胃，骑术利头脑，诸如此类。如若思想不能集中，可让他学数学；因为在演算时思想稍有旁骛，就须重新做起。如若不善于析难辨异，可让他学经院哲学，因为那些哲学家无不讲究细节。如若他粗枝大叶，不善于以一事论证和阐述另一事，可让他读律师的案卷。由此可见，心智方面的任何缺陷都有良方可治。

- 译文 3（曹明伦 译）

读书之用有三：一为怡神旷心，二为增趣添雅，三为长才益智。怡神旷心最见于蛰伏幽居，增趣添雅最见于高谈雄辩，而长才益智则最见于处事辩理。虽说有经验者能就一事一理进行处置或分辨，但若要通观全局并运筹帷幄，则还是博览群书者最能胜任。读书费时太多者皆因懒散，寻章摘句过甚者显矫揉造作，全凭书中教条断事者则乃学究书痴。天资之改善须靠读书，而学识之完美须靠实践；因为天生资质犹如自然花木，需要用学识对其加以修剪，而书中所示则往往漫无边际，必须用经验和阅历界定其经纬。讲究实际者鄙薄读书，头脑简单者仰慕读书，唯英明睿智者运用读书，这并非由于书不示人其用法，而是因为乃一种在书之外并高于书本的智慧，只有靠观察方可得之。读书不可存心吹毛求疵，不可尽信书中之论，亦不可为己言掠词夺句，而应该斟酌推敲，钩深致远。有些书可浅尝辄止，有些书可囫囵吞枣，但有些书则须细细咀嚼、慢慢消化；换言之，有些书可只读其章节，有些书可大致浏览，有些书则须通篇细读并认真领悟。有些书还可以请人代阅，只取代阅人所作摘录节要；但此法只适用于次要和无关紧要读书，因浓缩之书如蒸馏之水淡而无味。读书可使人充实，讨论可使人敏锐，笔记则可使人严谨；故不常作笔记者须有过目不忘之记忆，不常讨论者须有通权达变之天资，而不常读书者则须有狡诈诡谲之伎俩，方可显其无知为卓有见识。读史使人明智，读诗使人灵透，数学使人精细，物理学使人深沉，伦理学使人庄重，逻辑修辞则为使人善辩，正如古人所云：学皆成性。不仅如此，连心智上的各种障碍都可以读适当之书而令其开豁。身体之百病皆有相宜的调养运动，如滚球有益于膀胱和肾脏，射箭有益于肺部和胸腔，散步有益于肠胃，骑马有益于大脑，等等；与此相似，若有人难聚神思，可令其研习数学，因在演算求证中稍一走神就得重来一遍；若有人不善辨异，可令其读经院哲学，因该派哲学家之条分缕析可令人不胜其烦；而若有人不善由果溯因之归纳，或不善于由因及果之演绎,则可令其阅读律师之卷。如此心智上之各种毛病皆有特效妙方。

- **译文 4（廖运范 译）**

读书能给人乐趣、文雅和能力。人们独居或退隐的时候,最能体会到读书的乐趣;谈话的时候,最能表现出读书的文雅;判断和处理事物的时候,最能发挥由读书而获得的能力。那些有实际经验而没有学识的人,也许能够一一实行或判断某些事物的细枝末节,但对于事业的一般指导、筹划与处理,还是真正有学问的人才能胜任。耗费过多的时间去读便是迟滞,过分用学问自炫便是矫揉造作,而全凭学理判断一切,则是书呆子的癖好。学问能美化人性,经验又能充实学问。天生的植物需要人工修剪,人类的本性也需要学问诱导,而学问本身又必须以经验来规范,否则便太迂阔了。技巧的人轻视学问,浅薄的人惊服学问,聪明的人却能利用学问。因为学问本身并不曾把它的用途教给人,至于如何去应用它,那是在学问之外、超越学问之上、由观察而获得的一种聪明呢!读书不是为着要辩驳,也不是要盲目信从,更不是去找寻谈话的资料,而是要去权衡和思考。有些书只需浅尝,有些书可以狼吞,有些书要细嚼慢咽,慢慢消化。也就是说,有的书只需选读,有的书只需浏览,有的书却必须全部精读。有些书不必去读原本,读读它们的节本就够了,但这仅限于内容不大重要的二流书籍;否则,删节过的往往就像蒸馏水一样,淡而无味。读书使人渊博,辩论使人机敏,写作使人精细。如果一个人很少写作,他就需要有很强的记忆力;如果他很少辩论,就需要有急智;如果他很少读书,就需要很狡猾,对于自己不懂的事情,假装知道。历史使人聪明,诗歌使人富于想象,数学使人精确,自然哲学使人深刻,伦理学使人庄重,逻辑学和修辞学使人善辩。总之,读书能陶冶个性。不仅如此,读书并且可以铲除一切心理上的障碍,正如适当的运动能够矫治身体上某些疾病一般。例如,滚球游戏有益于肾脏,射箭有益于胸部,散步有益于肠胃,骑马有益于头部,等等。因此,假若一个人心神散乱,最好让他学习数学,因为在演算数学题目的时候,一定得全神贯注,如果注意力稍一分散,就必得再从头做起。假若一个人拙于辨别差异,就让他去请教那些演绎派的大师们,因为他们正是剖析毫发的人。假若一个人心灵迟钝,不能举一反三,最好让他去研究律师的案件。所以,每一种心理缺陷都有一种特殊的补救良方。

- **译文 5（水天同 译）**

读书为学的用途是娱乐、装饰和增长才识。在娱乐上学问的主要用处是幽居养静;在装饰上学问的用处是辞令;在长才上学问的用处是对于事务的判断和处理。因为富于经验的人善于实行,也许能够对个别的事情一件一件地加以判断;但是最好的有关大体的议论和对事务的计划与布置,乃是从有学问的人来的。在学问上费时过多是偷懒;把学问过于用作装饰是虚假;完全依学问上的规则而断事是书生的怪癖。学问锻炼天性,而其本身又受经验的锻炼,盖人的天赋有如野生的花草,他们需要学问的修剪;而学问本身,若不受经验的限制,则其所指示的未免过于笼统。多诈的人藐视学问,愚鲁的人羡慕学问,聪明的人运用学问;因为学问的本身并不教人如何用它们;这种运用之道乃是学问以外、学问以上的一种智能,是由观察体会才能得到的。不要为了辩驳而读书,也不要为了信仰与盲从;也不要为了言谈与议论;要以能权衡轻重、审查事理为目的。有些书可供一尝,有些书可以吞下,有不多的几部书则应咀嚼和消化;这就是说,有些书只要读读它们的一部分就够了,有些书可以全读,但是不必过于细心地读;还有不多的几部书则应当全读、勤读,而且用心地读。有些书也可以请代表去读,并且由别人替我作出节要来;但是这种办法只适于次要的议论和次要的书籍;否则录要的书就和蒸馏的水一样,都是无味的东西。阅读使人充实,会谈使人敏捷,写作与笔记使人精确。因此,如果一个人写得很少,那么他就必须有很好的记性;如果他很少与人会谈,那么他就必须有很敏捷的机智;并且假如他读书读得很少的话,那么他就必须要有很大的狡黠之才,才可以强不知以为知。史鉴使人明智;诗歌使人巧慧;数学使人精细;博物使人深沉;伦理之学使人庄重;逻辑与修辞使人善辩。"学问变化气质。"不仅如此,精神上的缺陷没有一种是不能由相当的学问来补救的,就如同肉体上各种的病患都有适当的运动来治疗似的。"地球"有益于结石和肾脏;射箭有益于胸肺;缓步有益于胃;骑马有益于头脑;诸如此类。同此,如果一个人心智不专,他最好研究数学;因为在数学的证理中,如果他的精神稍有不专,他就非从头再做不可。如果他的精神不善于辨别异同,那么它最好研究经院学派的著作,因为这一派的学者是条分缕析的人。如果他不善于推此知彼、旁征博引,他最好研究律师们的案卷。如此看来,精神上的各种缺陷都可以有一种专门的补救之方了。

- **译文 6**(姚宗立 译)

　　学习以获乐趣,以装饰门面,以求才能。为获乐趣的学习主要在个人独处之中;为装饰门面的学习表现在言谈之中;而求才能的学习用于鉴别与处理事务之中。虽然有经验的人能够处理或逐一判定事物细节,然而对事物的总体看法和筹划处置安排却主要来自那些好学之士。在读书上花太多的时间却是一种惰性。把读书过多地使用于装饰门面是虚伪卖弄。仅仅是按书本条条去鉴别事物则是学究的教条习惯。学习弥补天生的不足之处,而又被经验所完善。天生的才能就像自然界的花草树木,需由学习来整枝培育。如果学习不以实践经验所规范,那么学习本身所给予的指导就太笼统、太一般了。有实际能力的人轻视学习,无知的人羡慕学习,而聪明的人运用学习,因为学习本身并不教导如何运用;学习的运用是超越学习本身的一种智慧,且高于学习,全由观察实践而获得。读书时不要存心挑碴与作者唱反调;但也不要全信,认为一切理所当然。读书时也不要寻章找句以壮谈吐,而要掂量思考。有些书只需浅尝辄止,另有些书可囫囵吞枣,而只有少数的书要细细品嚼和消化。那就是说,有些书只需读其中的一部分,另一些书粗略读一下,只是少数的书要全读,而且要集中精力,勤奋攻读。有些书可请别人代读,摘取他人所作的要点精化。但这仅限于那些主题不很重要、价值较低的书籍。否则,经别人摘录复述的书就像蒸馏水一样索然无味了。读书使人完善充实;交谈使人敏捷机智;边读书边作笔记使人精确、严谨。因此,一个人很少作笔记的话,那么他必须要有很强的记忆力。如果他很少与人商谈,那么他必须有天生的机智。如果他很少读书,那么他必须手腕高超,方能显示出他似乎懂得他不知的东西。读历史使人聪明,读诗使人富有灵感。数学使人精确,自然哲学使人深刻,伦理学使人庄重,逻辑学和修辞学使人善辩。总之,学习影响到人的性格。人的才智并不是没有障碍梗阻,但可被适当的学习所排除。正如身体上的疾病可用适当的运动所消除一样。玩保龄球对腰肾有利,射箭对胸肺有利,散步对肠胃有利,骑马对头脑有利,其他此类运动也是如此。因此,如果某人心智跑神,就让他学习数学。因为在数学演算中他心里不集中,稍有走神,他便须从头再来。如果某人的智力不善于辨识差异,则让他学那些经院学究们,他们都是些吹毛求疵的人。如果某人不善于用一事物去证明和阐释另一事物,则让他学习律师的案例。这样,人们头脑中的每一个缺陷都能找到一种特方补救。

3. "Of Marriage and Single Life" by Francis Bacon

The Original

He that hath wife and children hath given hostages to fortune; for they are impediments to great enterprises, either of virtue or mischief. Certainly the best works, and of greatest merit for the public, have proceeded from the unmarried or childless men, which both in affection and means have married and endowed the public. Yet it were great reason that those that have children should have greatest care of future times, unto which they know they must transmit their dearest pledges. Some there are who, though they lead a single life, yet their thoughts do end themselves, and account future times impertinences. Nay, there are some other that account wife and children but as bills of charges. Nay more, there are some foolish rich covetous men that take a pride in having no children, because they may be thought so much the richer. For perhaps they have heard some talk, "Such one is a great rich man," and another except to it, "Yeah, but he hath a great charge of children"; as if it were an abatement to his riches. But the most ordinary cause of a single life is liberty, especially in certain self-pleasing and humorous minds, which are so sensible of every restraint; as they will go near to think their girdles and garters to be bonds and shackles. Unmarried men are best friends, best masters, best servants, but not always best subjects, for if they be facile and corrupt, you shall have a servant five times worse than a wife. For soldiers, I find the generals commonly in their hortatives put men in mind of their wives and children; and I think the despising of marriage amongst the Turks maketh the vulgar soldier more base. Certainly wife and children are a kind of discipline of humanity; and single men, though they be many times more charitable, because their means are less exhausted, yet, on the other side, they are more cruel and hard-hearted (good to make severe inquisitors), because their tenderness is not so oft called upon. Grave natures, led by custom, and therefore constant, are commonly loving husbands, as was said of Ulysses, Vetulam suam practulit immortalitati. Chaste women are often proud and forward, as presuming upon the merit of their chastity. It is one of the best bonds, both of chastity and obedience, in the wife if she thinks her husband wise, which she will never do if she finds him jealous. Wives are young men's mistresses, companions for middle age, and old men's nurses, so as a man may have a quarrel to marry when he will. But yet he was reputed one of the wise men that made answer to the question when a man should marry: "A young man not yet, an elder man not at all". It is often seen that bad husbands have very good wives; whether it be that it raiseth the price of their husbands' kindness when it comes, or that the wives take a pride in their patience. But this never fails, if the bad husbands were of their own choosing against their friends' consent; for then they will be sure to make good their own folly.

培根《论结婚与独身》(《论婚姻》)译文比读

• 译文1：论结婚与独身（水天同 译）

　　有妻与子的人已经向命运之神交了抵押品；因为妻与子是大事的阻挠物，无论是大善举或大恶行。无疑地，最好，最有功于公众的事业是出自无妻或无子的人的；这些人在情感和财产两方面都可说是娶了公众并给以奁资了。然而依理似乎有子嗣的人应当最关心将来，他们知道他们一定得把自己最贵重的保证交代给将来。有些人虽然过的是独身生活，他们的思想却仅限于自身，把将来认为无关紧要。并且有些人把妻与子认为仅是几项开销。尤有甚者，有些愚而富的悭吝人竟以无子嗣自豪，以为如此则他们在别人眼中更显得富有了。也许他们听过这样的话：一人说，"某某人是个大富翁"，而另一个人不同意地说，"是的，可是他有很大的儿女之累"，好像儿女是那人财富的削减似的。然而独身生活最普通的原因则是自由，尤其在某种自喜而且任性的人们方面为然，这些人对于各种约束都很敏感，所以差不多连腰带袜带都觉得是锁链似的。独身的人是最好的朋友、最好的主人、最好的仆人，但是并非最好的臣民；因为他们很容易逃跑，差不多所有逃跑的人都是独身的。独身生活适于僧侣之流，因为慈善之举若先须注满一池，则难于灌溉地面也。独身于法官和知事则无甚关系，因为假如他们是易欺而贪污的，则一个仆人之恶将五倍于一位夫人之恶也。至于军人，窃见将师激励士卒时，多使他们忆及他们的妻子儿女；又窃以为土耳其人之不尊重婚姻使一般士兵更为卑贱也。妻子和儿女对于人类确是一种训练；而独身的人，虽然他们往往很慷慨好施，因为他们的钱财不易消耗，然而在另一方面他们较为残酷狠心（作审问官甚好），因为他们不常有用仁慈之处也。庄重的人，常受风俗引导，因而心志不移，所以多是情爱甚笃的丈夫；如古人谓攸立西斯："他宁要他的老妻而不要长生"者是也。贞节的妇人往往骄傲不逊，一若他们是自恃贞节也者。假如一个妇人相信她的丈夫是聪慧的，那就是最好使她保持贞操及柔顺的维系；然而假如这妇人发现丈夫妒忌心重，她就永不会以为他是聪慧的了。妻子是青年人的情人、中年人的伴侣、老年人的看护。所以一个人只要他愿意，任何时候都有娶妻的理由。然而有一个人，人家问他，人应当在什么时候结婚？他答道："年轻的人还不应当，年老的人全不应当。"这位也被人称为智者之一。常见不良的丈夫多有很好的妻子；其原因也许是因为这种丈夫的好处在偶尔出现的时候更显得可贵，也许是因为做妻子的以自己的耐心自豪。但是这一点是永远不错的，就是这些不良的丈夫必须是做妻子的不顾亲友之可否而自己选择的，因为如此她们就一定非补救自己的失策不可也。

- 译文2：论婚姻（何新 译）

成了家的人,可以说对于命运之神付出了抵押品。因为家庭难免拖累于事业,使人的许多抱负难以实现。

所以最能为公众献身的人,往往是那种不被家室所累的人。因为只有这种人才能够把他的全部爱情与财产都奉献给唯一情人——公众。而那种有家室的人恐怕只愿把最美好的祝愿保留给自己的后代。

有的人在结婚后仍然愿意继续过独身生活。因为他们不喜欢家庭,把妻子儿女看作经济上的累赘。还有一些富人甚至以无子嗣为自豪。也许他们是担心,有了子女就会瓜分现有的财产吧。

有一种人过独身生活是为了保持自由,以避免受约束于对家庭承担的义务和责任。但这种人可能会认为腰带和鞋带也难免是一种束缚呢!

实际上,独身者也许可以成为最好的朋友、最好的主人、最好的仆人,但很难成为最好的公民。因为他们随时可以逃走,所以差不多一切流窜犯都是无家者。

作为献身宗教的僧侣,是有理由保持独身的。否则他们的慈悲就将先布施于家人而不是供奉于上帝了。作为法官与律师,是否独身关系并不大。因为只要他们身边有一个坏的幕僚,其进谗言的能力就足以抵上五个妻子。作为军人,有家室则是好事,家庭的荣誉可以激发他们的责任感和勇气。这一点可以从土耳其的事例中得到反证——那里的风俗不重视婚姻和家庭,结果他们士兵的斗志很差。

对家庭的责任心不仅是对人类的一种约束,也是一种训练。那种独身的人,虽然他们乐善好施,但实际上往往是心肠很硬的,因为他们不懂得怎样去爱他人。

一种好的风俗能教化出情感坚贞严肃的男子汉,如像优里西期(Ulysses)那样,他曾抵制美丽女神的诱惑,而保持了对妻子的忠贞。

一个独身的女人常常是骄横的。因为她需要显示,她的贞节似乎是自愿保持的。

如果一个女人为丈夫的聪明优秀而自豪,那么这是使她忠贞不渝的最好保证。但如果一个女人发现她的丈夫是妒忌多疑的,那么她将绝不会认为他是聪明的。

在人生中,妻子是青年时代的情人、中年时代的伴侣、暮年时代的守护。所以在人的一生中,只要有合适的对象,任何时候结婚都是有道理的。

但也有一位古代哲人,对于人应当在何时结婚这个问题是这样说的:"年纪少时还不应当,年纪大时已不必要。"

美满的婚姻是难得一遇的。常可见到许多不出色的丈夫却有一位美丽的妻子。这莫非是因为这种丈夫由于具有不多的优点,反而更值得被珍视吗? 也许因为伴随这种丈夫,将可以考验一个妇人的忍耐力吧? 如果这种婚姻出自一个女人的自愿选择,甚至是不顾亲友的劝告而选择的,那么就让她自己去品尝这枚果实的滋味吧。

4. A Visit with the Folks

The Original

Periodically I go back to a churchyard cemetery on the side of an Appalachian hill in northern Virginia to call on family elders. It slows the juice down something marvelous.

They are all situated right behind an imposing brick church with a tall square brick belltower best described as honest but not flossy. Some of the family elders did construction repair work on that church and some of them, the real old timers, may even have helped build it, but I couldn't swear to that because it's been there a long, long time.

The view, especially in early summer, is so pleasing that it's a pity they can't enjoy it. Wild roses blooming on fieldstone fences, fields white with daisies, that soft languorous air turning the mountains pastel blue out toward the West.

The tombstones are not much to look at. Tombstones are never in my book, but they do help in keeping track of the family and, unlike a family, they have the virtue of never chafing at you.

This is not to say they don't talk after a fashion. Every time I pass Uncle Lewis's I can hear it say, "Come around to the barber shop, boy, and I'll cut that hair." Uncle Lewis was a barber. He left up here for a while and went to the city, Baltimore. But he came back after the end. Almost all of them came back finally, those that left, but most stayed right here all along.

Well, not right here in the churchyard, but out there over the field, two, three, four miles away. Grandmother was born just over that rolling field out there near the woods the year the Civil War ended, lived most of her life about three miles out the other way there near the mountain, and has been right here near this old shade tree for the past 50 years.

We weren't people who went very far. Uncle Harry, her second child, is right beside her. A carpenter. He lived 87 years in these parts without ever complaining about not seeing Paris. To get Uncle Harry to say anything, you have to ask for directions.

"Which way is the schoolhouse?" I asked, though not aloud of course.

"Up the road that way right good piece," he replies, still the master of indefinite navigation whom I remember from my boyhood.

It's good to call on Uncle Lewis, grandmother and Uncle Harry like this. It improves your perspective to commune with people who are not alarmed about the condition of NATO or whining about the flabbiness of the dollar.

The elders take the long view. Of course, you don't want to indulge too extensively in that long view, but it's useful to absorb it in short doses. It corrects the blood pressure and puts things in more sensible light.

第九章 英汉互译原理应用比较

After a healthy dose of it, you realize that having your shins kicked in the subway is not the gravest insult to dignity ever suffered by common humanity.

Somewhere in the vicinity is my great-grandfather who used to live back there against the mountain and make guns, but could never find him. He was born out that way in 1871—James Monroe was President then—and I'd like to find him to commune a bit with somebody of blood kin who was around when Andrew Jackson was in his heyday.

After Jackson and Abraham Lincoln and the Civil War, he would probably not be very impressed about much that goes on nowadays, and I would like to get a few resonances off his tombstone, a cool frisson of content maybe for a great-grandchild who had missed all the really perilous times.

Unfortunately, I am never able to find him, but there is Uncle Irvey, grandmother' oldest boy. An unabashed Hoover Republican. "Eat all those string beans, boy," I hear as I nod at his tombstone.

And here is surprise, Uncle Edgar. He has been here for years, but I have never bumped into him before. I don't dare disturb him, for he is an important man, the manager of the baseball team, and his two pitchers. My Uncle Harold and my Cousin-in-law Howard, have both been shelled on the mound and Uncle Edgar has to decide whether to ask the shortstop if he knows anything about pitching.

My great-grandfather who made guns is again not to be found, but on the way out I pass the tombstone of another great-grandfather whose distinction was that he left an estate of $3.87. It is the first time I have passed this way since I learned of this, and I smile his way, but something says, "In the long run, boy, we all end up as rich as Rockefeller," and I get into the car and drive out onto the main road, gliding through fields white with daisies, past fences perfumed with roses, and am rather more content with the world.

《故亲访记》(《探访故亲》)译文比读

- **译文1：故亲访记**

每隔一段时间,我都要回北弗吉尼亚一趟,回到阿巴拉契亚山一座小山丘的山坡上,在那儿的教堂公墓里参拜家族中的先辈。这样做可以让人的肝火盛气大大消减。

各位父老的坟墓就在一座引人注目的砖砌教堂后面,教堂的钟塔方方正正,高高耸立,完全可以说是朴实无华。家里先辈中曾有人对这座教堂做过修缮,那些活得更久远的老一辈人甚至还在创建教堂时出过一把力,可这我不敢打包票,因为那是很久很久以前的事情了。

此处的景色,初夏时节尤其宜人,各位父老自己不能领略实在可惜。散石砌成的地界上野玫瑰繁花盛开,田野里是白茫茫的一片雏菊花,那种柔情倦意的气氛直把山中的碧蓝色延展到西天。

先辈的墓碑看上去倒不起眼。我读书从来没有读到过写墓碑的事,可是这墓碑的确可以帮你了解家族的情况,而且它们又和家里人不一样,不训斥人。

说它们不训斥人并不是说它们就怎么也不说话。每次路过路易斯大叔的坟前,我都听到墓碑在说:"小伙子,到理发店来,我把你那长发剪掉。"路易斯大叔是理发的,曾有一段时间离乡进城,去了巴尔的摩,但最后还是回来了。他们最后都回来了,只要出去都要回来,而绝大多数人就只待在这个地方过了一辈子。

当然,他们并不是就待在这儿的教堂庭院里,而是在田那边两三里、三四里以外的地方。我奶奶就是在内战打完的那一年在这一大片田那边的树林旁出生的。她一辈子基本上就生活在那边三里开外的山跟前,现在就埋在这儿靠近这株大树的地方,已经有 50 年了。

我们这儿的人都不出远门。我叔叔哈里是奶奶的二儿子,现在就埋在她身边。他生前干木匠,活了 87 岁,一直在这一带,一辈子都没有因为没逛过巴黎发过一句牢骚。要让哈里叔叔开口说什么话,你就得向他问路。

"到学堂怎么走?"我问他,不过声音当然压得低低的。

"就沿这条路往那边,还有一大截儿呢,"他回答道,依旧像是我小时候记忆中引航天涯的老手。

能这样参拜路易斯大叔、奶奶和哈里叔叔,我感觉很不错。跟这些不为北约目前的境况提心吊胆,不因美元贬值而哀叫呜咽的人们交流思想,这能叫人看事情的眼光更加合理、敏锐。

老一辈看事情从远处着眼。当然,你并不想方方面面、时时处处都看得那么远,可是稍微吸取一点他们的经验也是有用的。这能让你保持血压正常,把事理看得更明白些。

吸取一点他们有益的经验以后,你就会发现,有人在地铁中朝你腿上踢了一脚,这对一般人的尊严算不上最大的污辱。

附近不知什么地方埋着我的曾祖父。他过去就生活在后面的山脚下,专门制造枪支,可是我就是找不到他的坟。1817 年他就在公墓外那边出生——当时总统是詹姆斯·门罗——我想找到曾祖父的坟墓,想和这位在安德鲁·杰克逊名噪一时的年代目睹了那段历史的血亲父老倾心交谈。

杰克逊、林肯以及内战时代过后,曾祖父也许对我们这时代发生的很多事情都不太有什么印象了,不过我想从他的墓碑上听到历史的回声,也许墓碑会微微战抖,对我这个曾孙表示轻视,因为真正充满危险的年代我一个也没有经历过。

很不幸,我始终没有找到他的墓碑,却看到了艾维大伯的坟。艾维大伯是奶奶的大儿子,是个彻头彻尾的共和党人。"孩子,把这些豇豆都吃掉,"我听墓碑说着,对着它直点头。

还有一个让我感到意外的发现:埃德加叔叔的名字。他已经埋在这里多年了,可是我以前从来没有碰到过他的墓碑。我不敢打扰他,因为他这个人举足轻重,是棒球队的总管。他的两个投球手——哈罗德叔叔和表兄霍华德两人都丢了很多分,所以爱德加叔叔不得不考虑是否需要问问,做游击手的叔叔懂不懂投球的规矩。

第九章 英汉互译原理应用比较

我那位造枪的曾祖父这次还是找不到。不过,走出公墓的时候我碰上了另一位曾祖的墓碑。这位曾祖与众不同之处就是他去世时身边只留下了三块八毛七分钱的家产。自从我了解了这件事以后,这是第一次从他坟前经过。我对他的生活方式感到好笑,可是却听到有什么东西在说,"孩子,说到底,我们最后都和洛克菲勒一样富有。"

我钻进汽车,开出公墓上了大路,在白茫茫的雏菊田间平缓地行驶,经过玫瑰飘香的一道道田界,心里更觉得与世无争。

● 译文2:探访故亲

弗吉尼亚北部阿巴拉契亚山脉的一个小山坡上,有一处教堂墓地。每隔一段日子,我都要回到那里探望家族里的先辈们。这种探访有一种奇妙的力量,能让人的心境归于平静。先辈们的墓地全都在一座庄严醒目的砖石教堂后面。高高耸立的方形钟楼也是砖石结构的,说它"朴实而不粗糙"是再合适不过了。家族先辈中有些参与过教堂的修缮工作,另一些人,那些真正的老祖宗们,或许还为教堂的建造出过力,但对此我可没有绝对的把握,因为教堂建在那里毕竟已经很久很久了。那儿的景色非常怡人,尤其是在初夏时节。石栅篱上的野蔷薇竞相开放,田野被雏菊染成一片白色,微醺的和风给群山抹上淡淡的蓝色,一直向西边延伸而去。先辈们无法欣赏这些美景,真是一桩憾事。那些墓碑倒是没什么好看的。在我看来,墓碑从来就没什么好看的。但它们确实有助于寻根问祖,而绝不会像现在的家人,总跟你唠叨个没完。但这并不是说他们总是"一声不吭"。每次走过刘易斯大叔的墓前,我都能听见这样的话,"回头到理发店来,孩子,我给你剪剪头。"刘易斯大叔是个理发的。有一段时间他曾离开家乡,到大都市巴尔的摩谋生,但最后还是回来了,几乎所有的人,我是说那些离开过的人们,最终都回来了,但大多数人一辈子都待在这里。对了,"这里"当然不是指这片墓地,而是乡间那边,离墓地二三英里或三四英里的地方。内战结束那年,祖母就出生在树林子附近那片起伏不平的地头。她大半辈子都在离林子大约三英里的大山边度过,如今安躺在这棵绿荫如盖的老树下也有五十年了。先辈们都不大出远门。就拿哈里大伯来说吧,他是祖母的二儿子,就葬在她的墓旁。他是个木匠,一辈子87年都在这一带度过,从未抱怨过自己没去过巴黎,见识见识外面的世界。要想让哈里大伯开口说点什么,你得向他问路才行。"去学堂走哪条路呀?"我问道,当然声音不大。"沿那条道一直走就行,还得走好一阵子呢,"他回答说。在我儿时的记忆中,他一直就是这个样子,总是那副好给别人指路却又指不清路的含糊口气。像这样探访刘易斯大叔、祖母和哈里大伯,感觉真好。他们既不会因为北约现状而忧心忡忡,又不会因为美元疲软而牢骚满腹,同这样的人倾心交谈能使你更加明察事理。先辈们大都看得开、想得远。当然,你并不想沉迷于用太长远的目光去看问题,但偶尔合理地用上一次大有裨益,这样可以使你心平气和,更加理智地看待各种事物。学会适当地把目光放开一点之后,你就会明白,在地铁里被人踹了一脚并不算是普通人所受的什么奇耻大辱。就在这附近哪个地方埋着我的一个曾祖父。生前他依山而居,还造过枪,但我一直没能找到他的墓。1817年他就出生在那里——当时的总统是詹姆斯·门罗——我极想找到他,好跟这位亲眼看见了安德鲁·杰克逊鼎盛时期的亲人好好聊上几句。这位曾祖父生活在杰克逊、亚伯拉罕·林肯当政时期,又经历了内战,对时下发生的事儿可能不会有太大的感触。但我仍想从墓碑中听他讲上几句,哪怕他会对我这个没经历过真正危难时世的曾孙表示出冷漠和不屑,会令我不寒而栗。遗憾的是,我始终没能找到他的墓,却碰到了祖母大儿子欧维大伯的墓。他是个铁杆胡佛派共和党人。"孩子,把那些菜豆全吃了。"我朝他的墓碑点头时,听见他这么说。这可是个意外的发现:埃德加大叔的墓。他埋在这里已有好些年了,可今天还是我第一次看见他的墓。我没敢惊动他,因为他是个大人物,棒球队经理。记得有一次,他的两个投手——我的哈罗德大叔和霍华德表姐夫,在投球区被对方连连安打得分,他只得决定去找游击手,问他有没有信心上场充当投手去投球。造枪的曾祖父的墓还是没找到,但离开墓地的时候我却发现了另一个曾祖父的墓。他的与众不同之处就是只留下了3.87美元的遗产。这是我听说这桩事后第一次从这儿经过。我笑他的寒酸,却听见有个声音在说,"从长远看,孩子,到最后我们都会跟洛克菲勒一样有钱的。"于是我钻进汽车,穿过被雏菊染白了的田野,经过蔷薇飘香的石栅篱,把车开到大路上。此刻,我对这个世界又多了几许满足。

5. 白蛇传

原文

脍炙人口的传统京剧《白蛇传》讲的是传自明朝的故事,白蛇精与青蛇精化作美女来到人间,白蛇精与一位书生相爱并生一子。禅师法海认为他们的结合违反传统婚姻,伤风败俗,他气急败坏,于是他派神兵神将前来捉拿白蛇精,并将她镇压在一座塔下面。后来,青蛇精在深山中修炼,习武多年,终于砸烂了那座塔,救出白蛇精。至此,白蛇精与丈夫、儿子又得团聚。在《白蛇传》剧中,蛇被赋予了崇高的人性。

The Legend of the White Snake(*The Legend of the White Snake Spirit*)译文比读

- **译文1**:*The Legend of the White Snake*

The Legend of the White Snake, one of the most popular traditional Beijing operas, is based on a story handed down from the Ming Dynasty (1368 – 1644). White Snake Spirit and Green Snake Spirit metamorphosed themselves into two beautiful girls and ventured into the human world. White Snake fell in love with a yong scholar and gave birth to a son. Fahai, a Budhist monk, regarded their union as a violation of the conventions regarding marriage and an example of moral degenation. Much enraged, he sent officers and soldiers from the heaven, who captured White Snake, and using magical powers he himself incarcerated her underneath a pagoda. For many years afterwards, Green Snake hid herself in deep mountains and gave herself rigorous spiritual and martial arts training. In the end she succeded in troppling the pagoda and rescued her mistress. Now White Snake was reunited with her husband and son.

The snake in the opera is endowed with the noble character of human nature.

- 译文 2：*The Legend of the White Snake Spirit*

The Legend of the White Snake Spirit, a very popular traditional Beijing opera, is the representation of a tale that has come down from the Ming Dynasty. The White Snake Spirit and the Green Snake Spirit came to the human world in the form of two beauties. Then the White Snake Spirit fell in love with a young scholar and born him a child. However, their union in love was considered by Fahai, the Zen Master a shameful act against the convention and customs of marriage. In fact, Fahai became wild at it and sent his all powerful soldiers of different ranks to capture the White Snake Spirit. Then he had her imprisoned under a pagoda. In time, and after years of self-preparation through martial exercises in the depth of the mountains, the Green Snake Spirit became strong enough to destroy the pagoda and rescue her sister. Eventually, the White Snake Spirit was able to reunite with her husband and child. In this story, the snake's character has been highly humanized.

6. 可爱的南京

原文

南京,她有层出不穷的风流人物和彪炳千秋的不朽业绩。大都会特有的凝聚力,吸引了无数风云人物、仁人志士在这里角逐争雄,一逞豪彦。从孙权、谢安到洪秀全、孙中山,从祖冲之、葛洪到李时珍、郑和,从刘勰、萧统到曹雪芹、吴敬梓,从王羲之、顾恺之到徐悲鸿、傅抱石,还有陶行知、杨廷宝等,中国历史上一批杰出的政治家、军事家、科学家、文学家、艺术家、教育家、建筑家等荟萃于此,在这块钟灵毓秀的土地上一圆他们的辉煌之梦。他们是中华民族的优秀儿女,巍巍钟山、滚滚长江养育了他们,为他们提供了施展抱负的舞台,他们也以自己的雄才大略、聪明智慧为中华民族的灿烂文明增添了流光溢彩的新篇章。

南京,她自新中国建立以来发生的巨大而深刻的变化更加使人欢欣鼓舞。从1949年4月23日始,人民真正成为这座古老城市的主人。金陵回春,古城新生,昔日饱尝的屈辱和灾难,至此如同梦魇终被摆脱。人民在自己的土地上辛勤劳作,把古老的南京装扮得面貌一新。特别是近十年以来,改革开放又给这座美丽的名城注入了新的活力,崭新的工业、通达的运输、如画的城市建设、兴盛的第三产业、多姿的文化生活,都使这个具有古都特色的现代都市焕发出勃勃英姿。孙中山先生所预言的:"南京将来之发展未可限量也",正在逐步成为现实。

南京,这座古老而年轻的历史文化名城,是多么的可爱!

"Nanjing—the Beloved City"("A Nanjing to Love")译文比读

- 译文 1: Nanjing—the Beloved City

Nanjing has witnessed the continuous emergence of many distinguished talents and noble hearts as well as monumental achievements that shone through the ages. Attracted by her special appeal, a great number of powerful figures and people actuated by high ideals have stayed in or frequented this metropolis to contend for the lead or to give play to their genius and virtues. Military commanders such as Sun Quan and Xie An; political leaders such as Hong Xiuquan and Dr. Sun Yat-sen; scientists like Zu Chongzhi, Ge Hong, Li Shizhen and Zhenghe; men of letters such as Liu Xie, Xiao Tong, Cao Xueqin and Wu Jingzi; artists like Wang Xizhi, Gu Kaizhi, Xu Beihong and Fu Baoshi; educators such as Tao Xingzhi; and architects like Yang Tingbao—all these renowned historical figures used to settle on this blessed land to have their splendid dreams fulfilled. The towering Purple Mountains and the billowing Yangtze River nurtured them and provided them with arenas in which to realize their aspirations. By virtue of their genius, vision, and sagacity, these best and brightest sons and daughters of the nation made spectacular contributions to the resplendent Chinese civilization.

The tremendous changes that have taken place in Nanjing since New China was founded are even more inspiring. On April 23, 1949, the people virtually took the place of the master of this ancient city. Balmy spring winds returned to bring new life to this historic city, of which the common people came to be the genuine masters. The night marish sufferings and humiliations of the past were left behind once and for all. The citizens of Nanjing have been working hard to give this age-old town a new appearance. Especially for the past ten years or more, the country's reform and opening-up policy has infused new vigor into this beautiful and famous city. Newly built industries, an efficient transportation network extending in all directions, picturesque urban construction, a booming tertiary industry, a varied and colorful cultural life, all these and more added charm and vitality to this modern metropolis, which retains somehow the ambiance and features of an ancient capital. The prophecy of Dr. Sun Yat-sen father of modern China that "Nanjing will have a future that knows no bounds" is becoming true.

Nanjing, an old city with a rich and celebrated past, yet vigorous in her new youth—how lovely she is!

- 译文2: **A Nanjing to Love**

Nanjing, a beautiful city with an endless succession of romantic elite and forever celebrated for her enduring achievements, has a special appeal exclusively possessed by the metropolis, an appeal that has gathered here for a hectic life of competition numerous personages of over-powering influence and great expectations. Here the history of China has seen the galaxy of outstanding figures in all fields of life, such as Hong Xiuquan and Sun Yat-sen in government, Sun Quan and Xie An in military affairs, Zu Chongzhi, Ge Hong, Li Shizhen and Zheng He in science, Liu Xie, Xiao Tong, Cao Xueqin and Wu Jingzi in literature, Wang Xizhi, Gu Kaizhi, Xu Beihong and Fu Baoshi in arts, Tao Xingzhi in education, and Yang Tingbao in architecture. Here on this inspiring land they came for the realization of their splendid dreams, dreams of the excellent children of the Chinese nation. Here the towering Mount Bell and the torrential Yangtze River nurtured them and provided them with the arena to make good their ambitions, and in return for this, they also used their great talent, strategy, and intelligence to contribute to the brilliant culture of the Chinese nation a new page overwhelming with bright colors.

Nanjing, an even greater encouragement for her enormous and profound changes that have taken place since the founding of the New Republic. On April 23,1949, the people virtually took the place of the master of this ancient city. Then, spring came back to revive this ancient town of Jinling, and the disgraceful infamy and sufferings, like a nightmare, was eventually shaken off. Here on their own land, the people worked diligently to dress up this historic city. Of special remark are the changes of the recent ten odd years, in which the policy of reform and opening to the outside world have filled the fair city with fresh vitality: entirely new industries, express transport, picturesque townscaping, upstarting service trade, colorful cultural lifestyle, all contribute to giving a sprightly stance to this modern metropolis with its features of an ancient capital. What Dr. Sun Yat-sen once predicted of it is being gradually realized: " Nanjing will have a future of florescence that is not yet to be told."

Nanjing, ancient and yet young as a historically and culturally renowned city, is right here to love!

7. Speech by Former British Prime Minister Edward Heath at Welcoming Banquet (25 May, 1974)

The Original

Respected Mr. Vice-Premier,

My Distinguished Chinese Hosts and Friends,

It is a great pleasure to be here in Peking and to have this occasion for thanking the government and the people of China for all the kindness and hospitality which they have shown me.

It was a keen disappointment when I had to postpone the visit which I had intended to pay to China in January.

I was all the more delighted when, as a result of the initiative of your government, it proved possible to reinstate the visit so quickly.

This visit gives me the opportunity which I have long sought, to see for myself the achievements of the Chinese people.

I have of course read of these achievements and many visitors to your country have told me about them—in particular Sir Alec Douglas-Home who came here as British Foreign Secretary in 1972, and before him, Sir Anthony Royle.

I also welcomed the opportunity of discussions with Ji Pengfei, Foreign Minister, when we welcomed him on his visit to London in June 1973.

There has been no doubt in my mind of the progress which you have achieved.

Now I shall be able to see it for myself and I know that this will be a most rewarding experience.

We in Britain have a social and political system which differs in many respects from your own.

It is the result of different experiences and a different tradition.

This system of ours does not always produce results of which we all approve.

People sometimes grumble at it and criticize it.

But it is a political system deeply rooted in the instincts of the British people.

We do not aim to impose our own ideas on other people.

We believe that it is right and necessary that people with different political and social systems should live side by side—not just in a passive way but as active friends.

British was among the first countries to recognize the People's Republic of China.

More recently, I was very glad that while I was Prime Minister we were able to make such marked progress towards better relations between our two countries.

I am thinking of the establishment of full diplomatic relations—and here I would pay a tribute to the work of our two Ambassadors, Mr. Sung Chih-huang in London and Sir John Addis here in Peking.

At the same time there has been a notable expansion of trade and of cultural exchanges.

I remember with great pleasure opening the remarkable exhibition of Chinese treasures in London, which more than a million people visited.

I also, like many others, my fellow countrymen, enjoyed the highly successful visit to Britain of the Shanghai acrobats.

Today I welcome the opportunity of exchanging views with the leaders of the Chinese Government about the world scene. I had the great honour this morning of a long talk with Chairman Mao Tsetung. Then, this afternoon, you and I, Mr. Vice-Premier, had a most fruitful discussion.

My own views on the place of Britain in the modern world are well-known.

The government which I led successfully negotiated British entry into the European Community.

I believe strongly that it is in the interests of my countrymen that Britain should remain an active and energetic member of the European Community.

Only in this way can we protect our own interests in an uncertain and changing world.

Only in this way can we play a part worthy of our past in working for peace among the nations and a more assured prosperity for all our peoples.

I believe equally that it is in the interests of the world as a whole that Europe should increasingly unite and speak with a common voice.

英国前首相爱德华·希思在欢迎宴会上的讲话(1974年5月25日)译文比读

- **译文 1**

尊敬的副总理先生：

尊贵的中国主人和朋友们：

我感到十分愉快，能够来到北京，并且有此机会向中国政府和中国人民表示感谢，感谢他们给予我的盛情款待。

我本来打算在今年1月访问中国，后来不得不推迟，这曾使我深感失望。

由于贵国政府的提议，这次访问才得以这样快地重新实现，这使我感到格外高兴。

这次访问使我有机会亲眼看一看中国人民所取得的成就，这是我长期向往的。

当然，我曾经读过关于这些成就的材料；许多访问过贵国的人，特别是1972年以英国外交大臣身份来华访问的亚历克·道格拉斯-霍姆爵士以及在他之前的安东尼·罗伊尔爵士也向我介绍过这些成就。

1973年6月，我们欢迎姬鹏飞外长访问伦敦的时候，我也很高兴能有机会同他进行会谈。

你们已经取得了进步，对此我毫不怀疑。

现在我将亲眼看到这些进步，而且我知道这是一次非常有益的经历。

我们英国的社会政治制度在许多方面都与你们的不同。这是不同经历和传统造成的。

我们这个制度所产生的结果并不都是我们大家所赞成的。

人们有时抱怨它、批评它。

但是这种政治制度已经在英国人民中深深扎根，成为他们的一种本能。

我们并不打算把自己的思想强加于人。

我们认为生活在不同政治和社会制度下的人民应该共处，不仅仅是消极地共处，而是积极地友好相处，这是正确的而且是必要的。

英国是最早承认中华人民共和国的国家之一。

后来在我任首相期间我们能够在改善两国关系方面取得如此显著的进展，我感到十分高兴。

我指的是建立完全的外交关系，我愿再次对我们的两位大使——驻伦敦的宋之光先生和驻北京的约翰·艾惕思爵士——所做的工作表示敬意。

与此同时，贸易和文化交往也有了显著的发展。

我极其愉快地回想起在伦敦为出色的中国文物展览会揭幕的情景，参观这个展览会的人数超过一百万。

像我的许多同胞一样，我也欣赏了上海杂技团在英国的十分成功的访问演出。

今天我很高兴能有机会同中国政府领导人就世界形势交换看法。今天上午，我极为荣幸地同毛泽东主席进行了长谈。今天下午，我又同你，副总理先生，进行了十分富有成果的会谈。

我本人对英国在现代世界上的地位的看法是众所周知的。

我所领导的政府通过成功的谈判使英国加入了欧洲共同体。

我强烈地认为,英国应该继续是欧洲共同体中一个积极的和充满活力的成员,这是符合我国人民利益的。

只有这样,我们才能在变化不定的世界中保护自己的利益。

我同样认为,欧洲应该加强团结,用一个共同的声音说话,这是符合世界利益的。

- 译文 2

尊敬的副总理先生:

尊贵的中国主人和朋友们:

我十分高兴能来到北京并有此机会感谢中国政府和中国人民给予我的盛情款待。

我曾深感失望地被迫推迟了原定于 1 月的访华计划。

使我感到格外高兴的是,由于贵国政府的提议,这次访问又能这样快地重新实现。

这次访问给了我寻求已久的机会,即亲眼看一看中国人民所取得的成就。

当然,我曾经读过关于这些成就的材料;许多访问过贵国的人也向我介绍过。其中特别值得一提的是 1972 年以英国外交大臣身份来华访问的亚历克·道格拉斯-霍姆爵士以及在他之前的安东尼·罗伊尔爵士。

我也很高兴曾有机会与姬鹏飞外长进行过会谈,那是 1973 年 6 月我们欢迎他访问伦敦的时候。

对你们已经取得的进步,我毫不怀疑。

现在我将亲眼看到这些进步了,我知道这种体验将对我非常有益。

我们英国的社会政治制度在许多方面都与你们的有所不同。这是因为我们有不同的经历和传统。

我们这个制度所产生的结果并非我们所有人都赞成。

有时人们会抱怨、批评它。

但是这种政治制度已经深深扎根于英国人民之中,已成为他们的本能。

我们并不打算把自己的思想强加于人。

我们认为有不同政治和社会制度的人民应该而且有必要肩并肩地生活,不是消极地生活,而是积极地友好相处。

英国是一个最早承认中华人民共和国的国家之一。

在更近些时候,让我感到十分高兴的是,在我任首相期间我们能够在改善两国关系方面取得如此显著的进展。

我是说我们建立了全面的外交关系——所以我愿在此对我们的两位大使所做的工作表示敬意。他们是驻伦敦的宋之光先生和驻北京的约翰·艾惕思爵士。

在此期间,两国贸易和文化交往也有显著发展。

我可以愉快地回想起曾在伦敦为重大的中国文物展览会揭幕,有一百万以上的人参观了这个展览会。

我像我的许多同胞一样,还欣赏了上海杂技团在英国的十分成功的访问演出。

我很高兴今天能有机会同中国政府领导人就世界形势交换看法。今天上午,我极为荣幸地同毛泽东主席进行了长谈,下午又同你——副总理先生——进行了十分富有成果的会谈。

我本人对英国在现代世界上的地位的看法是众所周知的。

我所领导的政府经过成功的谈判使英国加入了欧洲共同体。

我坚信,英国应该继续作为欧洲共同体中一个积极而且充满活力的成员,这符合我国人民的利益。

只有这样,我们才能在风云莫测、变化不定的世界保护自己的利益。

我同样认为,欧洲应该加强团结,用一个共同的声音说话,这有利于整个世界。

8. Speech by President Nixon of the United States at the Welcoming Banquet (21 February 1972)

The Original

Mr. Prime Minister and all of your distinguished guests this evening,

On behalf of all of your American guests, I wish to thank you for the incomparable hospitality for which the Chinese people are justly famous throughout the world. I particularly want to pay tribute, not only to those who have prepared the magnificent dinner, but also to those who have provided the splendid music. Never have I heard American music played better in a foreign land.

Mr. Prime Minister, I wish to thank you for your very gracious and eloquent remarks. At this very moment through the wonder of telecommunications, more people are seeing and hearing what we say than any other such occasion in the whole history of the world. Yet, what we say here will not be long remembered. What we do here can change the world.

As you said in your toast, the Chinese people are a great people, the American people are a great people. If our two people are enemies, the future of this world we share together is dark indeed. But if we can find common ground to work together, the chance for world peace is immeasurably increased.

In the spirit of frankness which I hope will characterize our talks this week, let us recognize at the outset these points: we have at times in the past been enemies. We have great differences today. What brings us together is that we have common interest which transcends those differences. As we discuss our differences, neither of us will compromise our principles. But while we cannot close the gulf between us, we can try to bridge it so that we may be able to talk across it.

So, let us, in these next five days, start a long march together, not in lockstep, but on different roads leading to the same goal, the goal of building a world structure of peace and justice in which all may stand together with equal dignity and in which each nation, large or small, has a right to determine its own form of government, free of outside interference or domination. The world watches. The world listens. The world waits to see what we will do. What is the world? In a personal sense, I think of my eldest daughter whose birthday is today. As I think of her, I think of all the children in the world, in Asia, in Africa, in Europe, in the Americas, most of whom were born since the date of the foundation of the People's Republic of China.

What legacy shall we leave our children? Are they destined to die for the hatreds which have plagued the old world, or are they destined to live because we had the vision to build a new world?

There is no reason for us to be enemies. Neither of us seeks the territory of the other; neither of us seeks domination over the other, neither of us seeks to stretch out our hands and rule the world.

Chairman Mao has written, "So many deeds cry out to be done, and always urgently; the world rolls on, time presses. Ten thousand years are too long, seize the day, seize the hour!"

This is the hour. This is the day for our two peoples to rise to the heights of greatness which can build a new and a better world.

In that spirit, I ask all of you present to join me in raising your glasses to Chairman Mao, to Prime Minister Chou, and to the friendship of the Chinese and American people which can lead to friendship and peace for all people in the world.

美国总统尼克松在欢迎宴会上的讲话(1972年2月21日)译文比读

- 译文1

总理先生，今天晚上在座的诸位贵宾：

我谨代表所有美国客人向你们表示感谢，感谢你们的无可比拟的盛情款待。中国人民以这种盛情款待闻名世界。我们不仅要特别赞扬那些准备了这次盛大晚宴的人，而且还要赞扬那些为我们演奏美好音乐的人。我在外国从来没有听到过演奏这么好的美国音乐。

总理先生，我要特别感谢你的非常盛情和雄辩的讲话。此时此刻，通过电讯的奇迹，看到和听到我们讲话的人比在整个世界历史上任何其他这样的场合都要多。不过，我们在这里所讲的话，人们不会长久记住，但我们在这里所做的事能改变世界。

正如你在祝酒时讲的那样，中国人民是伟大的人民，美国人民是伟大的人民。如果我们两国人民互相为敌，那么我们共同居住的这个世界的前途的确很暗淡。但是，如果我们能够找到进行合作的共同点，那么实现世界和平的机会就将无可估量地大大增加。

我希望我们这个星期的会谈将是坦率的。本着这种坦率的精神，让我们一开始就认识到这样几点：过去一些时候我们曾经是敌人。今天我们有巨大的分歧。使我们走到一起的，是我们有超越这些分歧的共同利益。在我们讨论我们的分歧时，我们哪一方都不会在自己的原则上妥协。但是，虽然我们不能弥合双方之间的鸿沟，我们却能够设法搭设一座桥，以便我们能够越过它进行会谈。

因此，让我们在今后的五天里开始一次长征吧，不是在一起迈步，而是在不同的道路上向同一个目标前进。这个目标就是建立一个和平和正义的世界结构，在这个结构中，所有的人都可以在一起享有同等的尊严；每个国家，不论大小，都有权力决定它自己政府的形式，而不受外来的干涉或统治。全世界在注视着。全世界在倾听着。全世界在等待着看我们将做些什么。这个世界是怎样的呢？就我个人来讲，我想到我的大女儿，今天是她的生日。当我想到她的时候，就想到全世界所有的儿童，亚洲、非洲、欧洲以及美洲的儿童，他们大多数都是在中华人民共和国成立以后出生的。

我们将给我们的孩子们留下什么遗产呢？他们的命运是要为那些使旧世界蒙受苦难的仇恨而死亡呢，还是由于我们有缔造一个新世界的远见而活下去呢？

我们没有理由要成为敌人。我们哪一方都不企图取得对方的领土；我们哪一方都不企图统治对方。我们哪一方都不企图伸手去统治世界。

毛主席写过："多少事，从来急；天地转，光阴迫。一万年太久，只争朝夕。"

现在就是只争朝夕的时候，是我们两国人民攀登那种可以缔造一个新的、更美好的世界的伟大境界的高峰的时候了。

本着这种精神，我请求诸位同我一起举杯，为毛主席，为周总理，为能够导致全世界所有人民的友谊与和平的中美人民之间的友谊，干杯。

- 译文2

总理先生，今天晚上在座的诸位贵宾：

我代表所有的美国来宾，衷心感谢你们中国人民这种举世闻名、名不虚传的无比盛情。我想要特别赞扬的，不仅是那些准备了这次盛大晚宴的厨师们，而且还有那些为我们演奏了这美好音乐的乐师们。我还从来没有听到过，美国的音乐在异国他乡演奏得这么动听。

总理先生，我衷心感谢您动情而又雄辩的讲话。此时此刻，通过奇妙的电讯传播工具，还有更多的人正在观看和收听我们的讲话，人数之众超过了整个世界历史上任何其他类似的场合。然而，我们在这里所讲的话，人们不会记得很久。我们在这里所做的却可以改变世界。

正如您在祝酒词中所说的那样，中国人民是伟大的人民，美国人民是伟大的人民。如果我们两国人民彼此为敌，那么我们所共处的这个世界的前途就会暗淡不堪。但是，如果我们能够找到共同点进行合作，那么维持世界和平的可能性就将无可估量地大大增加。

本着坦诚的精神，本着我希望能体现本星期会谈特点的坦诚精神，让我们一开始就认识到这样几点：过去曾经彼此为敌，今天我们仍有重大分歧。我们之所以走到一起，是因为我们所有的共同利益超越了分歧。我们在讨论双方分歧时，哪一方都不会在原则上妥协。但是，我们虽不能弥合双方之间的鸿沟，却能够设法搭设一座桥梁，从而通过这座桥梁进行对话。

因此，让我们在今后的五天里开始一次长征吧，不是齐步迈进，而是在不同的道路上走向同一个目标。这个目标就是建立一个和平、正义的世界格局,从而使世界上所有的人在一起都可以享有同等的尊严;每个国家,不论大小,都有权决定它自己的政治体制,而不受外来的干涉或统治。全世界都在注目观看,全世界都在侧耳倾听,全世界都在等着看我们如何作为。这个世界是谁呢?就我个人来讲,我想到的是今天就过生日的大女儿。想到她的时候,我就会想到全世界所有的孩子,想到亚洲、非洲、欧洲以及美洲的孩子,他们大多数都出生在中华人民共和国成立以后。

我们将给孩子们留下什么遗产?他们的命运将是因瘟疫般传遍旧世界的仇恨而死,还是因为我们有缔造新世界的远见卓识而生?

我们没有理由彼此为敌。我们哪一方都不觊觎对方的领土;我们哪一方都不企图统治对方。我们哪一方都不企图伸手去统治世界。

毛主席写过:"多少事,从来急;天地转,光阴迫。一万年太久,只争朝夕。"

现在正是只争朝夕的时候,现在正是我们两国人民登上宏伟的高峰,从而能够缔造一个新的、更美好的世界的日子。

本着这种精神,我请求诸位同我一起举杯,为毛主席,为周总理,为能使全世界所有人民友好相待、和平相处的中美人民之间的友谊,干杯。

9. 邓小平1992年南方谈话

原文

在这短短的十几年内,我们国家发展得这么快,使人民高兴、世界瞩目,这就足以证明三中全会以来路线、方针、政策的正确性,谁想变也变不了。说过去说过来,就是一句话,坚持这个路线、方针、政策不变。改革开放以来,我们立的章程并不少,而且是全方位的。经济、政治、科技、教育、文化、军事、外交等各个方面都有明确的方针和政策,而且有准确的表述语言。这次十三届八中全会开得好,肯定农村家庭联产承包责任制不变。一变就人心不安,人们就会说中央的政策变了。农村改革初期,安徽出了个"傻子瓜子"问题。

当时许多人不舒服,说他赚了一百万,主张动他。我说不能动,一动人们就会说政策变了,得不偿失。像这一类的问题还有不少,如果处理不当,就很容易动摇我们的方针,影响改革的全局。城乡改革的基本政策,一定要长期保持稳定。当然,随着实践的发展,该完善的完善,该修补的修补,但总的要坚定不移。即使没有新的主意也可以,就是不要变,不要使人们感到政策变了。有了这一条,中国就大有希望。

Speech by Deng Xiaoping During His Visit in Shenzhen in 1992 译文比读

• 译文1 (选自《北京周报》)

In the short span of the past 10-plus years, the rapid development of our country has delighted the people and focused world attention. This fact suffices to prove the correctness of the line, principles and policies adopted since the Third Plenary Session of the 11th CPC Central Committee. Nobody can change this even if he wants to. After all that's been said, one sentence sums it up: stick to this line and these principles and policies. Since the reform and opening policy was carried out, we have formulated quite a few statutes, which are all-inclusive. Clear-cut guidelines and policies have been worked out and expressed in accurate language concerning the economy, politics, science and technology, education, culture and military and foreign affairs. The recent Eighth Plenary Session of the 13th CPC Central Committee was a successful meeting. It affirmed that rural household contract responsibility system with remuneration linked to output should remain unchanged. Any change in that system might cause unease among the people, who would assert that Party Central Committee had altered its policy. In the initial period of the rural reform, there emerged in Anhui Province the issue of the so-called "Idiot's Melon Seeds".

At that time, many people felt uncomfortable with this man who made a profit of 1 million yuan. They called for a struggle against him. I said that he should not be touched, because such a move might cause people to claim that the policy had changed, and the loss would far outweigh the gain. There are many more issues of this kind, and if not properly handled, they could easily shake our policies and affect the overall situation of reform. The basic policies for urban and rural reform must be kept stable for a long time to come. Of course, as the reform is implemented, these policies should be improved or amended wherever necessary. But we should remain unwavering in our general direction. It is all right even if there are no new ideas. The main thing is that we don't change these policies and don't let people feel our policies have altered. Then, there will be great hopes for China.

- 译文2（选自《中国建设》）

In the short span of the last dozen years, the rapid development of our country has delighted the people and attracted world attention. This suffices to prove the correctness of the line, principles and policies adopted since the Third Plenary Session of the 11th CPC Central Committee. No one could change them, even if he wanted to. After all that's been said, I can sum up our position in one sentence: we shall keep to this line and these principles and policies. Since we introduced the reform and the open policy, we have drawn up many rules and regulations covering all fields of endeavor. Clear-cut guidelines and policies concerning economic and political affairs, science and technology, education, culture and military and foreign affairs have been worked out and expressed in precise terms. The recent Eighth Plenary Session of the 13th CPC Central Committee was a success. It declared that the rural household contract responsibility system with remuneration linked to output should remain unchanged. Any change in that system would cause concern among the people, who would say that the Central Committee had altered its policy. In the initial stage of the rural reform, there emerged in Anhui Province the issue of the "Fool's Sunflower Seeds".

Many people felt uncomfortable with this man who had made a profit of 1 million yuan.

They called for action to be taken against him. I said that no action should be taken, because that would make people think we had changed our policies, and the loss would outweigh the gain. There are many problems like this one, and if we don't handle them properly, our policies could easily be undetermined and overall reform affected. The basic policies for urban and rural reform must be kept stable for a long time to come. Of course, as the reform progresses, some of these policies should be improved or amended as necessary. But we should keep firmly to our general direction. It doesn't matter much whether we can come up with new ideas. What matters is that we should not change our policies and should not make people feel that we are changing them. Then, the prospects for China will be excellent.

- 译文 3 （本书编者 译）

Over the short period of the last ten and more years, our country has developed so rapidly, which has delighted our people and attracted the world attention. This is adequate evidence to show that since the Third Plenary Session of the 11th CPC Central Committee, our lines, principles and policies have been correct in nature. Whoever wants to change them will fail. Whatever we may say, it ends up with one sentence: we shall adhere to this line and these principles and policies. Since the beginning of reform and opening-up, we have decided on quite a few rules, and they are all-encompassing. In economy, politics, science and technology, education, culture, military and foreign affairs, and all other aspects, we have already got definite guidelines and policies, which are expressed in exact language. The recent Eighth Plenary Session of the 13th CPC Central Committee was a success, for it affirmed that the rural household contract responsibility system would remain unchanged. Any change in that system would cause anxieties among the people, who would then say that the Central Committee's policies had been changed. During the beginning period of the rural reform, there in Anhui Province popped up the problem of the "Idiot's Crack Seeds".

At that time, many people felt uneasy with that man, saying that he had made one million yuan, and they believe action should be taken against him. I said that no action should be taken, for otherwise people would say that we had changed our policy, and that would not be anything profitable. There are many problems like this, and if not handled properly, they could easily undermine our policies and affect the overall situation of our reform. The guidelines in our policy for urban and rural reform must be kept stable for a long time to come. Of course, as the actual reform is carried on, necessary improvement and amending is natural. But the general policy must be kept steady. It's all right even if there are no new ideas. With this guaranteed, China will certainly have a promising future.

三、诗 歌

（一）英诗中译

1. The Solitary Reaper（William Wordsworth）

Behold her, single in the field,
Yon solitary Highland Lass!
Reaping and singing by herself;
Stop here, or gently pass!
Alone she cuts and binds the grain
And sings a melancholy strain;
O listen! For the vale profound
Is overflowing with the sound.

No nightingale did ever chant
More welcome notes to weary bands
Of travelers in some shady haunt,
Among Arabian sands;
A voice so thrilling ne'er was heard
In spring-time from the Cuckoo-bird,
Breaking the silence of the seas
Among the farthest Hebrides.

Will no one tell me what she sings?
Perhaps the plaintive numbers flow
For old, unhappy, far-off things,
And battles long ago:
Or is it some more humble lay,
Familiar matter of to-day?
Some natural sorrow, loss, or pain,
That has been, and may be again?

Whate'er the theme, the maiden sang
As if her song could have no ending;
I saw her singing at her work,
And o'er the sickle bending;

I listen'd, motionless and still;
And, as I mounted up the hill
The music in my heart I bore,
Long after it was heard no more.

《割麦女》(《孤独的收割人》)译文比读

- **译文1：割麦女（郭沫若 译）**

你看她,一个人在地上,
那个孤独的山地姑娘!
独自割麦,独自在唱歌;
停在这儿,或者轻轻走过!
她一个人割着捆着麦子,
唱着一个凄凉的调子;
哦听吧!这山谷深深,
弥漫着她的歌声。
夜鸣莺在阿剌伯的沙漠里面,
在幻洲的某些树荫,
为疲倦的商旅所欢迎,
从没有唱得这样好听;
春天时分杜鹃鸟鸣
在极远的希伯里德司群岛
叫破了海洋的沉静,
从没叫出这样甜的声音。
没有人告诉我她唱的是什么,
或许是古老的不幸的悲歌
歌唱着遥远的事物,
歌唱着古代的战祸;
或许是流传民间的歌谣
歌唱着今天的口碑传说?
是一些难免的悲哀、死亡或苦痛,
以前有过,将来也会遇着。
不问内容如何,那姑娘在唱,
她的歌好像总唱不完,
我看一面唱一面工作,
弯着腰伏在镰刀上面;
我立着静静地倾听;

待我已经登上了丘陵,
歌声早已不再听闻,
幽韵却总缭绕着我的心。

- **译文 2：割麦女（卞之琳 译）**

看她,在田里独自一个,
那个苏格兰高原的少女!
独自在收割,独自在唱歌;
停住吧,或者悄悄走过去!
她独自割麦,又把它捆好,
唱着一只忧郁的曲调;
听啊! 整个深邃的谷地
都有这一片歌声在洋溢。
从没有夜莺能够唱出
更美的音调来欢迎结队商,
疲倦了,到一个荫凉的去处
就在阿拉伯沙漠的中央;
杜鹃鸟在春天叫得多动人,
也没有这样子荡人心魂,
尽管它惊破了远海的静悄,
响彻了赫伯里底斯群岛。
她唱的是什么,可有谁说得清?
哀怨的曲调里也许在流传
古老、不幸、悠久的事情,
还有长远以前的征战;
或者她唱的并不特殊,
只是今日的家常事故?
那些天然的丧忧、哀痛,
有过的,以后还会有的种种?
不管她唱的是什么题目,
她的歌好像会没完没了;
我看见她边唱边干活,
弯着腰,挥动她的镰刀——
也不动,听了许久;
后来,当我上山的时候,
我把歌声还记在心上,
虽然早已听不见声响。

- 译文3：孤独的收割人（黄杲炘 译）

看哪，那孤独的高地姑娘——
形单影只地在那边田野里！
她独个儿收割，独个儿唱。
停下吧，要么轻轻离去！
她一个人割，一个人捆着！
嘴里还唱着支忧郁的歌子；
听啊！这幽深的山谷里面，
都已被她哀伤歌声充满。
旅行在阿拉伯沙漠中的人，
疲乏地歇息在荫凉的地方；
夜莺的歌虽然受他们欢迎，
却比不上这姑娘的歌唱；
春天里，杜鹃一声声号啼，
在最远的赫布里底岛响起，
打破了岛屿间海上的寂静——
但姑娘的歌声比这激动人心。
谁能告诉我她在唱什么歌曲？
也许这绵绵不绝的哀歌声
唱那早已过去的辛酸往事，
和很久很久以前的战争；
要不，她唱那通俗的小曲——
如今，人们都熟悉的东西？
或者是痛苦、损失和悲哀？——
它们曾发生，还可能重来。
不管这姑娘歌中唱的是什么，
她的歌儿都好像没完没了；
我看着她一边唱一边干着——
她弯着腰，挥动着镰刀；
不动默默听着她唱；
过后，我走上前面的山冈，
虽然耳中已听不见这歌唱，
可那曲调还久久留在心上。

2. My Luve Is like a Red, Red, Rose（Robert Burns）

O, my luve is like a red, red rose,

That's newly sprung in June.
O, my luve is like the melodie,
That's sweetly play'd in tune.
As fair art thou, my bonie lass,
So deep in luve am I,
And I will luve thee still, my dear,
Till a' the seas gang dry.
Till a' the seas gang dry, my dear,
And the rocks melt wi' the sun!
And I will luve thee still, my dear,
While the sands o' life shall run.
And fare thee weel, my only luve!
And fare thee weel, a while!
And I will come again, my luve,
Tho' it were ten thousand mile!

《我的爱人像朵红红的玫瑰》(《红玫瑰》)译文比读

- **译文1：我的爱人像朵红红的玫瑰（王佐良 译）**

呵,我的爱人像朵红红的玫瑰,
六月里迎风徐开；
呵,我的爱人像支甜甜的曲子,
奏得合拍又和谐。
我的好姑娘,多么美丽的人儿!
请看我,多么深挚的爱情!
亲爱的,我永远爱你,
纵使大海干涸水流尽。
纵使大海干涸水流尽,太阳将岩石烧作灰尘,
亲爱的,我永远爱你,
只要我一息尤存。
珍重吧,我唯一的爱人,
珍重吧,让我们暂时离别,但我定要回来,
哪怕千里万里!

- **译文2：红玫瑰（郭沫若 译）**

吾爱吾爱红玫瑰,
六月初开韵晓风；
吾爱吾爱如管弦,

其声悠扬而玲珑；
吾爱吾爱美而殊，
我心 爱你 永不渝，
直到四海海水枯；
直到四海海水枯，
岩石融化变成泥，
只要我还有口气，
我心 爱你 永不渝，
暂时告别我心肝，
请你不要把心耽！
纵使相隔十万里,踏破地皮也要还。

3. Liberty, Love！（Petöfi Sándor）

- 匈牙利语英译文

Liberty, love！
These two I need.
For my love I will sacrifice life,
For liberty I will sacrifice my love.

- 匈牙利语原文

Szabadság, szerelem！
E kettökell nekem.
Szerelmemért föláldozom
Az életet,
Szabadságért föláldozom
Szerelmemet.

《自由爱情》译文比读

- 译文1（殷夫 译）

生命诚可贵
爱情价更高
若为自由故
两者皆可抛

- 译文2（茅盾 译）

我一生最宝贵:恋爱与自由。
为了恋爱的缘故,生命可以舍去;
但为了自由的缘故,我将欢欢喜喜地把恋爱舍去。

- 译文 3（孙用 译）

自由、爱情
我要的就是这两样
为了爱情,我牺牲我的生命
为了自由,我又将爱情牺牲

- 译文 4（周作人 译）

欢乐自由,为百物先
吾以爱故不惜舍身
并乐蠲爱
为自由也

- 译文 5（兴万生 译）

自由与爱情!
我都为之倾心。
为了爱情,
我宁愿牺牲生命,
为了自由,我宁愿牺牲爱情。

（二）中诗英译

1. 枫桥夜泊

月落乌啼霜满天,
江枫渔火对愁眠。
姑苏城外寒山寺,
夜半钟声到客船。

译文比读

- 译文 1（许渊冲 译）

Mooring at Night by Maple Bridge

The moon goes down, crows caw under the frosty sky,
Dimly-lit fishing boats 'neath maples sadly lie.
Beyond the Gusu walls the Temple of Cold Hill
Rings bells which reach my boat, breaking the midnight still.

- 译文 2（许渊冲 译）

Mooring by Maple Bridge at Night

At moonset cry the crows, streaking the frosty sky;

Dimly-lit fishing boats 'neath maples sadly lie.

Beyond the city walls, from Temple of Cold Hill

Bells break the ship-borne roamer's dream and midnight still.

- 译文 3 （文殊 译）

Mooring for the Night at Maple Bridge

The moon is setting, crows caw in the frosty cold air;

Maples and fishing lights—the sight brings melancholy as I lie in bed.

From Hanshan Temple outside the City of Gusu

The sounds of the midnight bell reach a traveller's boat.

- 译文 4 （文殊 译）

Anchored at Night by the Maple Bridge

The moon is setting, rooks disturb the frosty air,

I watch by mapled banks the fishing-torches flare.

Outside the Suzhou wall, from Hanshan Temple's bell,

I hear its sound aboard and feel its midnight spell.

- 译文 5 （Burton Watson 译）

Tying Up for the Night at Maple River Bridge

Moon setting, crows cawing, frost filling the sky,

Through river maples, fishermen's flares confront my uneasy eyes.

Outside Gusu City, Cold Mountain Temple—

Late at night the sound of its bell reaches a traveller's boat.

- 译文 6 （万昌盛 译）

Mooring at Night by Maple Bridge

The raven calls, the moon descends the sky with frost all white,

Near the bank maple, by a lamp I lie awake in sorrow.

And outside Gusu City, from Bleak Hill Temple, flow,

Out to the mooring boat the distant chimes of midnight.

- 译文 7 （卓振英 译）

Mooring at the Maple Bridge for the Night

The moon is set, the crows decrying dark and frosty skies;

The maples vague, the fishing lamps are blinking ere mine eyes.

The ringing bells from Hanshan Temple outside Gusu float

Afar at mid-night to the sad and troubl'd napper's boat.

- 译文 8 （张廷琛 译）

Mooring at Night by Maple Bridge

The setting moon, a cawing crow, the frost filled the sky;

River maples, fishermen's flares, and troubled sleep.

From the Cold Mountain Temple, outside Suzhou,

The tolling of the midnight bell reaches the wanderer's boat.

- 译文 9 （杜争鸣 译）

A Night Mooring by the Maple Bridge

The moon is down, crows cry, and frost fills up the sky;

By bank maples, fishing lights, with sorrow I lie.

Beyond Gusu town from the Temple of Hanshan,

Come at midnight the bell to my boat from strange land.

- 译文 10 （王守义、约翰·诺弗尔 译）

Anchored at Night near Maple Bridge

The old moon is going down

And the crows make a ruckus

The world is covered with frost

There are maples on the riverbank

And the lights of fishing boats

Drift with the current

I fall into a sad sleep

The monastery on Cold Mountain

It is outside the town of Gusu

The sound of its bell

Touches the guest boat at midnight

- 译文 11 （王力伟 译）

Night Mooring near Maple Bridge

The crows caw at moonset while the frost is heavy in the air,

Maples' bough and fishermen's fires trouble my sleep.

From Hanshan Temple outside Suzhou town,

The sound of the midnight bell reaches the boat.

- 译文 12（王大濂 译）

A Night Mooring by Maple Bridge

Moon's down, crows cry and frosts fill all the sky;

By maples and boat lights, I sleepless lie.

Outside Gusu Cold-Hill Temple's in sight;

Its ringing bells reach my boat at mid-night.

- **译文 13 （陆佩弦 译）**

Overnight Mooring at the Maple Bridge

A cawing rook, a drooping moon, a frosty sky,

And fishing lights dart grief into my sleepless eye.

From the Han Shan Shrine outside the walls of Gu-su,

Come midnight tollings to my lone boat moored nearby.

- **译文 14 （Wai-Lim Yip 译）**

Night-Mooring at Maple Bridge)

Moondown: crows caw. Frost, a skyful.

River maples, fishing lamps, sad drowsiness.

Beyond Su-chou City, the Cold Mountain Temple

Rings its midnight bell, reaching this visitor's boat.

- **译文 15 （Gary Snyder 译）**

Maple Bridge Night Mooring

Moon set, a crow caws

    frost fills the sky

River, maple, fishing-fires

    cross my troubled sleep.

Beyond the walls of Soochow

    from Cold Mountain temple

The midnight bell sounds

    reach my boat.

- **译文 16 （张炳星 译）**

Mooring at Night by the Maple Bridge

The moon is setting in the west.

Crows are crying to their best.

The sky is overcast with hoard frost.

On the river of maple,

watching fishing boat's lights

I can hardly close my sad eyes,

While the bell of Hanshan Temple

outside the ancient Gusu gate

at midnight reaches my boat.

- **译文 17 （Witter Bynner 译）**

A Night-Mooring near Maple Bridge

While I watch the moon go down, a crow caws through the frost;

第九章 英汉互译原理应用比较

Under the shadows of maple-trees a fisherman moves with his torch;
And I hear, from beyond Suzhou, from the temple on Cold Mountain,
Ringing for me, here in my boat, the midnight bell.

• 译文 18（Translator Unknown）

Parking My Boat in Maple Bridge at Night

As the moon goes down, a crow calls through the frost
Under Maple Bridge a fisherman's lamp troubles my sleep
And I hear, from beyond Suzhou's walls, from Cold Mountain Temple
Ringing for me, here in my boat, the midnight bell

• 译文 19 （Translator Unknown）

A Night Mooring by Maple Bridge

Moon sets, crows cry and frost fills all the sky;
By maples and boat lights, I sleepless lie.
Outside Suzhou Hanshan Temple is in sight;
Its ringing bells reach my boat at midnight.

• 译文 20 （Translator Unknown）

Mooring at Night by Maple Bridge

The setting moon, a cawing crow, the frost filled sky;
River maples, fisherman's flares, and troubled sleep.
From the Cold Mountain Temple, outside Suzhou;
The tolling of the midnight bell reaches the wanderer's boat.

• 译文 21 （Translator Unknown）

Night Mooring at Maple Bridge

The moon's down, the crows cry and the sky's full of frost
Under the riverside maples, lit by the fishing lamps, my sadness keeps me awake
Beyond the old Suzhou town, the midnight pealing of Han Shan Temple's bell reaches this visitor on his boat

• 译文 22 （张华 译）

A Night Mooring near Maple Bridge

As I watch the moon go down, a crow caws through the frost;
Under the shadows of maple trees a fisherman moves with his torch;
And I hear, from beyond Suzhou, from the temple on Cold Mountain,
Ringing for me, here in my boat, the midnight bell.

• 译文 23 （Translator Unknown）

Mooring at Night by the Maple Bridge

As the moon goes down a raven calls, frost fills the sky.

Riverside maples and a fisherman's fire enter my restless sleep.

Just then beyond the walls of Suzhou, at the Cold Mountain Temple,

The midnight bell rings, and (the sound) reaches my boat.

- 译文 24 （Michael P. Garofalo 译）

Night Mooring at Maple Bridge

The moon's low, a crow caws,

The landscape's laced with frost.

Under the riverside maples,

Lit by fishing lamps,

My sadness keeps me from sleep.

Beyond old Suzhou town,

Down to the traveler's boats,

Han Shan's Temple bell

Rings clear—

Right at midnight.

- 译文 25 （陆志韦 译）

Night Mooring at the Maple Bridge

The moon goes down, a raven cries, frost fills the sky.

River maples, fishing lanterns—facing sadness I lie.

Outside of the Gusu City is the Hanshan Temple.

At midnight a bell rings; it reaches the traveler's boat.

- 译文 26 （Translator Unknown）

Mooring at Night by Maple Bridge

The Crows caw to the falling moon;

The frosty air fills the sky.

The fisher's lights gleam, the maples croon;

With much sorrow I lie.

On the outskirts of Suzhou Town

From Hanshan Temple, hark!

The midnight vesper bells come down,

Wafting to rover's bark.

- 译文 27 （Translator Unknown）

Night Mooring at Maple Bridge

From Han Shan Temple outside the town of Suzhou, the sound of night bell reached as far as my boat

- 译文 28 （刘军平 译）

Mooring by the Maple Bridge at Night

When the moon is down, the raven crows with sky frostbite,

The bank maples and the fishing flares see a sleepless night.

At Hanshan Temple outside Suzhou the bell chimes deep and strong,

Midnight echoes reach the roamer's boat lone and long.

2. 静夜思

床头明月光,疑是地上霜。

举头望明月,低头思故乡。

译文比读

- 译文 1 （徐忠杰 译）

In the Still of the Night

I descry bright moonlight in front of my bed.

I suspect it to be hoary frost on the floor.

I watch the bright moon, as I tilt back my head.

I yearn, while stooping, for my homeland more.

- 译文 2 （许渊冲 译）

A Tranquil Night

Abed, I see a silver light,

I wonder if it's frost aground.

Looking up, I find the moon bright;

Bowing, in homesickness I'm drowned.

- 译文 3 （Witter Bynner 译）

In the Quiet Night

So bright a gleam on the foot of my bed—

Could there have been a frost already?

Lifting my head to look, I found that it was moonlight.

Sinking back again, I thought suddenly of home.

- 译文 4 （Herbert A. Giles 译）

Night Thoughts

I wake, and moonbeams play around my bed,

Glittering like hoar-frost to my wandering eyes;

Up towards the glorious moon I raise my head,

Then lay me down—and thoughts of home arise.

- 译文 5（S. Obata 译）

On a Quiet Night

I saw the moonlight before my couch,

And wondered if it were not the frost on the ground.

I raised my head and looked out on the mountain moon,

I bowed my head and thought of my far-off home.

- 译文 6（W. J. B. Fletcher 译）

The Moon Shines Everywhere

Seeing the Moon before my couch so bright

I thought hoar frost had fallen from the night.

On her clear face I gaze with lifted eyes:

Then hide them full of Youth's sweet memories.

3. 自君之出矣

自君子出矣

不复理残机

思君如满月

夜夜减清辉

译文比读

- 译文 1（Herbert A. Giles 译）

AN ABSENT HUSBAND

Since my lord left—ah me, unhappy hour! —

The half—spun web hangs idly in my bower;

My heart is like the full moon, full of pains,

Save that 'tis always full and never wanes.

- 译文 2（W.J.B. Fletcher 译）

LONGING

Since, ah! you went away,

What grief my mind can sway?

　　I yearn like the moon at full:

Am duller day by day!

- 译文 3（Henry H. Hart 译）

ABSENCE

Ever since the day

You went,

And left me here alone,

My lord,

The world is changed!

Upon the loom

The web, half woven, hangs

Untouched.

My thoughts

Are all of you,

And I am like you silver moon,

Whose glory wanes

And grows more pale

Each night!

4. 天净沙·秋思

枯藤老树昏鸦,

小桥流水人家,

古道西风瘦马。

夕阳西下,

断肠人在天涯。

译文比读

Sunny Sand · Autumn Thoughts

- 译文 1 （Schleep 译）

Dry vine, old tree, crows at dust,

Low bridge, stream running, cottages,

Ancient road, west wind, lean nag,

The sun westering

And one with breaking heart at the sky's edge.

- 译文 2 （翁显良 译）

Crows hovering over rugged trees wreathed with rotten vine—the day is about done. Yonder is a tiny bridge over a sparkling stream, and on the far bank, a pretty little village. But the traveler has to go on down this ancient road, the west wind moaning, his bony horse groaning, trudging towards the sinking sun, farther and farther away from home.

- 译文 3 （丁祖馨、Burtton Raffel 译）

Withered vines hanging on old branches,
Returning crows croaking at dusk.
A few houses hidden past a narrow bridge,
And below the bridge quiet creek running.
Down a worn path, in the west wind,
A lean horse comes plodding.
The sun dips down in the west,
And the lovesick traveler is still at the end of the world.

- 译文 4 （杜争鸣 译）

Dried vines cling to an aged tree with evening crows;
By a small bridge over a stream are some homes.
Along an old road swept by west wind comes a lean horse.
As the evening sun to the west sets,
The heart-broken man is now at the world's edge.

5. 赏中秋(苏州评弹词)

[许仙](唱)
七里山塘景物新,
秋高气爽净无尘。
今日里是欣逢佳节同游赏,
半日偷闲酒一樽。
云儿片片升,船儿缓缓行,
酒盅儿举不停,脸庞儿醉生春,
情致缠绵笑语温。娘子呀!
我是不知几世来修到,
方能够缔结丝萝攀了你这女千金,
好比那得水鱼儿有精神,
我是暮暮朝朝忘不了你白素贞。
[白素贞](唱)
官人言太重,为妻心不宁,
夫妻原一体,何分我与君,
哪有夫妇之间来论什么恩?
官人啊,如水流年须珍惜,
莫教误了少年身。
只要勤勤恳恳成家业,

方能喜喜欢欢度光阴。
但愿夫妻好比秋江水,
心与秋江一样清,
一清到底见鱼鳞;
但愿君心似我心,
心心相印心连心。
官人啊,一年几见当头月,
但愿得花常好;
［许仙］(唱)
但愿月长明;
［白素贞］(唱)
人长寿;
［许仙］(唱)
松常青;
［白素贞］(唱)
但愿千秋百岁长相亲;
［许仙］(唱)
地久天长永不分。

译文比读

Sightseeing on the Mid-Autumn Day
- **译文 1（汪榕培 译）**

Xu Xian:
The seven-li Shantang street, a refreshing scene,
The mid-autumn sky is high, the air clear and clean.
Such a date out with my lady makes me so pleased,
As I can sit over a glass for hours released.
Under rising clouds my boat moves but not rushed,
With glasses raised and raised I feel as if blushed.
Tender is my feeling as I smile, tender to my lady:
What blessing, of which world I've had I know not,
To have such an invaluable babe as you in my lot.
Like a fish returning to fresh water, I'm rejuvenated,
For this I'd keep you in my heart, always venerated.
Bai Suzhen:
Dear husband, your over-praise stirs my heart;

In our wedlock, why talk of you and me apart?
Formality of gratitude goes beyond the union of love,
My man, good time flies fast and is for us to cherish,
So we shouldn't let our youth for nothing perish.
If we just work with diligence for our home and career,
We'd sure live a happy life sparkled with cheer.
I wish you and me can resemble the autumn tide,
With our hearts seen clear and nothing to hide,
Clear to show the scales of fish below on the side.
I wish your heart feels as my own would do,
And we can feel heart to heart even if in two.
My husband, such a good moon is seen all time rare,
And I just wish the flowers will always look so fair.

Xu Xian:

Wish the moon will always be brightly shone.

Bai Suzhen:

And we'll live on and on;

Xu Xian:

As the pine, always green;

Bai Suzhen:

For eternity, we'll hold each other dear;

Xu Xian:

For as long as the world, together near.

● 译文2（杜争鸣 译）

Xu Xian:

The seven-li Shantang street is fresh and clean,
With the mid-autumn sky so serene.
On a day so fine,
We are enjoying ourselves
And drinking sips of wine.
Under the floating clouds,
Our boat is moving slow and steady.
Toast after toast,
I feel that I am half-drunken.
And start to speak to my wife in a smile:
Oh, my dear wife,

What blessing from the world unknown

Has knit the tie between you and me!

Like a fish swimming freely in the stream,

I have you in sight by day and in my dream.

Bai Suzhen:

My dear man, your flattering

Has put me ill at ease;

In our married life,

There is no need to speak of you and me;

Gratitude is not the word for man and wife.

My dear man,

Take good care of time and tide,

And do not let your prime of youth slide.

If you work hard for our home and career,

We're sure to live a life sparked with cheer.

O that we resemble the autumn tide,

As clean as our linked hearts,

So clean that you can see the scales of the fish.

O that your heart is like my heart,

And the two of us feel heart to heart.

My dear man,

We can seldom see such a bright moon,

And so let's hope that flowers are always in bloom,

Xu Xian:

Let's hope that the moon is always shining bright,

Bai Suzhen:

We shall live a long life,

Xu Xian:

And the pine trees are always green.

Bai Suzhen:

Let's hope that we shall always love each other.

Xu Xian:

And we shall always stay together.

Such a date out with my lady makes me so pleased,

As I can sit over a glass for hours released.

Under rising clouds my boat moves but not rushed,

With glasses raised and raised I feel as if blushed.
Tender is my feeling as I smile, tender to my lady:
What blessing, of which world I've had I know not,
To have such an invaluable babe as you in my lot.
Like a fish returning to fresh water, I'm rejuvenated,
For this I'd keep you in my heart, always venerated.

第十章 英汉互译原理综合实践

一、英汉互译原理在散文中的应用

(一) 英译中

1. Genius at Work

Henry Ford didn't always pay attention in school. One day, he and a friend took a watch apart. Angry and upset, the teacher told him both to stay after school. Their punishment was to stay until they had fixed the watch. But the teacher did not know young Ford's genius. In ten minutes, this mechanical wizard had repaired the watch and was on this way home. Ford was always interested in how things worked. He once plugged up the spout of a teapot and placed it on the fire. Then he waited to see what would happen. The water boiled and, of course, turned to steam. Since the steam had no way to escape, the teapot exploded. The explosion cracked a mirror and broke a window. The young inventor was badly scalded. Ford's year of curiosity and tinkering paid off. He dreamed of a horseless carriage. When he built one, the world of transportation was changed forever.

2. Love Your Life

However mean your life is, meet it and live it; do not shun it and call it hard names. It is not so bad as you are. It looks poorest when you are richest. The fault-finder will find faults in paradise. Love your life, poor as it is. You may perhaps have some pleasant, thrilling, glorious hours, even in a poor-house. The setting sun is reflected from the windows of the alms-house as brightly as from the rich man's abode; the snow melts before its door as early in the spring. I do not see but a quiet mind may live as contentedly there, and have as cheering thoughts, as in a palace. The town's poor seem to me often to live the most independent lives of any. Maybe they are simply great enough to receive without misgiving. Most think that they are above being supported by the town; but it often happens that they are not above supporting themselves by dishonest means, which should be more disreputable. Cultivate poverty like a garden herb, like sage. Do not trouble yourself much to get new things, whether clothes or friends. Turn the old, return to them. Things do not change; we change. Sell your clothes and keep your thoughts.

3. The Cobbler and the Banker

A cobbler passed his time in singing from morning till night; it was wonderful to see, wonderful to hear him; he was more contented in shoes, than was any of the seven sages. His neighbor, on the contrary, who was rolling in wealth, sung but little and slept less. He was a banker; when by chance he fell into a doze at day-break, the cobbler awoke him with his song. The banker complained sadly that providence had not made sleep a saleable commodity, like edibles or drinkables. Having at length sent for the songster, he said to him, "How much a year do you earn, master Gregory?" "How much a year, sir?" said the merry cobbler, laughing, "I have reckon in that way, living as I do from one day to another; somehow I manage to reach the end of the year; each day brings its meal." "Well then! How much a day do you earn, my friend?" "Sometimes more, sometimes less; but the worst of it is—and, without that our earnings would be very tolerable—a number of days occur in the year on which we are forbidden to work; and the curate, moreover, is constantly adding some new saint to the list." The banker, laughing at his simplicity, said, "In the future I shall place you above want. Take this hundred crowns, preserve them carefully, and make use of them in time of need." The cobbler fancied he beheld all the wealth which the earth had produced in the past century for the use of mankind. Returning home, he buried his money and his happiness at the same time, no more singing; he lost his voice, the moment he acquired that which is the source of so much grief. Sleep quitted his dwelling; and cares, suspicions, and false alarms took its place, all day, his eye wandered in the direction of his treasure; and at night, if some stray cat made a noise, the cat was robbing him. At length the poor man ran to the house of his rich neighbor; "Give me back," said he, "sleep and my voice, and take your hundred crowns."

4. The Life I Desired

That must be the story of innumerable couples, and the pattern of life it offers has a homely grace. It reminds you of a placid rivulet, meandering smoothly through green pastures and shaded by pleasant trees, till at last it falls into the vast sea; but the sea is so calm, so silent, and so indifferent, that you are troubled suddenly by a vague uneasiness. Perhaps it is only by a kink in my nature, strong in me even in those days that I felt in such an existence the share of the great majority, something amiss. I recognized its social value. I saw its ordered happiness, but a fever in my blood asked for a wilder course. There seemed to me something alarming in such easy delights. In my heart was desire to live more dangerously. I was not unprepared for jagged rocks and treacherous shoals if I could only have change and the excitement of unforeseen.

5. A Few Thoughts of Sleep

This is an article for the reader to think of when he or she is warm in bed, a little before he goes to sleep, the clothes at his ear, and the wind moaning in some distant crevice.

"Blessings," exclaimed Sancho, "on him that first invented sleep! It wraps a man all round like a cloak." It is a delicious moment certainly—that of being well nestled in bed, and feeling that you shall drop gently to sleep. The good is to come, not past: the limbs have been just tired enough to render the remaining in one posture delightful: the labour of the day is done.

It is said that sleep is best before midnight: and Nature herself, with her darkness and chilling dews, informs us so. There is another reason for going to bed betimes; for it is universally acknowledged that lying late in the morning is a great shortener of life. At least, it is never found in company with longevity. It also tends to make people corpulent. But these matters belong rather to the subject of early rising than of sleep.

……

The most complete and healthy sleep that can be taken in the day is in summer-time, out in a field. There is, perhaps, no solitary sensation so exquisite as that of slumbering on the grass or hay, shaded from the hot sun by a tree, with the consciousness of a fresh but light air running through the wide atmosphere, and the sky stretching far overhead upon all sides, Earth, and heaven, and a placed humanity seem to have the creation to themselves. There is nothing between the slumberer and the naked and glad innocence of nature.

Sleep is most graceful in an infant; soundest, in one who has been tired in the open air; completest, to the seaman after a hard voyage; most welcome, to the mind haunted with one idea; most touching to look at, in the parent that has wept; lightest, in the playful child; proudest, in the bride.

6. The Literature of Knowledge and the Literature of Power

What is it that we mean by literature? Popularly, and amongst the thoughtless, it is held to include everything that is printed in a book. Little logic is required to disturb that definition. The most thoughtless person is easily made aware that in the idea of literature on essential element is some relation to a general and common interest of man—so that what applies only to a local, or professional, or merely personal interest, even though presenting itself in the shape of a book, will not belong to literature. So far the definition is easily narrowed; and it is as easily expanded. For not only is much that takes a station in books not literature, but inversely, much that really is literature never reaches a station in books. The weekly sermons of Christendom, that vast pulpit literature which acts so extensively upon the popular mind—to warn, to uphold, to renew, to comfort, to alarm—does not attain the sanctuary of libraries in the ten-thousandth part of its extent. The drama again—as, for instance, the finest part of Shakespeare's plays in England, and all leading Athenian plays in the noontide of the Attic stage—operated a literature on the public mind, and were (according to the strictest letter of that term) published through the audiences that witnessed their representation sometime before they were published as things to be read; and they were published in this scenical mode of publication with much more effect than they could have had as books during ages of costly copying or of costly printing.

Books, therefore, do not suggest an idea co-extensive and interchangeable with the idea of literature, since much literature, scenic, forensic, or didactic (as from lectures and public orators), may never come into books, and much that does come into books may connect itself with no literary interest. But a far more important correction, applicable to the common vague idea of literature, is to be sought, not so much in a better definition of literature, as in a sharper distinction of the two functions which it fulfils. In that great social organ which, collectively, we call literature, there may be distinguished two separate offices, that may blend and often do so, but capable, severally, of a severe insulation, and naturally fitted for reciprocal repulsion. There is, first, the literature of knowledge, and, secondly, the literature of power. The function of the first is to teach; the function of the second is to move: the first is a rudder; the second an oar or a sail. The first speaks to the mere discursive understanding; the second speaks ultimately, it may happen, to the higher understanding, or reason, but always through affections of pleasure and sympathy. Remotely it may travel towards an object seated in what Lord Bacon calls dry light; but proximately it does and must operate—else it ceases to be literature of power—on and through that humid light which clothes itself in the mists and glittering iris of human passions, desires, and genial emotions. Men have so little reflected on the higher functions of literature as to find it a paradox if one should describe it as a mean or subordinate purpose of books to give information. But this is a paradox only in the sense which makes it honorable to be paradoxical. Whenever we talk in ordinary language of seeking knowledge, we understand the words as connected with something of absolute novelty. But it is the grandeur of all truth which can occupy a very high place in human interests that it is never absolutely novel to the meanest of minds: it exists eternally, by way of germ or latent principle, in the lowest as in the highest, needing to be developed but never to be planted. To be capable of transplantation is the immediate criterion of a truth ranges on a lower scale. Besides which, there is a rarer thing than truth, namely, power, or deep sympathy with truth. What is the effect, for instance, upon society, of children? By the pity, by the tenderness, and by the peculiar modes of admiration, which connect themselves with the helplessness, with the innocence, and with the simplicity of children, not only are the primal affections strengthened and continually renewed, but the qualities which are dearest in the sight of heaven—the frailty, for instance, which appeals to forbearance, the innocence which symbolizes the heavenly, and the simplicity which is most alien from the worldly—are kept up in perpetual remembrance, and their ideals are continually refreshed. A purpose of the same nature is answered by the higher literature, viz., the literature of power. What do you learn from Paradise Lost? Nothing at all. What do you learn from a cookery book? Something new, something that you did not know before, in every paragraph. But would you therefore put the wretched cookery-book on a higher level of estimation than the divine poem? What you owe to Milton is not any knowledge, of which a million separate items are still but a million of advancing steps on the same earthly level; what you owe is power, that is, exercise and expansion to your own latent capacity of sympathy with the infinite, where every pulse and each separate influx is a step upwards, a step ascending as upon a Jacob's ladder from earth to mysterious altitudes above the earth. All the steps of knowledge, from first to last, carry you further on the same plane, but could never raise you one foot above your ancient level of earth; whereas the very first step in power is a flight, is an ascending movement into another element where earth is forgotten.

7. How to Grow Old

In spite of the title, this article will really be on how not to grow old, which, at my time of life, is a much more important subject. My first advice would be to choose your ancestors carefully. Although both my parents died young, I have done well in this respect as regards my other ancestors. My maternal grandfather, it is true, was cut off in the flower of his youth at the age of sixty-seven, but my other three grandparents all lived to be over eighty. Of remoter ancestors I can only discover one who did not live to a great age, and he died of disease which is now rare, namely, having his head cut off. A great-grandmother of mine, who was a friend of Gibbon, lived to the age of ninety-two, and to her last day remained a terror to all her descendants. My maternal grandmother, after having nine children who survived, one who died in infancy, and many miscarriages, as soon as she became a widow devoted herself to women's higher education. She was one of the founders of Girton College, and worked hard at opening the medical profession to women. She used to relate how she met in Italy an elderly gentleman who was looking very sad. She inquired the cause of his melancholy and he said that he had just parted from his two grandchildren. "Good gracious," she exclaimed, "I have seventy-two grandchildren, and if I were sad each time I parted from one of them, I should have a dismal existence!" "Madre snaturale," he replied. But speaking as one of the seventy-two, I prefer her recipe. After the age of eighty she found she had some difficulty in getting to sleep, so she habitually spent the hours from midnight to a. m. in reading popular science. I do not believe that she ever had time to notice that she was growing old. This, I think, is the proper recipe for remaining young. If you have wide and keen interests and activities in which you can still be effective, you will have no reason to think about the merely statistical fact of the member of years you have already live, still less of the probable brevity of your future.

As regards health, I have nothing useful to say since I have little experience of illness. I eat and drink whatever I like, and sleep when I cannot keep awake. I never do anything whatever on the ground that it is good for health, though in actual fact the things I like doing are mostly wholesome.

Psychologically there are two dangers to be guarded against in old age. One of these is undue absorption in the past. It does not do to live in memories, in regrets for the good old days, or in sadness about friends who are dead. One's thoughts must directed to the future, and to things about which there is something to be done. This is not always easy; one's own past is a gradually increasing weight. It is easy to think to oneself that one's emotions used to be more vivid than they are, and one's mind more keen. If this is true it should be forgotten, and if it is forgotten it will probably not be true.

The other thing to be avoided is clinging to youth in the hope of sucking vigor from its vitality. When your children are grown up they want to live their own lives, and if you continue to be as interested in them as you were when they were young, you are likely to become a burden to them, unless they are unusually callous. I do not mean that one should be without interest in them, but one's interest should be contemplative and, if possible, philanthropic, but not unduly emotional. Animals become indifferent to their young as soon as their young can look after themselves, but human beings, owing to the length of infancy, find this difficult.

I think that a successful old age is the easiest for those who have strong impersonal interests involving appropriate activities. It is in this sphere that long experience is really fruitful, and it is in this sphere that the wisdom born of experience can be exercised without being oppressive. It is no use telling grown-up children not to make mistakes, both because they will not believe you, and because mistakes are an essential part of education. But if you are one of those who are incapable of impersonal interests, you may find that your life will be empty unless you concern yourself with your children and grandchildren. In that case you must realize that while you can still render them material service, such as making them an allowance or knitting them jumpers, you must not expect that they will enjoy your company.

Some old people are oppressed by the fear of death. In the young there is a justification for this feeling. Young men who have reason to fear that they will be killed in battle may justifiably feel bitter in the thought that they have been cheated of the best things that life has to offer. But in an old man who has known human joys and sorrows, and has achieved whatever work it was in him to do, the fear of death is somewhat abject and ignoble. The best way to overcome it—so at least it seems to me—is to make your interest gradually wider and more impersonal, until bit by bit the walls of the ego recede, and your life becomes increasingly merged in the universal life. An individual human existence should be like a river—small at first, narrowly contained within its banks, and rushing passionately past boulders and over waterfalls. Gradually the river grows wider, the banks recede, the waters flow more quietly and in the end, without any visible break, they become merged in the sea, and painlessly lose their individual being. The man who, in old age, can see his life in this way, will not suffer from the fear of death, since the things he cares for will continue. And if, with the decay of vitality, weariness increases, the though of rest will be not unwelcome. I should wish to die while still at work, knowing that others will carry on what I can no longer do, and content in the thought that what was possible has been done.

8. From These Weary Bones I Cry

My grandmother's father was just a boy when the whitemen came to the cold flowing waters of wounded Knee Creek, their pale faces masked with mean. Alone, he shivered naked on the packed dirt floor of his mother's cabin, staring wide-eyed through the chinks at the snow spotted banks of the familiar creek. The snow had been white, whiter even than the faces of the devils, so white it would glow like many fireflies at night when the sky was purple smoke. This day, however, it had darkened, stained so red it was nearly black. The moans and cries of the dying rose up in horrible, thunderous song that the land could not forget (even now, it is said, they can be heard sometimes, as the earth stirs fretfully in troubled sleep). In the shattering stillness that followed the storm of gunshot, the blackened snow blew cold over stiff, bloodied corpses, their eyes blank and unseeing, empty as the colorless winter sky. Our blood spilled there, my great grandfather moaned to me sometimes in the heart of the night. Our blood spilled out and was eaten by the earth, and we died on the plains with their guns still smoking. They shot holes in the heads of the dead and in the hearts of the living and so there was none to survive. All the rest of my days I didn't forget. I lived to be an old man, but when I died I saw the hurt of Wounded Knee.

The forgotten cries of the dead mingled with the wind that snaked into my room, and I could not tell which was which. I would clutch the damp, twisted sheets and tell myself it was sweat, not blood that had soaked through the thin worn cloth; that the sting in my eyes was caused by tears, and not the harsh hungry bite of blood-blackened snow.

In the deepest South, where the wind whispers through trees black with the memory of charred dark flesh and the earth is heavy with the burden of unmarked Negro graves, it is whispered that a child with a caul over his face will have the ability to see the waling dead. But I was born where whispers could not be heard, in the stark neat whiteness of a northern hospital. What are you talking about a caul, my mother will say if I asked her, I was so tired after two days of labor eight pounds fifteen ounces and on the fourth of July too. Anyway it is not if I see them but more that I sense their perpetual presence, the threadbare remnants of their memories. It is as if, born in the shadow of the past, my veins carry not only the blood of my ancestors but their hurt and hunger as well.

9. F. Engels, Speech at the Grave of Karl Marx, Highgate Cemetery, London, March 17, 1883

On the 14th of March, at a quarter to three in the afternoon, the greatest living thinker ceased to think. He had been left alone for scarcely two minutes, and when we came back we found him in his armchair, peacefully gone to sleep—but forever.

"An immeasurable loss has been sustained both by the militant proletariat of Europe and America, and by historical science, in the death of this man. The gap that has been left by the departure of this mighty spirit will soon enough make itself felt.

"Just as Darwin discovered the law of development of organic nature, so Marx discovered the law of development of human history: the simple fact, hitherto concealed by an overgrowth of ideology, that mankind must first of all eat, drink, have shelter and clothing, before it can pursue politics, science, art, religion, etc.; that therefore the production of the immediate material means of subsistence and consequently the degree of economic development attained by a given people or during a given epoch form the foundation upon which the state institutions, the legal conceptions, art, and even the ideas on religion, of the people concerned have been evolved, and in the light of which they must, therefore, be explained, instead of vice versa, as had hitherto been the case.

"But that is not all. Marx also discovered the special law of motion governing the present-day capitalist mode of production and the bourgeois society that this mode of production has created. The discovery of surplus value suddenly threw light on the problem, in trying to solve which all previous investigations, of both bourgeois economists and socialist critics, had been groping in the dark.

"Two such discoveries would be enough for one lifetime. Happy the man to whom it is granted to make even one such discovery. But in every single field which Marx investigated—and he investigated very many fields, none of them superficially—in every field, even in that of mathematics, he made independent discoveries.

"Such was the man of science. But this was not even half the man. Science was for Marx a historically dynamic, revolutionary force. However great the joy with which he welcomed a new discovery in some theoretical science whose practical application perhaps it was as yet quite impossible to envisage, he experienced quite another kind of joy when the discovery involved immediate revolutionary changes in industry and in historical development in general. For example, he followed closely the development of the discoveries made in the field of electricity and recently those of Marcel Deprez.

"For Marx was before all else a revolutionist. His real mission in life was to contribute, in one way or another, to the overthrow of capitalist society and of the state institutions which it had brought into being, to contribute to the liberation of the modern proletariat, which he was the first to make conscious of its own position and its needs, conscious of the conditions of its emancipation. Fighting was his element. And he fought with a passion, a tenacity and a success such as few could rival. His work on the first *Rheinische Zeitung* (1842), the *Neue Rheinische Zeitung* (1848 – 1849), the *New York Tribune* (1852 – 1861) and so on, and in addition to these a host of militant pamphlets, work in organisations in Paris, Brussels and London, and finally, crowning all, the formation of the great International Working Men's Association—this was indeed an achievement of which its founder might well have been proud even if he had done nothing else.

"And, consequently, Marx was the best-hated and most calumniated man of his time. Governments, both absolutist and republican, deported him from their territories. Bourgeois, whether conservative or ultra-democratic, vied with one another in heaping slanders upon him. All this he brushed aside as though it were cobweb, ignoring it, answering only when extreme necessity compelled him. And he died beloved, revered and mourned by millions of revolutionary fellow-workers—from the mines of Siberia to California, in all parts of Europe and America—and I make bold to say that though he may have had many opponents he had hardly one personal enemy.

"His name will endure through the ages, and so also will his work!"

(二)中译英

1. 加德满都的狗(节选)(季羡林)

我小时候住在农村,终日与狗为伍。一点也没有感觉到狗这种东西有什么稀奇的地方。但是狗却给我留下了极其深刻的印象。我母亲逝世以后,故乡的家中已经空无一人。

她养的一条狗——连它的颜色我现在都回忆不清楚了——却仍然日日夜夜卧在我们门口,守着不走。女主人已经离开人世,再没有人喂它了。它好像已经意识到这一点。但是它却坚决宁愿忍饥挨饿,也绝不离开我们那破烂的家门口。黄昏时分,我形单影只从村内走回家来,屋子里摆着母亲的棺材,门口卧着这一只失去了主人的狗,泪眼汪汪地望着我这个失去了慈母的孩子,有气无力地摇摆着尾巴,嗅我的脚。茫茫宇宙,好像只剩下这只狗和我。此情此景,我连泪都流不出来了,我流的是血,而这血还是流向我自己的心中。我本来应该同这只狗相依为命,互相安慰。但是,我必须离开故乡,我又无法把它带走。离别时,我流着泪紧紧地搂住了它,我遗弃了它,真正受到良心的谴责。几十年来,我经常想到这一只狗。直到今天,我一想到它,还会不由自主地流下眼泪。我相信,我离开家以后,它也绝不会离开我们的门口。它的结局我简直不忍想下去了。母亲有灵,会从这一只狗身上得到我这个儿子无法给她的慰藉吧。

从此,我爱天下一切狗。

2. 中国文化

中国有着五千年的文明史。在这漫长的历史进程中,中国人民创造了灿烂的中华文化。早在四五千年前的新石器时代,我们的祖先就在江苏、河北、河南一带从事养蚕和生产丝绸;秦汉时期,我国在世界上最早开始种植茶树、生产茶叶,唐代的陆羽撰写了世界上第一部关于茶叶的专著——《茶经》。世界上最早形成完整的农业耕作理论的国家是我国。公元六世纪,我国古代著名农业科学家贾思勰撰写的科学典籍《齐民要术》是世界上被完整地保存下来的最早的一部农书。世界上最早发明瓷器的国家是我国。至迟在东汉时已发明了瓷器,三国以后,瓷器制造业迅速发展了起来;而欧洲十八世纪初才造出真正的瓷器。世界上最早发明指南针、造纸术、印刷术、火药的国家是我国,而我国的万里长城是世界上最伟大的古军事防御工程。世界中世纪造船业最发达的国家是我国;世界上最早进行大规模远洋航行的国家是我国(郑和七下西洋);世界上最古老、保存最完善的石拱桥是我国河北省的赵州桥;世界上第一架测天仪器是我们祖先在公元前四世纪发明创制的浑天仪;世界上最早使用麻醉剂进行外科手术的是我国公元二世纪的名医华佗;世界上最早出现的诗歌总集是我国公元前六世纪编定的《诗经》;世界上最大的古代百科全书是我国明朝的《永乐大典》。这一系列的"最早"和"第一"都是我国五十六个民族的人民共同创造出来的。中国是一个山川秀丽、历史悠久的国家,在政治、文化以及其他领域出现了许许多多杰出的人物。

3. 让我们共同缔造一个更美好的世界(节选)(江泽民)

饱经沧桑的二十世纪仅剩下几个春秋,人类即将跨入充满希望的二十一世纪。在这临近世纪之交的时刻,各国领导人从四面八方来到这里,纪念当代具有普遍性、权威性的政府间国际组织——联合国成立五十周年,是很有意义的。我们可以利用这个机会,站在更高的立足点上,回顾过去,展望未来,共同探讨如何实现联合国所肩负的崇高使命。

五十年前,正当世界反法西斯战争取得伟大胜利之时,联合国诞生了。这是国际关系史上的重大事件。在本世纪上半叶,不到三十年就爆发了两次世界大战,给人类带来空前的浩劫和惨痛的教训。联合国宪章的制定和联合国组织的创建,适应了时代进步的客观需要,体现了各国人民渴求消除战争劫难的强烈愿望,反映了人类要求建立一个和平、平等、合作和繁荣的新世界的美好理想。

……

中国是一个历史悠久、人口众多的国家,创造了灿烂的古代文明,对人类做出了重大的贡献。十九世纪中叶以后,中国逐步变成贫穷落后的半殖民地半封建社会。中国人民为了捍卫国家的独立、主权和统一,实现民族振兴,进行了长期不屈不挠的斗争,终于在一九四九年建立了中华人民共和国。现在,中国人民正在沿着建设有中国特色社会主义的道路阔步前进,正在集中精力发展经济,提高自己的生活水平。中国人民热爱和平,渴望发展,愿意同世界各国人民发展友好合作关系,坚持奉行独立自主的和平外交政策。中国发展和强大起来,也绝不谋求霸权,绝不会对任何国家构成威胁,而且它作为维护世界和平与稳定的重要力量,必将对人类做出更大的贡献。如果占世界人口近四分之一的中国不发展,长期贫困落后下去,那就会给亚太地区乃至世界的和平与稳定带来严重影响。

……

我们这一代政治家,对世界和平、发展与进步事业肩负着继往开来的历史使命,任重而道远。历史既公正,又无情。我们绝不能辜负世界人民的殷切期望。让我们携起手来,为迎接新世纪的到来,为缔造一个更美好的世界而共同努力!

4. 拙政园

拙政园布局以水为主,水面约占全园面积的三分之一。东部地势空旷,平冈草木,芙蓉榭、天泉亭等点缀其间。中部是全园的精华所在。若从中部小巷入,进大门,即可见一座黄石假山半遮景物,造园学上称为障景。绕曲廊,过小桥,可见主厅远香堂。远香堂又如障景,再次将满池景致遮掩。"远香"取周敦颐《爱莲说》"香远益清",表示了园主自谓高洁之意。堂北池中遍植荷花,荷花时节,清香送远,淡雅怡人。远香堂是一座四面厅,在堂内观望,四方景观犹如长卷,依次展开——东有绣绮亭,西接倚玉轩,北临荷池,雪香云蔚亭隔岸耸立在小山上,与远香堂恰为对景。西侧隔水为荷风四面亭,西北角是重檐歇山顶的见山楼。旱船"香洲",船头为石砌平台,前舱如亭,中舱如阁,后舱则为一楼,亭台楼阁四种样式合一,高低错落。旱船东南是著名的廊桥"小飞虹"横卧水面,十分雅致。过西侧走廊洞门,即是西部,但见水廊透迤,楼台倒影,清幽恬静。尤其是精巧的鸳鸯厅,南北两侧分别悬挂着由清代后期两位苏州状元题名的"卅六鸳鸯馆"和"十八曼陀罗花馆"的匾额。昆曲大师俞振飞先生少年时就常随其父在此拍曲演唱。

水池之西的留听阁,取李商隐"秋阴不散霜飞晚,留得残荷听雨声"诗意而名,阁内有银杏木透雕松、竹、梅、鹊飞罩。临池而建的扇亭,平面犹如一把打开的折扇,为符"扇"意,亭内的门窗与石桌、石凳均为扇形。其名取苏东坡词意,为"与谁同坐轩"。水池北侧为倒影楼,楼下称拜文揖沈之斋,内置沈周、文徵明石刻小像,北面六扇银杏木屏门板上刻有郑板桥画竹石图及题跋。再西,今辟为盆景园,汇集了苏派盆景50余个品种近万盆,花开花落,姹紫嫣红;松柏挺立,四季常青。

5. 乘雪橇小游

我安顿好小宝贝们呼呼入睡以后,就陪伴着妹妹苏珊上了牛拉雪橇,送她回家。我们俩欢快地在一起,舒舒服服地挤在简陋的雪橇里。雪橇底层铺着干净的稻草,稻草上盖着漂亮的毛毯,还有枕头可以依靠。我们严严实实地裹着苏格兰方格呢风衣,不畏寒冷,一路上谈笑风生。虽然我们的雪橇犹如劣马破车,很不雅观,缓缓蠕动像送葬一般,但我们那高兴的劲头儿并不亚于乘坐在两匹高大的栗色骏马所拉的豪华车上。我们的华盖是白雪覆盖的青松、铁杉、柏树和茫茫的密林。我们的灯火是黯淡的星星和那透过水雾、透过银色的雪云露出的如水的月光。此时此地,欢乐的哼唧声和孩子们无忧无虑的嬉闹声打破了密林的一片寂静。雪橇压过积雪覆盖的落枝卧木,颠簸起伏。万籁俱寂,只有犟牛的沉重脚步声和雪橇隆隆声。

林中最美的时刻是当暴风雪过后,所有的粗枝细杆统统都被羽毛似的积雪所覆盖。腐烂程度不等的木材、连根拔起的树木和残枝塞满了的坑洼路面,似乎都被神气的魔棒点过一样,旧貌换了新装。无比的纯洁、柔和光泽取代了纷繁杂乱和植腐糜烂。大雪过后,林中漫游是乡村赐予我最美的享受之一,无论是在正午时分,在万里无云的蔚蓝天空里,有灿烂的阳光照亮着沾在树木、地面上或悬挂在常青树中的璀璨珠粒,把扇形的枝杈变成羽绒的叶片,呈现出非常奇特的形状;或是当盈盈月儿,如霜的星光泻在丛林雪染的树梢上,偶尔也透过薄雾轻纱,光彩耀眼。树林把薄雾变成闪烁的白霜,白霜用水晶的粒珠装裹着条条细枝小叉。柔和的清风摇曳着更加轻巧的雪花,让它无声无息,纷纷飘下。除此之外,万物都凝固了,只有我们的雪橇——铃儿叮当,欢快悠扬。

6. 匆匆(朱自清)

燕子去了,有再来的时候;杨柳枯了,有再青的时候;桃花谢了,有再开的时候。但是,聪明的,你告诉我,我们的日子为什么一去不复返呢?——是有人偷了他们吧:那是谁?又藏在何处呢?是他们自己逃走了吧:现在又到了哪里呢?

我不知道他们给了我多少日子;但我的手确乎是渐渐空虚了。在默默里算着,八千多日子已经从我手中溜去;像针尖上一滴水滴在大海里,我的日子滴在时间的流里,没有声音,也没有影子。我不禁头涔涔而泪潸潸了。

去的尽管去了,来的尽管来着;去来的中间,又怎样地匆匆呢?早上我起来的时候,小屋里射进两三方斜斜的太阳。太阳他有脚啊,轻轻悄悄地挪移了;我也茫茫然跟着旋转。于是——洗手的时候,日子从水盆里过去;吃饭的时候,日子从饭碗里过去;默默时,便从凝然的双眼前过去。我觉察他去得匆匆了,伸出手遮挽时,他又从遮挽着的手边过去,天黑时,我躺在床上,他便伶伶俐俐地从我身上跨过,从我脚边飞去了。等我睁开眼和太阳再见,这算又溜走了一日。我掩着面叹息。但是新来的日子的影儿又开始在叹息里闪过了。

在逃去如飞的日子里,在千门万户的世界里的我能做些什么呢?只有徘徊罢了,只有匆匆罢了;在八千多日的匆匆里,除徘徊外,又剩些什么呢?过去的日子如轻烟,被微风吹散了,如薄雾,被初阳蒸融了;我留着些什么痕迹呢?我何曾留着像游丝样的痕迹呢?我赤裸裸来到这世界,转眼间也将赤裸裸地回去吧?但不能平的,为什么偏要白白走这一遭啊?

你聪明的,告诉我,我们的日子为什么一去不复返呢?

7. 这是一个美丽地方

烟波浩渺的太湖,点点帆影,渔歌唱晚,青山绿水相拥,在三万六千顷的太湖中有一个宛如人间仙境的地方——那就是康熙御茶碧螺春的发祥地,被人们誉为天堂中天堂的苏州市东山镇。

东山是历史文化名镇和全国环境优美乡镇,是国务院规划的太湖风景区的重要区域。它位于苏州市区西南处,是延伸到太湖里的一座三面环水的半岛,地形呈蝙蝠状,被古人誉为洞天福地。总面积96.6平方公里,常住人口5.3万余人,这里交通网络四通八达,沿太湖大道、东山大道、木东公路三条主干道在此汇合。驱车十分钟即可到达环城高速道口,20分钟就可到达苏州市中心及沪宁、苏嘉杭高速道口,距上海虹桥机场120公里、浦东国际机场170公里、上海港口150公里。

东山的历史可追溯至远古的旧石器时代,久远的历史饱蘸了吴文化深厚的内涵,南宋初年,北方的豪门,甚至还有皇族,为躲避中原战乱,纷纷南迁,那随之而来的中原文化给古老的东山注入了新的活力,古镇的屋檐下走出了一代又一代的名臣贤达、文人雅士,仅明清两朝就诞生了以明代宰相王鏊为代表的状元、进士43人,知县以上官员多达149人。明清时,东山很多乡民成了行走江湖的商人,他们意气风发、善于经营,与此后闻名的晋商、徽商相比毫不逊色,被人们称为"钻天洞庭"。当代更是名人辈出,有省部级以上干部18名,高级知识分子、教授286名,研究员30名,其他具有高级职称的地市级领导约600名,曾任国家劳动保障部部长的郑斯林、上海市人大常委会主任的叶公琦、广东省省长的朱森林等国家和省部级领导人,中国科学院院士王守武、王守觉、王大珩、何泽慧、程庆国,均为东山籍人。时任中共中央组织部部长的宋平赞誉东山为"进士之乡,教授之镇"。

东山是著名的旅游风景区,山之阳刚,水之清柔,美丽的太湖风光令人流连忘返。拥有古紫金庵、雕花大楼、席家花园、陆巷古村等一大批省、市级文物保护单位22处。三山岛的远古文化和其宛如世外桃源的生态环境,已成为沿太湖地区自助游的首选。它们像一颗颗璀璨的明珠,闪烁着历史和文化的神秘光彩。

近年来,东山镇党委、政府充分利用其独特的地理环境和优美的自然风光大做山水文章。加大了三产的规划和投入,投巨资开发了沙滩山茶舫、古尚锦茶舫、岱湖山庄、金龙生态园、灵源景区、碧螺景区、雨花景区等多个旅游观光项目。陆巷古村是全国为数不多保护完好的古村落之一,东山镇对古村落内的古宅、古街、小巷等进行了保护性的修复和改造,使昔日的宰相故里,萌发出新的生机。

当你轻轻推开老街上那一处处不起眼的门,或许里面就隐匿着一座被岁月遗忘的庭院,而它的主人呢,或已出门访友,或许正乘着午后的暖阳,在读书、品茶、观云、作画、种瓜……

东山镇是康熙御茶碧螺春的原产地保护区,月月有花,季季有果,是著名的花果山、鱼米乡,盛产各类名特优花果20多种,盛产银鱼、白鱼、白虾、太湖大闸蟹、莼菜等各类水产品200多种,是江苏省重要的常绿果树生产基地。优越的自然生态环境,培植了果品、茶叶、蔬菜、水产、湖羊五大农产品无公害(绿色)生产基地。"古尚锦""碧螺"牌碧螺春茶叶、"碧螺"牌枇杷、杨梅;"雨花绿"牌番茄、黄瓜;"太湖叶"牌莼菜等10多个产品,获得了无公害农产品及绿色食品使用证书。同时东山镇已成为太湖大闸蟹的主产区,最高日成交量达20000多公斤。太湖活蚬更是名声远扬,成为日本餐桌上的佳肴,获得了日本进出口免检产品的殊荣。

有着悠久历史文化的东山古镇,今日又是一个新兴的现代化科技工业重镇。规划建立了10平方公里的东山镇科技工业园,区内所有基础设施均参照苏州工业园区进行配套,已开发面积5平方公里,进驻中外企业近百家。已形成了电子电器、机械制造、塑料、印刷包装、医用器材、生物工程等五大行业。客户来自全国二十多个省市及新加坡、日本、韩国等多个国家以及中国香港、台湾等多个地区。东山已成为苏州城南工业带中的一个新亮点。

在加强硬环境建设的科学、合理布局的同时,东山镇更注重软环境的建设。他们千方百计地营造亲商、安商、富商的良好氛围。完善了金融、医疗、教育网络。东山宾馆、山水度假村等高档的休闲度假场所近在咫尺。天然气、日供20000吨优质自来水的自来水厂和日处理污水5000吨的污水处理厂等商用生活基础设施为你提供各种便利。东山镇人民政府按照国家政府规定,结合本地实际,出台了一系列招商引资的优惠政策,他们专门成立了招商办公室,并会同工商、税务等单位建立了从立项、报批、注册到登记的一条龙服务体系。

1996年新加坡内阁资政李光耀下榻东山,看到东山美丽的景色,陶醉于这方湖光山色之中,欣然题写了"这是一个美丽的地方,永远使人心旷神怡"的佳句作为永久留念。

如果说,莫厘峰是一位智者,默默地谱写着历史的春秋,那太湖柔美的波涛是一道琴弦,吟唱着吴风越雨的沧桑,那长长的东山老街就是一支竹笛,吹奏着历史、文化的繁华;而东山古镇就像是一位踏着晨雾采茶归来的碧螺仙子,她婀娜着美丽的身姿,吟哦着吴歌,风情万种,款款走进你的梦里……

8. 七彩梦笔——桥与史迹传说

苏州的桥,不仅是站立在水巷里,它们还牢牢站立在悠远的历史长河中。它们不仅跨越了河流,还跨越了历史。是桥,把苏州古老优秀的文化从千百年前传递到现在。

我们读桥,就是在读历史;我们走过桥,就是走过历史。岁月湮远,朝代递嬗,一座座古桥穿越时空,联系古今。我们今天正在走着的桥,也许吴王们傲笑着走过,伍子胥叹息着走过,梁鸿孟光牵着手走过,陆逊沉思着走过,陆羽捧着野茶走过,张继、杜荀鹤、白居易、倪瓒们吟哦着走过,范仲淹、苏轼们神色凝重地走过,沈周、文徵明、唐寅、祝允明、张灵们摇着折扇走过……

古人们走过的桥,我们在走着,古人们没有走过的路,也正在由我们走着。千年百代,像风一样从桥洞里吹过,当我们拾级登临,盘桓在一座座古朴的桥上时,便会与一位古代的圣贤俊杰悠然心会。这桥,是现实的桥,是历史的桥,也是我们心上的桥呵。

9. 中国民居概述

公元2000年,在联合国教科文组织第24届世界遗产委员会会议上,中国安徽省境内的古村落西递和宏村被正式列入《世界文化遗产名录》;是年初春,受命世界遗产委员会的日本专家大河直躬博士做实地考察后高度评价说:"像宏村这样的乡村景观可以说是举世无双的……西递村还保存了精致如画的古街巷,这在世界上也不多见。"此前的1997年,云南丽江古城和山西平遥古城分别被列为世界文化遗产;著名的江南水乡江苏周庄也正在申报之中。中国传统民居正在不断地向世界撩开面纱,逐渐成为中国走向世界、世界了解中国的大舞台。

中国疆域辽阔、地形复杂、气候多样,加之民族众多、文化各异,因而传统民居聚落和民居建筑也形态繁多、异彩纷呈。本书以生活在传统民居中的人的习俗、行为特征与空间模式的互动来选择较有代表性、覆盖面较广的若干聚落实例予以介绍,大体上分为院落式民居、楼居式民居和穴居式民居几种。

二、英汉互译原理在小说中的应用

(一) 英译中

1. *Forsyte Saga* (Excerpts of Chapter I)

(1) Those privileged to be present at a family festival of the Forsytes have seen that charming and instructive sight—an upper-middle-class family in full plumage. But whosoever of these favoured persons has possessed the gift of psychological analysis (a talent without monetary value and properly ignored by the Forsytes), has witnessed a spectacle, not only delightful in itself, but illustrative of an obscure human problem. In plainer words, he has gleaned from a gathering of this family—no branch of which had a liking for the other, between no three members of whom existed anything worthy of the name of sympathy—evidence of that mysterious concrete tenacity which renders a family so formidable a unit of society, so clear a reproduction of society in miniature. He has been admitted to a vision of the dim roads of social progress, has understood something of patriarchal life, of the swarmings of savage hordes, of the rise and fall of nations. He is like one who, having watched a tree grow from its planting—a paragon of tenacity, insulation, and success, amidst the deaths of a

hundred other plants less fibrous, sappy, and persistent—one day will see it flourishing with bland, full foliage, in an almost repugnant prosperity, at the summit of its efflorescence.

(2) On June 15, 1886, about four of the afternoon, the observer who chanced to be present at the house of old Jolyon Forsyte in Stanhope Gate, might have seen the highest efflorescence of the Forsytes.

This was the occasion of an "at home" to celebrate the engagement of Miss June Forsyte, old Jolyon's granddaughter, to Mr. Phillip Bosinney. In the bravery of light gloves, buff waistcoats, feathers, and frocks, the family were present—even Aunt Ann, who now but seldom left the corner of her brother Timothy's green drawing-room, where, under the aegis of a plume of dyed pampas grass in a light blue vase, she sat all day reading and knitting, surrounded by the effigies of three generations of Forsytes. Even Aunt Ann was there; her inflexible back and the dignity of her calm old face personifying the rigid possessiveness of the family idea.

(3) When a Forsyte was engaged, married, or born, the Forsytes were present; when a Forsytes died, but no Forsyte had as yet died; they did not die; death being contrary to their principles, they took precautions against it, the instinctive precautions of highly vitalized persons who resent encroachments on their property.

About the Forsytes mingling that day with the crowd of other guests, there was a more than ordinarily groomed look, an alert, inquisitive assurance, a brilliant respectability, as though they were attired in defiance of something. The habitual sniff on the face of Soames Forsyte had spread through their ranks; they were on their guard.

2. *Winesburg, Ohio*

Type of work: Short stories
Author: Sherwood Anderson (1876 - 1941)
Type of plot: Psychological realism
Time of plot: Late nineteenth century
Locale: Winesburg, Ohio
First published: 1919

- **Critique**:

Winesburg, Ohio has the stature of a modern classic. It is at once beautiful and tragic, realistic and poetic. Without being a novel in the usual sense of the word, the connected stories have the full range and emotional impact of a novel. In simple, through highly skillful and powerful language, Sherwood Anderson has told the story of a small town and the lonely, frustrated people who live there. Though regional in its setting and characters, the book is also intensely American. No one since Anderson has succeeded in interpreting the inner compulsions and loneliness of the national psyche with the same degree of accuracy and emotional impact

- **The story:**

Young George Willard was the only child of Elizabeth and Tom Willard. His father, a dull, conventional, insensitive man, owned the local hotel. His mother had once been a popular young bell. She had never loved Tom Willard, but the young married women of the town seemed to her so happy, so satisfied, that she had married him in the hope that marriage would somehow change her own life for the better. Before long she realized that she was caught in the dull life of Winesburg, her dreams turned to drab realities by her life with Tom Willard.

The only person who ever understood her was Dr. Reefy. Only in his small, untidy office did she feel free; only there did she achieve some measure of self-expression. Their relationship, doomed from the start, was nevertheless beautiful, a meeting of two lonely and sensitive people. For Dr. Reefy, too, had his sorrow. Once, years ago, a young girl, pregnant and unmarried, had come to his office, and shortly afterward he had married her. The following spring she had died, and from then on Dr. Reefy went around making little paper pills and stuffing his pockets with them. On the pieces of paper he had scribbled his thoughts about the beauty and strangeness of life.

Through her son George, Elizabeth Willard hoped to express herself, for she saw in him the fulfillment of her own hopes and desires. More than anything, she feared that George would settle down in Winesburg. When she learned that he wanted to be writer, she was glad. Unknown to her husband, she had put away money enough to give her son a start. But before she could realize her ambition, Elizabeth Willard died. Lying on her bed, she did not seem dead to either George or Dr. Reefy. To both she was extremely beautiful. To George, she did not seem like his mother at all. To Dr. Reefy, she was the woman he had loved, now the symbol of another lost illusion.

Many people of the town sought out George Willard; they told him of their lives, of their compulsions, of their failure. Old Wing Biddlebaum, the berry picker, years before had been a schoolteacher. He had loved the boys in his charge, and he had been, in fact, one of those few teachers who understand young people. But one of his pupils, having conceived a strong affection for his teacher, had accused him of homosexuality. Wing Biddlebaum, though innocent, was driven out of town. In Winesburg, he became the best berry pecker in the region. But always the same hands that earned his livelihood were a source of wonder and fear to him. When George Willard encountered him in the berry field Wing's hands went forward as if to caress the youth. But a wave of horror swept over him, and he hurriedly thrust them into his pockets. To George, also, Wing's hands seemed odd, mysterious.

Kate Swift, once George's teacher, saw in him a future writer. She tried to tell him what writing was, what it meant. George did not understand exactly, but he understood that Kate was speaking, not as his teacher, but as a woman. One night, in her house, she embraced him, for George was now a young man with whom she had fallen in love. On another night, when all of Winesburg seemed asleep, she went to his room. But just as she was on the point of yielding to him, she struck him and ran away, leaving George lonely and frustrated.

Kate lived across the street from the Presbyterian church. The pastor, Reverend Curtis Hartman, accidentally had learned that he could see into Kate's room from his study in the bell tower of the church. Night after night he looked through the window at Kate in her bed. He wanted at first to prove his faith, but his flesh was weak. One night, the same night Kate had fled from George Willard, he saw her come into her room. He watched her. Naked, she threw herself on the bed and furiously pounded the pillow. Then she arose, knelt, and began to pray. With a cry, the minister got up from his chair, swept the Bible to the floor, smashed the glass in the window, and dashed out into the darkness. Running to the newspaper office, he burst in upon George. Wild-eyed, his fist dripping blood, he told the astonished young man that God had appeared to him in the person of a naked woman, that Kate Swift was the instrument of the Almighty, and that he was saved.

Besides Kate Swift, there were other women in George's life. There was Helen White, the banker's daughter. One night George and Helen went out together. At first they laughed and kissed, but then a strange new maturity overcame them and kept them apart. Louis Trunnion, a farm girl, wrote to George, saying that she was his if he wanted her. After dark he went out to the farm and they went for a walk. There, in a berry field, George Willard enjoyed the love that Helen White had refused him.

Like Louis Trunnion, Louise Bentley also wanted love. Before going to live in Winesburg, Louise had lived on a farm, forgotten and unloved by a greedy, fanatical father who had desired a boy instead of a daughter. In Winesburg she live with the Hardy family while she went to school. She was a good student, praised by her teachers, but she was resented by the two Hardy girls, who believed that Louise was always showing off. More than ever, she wanted someone to love. One day she sent young John Hardy a note, and a few weeks later she gave herself to him. When it became clear that she was pregnant, Louise and John were married. John reproached her for cruelty toward her son David. She would not nurse her child and for long periods of time she would ignore him. Since she had never really loved her husband, nor he her, the marriage was not a happy one. At last she and John separated, and shortly afterward her father took young David to live with him on the farm.

Old Jesse Bentley was convinced that God had manifested himself in his grandchild, that the young David, like the Biblical hero, would be a saviour, the conqueror of the Philistines who owned the land Jesse Bentley wanted for himself. One day the old man took the boy into the fields with him. Young David had brought along a little lamb, and the grandfather prepared to offer the animal as a sacrifice to the Almighty. The youngster, terrified, stuck his grandfather and ran away, never to return to Winesburg.

The time came when George Willard had to choose between staying in Winesburg and starting out on his career as a writer. Shortly after his mother's death, George got up early one morning and walked to the railroad station. There, with the postmistress' expression of good luck in his ears, he boarded the train and left Winesburg behind him.

3. *The Honorary Consul* (Excerpt 1)

Not one of the characters in this book is based on a living character, from the British Ambassador to the old man Jose. The province and the city in Argentina where the scene is principally set bear, of course, resemblances to a real city and a real province. I have left them nameless because I wished to take certain liberties and not to be tied down to the street plan of a particular city or the map of a particular province.

For Victoria Ocampo with love,

And in memory of the many happy weeks

I have passed at San Isidro and Mar del Plata

Doctor Eduardo Plarr stood in the small port on the Parana, among the rails and yellow cranes, watching where a horizontal plume of smoke stretched over the Chaco. It lay between the red bars of sunset like a stripe on a national flag. Doctor Plarr found himself alone at that hour except for the one sailer who was on guard outside the maritime building. It was an evening which, by some mysterious combination of failing light and the smell of an unrecognized plant, brings back to some men the sense of childhood and of future hope and to others the sense of something which has been lost and nearly forgotten.

The rails, the cranes, the maritime building—these had been what Doctor Plarr first saw of his adopted country. The years had changed nothing except by adding the line of smoke which when he arrived here first had been hung out along the horizon on the far side of the Parana. The factory that produced it had not been built when he came down from the northern republic with his mother more than twenty years before on the weekly service from Paraguay.

4. *The Honorary Consul* (Excerpt 2)

He remembered his father as he stood on the quay at Asuncion beside the short gangway of the small river boat, tall and grey and hollow-chested, and promisedwith a mechanical optimism that he would join them soon. In a month—or perhaps three—hope creaked in his throat like a piece of rusty machinery.

It seemed in no way strange to the fourteen-year-old boy, though perhaps a little foreign, that his father kissed his wife on her forehead with a sort of reverence, as though she were a mother more than a be-mate. Doctor Plarr had considered himself in those days quite as Spanish as his mother, while his father was very noticeably English-born. His father belonged by right—and not simply by passport, to the legendary island of snow and fog, the country of Dichens and of Conan Dyle, even though he had probably retained few genuine memories of the land he had left at the age of ten. A picture book, which had been bought for him at the moment before embarkation by his parents, had survived—London Panorama—and Henry Plarr used often to turn over for his small son Eduardo the pages of flat grey photographs showing Buckingham Palace, the Tower of London, and a vista of Oxford Street, filled with hansoms and horse-drawn cabs and ladies who clutched long skirts. His father, as Doctor Plarr realized much later, was an exile, and this was a continent of exiles—of Italians, of Czechs, of Poles, of Welsh, of English. When Doctor Plarr as a boy read a novel of Dickens he read it as a foreigner might do, taking it all for contemporary truth for want of any other evidence, like a Russian who believes that the bailiff and the coffin-maker still follow their unchanged vocations in a world where Oliver Twist is somewhere imprisoned in a London cellar asking for more.

At fourteen he could not understand the motives which had made his father stay behind on the quay of the old capital on the river. It took more than a few years of life in Buenos Aires before he began to realize that the existence of an exile did not make for simplicity—so many documents, so many visits to government offices. Simplicity belonged by right to those who were native-born, those who could take the conditions of like, however bizarre, for granted. The Spanish language was Roman by origin, and the Romans were a simple people. Machismo—the sense of masculine pride—was the Spanish equivalent of virtus. It had little to do with English courage or a stiff upper lip. Perhaps his father in his foreign way was trying to imitate machismo when he chose to face alone the daily increasing dangers on the other side of the Paraguayan border, but it was only the stiff lip when showed upon the quay.

The young Plarr and his mother reached the river port at amost this hour of the evening on their way to the freat noisy capital of the republic in the south (their departure having been delayed some hours by a political demonstation), and something in the scene—the old colonial houses, a crumble of stucco in the street behind the waterfront—two lovers embracing on a bench—a moonstruck statue of a naked woman and the bust of an admiral with a homely Irish name—the electric light globes like great ripe fruit above a soft-drink stand—became lodged in the young Plarr's mind as a symbol of unaccustomed peace, so that, at long last, when he felt and rugent need to escape from somewhere from the skyscrapers, the traffic blocks, the sirens of polic-care and ambulances, the heroic statues of liberators on horseback, he chose to come back to this small northern city to work, with all the prestige of a qualified doctor from Benos

Aires. Not one of his friends in the capital or his coffee-house acquaintances came near to understanding his motive: he would find a hot humid unhealthy climate where nothing ever happened, not even violence.

"Perhaps it's unhealthy enough for me to build a better practice," he would reply with a smile which was quite as unmeaning—or false—as his father's expression of hope.

In Buenos Aires, during the long years of separation, they had received one letter only from his father. It was addressed on the envelope to both of them, Snora e hijo. The letter had not come through the post. They found it stuck under the door of their apartment on a Sunday evening about four years after their arrival when they returned from the cinema where they had watched *Gone with the Wind* for the third time. His mother never missed a revial, perhaps because the old film and the old stars made civil war seem for a few hours something static and undangerous. Clark Gable and Vivien Leigh bobbed up again through the years in spite of all the bullets.

The envelope was very dirty and scrumpled and it was marked "By hand", but they were never to learn by whose hand. It was not written on their old notepaper, which had been elegantly stamped in Gothic type with the name of the estancia, but on the line leaves of a cheap notebook. The letter was full, like the voice on the quay had been, of pretended hope— "things", his father wrote, were bound to settle down soon; it ws undated, so perhaps the "hope" had been exhausted for a long time before the letter arrived. They never heard from his father again; not even a report of a rumour reached them either of his imprisonment or of his death. He had concluded the letter with Spanish formality, "It is my great comfort that the two whom I love best in the world are both in safety, your affectionate husband and father, Henry Plarr."

5. *The Island of Dr. Moreau* (Excerpt 1)

On 1 February 1887 the Lady Vain was lost by collision with a derelict when about the latitude 1 S. and longitude 107°W.

On 5 January 1888—that is, eleven months and four days after, my uncle, Edward Prendick, a private gentleman, who certainly went aboard the Lady Vain at Callao, and who had been considered drowned, was picked up in latitude 5°3' S. and longitude 101° W. in a small open boat, of which the name was illegible, but which is supposed to have belonged to the missing schooner Ipecacuanha. He gave such a strange account of himself that he was supposed demented. Subsequently, he alleged that his mind was a blank from the moment of his escape from the Lady Vain. His case was discussed among psychologists at the time as a curious instance of the lapse of memory consequent upon physical and mental stress. The following narrative was found among his papers by the undersigner—his nephew and only heir, but it was not accompanied by any definite request for publication.

The only island known to exist in the region in which my uncle was picked up is Noble's Isle, a small volcanic islet, and uninhabited. It was visited in 1891 by H. M. S. Scorpion. A party of sailors then landed, but found nothing living thereon except certain curious white moths, some hogs and rabbits, and some rather peculiar rats. No specimen was secured of these. So that this narrative is without confirmation in its most essential particular. With that understood, there seems no harm in putting this strange story before the public, in accordance, as I believe, with my uncle's intentions. There is at least this much in its behalf: my uncle passed out of human knowledge about latitude 5° S. and longitude 105° W., and reappeared in the same part of the ocean after a space of eleven months. In some way he must have lived during the interval. And it seems that a schooner called the Ipecacuanha, with a drunken captain, John Davis, did start from Africa with a puma and certain other animals aboard in January 1887, that the vessel was well-known at several ports in the South Pacific, and that is finally disappeared from those sees (with a considerable amount of copra aboard) sailing to its unknown fate from Banya in December 1887, a date that tallies entirely with my uncle's story.

6. *The Island of Dr. Moreau* (Excerpt 2)

In the evening I started, and drove out to sea before a gentle wind from the southwest, slowly, steadily; and the island grew smaller and smaller, and the lank spire of smoke dwindled to a finer and finer line against the hot sunset. The ocean rose up around me, hiding that low, dark patch from my eyes. The daylight, the trailing glory of the sun, went streaming out of the sky, was drawn aside like some luminous curtain, and at last I looked into the blue gulf of immensity which the sunshine hides, and saw the floating hosts of the stars. The sea was silent, the sky was silent.

I was alone with the night and silence.

So I drifted for three days, eating and drinking sparingly, and meditating upon all that had happened to me—not desiring very greatly then to see men again. One unclean rag was about me, my hair a black tangle: no doubt my discoverers thought me a madman.

It is strange, but I felt no desire to return to mankind. I was only glad to be quit of the foulness of the Beast People.

And on the third day I was picked up by a brig from Apia to San Francisco. Neither the captain nor the mate would believe my story, judging that solitude and danger had made me mad; and fearing their opinion might be that of others, I refrained from telling my adventure further, and professed to recall nothing that had happened to me between the loss of the Lady Vain and the time when I was picked up again—the space of a year.

I had to act with the utmost circumspection to save myself from the suspicion of insanity.

My memory of the Law, of the two dead sailors, of the ambuscades of the darkness, of the body in the canebrake, haunted me; and, unnatural as it seems, with my return to mankind came, instead of that confidence and sympathy I had expected, a strange enhancement of the uncertainty and dread I had experienced during my stay upon the island. No one would believe me; I was almost as queer to men as I had been to the Beast People. I may have caught something of the natural wildness of my companions. They say that terror is a disease, and anyhow I can witness that for several years now a restless fear has dwelt in my mind—such a restless fear as a half-tamed lion cub may feel.

My trouble took the strangest form. I could not persuade myself that the men and women I met were not also another Beast People, animals half wrought into the outward image of human souls, and that they would presently begin to revert—to show first this bestial mark and then that. But I have confided my case to a strangely able man—a man who had known Moreau, and seemed half to credit my story; a mental specialist—and he has helped me mightily, though I do not expect that the terror of that island will ever altogether leave me. At most times it lies far in the back of my mind, a mere distant cloud, a memory, and a faint distrust; but there are times when the little cloud spreads until it obscures the whole sky. Then I look about me at my fellow-men; and I go in fear. I see faces, keen and bright; others dull or dangerous; others, unsteady, insincere—none that have the calm authority of a reasonable soul. I feel as though the animal was surging up through them; that presently the degradation of the Islanders will be played over again on a larger scale.

I know this is an illusion; that these seeming men and women about me are indeed men and women—men and women for ever, perfectly reasonable creatures, full of human desires and tender solicitude, emancipated from instinct and the slaves of no fantastic Law—beings altogether different from the Beast Folk. Yet I shrink from them, from their curious glances, their inquiries and assistance, and long to be away from them and alone. For that reason I live near the broad free downland, and can escape thither when this shadow is over my soul; and very sweet is the empty downland then, under the wind-swept sky.

When I lived in London the horror was well-nigh insupportable. I could not get away from men: their voices came through windows; locked doors were flimsy safeguards. I would go out into the streets to fight with my delusion, and prowling women would mew after me; furtive, craving men glance jealously at me; weary, pale workers go coughing by me with tired eyes and eager paces, like wounded deer dripping blood; old people, bent and dull, pass murmuring to themselves; and, all unheeding, a ragged tail of gibing children. Then I would turn aside into some chapel—and even there, such was my disturbance, it seemed that the preacher gibbered "Big Thinks", even as the Ape-man had done; or into some library, and there the intent faces over the books seemed but patient creatures waiting for prey. Particularly nauseous were the blank, expressionless faces of people in trains and omnibuses; they seemed no more my fellow-creatures than dead bodies would be, so that I did not dare to travel unless I was assured of being alone. And even it seemed that I too was not a reasonable creature, but only an animal tormented with some strange disorder in its brain which sent it to wander alone, like a sheep stricken with gid.

This is a mood, however, that comes to me now, I thank God, more rarely. I have withdrawn myself from the confusion of cities and multitudes, and spend my days surrounded by wise books—bright windows in this life of ours, lit by the shining souls of men. I see few strangers, and have but a small household. My days I devote to reading and to experiments in chemistry, and I spend many of the clear nights in the study of astronomy. There is—though I do not know how there is or why there is—a sense of infinite peace and protection in the glittering hosts of heaven. There it must be, I think, in the vast and eternal laws of matter, and not in the daily cares and sins and troubles of men, that whatever is more than animal within us must find its solace and its hope. I hope, or I could not live.

And so, in hope and solitude, my story ends.

（二）中译英

1.《香魂女》(节选)

节选一

做香油和做啤酒一样,讲究水!

没有崂山矿泉水,青岛啤酒就不会享誉国际;同样,没有香魂塘里的水,郜二嫂的油坊也不会让那么多人着迷!

香魂塘里的水是有些奇!

这水塘坐落在郜家营村南,方形,百米宽窄,最深处不过一丈,然即是再大旱年,塘水也不见稍减,据说塘底通着什么暗河。塘中夏日长满荷叶,花开时香裹全村,然水凉得怕人,很少有人愿意下去摸藕,偶有人敢试,也是下水片刻便牙齿发颤嘴唇乌青地慌忙爬上来。塘水颇清,却无鱼无虾无鳖等生存,且喝到嘴里又有一股苦涩味,极像是放了一种什么草药。村里的牛羊猪狗再渴,从不喜欢喝这塘里的水。可就是这塘水用来做小磨香油,特别好。会使油色橙黄微红,味甜润,入口清香醇爽。用这油来煎炸食品和调制凉拌菜肴,可去腥膻而生奇香,使人口生津液食欲大增,若用来配制中药,可滋阴、清热解毒、壮精髓、润脾胃;若用来熬膏外敷,具有凉血、止痛、生肌等功效。

郜二嫂的香魂油坊就坐落在香魂塘畔,油坊大门面南,出门五十步既是塘岸。

节选二

这么多年来,正是由于实忠的这份恋情,才使她对生活还怀着希望,才使她有了去开油坊挣钱的兴趣。差不多从他一到郜家起,她就注意到了住在这个村中的小货郎任实忠,他那时常挑一个不大的货郎担在本村和邻村间转悠,担子上有糖人、有头绳、有顶针和她喜欢的许多小东西,但她无钱买,她只能跟在他担子后面看。他自然也注意到了她,有时,他会在无人的时候,从自己的货郎上捡一块糖或一节头绳扔给她这个可怜的童养媳。他向她表示关切,她向他表示感激,两人的友谊从那时悄悄建立,这友谊继续发展,终于在若干年后越过了那个界限。不过这份爱恋不可能有一个美好的结果,她不是那种敢于不要名誉的女人,他也没有可以养活一个女人的家产,于是这爱便必须在极秘密的状态下存在。为了掩盖这份爱,两人都费尽了心机,有时为了获得一次见面的机会,不得不忍痛去演互相仇恨的戏。那个酷热的前天,两人夜间的来往有些频繁,为了不使人起疑,他们精心策划了一个"阴谋":任实忠故意在一个下午去她家的菜园里偷拔了两个萝卜,她看见后大叫大喊,立即告诉了丈夫,并和丈夫一起骂上实忠的门前,把实忠"贼呀!""小偷呀!""不要脸呀!"狗血淋头地骂了一顿。在丈夫郜二东挥着拐杖上前轮了实忠一杖的同时,她也上前抓破了实忠的胳膊,以此在村人面前造成一种两家有冤有仇的印象,巧妙地蒙住了村人的眼睛。那日过去几天后的一个夜里,当她重又躺在实忠的怀里时,又心疼至极地去抚摸他胳膊上的伤口。当她怀上实忠的女儿——芝儿时,因为知道这孩子不会再得什么遗传病,可又要把这孩子说成是郜二东的,她苦想了多少办法,在村里和家里编了多少谎话!先说算命先生算卦讲,正月怀胎的孩子,老天爷正是高兴的时候,不让他们带残带病出生;又说城里的名医讲了,老辈人的遗传病,并不是要传给所有的后代,有的子女照样正常;再说夜里做了一梦,梦见送子娘娘讲,既然已有一个得癫痫病的儿子,下一个孩子该让他聪明伶俐了!正是由于做了这些舆论准备,当模模样样芝儿出生后,才没引起村人和二东的怀疑,人们才称赞这是她守妇道的报应和福气……

2.《月牙儿》(节选)(老舍)

是的,我又看见月牙儿了,带着点寒气的一钩儿浅金。多少次了,我看见跟现在这个月牙儿一样的月牙儿;多少次了。它带着种种不同的感情,种种不同的景物,当我坐定了看它,它一次一次地在我记忆中的碧云上斜挂着。它唤醒了我的记忆,像一阵晚风吹破一朵欲睡的花。

那第一次,带着寒气的月牙儿确是带着寒气。它第一次在我的云中是酸苦,它那一点点微弱的浅金光儿照着我的泪。那时候我也不过是七岁吧,一个穿着短红棉袄的小姑娘。戴着妈妈给我缝的一顶小帽儿,蓝布的,上面印着小小的花,我记得。我倚着那间小屋的门垛,看着月牙儿。屋里是药味、烟味、妈妈的眼泪、爸爸的病;我独自在台阶上看着月牙,没人招呼我,没人顾得给我做晚饭。我晓得屋里的惨凄,因为大家说爸爸的病……可是我更感觉自己的悲惨,我冷饿,没人理我。一直我立到月牙儿落下去。什么也没有了,我不能不哭。可是我的哭声被妈妈的压下去;爸,不出声了,面上蒙了块白布。我要掀开白布,再看看爸,可是我不敢。屋里只是那么点点地方,都被爸占了去。妈妈穿上白衣,我的红袄上也罩了个没缝襟边的白袍,我记得,因为不断地撕扯襟边上的白丝儿。大家都很忙,嚷嚷的声儿很高,哭得很恸,可是事情并不多,也似乎值不得嚷:爸爸就装入那么一个四块薄板的棺材里，到处都是缝子。然后，五六个人把他抬了走。妈和我在后边哭。我记得爸，记得爸的木匣。那个木匣结束了爸的一切：每逢我想起爸来，我就想到打开那个木匣不能见着他。但是，那木匣是深深地埋在地里，我明知在城外哪个地方埋着它，可又像落在地上的一个雨点，似乎永难找到。

3.《我这一辈子》(节选)（老舍）

我幼年读过书，虽然不多，可是足够读七侠五义与三国演义什么的。我记得好几段聊斋，到如今还能说得很齐全动听，不但听的人都夸奖我的记性好，连我自己也觉得应该高兴。可是，我并念不懂聊斋的原文，那太深了；我所记得的几段，都是由小报上的"评讲聊斋"念来的——把原文变成白话，又添上些逗哏打趣，实在有个意思！

我的字写得也不坏。拿我的字和老年间衙门里的公文比一比，论个儿的匀适，墨色的光润，与行列的齐整，我实在相信我可以做个很好的"笔帖式"。自然我不敢高攀，说我有写奏折的本领，可是眼前的通常公文是准保能写到好处的。

凭我认字与写的本事，我本该去当差。当差虽不见得一定能增光耀祖，但是至少也比做别的事更体面些。况且呢，差事不管大小，多少总有个升腾。我看见不止一位了，官职很大，可是那笔字还不如我的好呢，连句整话都说不出来。这样的人既能做高官，我怎么不能呢？

可是，当我十五岁的时候，家里教我去学徒。五行八作，行行出状元，学手艺原不是什么低搭的事；不过比较当差稍差点劲儿罢了。学手艺，一辈子逃不出手艺人去，即使能大发财源，也高不过大官儿不是？可我并没和家里闹别扭，就去学徒了；十五岁的人，自然没有多少主意。况且家里老人还说，学满了艺，能挣上钱，就给我说亲事。在当时，我想象着结婚必是件有趣的事。那么，吃上二三年的苦，而后大人似的去耍手艺挣钱，家里再有个小媳妇，大概也很下得去了。

4.《孔乙己》（节选）

孔乙己是站着喝酒而穿长衫的唯一的人。他身材很高大；青白脸色，皱纹间时常夹些伤痕；一部乱蓬蓬的花白的胡子。穿的虽然是长衫，可是又脏又破，似乎十多年没有补，也没有洗。他对人说话，总是满口之乎者也，教人半懂不懂的。因为他姓孔，别人便从描红纸上的"上大人孔乙己"这半懂不懂的话里，替他取下一个绰号，叫作孔乙己。孔乙己一到店，所有喝酒的人便都看着他笑，有的叫道，"孔乙己，你脸上又添上新伤疤了！"他不回答，对柜里说，"温两碗酒，要一碟茴香豆。"便排出九文大钱。他们又故意地高声嚷道，"你一定又偷了人家的东西了！"孔乙己睁大眼睛说，"你怎么这样凭空污人清白……""什么清白？我前天亲眼见你偷了何家的书，吊着打。"孔乙己便涨红了脸，额上的青筋条条绽出，争辩道，"窃书不能算偷……窃书！……读书人的事，能算偷吗？"接连便是难懂的话，什么"君子固穷"，什么"者乎"之类，引得众人都哄笑起来：店内外充满了快活的空气。

听人家背地里谈论，孔乙己原来也读过书，但终于没有进学，又不会营生；于是愈过愈穷,弄到将要讨饭了。幸而写得一笔好字,便替人家抄抄书,换一碗饭吃。可惜他又有一样坏脾气,便是好吃懒做。坐不到几天,便连人和书籍纸张笔砚,一齐失踪。如是几次,叫他抄书的人也没有了。孔乙己没有法,便免不了偶然做些偷窃的事。但他在我们店里,品行却比别人都好,就是从不拖欠;虽然间或没有现钱,暂时记在粉板上,但不出一月,定然还清,从粉板上拭去了孔乙己的名字。

孔乙己喝过半碗酒,涨红的脸色渐渐复了原,旁人便又问道,"孔乙己,你当真认识字吗?"孔乙己看着问他的人,显出不屑置辩的神气。他们便接着说道,"你怎的连半个秀才也捞不到呢?"孔乙己立刻显出颓唐不安模样,脸上笼上了一层灰色,嘴里说些话;这回可是全是之乎者也之类,一些不懂了。在这时候,众人也都哄笑起来:店内外充满了快活的空气。

5.《看护》(微型小说)

孤傲清高的庄教授,终于耐不住寂寞,不觉忿忿然了。他是名牌大学的名教授,到国外讲学时生了病都未曾受到这般的冷落,高级知识分子名义上享受高级干部的待遇,可他这个"高知"怎么能跟对面床上的"高干"相比呢?人家床边老有处长、科长之类的干部伺候着,间或还有一两位漂亮的女人来慰问一番。床头柜和窗台上堆满了高级食品,有六个小伙子分成三班,昼夜二十四小时守护着他。医生、护士查病房也是先看那位财大势大的所谓王经理,后看他这个不是毫无名气的化学系教授,如果检查经理的病情用半个小时,检查他最多用十分钟。他的床边总是冷冷清清,儿子在几千公里以外搞他的导弹,女儿在国外上学,只有老伴每天挤公共汽车给他送点饭来,为他灌上一暖瓶热水。系里更是指望不上,半个月能派人来探望他一次就很不错了。人一落到这步境地最没有用就是学问、名气和臭架子。庄教授偏偏放不下他的身份,每天冲墙躺着,对王经理床边的一切不闻不问不看。鬼知道这位是什么经理? 现在"公司"遍地有,成千上万的大单位可以叫"公司",一两个人也可以戳起一块"公司"的招牌……

这一天王经理突然病势恶化,医生通知准备后事。他床边围着的人就更多了,连气宇轩昂的刘副经理也来了,他不愿假惺惺地用些没用的空话安慰一个快死的人。先沉默了一会儿,然后说了几句很实在的话,询问经理有什么要求,还有什么不放心的事情,他对垂死者提出的所有问题都满口答应。该说的话都说完了,便起身告辞,着手去安排经理的后事。看护王经理的人呼啦都站起身,撇下病人,争先恐后地去搀扶刘副经理,有的头前开门,有的跟在身边赔笑,前呼后拥,甚是威风。刘副经理勃然大怒:"我又不死,你们扶着我干什么?"

庄教授破例转过脸来,见孤零零的王经理奄奄待毙,两滴泪珠横着落在枕头上,他庆幸自己是"高知",不是"高干"。知识和钢笔到死也不会背叛他……

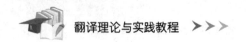

三、英汉互译原理在诗歌中的应用

（一）英译中

1. Right Here Waiting（Richard Max）

Oceans apart, day after day

And I slowly go insane

I hear your voice, on the line

But it doesn't stop the pain

If I see you next to never

How can we say forever

Wherever you go

Whatever you do

I will be right here waiting for you

Whatever it takes

Or how my heart breaks

I will be right here waiting for you

I took for granted

all the times

That I thought would last somehow

I hear your laughter

I taste the tears

But I can't get near you now

Oh, can't you see it baby

You've got me goin' crazy

Wherever you go

Whatever you do

I will be right here waiting for you

Whatever it takes

Or how my heart breaks

I will be right here waiting for you

I wonder how we can survive

This romance

But in the end if I'm with you
I'll take the chance
Oh, can't you see it baby
You've got me goin' crazy
Wherever you go
Whatever you do
I will be right here waiting for you
Whatever it takes
Or how my heart breaks
I will be right here waiting for you

2. Your Eyes (Heinrich Hein)

Your eyes, in their deep heavens,
Possess me, and will not depart;
A sea of blue thoughts, rushing,
Pouring over my heart.

（二）中译英

1. 十年（流行歌曲）

如果那两个字没有颤抖
我不会发现我难受
怎么说出口也不过是分手
如果对于明天没有要求
牵牵手就像旅游
成千上万个门口总有一个人要先走
怀抱既然不能逗留
何不在离开的时候
一边享受一边泪流
十年之前
我不认识你你不属于我
我们还是一样陪在一个陌生人左右
走过渐渐熟悉的街头
十年之后
我们是朋友还可以问候
只是那种温柔再也找不到拥抱的理由

情人最后难免沦为朋友
直到和你做了多年朋友
才明白我的眼泪
不是为你而流也为别人而流

2. 苏州园林题诗

(1) 赞苏州(1)(郑孝燮)

粉墙隔取闹中静
城市幽居世外源
峰岭溪池藏意蕴
亭廊轩榭远尘凡
竹藤花木弄清影
春夏秋冬却暑寒
凝固无声丝竹曲
知音天下谐人寰

(2) 赞苏州(2)(郑孝燮)

画境诗情形与神
苏州绝胜古园林
天开人造小中大
遗产根深民族魂

(3) 虞美人·馆娃宫怀古 (罗哲文)

灵岩山寺青青草,细雨流光照。吴山隐约下余晴。烟树迷离人散,渐黄昏。馆娃宫殿今何在,遗比几更改,年年岁岁旧情思,响屐廊声飘向有谁知。

注:馆娃宫为两千多年前苏州之名园,全国最早的帝王宫苑之一。

(4) 苏州风景园林诗赞 (孟兆祯)

天人合一龙脉宗
太湖西山育吴风
计成园冶立巨著
城市山林永世荣

(5) 响屐廊 (孟兆祯)

灵岩山石架空廊
瓦甏底托共鸣箱
梗榫结构薄地板
跫跫曼舞踢踏王

(6) 环秀山庄赞 (孟兆祯)

勺水巷山巍峨观

引流钳峦幽谷穿

因近求高岩壁立

环洞飞梁俨大千

3. 唐诗选译

（1）锄禾（李绅）

锄禾日当午，

汗滴禾下土；

谁知盘中餐，

粒粒皆辛苦。

（2）题都城南庄（崔护）

去年今日此门中，

人面桃花相映红。

人面不知何处去，

桃花依旧笑春风。

（3）登高（杜甫）

风急天高猿啸哀，渚清沙白鸟飞迴。

无边落木萧萧下，不尽长江滚滚来。

万里悲愁尝作客，百年多病独登台。

艰难苦恨繁霜鬓，潦倒新停浊酒杯。

（4）春怨（金昌绪）

打起黄莺儿，

莫教枝上啼。

啼时惊妾梦，

不得到辽西。

4. 苏州五洲心连心（儿童舞蹈）

（一）

同一个月亮天上挂，

同一个太阳放光华，

同一个地球连着你我他。

世界不算大，

苏州连着五大洲，

朋友遍天下！

啦……朋友遍天下。

（二）

同一片蓝天飞彩霞，
同一片大地开鲜花，
同一个星球连着你我他。
世界是一家。
苏州连着五大洲，
朋友遍天下！
啦……朋友遍天下。

5．苏州情缘

来了，来了，又来了，寒山寺

古运河之水渊源于北京

杨柳依依

黄昏的枫桥　钟声缭绕

苏州迎来了美丽的夜晚

故乡啊　故乡啊　我的故乡——苏州

来了，来了，又来了，美丽的水乡

古运河之水流向杭州

梧桐树荫　人们享受着绿意

如梭的船家　你奔向何方

拥抱苏州温柔的夜色

四、英汉互译原理在应用文中的应用

1．便笺（Notepaper）

（1）请假条（Request for Leave）

院办公室张秘书：

　　因祖父病重，欲回家探望，请假一周，从本月二日起至八日止。现附上父亲发来的电报，以资证明，敬请批准为盼。请假期间所缺功课，返校后定努力补上。
此致
　　敬礼

05(1)习凿齿
2007年11月2日

（2）借条（Forms of IOU）

今借到

公司财务科人民币壹佰元整。

此据

×××（人名）

二〇〇七年十月十二日

（注：I. O. U. 也可写成 IOU，是"I owe you"的缩写）

2. 邀请函（Letter of Invitation）

（1）朋友赴宴邀请（Inviting a Friend to Dinner）

Dear Lorna,

　　Will you and Mr. West have dinner with us on Tuesday, the fifth of May, at seven o'clock?

　　It's a long time since we have had the pleasure of seeing you and we do hope you can come.

　　　　　　　　　　　　　　　　　　　　　　　Sincerely yours,

　　　　　　　　　　　　　　　　　　　　　　　Elizabeth K. Benton

（2）应邀（Acceptance）

Dear Mrs. Benton,

　　West and I will be delighted to dine with you on Tuesday, the fifth of May, at seven o'clock. How nice of you to ask us!

　　We are both looking forward with great pleasure to seeing you and Dr. Benton again.

　　　　　　　　　　　　　　　　　　　　　　　Very sincerely yours,

　　　　　　　　　　　　　　　　　　　　　　　Lorna

(3) 谢却（Regret）

Dear Mrs. Benton,

  I've been putting off this note until the last possible moment, hoping and hoping West would get back from Nanjing in time for your dinner party. But now I must regretfully write that he'll still be out of town on Tuesday, the fifth; and we therefore cannot accept your kind invitation for dinner that day.

  It was sweet of you to ask us; and I know West will be as sorry as I am to miss an evening with you and Dr. Benton. We know how delightful such evenings at your house usually are!

Sincerely yours,
Lorna

(4) 婚礼邀请信（Wedding Invitation）

Dear Betty,

  David and I have set the date—and we want you to be the first to know it! We're going to be married very quietly at the Community Church on Thursday, June the twelfth, at noon. We're asking only a few people—just our nearest relatives and our very special friends.

  Can you be at the house about eleven, Betty, and go to the church with us? Then we'll all come back here after the ceremony; mother's giving a little wedding breakfast for us.

  Let's hope it's a bright sunny day on the twelfth!

Best wishes,
Helen

3. 信息咨询（Asking for Information）

亲爱的先生：

  我于 1998 年 8 月毕业于东南大学，主修工程学。目前在苏州大学担任助教兼实验员。为进修深造，我希望进入马萨诸塞理工学院工程研究生院攻读理学硕士学位。贵院有悠久的历史和优良的学风，师资力量雄厚，教学设备精良，享有很高的国际声誉。能在这样一所理想的高等学府深造，实为一件无上光荣的事情。长期以来我一直向往着能够有幸被录取在麻省理工学院学习。

  我很想知道贵院招收研究生的情况，不知您能否给我寄来报名表和有关材料。

  盼您早日复信。

李峰 敬上

4. 商业合同（Business Contract）

合　同

本合同由香港胜利电器贸易有限公司（下称"卖方"），按香港法律正式组织和存在的公司，总部设在香港_____，与尼日利亚泛非贸易有限公司（下称"买方"），按尼日利亚法律正式组织和存在的公司，总部设在尼日利亚_____，于 1988 年 12 月 8 日签订，合同如下：

卖方欲出口下述产品到下面规定的地方去，而买方欲进口所述货物在所述地方出售。

货　　名："胜利"牌 VEC—886 型手提式收录两用机。

数　　量：5 000 台，按照制造商标准包装。

价　　格：总额港币 1 000 000 元，FOB 香港净价为每台港币 200 元。

装　　运：1989 年 8 月，但须在 5 月底收到信用证。

付款方式：由买方开出的、保兑的、不可撤销的信用证。

备　　注：本合同能否执行取决于在香港和尼日利亚取得必要的各种许可证。假如买方要求加上保险，则只保平安险和水渍险。包括唛头、入港等装运细节必须在 1989 年 7 月 20 日之前告知卖方。这批货物只能在尼日利亚和西非其他地方出售。

买方：泛非贸易有限公司　　　　　　　卖方：胜利电器有限公司

　　（签字）　　　　　　　　　　　　　　（签字）

5. 通知、公告（Notice and Announcement）

（1）报告会通知（Notice About a Report Meeting）

外文系主办报告会

主讲人：×××教授

题　目：访美观感

地　点：外文系 101 教室

时　间：2007 年 10 月 21 日星期三下午 3 点半

　欢迎大家届时参加。

系办公室

2007 年 10 月 21 日

（2）停水通知 （Notice of Water Supply Suspension）

> 由于自来水管检修，明天从早晨 7 点至晚上 11 点停水，特此通知。
>
> 总务处
> 2007 年 11 月 2 日

（3）公告 （Announcement）

> 根据十一届人大一次会议批准的《国务院机构改革方案》，组建中华人民共和国环境保护部，不再保留国家环境保护总局。原国家环境保护总局网站于 2008 年 3 月 18 日正式更名为中华人民共和国环境保护部网站，域名变更为 WWW. MEP. GOV. CN。
>
> 新域名自 2008 年 3 月 25 日起启用。
>
> 特此公告。
>
> 中华人民共和国环境保护部
> 2008 年 3 月 18 日

6．证书（Certificate）

（1）学位证书 （Certificate of Degree）

> THE UNIVERSITY OF EDINBURGH
> This is to certify that
> David Smith
> was duly admitted to the degree of
> Bachelor of Arts
> in the University of Edinburgh on
> 18 December, 1988
>
> Chancellor
> Registrar

（2）公证书 （Notarial Certificate）

> (2007)浙温证字第 011023 号
>
> 兹证明廖阿珍(女,一九六六年三月九日出生)与程安重(男,一九六三年十一月一日出生)于一九八九年三月二十日在浙江省温州市登记结婚,于二〇〇四年十月二十八日在温州市鹿城区人民法院调解离婚。根据温州市鹿城区人民法院(2004)鹿一民初字第 121 号民事调解书,廖阿珍与程安重的婚生女程琳(女,一九八九年六月十日出生)归女方廖阿珍抚养。
>
> 中华人民共和国浙江省温州市中信公证处
> 公证员
> 二〇〇七年三月三十日

7. 合作倡议(Proposal for Cooperation)

(1) 出版社合作倡议(A Publisher's Proposal for Cooperation)

现代教育出版社是中国政府为了加快中国出版事业的发展,使中国教育图书出版尽快与世界接轨,而新成立的一家国家级大型的教育图书出版专业机构。下设有中国小学、中学、大学教材出版中心,教育助学读物出版中心,教育辞书工具书出版中心,世界教育图书出版中心,世界优秀图书读物译作中心等10个出版中心。本社成立的目的就是形成中国教育图书出版的主要基地。本社已组建强大的编辑队伍、专业化的翻译人员、广泛的发行网络,并开始向世界翻译引介了大量的国际教育类图书。

贵社出版的图书在国际上有着广泛的影响,本社热切希望与贵社建立良好的合作关系。合作关系包括以下内容:

一、共享出版信息。定期互换最新出版图书目录,如有需要,可提供已出版图书的详细信息。

二、建立版权合作渠道,一方如需翻译出版另一方的图书,对方应优先赋予版权。版权转让费双方协商,并签订相关合同。

三、建立互访机制。如一方提出访问要求,另一方应为访方提供访问便利,所有访问费用均由访问方承担。

四、其他合作。

本社热切希望能与贵社建立长期的、密切的合作关系,为繁荣出版事业、加强文化交流、实现互利双赢提供一个良好的稳定的平台。

现代教育出版社
社长:宋一夫

(2) 公司合作倡议(A Company's Proposal for Cooperation)

上海上外(集团)公司简介

上海上外(集团)公司是由上海外国语大学创办,经上海市教卫办批准的由市工商管理局注册登记的全市高校系统第一家综合性集团公司。它依托上海外国语大学人才、信息等综合优势,按现代企业制度规范操作运行。恪守"依法经营、信誉第一、优质服务、利国利民"的企业宗旨,努力把集团公司办成具有较强实力和外语特色的科技经济实体。

上外(集团)公司现有总资产5千万元,拥有8个子公司,主要经营外语音像制品、外语教材、报刊杂志、翻译服务、涉外劳务培训和组织国内外旅游等。为适应市场经济的激烈竞争,上外(集团)公司将不断扩大和增强实力,创造条件,争取在科技项目开发、国内外贸易、国际旅游、房地产开发等方面经营,愿与社会各界广泛合作,尽快在境内外投资兴办一批合资、合作企业。

上外(集团)公司热忱欢迎海内外各界仁人志士前来洽谈业务,长期合作,共创大业。

8. 学生守则（Rules for the Students）

(1) 热爱祖国,热爱人民,拥护中国共产党,努力学习,准备为社会主义贡献力量。
(2) 按时到校,不迟到,不早退,不旷课。
(3) 专心听讲,勤于思考,认真完成作业。
(4) 坚持锻炼身体,积极参加文娱活动。
(5) 讲究卫生,不吸烟,不喝酒,不随地吐痰。
(6) 积极参加劳动,生活俭朴。
(7) 遵守学校纪律,遵守公共秩序,遵守国家法令。
(8) 尊敬师长,团结同学,对人有礼貌,不骂人,不打架。
(9) 热爱集体,爱护公物,不做对集体和别人有害的事。
(10) 谦虚诚实,有错即改。

9. 年度工作总结（Annual Summing-Up Report）

中小学外语教学研究会工作总结

2007年已经过去了,为克服缺点,发扬优点,改进今后的工作,我们把过去一年中所做的工作总结如下:

由于全体会员的团结合作,我们完成了以下几项工作:

(1) 我们发展了新会员。会员人数由105人增加到198人。
(2) 今年举行了8次公开课。促进了教师相互学习,改进了教法。
(3) 每月举办了一次座谈会,与会者交流了教学经验和技巧,讨论了在教改中遇到的问题。
(4) 为提高新教师素质,举办了一期短训班。
(5) 在工人文化宫建立了"英语角",教师、学生可以与外国旅游者一起练习口语。
(6) 邀请了国内外学者、专家做学术讲座,以促进交流教学经验和获得外语教学的最新信息。
(7) 出版了两本英语教学论文集,赢得了中小学教师的一致好评。

10. 序、后记和内容提要（Foreword, Afterword and Summaries）

(1)《走进上海朱家角》序（蒋耀,上海市青浦区区长）

上海名镇朱家角,位于上海市西郊美丽的淀山湖畔,是上海市与江苏、浙江两省交界处青浦区的重镇。她以历史悠久、物产丰富、风景优美、民风淳朴而素负盛名,以江南水乡风情保留完整而著称。作为生活在这里的朱家角人,我们感到无比的自豪。

朱家角是上海古文明的发源地,六千多年前就有先民在这里开荒种植。三国时期为东吴所辖,唐宋时期趋以繁荣,宋元时期形成集市,名朱家村。明代万历年间正式建镇,名珠街阁,又名珠溪。以后称朱家角,明清时期成为江南地区著名的商镇。明末清初,发达的布业带动米业、油业,朱家角百业兴旺。随后资本主义萌芽显现,直至近现代的经济发展。朱家角的演进是一幅秀美壮丽的历史长卷。

当前,随着上海现代大都市的发展,保护和继承朱家角历史文化遗产,越来越受到人们的关注。朱家角曾荣获上海市四大名镇的称号;2006年,又是上海市唯一荣获中国最值得外国人去的50个地方金奖;今年,还将申报中国历史文化名镇。朱家角人决心在建设新郊区、新农村的进程中立足当前、着眼长远,对古镇的历史文脉、文化底蕴、风貌建筑、风土人情,本着正确处理保护与传承、保护与利用、保护与发展的关系,具体规划、加大投入、组织实施,既要保护朱家角的江南水乡风貌,又要改善群众的生活环境。在保护中扩大利用,以利用推动保护,使保护和利用走上良性发展的轨道,使朱家角的传统历史文脉在发展中生生不息、发扬光大。

临近丹桂飘香时节,《走进上海朱家角》与广大读者见面了。她创意新颖,以特有的视角深入品味朱家角的历史、文脉、风貌、习俗。以图文并茂的形式使您在受到视觉冲击的同时,感受到朱家角人崇文重德、兼容并包的人文精神,使您了解世代朱家角人繁衍生息创造历史、创造文化的轨迹,彰显人本思想对于社会发展的贡献。

朱家角保护历史文化遗产的工作,需要向先进地区学习,我们亟待专家、学者、志士仁人莅临指教。当我们奉上这本画册时,真诚地说一声:纯朴热情的朱家角人欢迎您!

2006年8月

(2)《海外掠影》(影集)序

"世上不缺少美,缺少的是发现。"——罗丹

说实在的,当建业君捧出一大摞照片交我欣赏时,真一时不敢相信,这全部出自他的摄影作品!

建业君,出身江南水乡。自幼得故乡之灵气,悟万物之美观。他少年得志,从政十数载,学历资历颇深。我觉得他一直很忙,马不停蹄,时间在他那里总嫌不够。他有强烈的责任心,总想把什么事情都做得完美。因此,他事业有成。

这样一个忙人,怎么会有暇拍摄出如此量大的照片,真是不可思议。带着这种疑问,细细品味他的摄作,方才悟出答案来。原来这些年他因学习和工作的需要,常旅迹天涯,行踪遍欧美亚太。在紧张的学习参观、洽商交流之余,抽暇拿出他的随身"傻瓜"袖珍相机,捕捉世界。用他的镜头,瞄准一切美好的失去,无论城市大观、建筑艺术、自然风光、环境艺术、园林景致、雕塑精品、风土人情,都一一摄入他的相机之中。虽然,摄影只是他的业余爱好,但他能以专业的审美观、独到的构图、精致的光线、秀逸的意境、丰富的内涵,将异国风情之美表现得淋漓尽致。他的作品绝无矫揉造作,却是那般清新自然,充分体现出他的艺术修养、文化底蕴和敏捷的洞察力。再则,用他的话来说,他不是为摄影而摄影,而是用相机记录下时代的信息、文明的脉搏,作为借鉴。这对他的事业无疑是一种极好的辅助。

狄德罗说:"有感情的地方就有美。"阅读他的作品,我体悟出他的感情美;阅读他的作品,我窥见他的另一面。如今,鳞选出一部分作品编印成册,以飨有人,可喜可贺!并愿建业君的快门不息,奉献出更多更美的照片来。

辛巳中秋 文翰于姑苏城南见博斋

(3)《我在政协这五年》内容提要

作者以担任第十届全国政协常委的亲身经历,以一个民主党派成员的视角,既从实践层面、以丰富的内容反映了一个民主党派成员的参政议政历程,更从理论层面、以深入的思

考探索了如何在政协这个平台上参政议政。

作者把民主党派成员、全国政协常委、教育学者、政府官员等多个角色有机统一起来，互相促进，形成了独特的参政议政风格、独到的思考和见解。

全书共收录作者五年中所提交的提案（含答复）81份，内容丰富；"参政感言"是作者历年参政议政的感受、体会和经验，思考深刻；"议政网事"是作者每年做客人民网、新华网等媒体与网友进行交流的实录摘要，生动鲜活；"媒体关注"收录了媒体对作者参政议政报道的目录，可资参考；"两会走笔"收录了作者两会期间的博客和政协大会发言，真实质朴。

本书叙述个人的参政历程，在一定程度上反映了中国民主政治的进程，具有史料与文献价值。同时，它也是为政协委员如何参政议政提供了可资借鉴的范例。

（4）《悲鸿南归——徐悲鸿绘画经典作品苏州特展》前言

苏州——中国南方的美丽城市，人们都说"上有天堂，下有苏杭"，在经济发展的大潮中，全国每个城市高楼林立，而苏州仍保持着它那中国古典式的建筑美，映衬着苏州的山明水秀，呈现我国文化的深刻内涵。

悲鸿出生在江苏省宜兴，距苏州很近，他和苏州也曾结下不解之缘，把苏州视作故乡。八年抗日战争，悲鸿居住在重庆山区和奔走于国内外开办筹赈画展以救济国内难民和烈士遗孤。抗日战争胜利以后，他又被派到北平接收国立北平艺专，忙于教学工作，但他对故乡和南方的怀念仍缠绕于心。直到解放后中华人民共和国成立，他担任中央美术学院院长。一九五三年全国第二届文艺工作者代表大会召开，他计划会议结束以后便去南方看看他怀念的地方和老朋友，但是没有料到，就在文代会的第一天他担任执行主席，从早到晚开了一整天会，晚上又奉命陪波兰代表晚宴，因劳累过度突发脑出血，抢救无效而逝世。

这次的苏州画展，我们徐悲鸿纪念馆极为重视，不仅因为苏州闻名于国内外，且因为苏州有着悲鸿一份深情，他和苏州著名油画家颜文樑先生是挚友，一九三三年悲鸿赴欧洲举办画展，耗时一年多，他在中央大学艺术系的课是请颜文樑先生代授的。他们在艺术上的主张相同，而且都先后在国立巴黎美术学校学习。悲鸿也曾在苏州美专讲演和教课，他送给颜文樑先生一幅很大的中国画，凝重地书写了"中流砥柱"四个字，还在旁添上了一行小字"素描者艺之操也"。美丽的苏州，真挚的友谊，曾经给予三十年代的悲鸿在痛苦中以温暖和抚慰。这次苏州画展，我们特意名之曰"悲鸿南归"，是为了补偿悲鸿生前未竟之志，也因此，在北京市文物局的大力支持下，我们对展览做了充分的准备，我们携带的巨幅油画《田横五百士》是悲鸿在欧洲学成归国后创作的第一幅大型油画。

我很欣幸，在我八十五岁的暮年能亲自护送悲鸿的原作赴苏州展览。这次携带的悲鸿四十八件原作都是悲鸿的精品，有油画、国画、素描、速写、水彩、粉画，这些作品都展现了悲鸿娴熟而精炼的艺术技巧、完美的造型、丰富的色彩和中西结合的创造，描写和反映了现实，是他所生活的时代的珍品。

悲鸿出生于贫困之家，他以坚强的毅力和无比的勤奋而走向了世界，对于今天的年轻人来说，也是一个榜样。

我预祝画展成功，并向苏州市领导以及为画展而工作的同志们表示深深的谢忱。

附录

第十章参考译文

一、英汉互译原理在散文中的应用

（一）英译中

1. 天才在工作

亨利·福特在学校里常常心不在焉。有一天,他和一个小朋友把一块手表拆开了。老师很生气,让他们放学后留下来,把表修好才能回家。当时这位老师并不知道小福特的天才。只用了十分钟,这位机械奇才就把手表修好,走在回家的路上了。

福特对各种东西的工作原理总是很感兴趣。曾有一次,他把茶壶嘴用东西堵住,然后把茶壶放在火炉上。他便站在一边等候着会出现什么情况。当然,水开后变成了水蒸气。因为水蒸气无处逸出,茶壶便爆炸了,因而打碎了一面镜子和一扇窗户。这个小发明家也被严重地烫伤了。

多年后,福特的好奇心和他的动手能力使他得到了回报。他曾经梦想着去制造一辆无马行进的车。他造成了一辆这样的车后,运输界发生了永久性的变化。

2. 热爱生活

不论你的生活如何卑贱,你要面对它生活,不要躲避它,更别用恶言咒骂它。它不像你那样坏。你最富有的时候,倒是看似最穷。爱找缺点的人就是到天堂里也能找到缺点。你要爱你的生活,尽管它贫穷。甚至在一个济贫院里,你也还有愉快、高兴、光荣的时候。夕阳反射在济贫院的窗上,像身在富户人家窗上一样光亮;在那门前,积雪同在早春融化。我只看到,一个从容的人,在哪里也像在皇宫中一样,生活得心满意足而富有愉快的思想。城镇中的穷人,我看,倒往往是过着最独立不羁的生活。也许因为他们很伟大,所以受之无愧。大多数人以为他们是超然的,不靠城镇来支援他们;可是事实上他们是往往利用了不正当的手段来对付生活,他们是毫不超脱的,毋宁是不体面的。视贫穷如园中之花而像圣人一样耕植它吧!不要找新的花样,无论是新的朋友或新的衣服,来麻烦你自己。找旧的,回到那里去。万物不变,是我们在变。你的衣服可以卖掉,但要保留你的思想。

3. 皮匠和银行家

一个皮匠从早到晚在唱歌中度过。无论见到他本人或听见他的歌声都使人觉得很愉快。他对于制鞋工作比当上了希腊七贤人还要满足。与此相反,他的邻居是个银行家,拥有万贯家财,却很少唱歌,晚上也睡得不好。他偶尔在黎明时分迷迷糊糊刚入睡,皮匠的歌声便把他吵醒了。银行家郁郁寡欢地抱怨上帝没有把睡眠也制成一种像食品或饮料那样可以买卖的商品。后来,银行家就叫人把这位歌手请来,问道:"格列戈里师傅,你一年赚多少钱?""先生,你问我一年赚多少钱吗?"快乐的皮匠笑道:"我从来不算这笔账,我是一天一天地过日子,总而言之坚持到年底,每天挣足三餐。""啊,朋友,那么你一天赚多少钱呢?""有时多一点,有时少一点;不过最糟糕的是一年中总有些日子不准我们做买卖,牧师又常常在圣徒名单上添新名字,否则我们的收入也还算不错。"银行家被皮匠的直率逗笑了,他说:"我要你从今以后不愁没钱用。这一百枚钱你拿去,小心放好,需要时拿来用吧。"皮匠觉得自己好像看到了过去几百年来大地为人类所需而制造出来的全部财富。他回到家中,埋藏好硬币,同时也埋葬了他的快乐。他不再唱歌了;从他得到这种痛苦的根源那一刻起,他的嗓子就哑了。睡眠与他分手;取而代之的却是担心、怀疑、虚惊。白天,他的目光尽朝埋藏硬币的方向望;夜间,如果有只迷途的猫弄出一点声响,他就以为是有人来抢他的钱。最后,这个可怜的皮匠跑到他那富有的邻居家里说:"把你的一百枚钱拿回去,还我的睡眠和歌声来。"

4. 我所追求的生活

这一定是世间无数对夫妻的生活写照,这种生活模式给人一种天伦之美。它使人想起一条平静的溪流,蜿蜒畅游过绿茵的草场,浓荫遮蔽,最后注入烟波浩渺的汪洋大海;但是大海太过平静,太过沉默,太过不动声色,你会突然感到莫名的不安。也许这只是我自己的一种怪诞想法,在那样的时代,这想法对我影响很深:我觉得这像大多数人一样的生活,似乎欠缺了一点儿什么。我承认这种生活有社会价值,我也看到了它那井然有序的幸福,但我血液里的冲动却渴望一种更桀骜不驯的旅程。这样的安逸中好像有一种叫我惊惧不安的东西。我的心渴望一种更加惊险的生活。只要生活中还能有变迁以及不可知的刺激,我愿意踏上怪石嶙峋的山崖,奔赴暗礁满布的海滩。

5. 睡眠小议

这篇文章是让读者暖暖和和躺在床上品赏的——这时候他或者她即将入睡,衣服放在耳边,风声在远方一个什么缝隙里呼啸。

"愿老天爷降福,"桑丘大声说道,"给那头一个发明睡觉的人!它把人浑身上下严严实实裹了起来,跟个大斗篷似的。"这真是一个甜蜜的时刻——你在床上舒舒服服安卧,觉得自己正在轻轻松松堕入睡乡。好处还在前头,并未过去:你受困足软,身体自自然然摆出一副惬意的姿态——一天的劳累结束了。

据说,子夜之前睡觉最好——这样的信息,造物主用她那黑沉沉的夜色、凉飕飕的露水,透漏给我们。及时登榻还另有一层理由,因为众口一词承认:早上赖在床上不起即等于大大缩短人的寿命。至少说,睡懒觉和长寿总难并行不悖,而且它还容易让人发胖。不过,此类问题与其归入睡眠这个题目之下,不如说与早起有关。

…………

婴儿的睡眠,最为优美;疲劳的人在户外睡眠,最为酣畅;水手在艰苦航程之后的睡眠,最为圆满;为某种意念所苦的人,对睡眠最为欢迎;哭泣后的母亲的睡眠,最动人心弦;一个顽皮小孩的睡眠,最为轻松;一个深受爱慕的新娘的睡眠,最为骄傲。

6. 知识的文学与力量的文学

我们所讲的文学究竟是指什么?通常人们会不假思索地认为一切书中所印之物都是文学。这种说法经不起深究。再糊涂的人也很容易弄明白,文学关照人类某种普遍的共同志趣,这是文学的要素——仅仅一个地方、一个行业或一个人的志趣,即使以书本的形式出现也算不上文学。文学的定义不难加以限制,同样也容易加以扩充。太多印成书本的东西不能称作文学;大量真正的文学之作从未跻身书林。基督教堂每周的布道词,数量庞大的教坛文学,或告诫,或鼓励,或安抚,或警告,广泛作用于民众心灵,能在图书殿堂中占有一席之位的恐怕百中无一。又譬如戏剧,英国莎士比亚最优秀的剧作,以及古希腊戏剧鼎盛时期的所有代表之作,在成为读本发表之前,早就在看演出的观众面前发表过了(根据"发表"一词最准确的意义),作为一种文学影响着公众的思想。这种舞台表演形式,在传抄或印刷价格昂贵的年代,效果更甚于书本。

书不等于文学,内涵不同,不可相互替代。众多文学,诸如舞台戏剧、法庭辩词及讲坛说教(讲学或演说),难以成书;成书之物本身可能并无多大文学趣味。要纠正普遍存在的关于文学的模糊观念,与其给它一个恰当的定义,不如把它的两个功用划分清楚。文学这个总称,就其重大的社会职能来说,可分为两种不同的类别:一是书本知识,一是力量文学。二者经常混为一谈,但分而论之,本质截然不同且相互排斥。前者意在传授知识;后者旨在感化心灵。前者是舵;后者是桨或帆。前者诉诸一般推理;后者往往通过愉悦和感悟,从根本上诉诸人更高的悟性或理性。远观,它穿过培根爵士所谓的"朴素之光",直达一物;近察,泛着蒙蒙水汽的幽光,还罩着人类七情六欲的薄雾轻纱、虹霓彩衣,但它必须穿透,否则就不是力量文学。人们对文学这种高级功用思之甚少,若有人认为传播知识只是书本的低级功用,便会以为那是谬言妄语。此言虽然有悖常理,但确实值得我们玩味。

我们求知获艺用的都是平常语言,涉及新奇事物,也能据理了解。人类公理,之所以为真理大道,就在于它并不奇玄,即使最微贱之人也能完全明了。作为胚芽或潜在的天性,它永远并存于最高贵者和最微贱者心中,只需培养,无需栽种。能被移栽,绝非真理大道,只有低级事理才以此为准。此外,还有种东西比真理更为神奇——那就是力量,或对真理的感悟。譬如,儿童对社会有何影响?儿童幼弱无能,天真无邪,纯朴无伪,令人顿生爱怜之心、叹慕之情,人之本性从而得到巩固与升华。唤醒宽容的柔弱、象征圣洁的天真和远离世俗的纯朴,这些也是上苍眼中最为宝贵的品质,存于永久的记忆之中,需要不断重温。高级文学,也即力量文学,功用就在于此。我们从《失乐园》中学到什么?什么也没有。从一本食谱学到什么呢？新东西，每段都有从前不知的东西。但是，你会因此判定这本翻烂的食谱就比那部美妙的诗篇更高明吗？从弥尔顿那学到的不是知识，因为知识，哪怕有一百万条，也依然是在尘世上开步一百万次罢了。从弥尔顿那得到的是力量，就是用潜在的悟性去感悟无限；在那里，每一个搏动，每一次倾注，都是朝着更高处攀升，好似顺着雅各的天梯攀登向上，从地面一步一步登上神秘的天庭。知识的一切步伐，自始至终，只是在同一层面上前进，永远不能使人从古老的地面上提升一步；而力量迈出的第一步就是飞升，飞向另一个境界——在那里，尘世的一切都被忘却。

7. 怎样才能活得老

题目虽然这么写，实际上本文所要谈的却是人怎样才可以不老。对于像我这样年纪大的人来说，这个问题就重要得多了。我的头一条忠告是，你可得要挑选好你的先人啊。我父母年纪轻轻就去世了，可是说到祖辈，我还是选得不错。我外祖父固然是在风华正茂之年就弃世了，当时他只有六十七岁，但是我的祖父、祖母和外祖母却都活到了八十岁以上。再往远一点说，在我的先人之中，我发现只有一位活得不长，他得了一种现在已不多见的病，那就是头让人砍掉了。我的一位曾祖母，和吉本是朋友，活到了九十二岁，她直到临终都使儿孙望而生畏。我外祖母有九个孩子活了下来，有一个孩子很小就死了，她还流产过多次。丈夫一死，她就致力于女子高等教育。她是戈登学院的创办人之一，曾竭力使医学专业对妇女开放。她常对人说，她在意大利碰到过一位愁容满面的先生，就问他为什么闷闷不乐，他说两个小孙孙刚刚离开他。"我的天哪！"我外祖母就说，"我孙子孙女有七十二个，要是每离开一个都要难过，我的生活可就太痛苦了"听了这话，老先生说，"Madre snaturale！"但是我作为七十二人中的一员，倒是赞成她的办法的。她年过八十就老睡不着觉，所以从午夜凌晨三点总要读些科普读物。我相信她从来没有功夫去注意到自己是在日益衰老。我认为，要想永葆青春，这是最好的办法。你要是有广泛的爱好和强烈的兴趣，而且还有能力参加一些活动，你就没有理由去考虑自己已经活了多少岁数这样的具体数字，更没有理由去考虑自己的余年大概是很有限的这种事情。

谈到健康问题，我就没有什么可说的了，因为我没怎么生过病。我想吃什么就吃什么，想喝什么就喝什么，眼睛睁不开了就去睡觉，从来不为对身体有益而搞什么活动，然而实际上我喜欢做的事大都是有助于增进身体健康的。

从心理方面来说，到了老年，有两种危险倾向需要注意防止。一是过分地怀念过去。老想着过去，总觉得过去怎么好怎么好，或者总是为已故的朋友而忧伤，这是不妥的。一个人应当考虑未来，考虑一些可以有所作为的事情。要做到这一点是不大容易的；自己过去的经历就是一个越来越沉重的包袱。人们往往会对自己说，我过去感情那么丰富，思想那么敏锐，现在不行了。如果真是这样的话，那就不要去想它，而如果你不去想它，情形就很可能不是这样了。

另一件需要避免的事就是老想和年轻人待在一起，希望从青年人的活力中汲取力量。孩子们长大之后，就希望独立生活，如果你还像他们年幼时那样关心他们，你就会成为他们的累赘，除非他们特别麻木不仁。我不是说一个人不应当关心孩子，而是说这种关心主要应该是多为他们着想,可能的话,给他们一些接济,而不应该过分地动感情。动物,一旦它们的后代能够自己照料自己,它们就不管了;但是人,由于抚养孩子的时间长,是难以这样做的。

我认为,如果老年人对于个人以外的事情怀有强烈的兴趣,并参加适当的活动,他们的晚年是最容易过得好的。在这一方面,他们由于阅历深,是能够真正做得卓有成效的,也正是在这一方面,他们从经验中得出的智慧既可以发挥作用,又不至使人感到强加于人。告诫成年的子女不要犯错误,那是没有用的,一来他们不听你的,二来犯错误本身也是受教育的一个重要方面。但是如果你这个人对于个人以外的事情不发生兴趣,就会感到生活空虚,要不你就老是惦记着儿孙。在这种情况下,你可要明白,虽然你还可以在物质方面给他们以帮助,比如给他们零用钱,或者为他们织毛衣,但你绝不要指望他们会喜欢跟你做伴。

有些老年人因怕死而惶惶不安。年轻人有这种情绪是情有可原的。如果青年人由于某种原因认为自己有可能在战斗中死去,想到生活所提供的最美好的东西自己全都无法享受,觉得受了骗,因而感到痛苦,这是无可指责的。但是对于老年人来说,他经历了人生的酸甜苦辣,自己能做的事情都做到了,怕死就未免有些可鄙,有些不光彩了。要克服这种怕死的念头,最好的办法——至少在我看来——就是逐渐使自己关心更多的事情,关心那些不跟自己直接有关的事情,到后来,个人所有的壁垒就会慢慢消失,个人的生活也就越来越和生活融合在一起了。人生应当像条河,开头河身狭小,夹在两岸之间,河水奔腾咆哮,流过巨石,飞下悬崖。后来河面逐渐展宽,两岸离得越来越远,河水也流得较为平缓,最后流进大海,与海水浑然一体,看不出任何界限,从而结束其单独存在的那一段历程,但毫无痛苦之感。如果一个人到了老年能够这样看待自己的一生,他就不会怕死了,因为他所关心的一切将会继续下去。如果随着精力的衰退,日见倦怠,就会觉得长眠未尝不是一件好事。我就希望在工作时死去,知道自己不能再做的事有人会继续做下去,并且怀着满意的心情想到自己能做到的事都已做到了。

8. 就是这些无奈的倦骨头让我痛哭

我外曾祖父还是个小孩的时候那些白人就来到了这已遭创伤的"膝盖河谷",来到了这流着冰冷河水的水域。他们苍白的脸上罩着一副没有表情的咨啬相。我外曾祖父独自一人在他母亲的小屋里那狭隘的泥土地上赤裸着身子瑟瑟发抖,睁大眼睛透过门缝盯着那熟悉的河谷残雪未消的两岸。雪过去一直是白色的,比那些鬼子的脸色还要白,白得就像青烟色夜空中的萤火虫在闪着光亮。可是,在这一天,雪色黯淡了下来,斑斑点点染着红色,甚至成了黑色。那些临死的人的呻吟和哭声响了起来,变成令人恐怖的如雷贯耳的悲歌,对此这片土地难以忘却(据说甚至现在有时也能听到,而且此时整个大地都辗转反侧难以入睡)。在疾风暴雨般的枪声过后,在那被打破的沉寂中,黯淡下来的白雪随着冷风遮盖了那些僵硬的尸体——此时他们眼睛茫然无色地睁着,却一无所见,就像冬天的天空那样苍白无色。我外曾祖父半夜里有时对我说,那里流满了我们的血,我们的血顿时浸染着大地,被泥土吸食——而且我们是死在平原上的,他们枪口的硝烟还没有散尽。他们把子弹打进了死人的头颅和活人的心口,所以没有一个人能幸免于难。我此后一辈子也没有忘记。我已经成了一个老人,可是我死的时候还看到了那"膝盖河谷"的伤痛。

那些已经被忘记的死人的哭声和风声搅在一起,像蛇一样溜进我的房间,我说不清哪些是风声,哪些是哭声。我总是紧紧抓住、拧着床单告诉自己说,是汗水浸透了那单薄破烂的棉被,而不是血水;我告诉自己我眼睛刺痛是因为流泪的缘故,而不是因为那血染变暗的白雪饿狼般的袭击。

在那最深远的南方,风声喃喃细语般穿过那些因为对炭黑色的肌肉记忆犹新而变黑的树林,刮过那因背负着那些无名的黑奴而变得沉重的大地,人们悄悄流传说,脸上有胎记的孩子能听到死人的号啕痛哭。可是我出生在一个听不到人们说悄悄话的地方,出生在一切都显得整齐苍白的一家北方的医院。对于你们说的胎记这件事儿,我要是问我母亲的话她就会说那是因为我太累了,因为我出生花了两天时间,生下来八磅零十五盎司,而且偏偏生在七月四号。不管怎么说,问题并不是我能不能看到他们,而是我能感到他们的存在,感到那些已经残缺不全的有关他们的往事。事情似乎是因为我出生在过去的阴影中,我的血脉里不仅流着我祖先的血,而且也遗留着他们的伤痛和饥饿感。

9. F. 恩格斯1883年3月17日在伦敦海格特公墓马克思墓前的讲话

3月14日下午两点三刻,当代最伟大的思想家停止思想了。让他一个人留在房里还不到两分钟,当我们进去的时候,便发现他在安乐椅上安静地睡着了——但已经永远地睡着了。

这个人的逝世,对于欧美战斗的无产阶级,对于历史科学,都是不可估量的损失。这位巨人逝世以后所形成的空白,不久就会使人感觉到。

正像达尔文发现有机界的发展规律一样,马克思发现了人类历史的发展规律,即历来为繁芜丛杂的意识形态所掩盖着的一个简单事实:人们首先必须吃、喝、住、穿,然后才能从事政治、科学、艺术、宗教等;所以,直接的物质生活资料的生产对于一个民族或一个时代一定的经济发展阶段来说便构成了基础,人们的国家设施、法律概念、艺术以至宗教观念就是从这个基础上发展起来的,因而也必须由这个基础来解释,而不是像过去那样做得相反。

不仅如此。马克思还发现了现代资本主义生产方式和它所产生的资产阶级社会的特殊的运动规律。由于剩余价值的发现,这里就豁然开朗了,而先前无论资产阶级经济学家或者社会主义批评家所做的一切研究都只是在黑暗中摸索。

一生中能有这样两个发现,该是足够了。即使只能有一个这样的发现,也已经是幸福的了。但是马克思在他所研究的每一个领域,甚至在数学领域,都有独到的发现,这样的领域是很多的,而且其中任何一个领域他都不是浅尝辄止。

他作为科学家就是这样。但是这在他身上远不是主要的。在马克思看来,科学是一种在历史上起推动作用的、革命的力量。任何一门理论科学中的每一个新发现——它的实际应用也许还根本无法预见——都使马克思感到衷心喜悦,而当他看到那种对工业、对一般历史发展立即产生革命性影响的发现的时候,他的喜悦就非同寻常了。例如,他曾经密切注视电学方面各种发现的进展情况,不久以前他还密切注视马塞尔·德普勒的发现。

马克思首先是一个革命家。他毕生的真正使命就是以这种或那种方式参加推翻资本主义社会及其所建立的国家设施的事业,参加现代无产阶级的解放事业,正是他第一次使现代无产阶级意识到自身的地位和需要,意识到自身解放的条件。斗争是他的生命要素。很少有人像他那样满腔热情、坚韧不拔和卓有成效地进行斗争。最早的《莱茵报》(1842年)、《新莱茵报》(1848—1849年)、《纽约每日论坛报》(1852—1861年),以及许多富有战斗性的小册子,在巴黎、布鲁塞尔和伦敦各组织中的工作,最后作为全部活动的顶峰,创立伟大的国际工人协会——老实说,协会的这位创始人即使没有别的什么建树,单凭这一成果也可以自豪。

正因为这样,所以马克思是当代最遭忌恨和最受诬蔑的人。各国政府——无论专制政府或共和政府,都驱逐他;资产者——无论保守派或极端民主派,都竞相诽谤他、诅咒他。他对这一切毫不在意,把它们当作蛛丝一样轻轻拂去,只是在万不得已时才给以回敬。现在他逝世了,在整个欧洲和美洲,从西伯利亚矿井到加利福尼亚,千百万革命战友无不对他表示尊敬、爱戴和悼念,而我敢大胆地说:他可能有过许多敌人,但未必有一个私敌。

他的英名和事业将永垂不朽!

(二) 中译英

1. Dogs in Katmandu (Extracted) (Ji Xianlin)

When I lived in the countryside as a small child, there were dogs all around, and so I got quite accustomed to them, never thinking of them as anything out of the common. Nevertheless, they have since left a most deep impression on me. After mother, the sole occupant of our country home, passed away, the dog she had raised—I've now even forgotten what color he was—continued to keep watch at the door, lying there day and night. He must have been aware that nobody was going to feed him after the death of his mistress. But he would rather endure the torments of hunger than forsake his post outside our run-down home. At dusk, when I arrived alone from somewhere in the village at our house, in which lay mother's coffin, the ownerless dog would fix his tearful eyes on me, the youngster who had just lost his loving mother, wag his tail feebly and sniff at my feet. It seemed as if he and I were left all alone in this vast universe. In face of the sad and dreary scene, I could shed no tears. What I shed was blood which flowed right into my innermost heart. I could have staved with him to live in mutual dependence and comfort each other in distress, but I had to quit my native place, unable to take him along with me. At the time of parting, I hugged him tightly with tears in my eyes. I fell terribly bad about having to desert him. He has since been in my mind for decades. Even today, I cannot restrain my tears whenever I think of him. I am certain he would never stop standing guard at our door even after I left. I cannot bear to imagine what fate befell him in the end. May mother's soul receive from this faithful dog the consolation that I, as her son, have not been able to offer her!

Since then, I have been fond of all dogs in the world.

2. Chinese Culture

In an extended course of 5 thousand years' development towards civilization, the Chinese people have created a splendid culture of their own. As early as four to five millennia ago in the New Stone Age, their ancestors began to raise silkworms for silk textiles. Then, during the Qin-Han period (221 BC – 220 AD), tea production first appeared, which was later recorded in the world's first book on tea, namely *Cha Jing* (or *The Classic Script on Tea*). And in the whole world, China is the earliest country to have a complete systematic theory of agriculture. In the 6th century, *Qimin Yaoshu* (Essential Techniques for the Peasantry), was written by a Chinese agriculturist name Jia Sixie, which is considered as one of the world's earliest books on farming kept intact today. China is also the first country of the world to invent pottery and porcelain, of which the latter appeared in the period of the East Han at the latest time possible (25 – 220 BC), though the fast development of porcelain as a trade began later in the Three-Kingdoms Period (220 – 280 BC). In contrast, it was not until the 18th century that genuine porcelain began to be produced in Europe. The world's earliest country to invent the compass, paper, printing techniques and powder is China. And China is also known for the world's greatest ancient defense project—the Great Wall, the most developed ship-making industry in the medieval time, the earliest cross-ocean navigation (Zheng He's seven west ocean expeditions), the perfectly kept world's oldest stone-arch bridge (Zhaozhou Bridge in Hebei Province), the earliest device for observing celestial changes (Huntianyi, armillary sphere), the earliest anesthetic drugs (used by Huatuo in the second century), the first poetry collection (*The Book of Odes* of the 6th century BC), and the greatest and earliest encyclopedia (*Yonghe Great Encyclopedia*). All these "earliests" and "firsts" were brought about by the Chinese people, composed of the Han people and fifty-five ethnic groups. Besides all these, China is a country of beautiful landscape embellished with fine mountains and rivers, and many outstanding persons have emerged through its extended course of history, in government, cultural affairs and other walks of life.

3. Let Us Join Hands and Work for a Better World (Excerpt) (Jiang Zemin)

In a few years time, mankind will bid farewell to the 20th century, a century full of vicissitudes, and enter the 21st century, a century full of promises. At this turn of centuries, it is of great significance that we are gathered here from all corners of the world to commemorate the 50th anniversary of the United Nations—the widely representative and authoritative inter-governmental organization of our age. We can use this opportunity to take a look at the past and the future from a higher plane and share our views on how to turn the lofty missions of the United Nations into reality.

Fifty years ago, when the world war against fascism came to its victorious conclusion, the United Nations was born, which was a major event in the history of international relations.

That the world went through two world wars in a short span of 30 years in the first half of the century left mankind not only unprecedented carnage and destruction, but also painful and thought-provoking lessons. The drawing up of the U. N. charter and the laughing of U. N. organizations met the needs of the times, reflect the strong desire of the world's people to eliminated the scourge of war, and mirrored the humanity's dream of building a new world of peace, equality, cooperation, and prosperity.

……

China is a populous country with a time-honored history. It is home of a splendid ancient civilization and a major contributor to human progress. Staring from the 19th century, China was reduced to a semi-colonial and semi-feudal society, increasingly impoverished and backward. The Chinese people waged a protracted and unyielding struggle to uphold the independence, sovereignty and unification of their country and to realize its rejuvenation, which culminated in the founding of People's Republic of China in 1949. Right now, the Chinese people are advancing with confident strides on the road of building socialism with Chinese characteristics, concentrate their energy on economic development and improvement of there living standards. Loving peace and desiring a development, the Chinese people are willing to cultivate friendly relations and cooperation with the people in the rest of the world and steadfastly pursue an independent foreign police of peace. Even when China becomes stronger and more developed, it will not seek hegemony or pose a threat to any one. On the contrary, China, as an important force making for the maintenace of world peace and stability, will make more greater contributions to mankind. If China, a country with a quarter of the world's population, remains underdeveloped in prolonged poverty and backwardness, that will cause serious consequences to peace and stability of the Asia-Pacific region and the world at large.

……

The political leaders of our age have on their shoulders the historical mission of carrying forward the cause of world peace, development and progress into the future. History is both fair and unmerciful, we must not fail the ardent expectation of the people throughout the world. Let's join hands and work together to embrace the the new century with a still better world.

4. The Humble Administrator's Garden

The garden concentrates on water, which occupies about one third of the total area. The garden is spacious in the east, dotted with the Lotus Pavilion, the Heaven Fountain Pavilion, etc. In the center is the garden's quintessence. Once entering the gate from the central lane, you will see a yellow granite artificial hill half-concealing the panorama, which is called "Scenic Obstacle" in horticulture. Through winding corridors and bridges, the Distant Fragrance Hall, the main hall comes into your eyes. The hall conceals the whole pond like another scenic obstacle. The hall derived its name from "more distant, more delicate the fragrance is" in the essay "On Loving Lotus" by Zhou Dunyi. North to the hall are fully growing lotus sending delicate fragrance afar. From the Distant Fragrance Hall you can see a fine view which looks like a scroll-painting unfolded successively: the Xiuqi Pavilion in the east, the Lotus Pond in the north, and the Snow-Cloud Clothing Pavilion erecting on the other side, making a contrast to the hall. Opposite to the west is the Lotus Wind Pavilion and in the northwest is the double-eave Tower of Mountain View. The cabins of the "Fragrant Isle", a land boat, bear the resemblance of a hall, pavilion and tower respectively, which are integrated harmoniously. Southeast to the boat is the well-known Small Rainbow Bridge, lying on the water with great exquisiteness. Through the west corridor gate you can see the winding waterside corridor with the reflections of buildings, showing great serenity. What's worth saying is the exquisite Hall of Mandarin Ducks. On its south and north sides are hung two horizontal plaques, inscribed by two native Number One Scholars of the late Qing Dynasty respectively, one of which reads "the House of Thirty Six Mandarin Ducks" and the other "the House of Patura". Yu Zhengfei, a master of Kunqu Opera, in his childhood, used to join in the singings here with his father.

The Cabinet of Lingering and Listening derived its name from the poem by Li Shangyin of the Tang Dynasty. In the cabinet are ginkgo-wood engraved pine, bamboo, plum blossom and magpie, symbolizing auspiciousness. The Pavilion of Folding Fan with its doors, windows, stone tables and stools all folding-fan shaped, is in accordance with its name, which derived from the idea "Who are sitting with me? The moon, the breeze, and I.", written by Su Dongpo of the Song Dynasty. North to the pond is the Building of Reflection. On its first floor stand the stone figures of Shenzhou and Wen Zhengming. On the north of ginkgo-wood screen are the inscriptions of "Bamboos and Rocks" by Zheng Banqiao, an eminent painter of Qing. Further westward is the Bonsai Garden, gathering nearly ten thousand pots from 50-plus varieties of Suzhou style, in which the flowers flourish in their brilliant purples and reds, as well as pines and cypresses staying evergreen.

5. A Sleigh Ride

I left the dear children all soundly sleeping and accompanied my sister Susan home in the ox-sleigh; we made a merry party comfortably nested in our rude vehicle, with a bed of clean straw, and a nice blanket over it, with pillows to lean against; we wrapped up in our Scotch paids, we defied the cold and chatted merrily away, not a whit less happy than if we had been rolling along in a carriage with a splendid pair of bays, instead of crawling along at a funeral pace, in the rudest of all vehicles with the most ungraceful of all steeds; our canopy, the snow-laden branches of pine, hemlock, and cedar, the dark forest around us, and our lamps the pale stars and watery moon struggling through "wrack and mist" and silver-tinged snow-clouds. Here then were we breaking the deep silence of the deep woods with the hum of cheerful voices and the wild mirth that bursts from the light-hearted children. No other sound was there except the heavy tread of the oxen and the lumbering sound of the sleigh as it jolted over the fallen sticks and logs that lay beneath the snow.

Nothing can surpass the loveliness of the woods after a snowstorm has loaded every bough and sprig with its feathery deposit. The face of the ground, so rough and tangled with a mass of uptorn trees, broken boughs, and timbers in every stage of decay, seems by the touch of some powerful magician's wand to have changed in character. Unrivalled purity, softness, and brilliancy, has taken the place of confusion and vegetable corruption. It is one of the greatest treats this country affords me, to journey through the thick woods after a heavy snowfall—whether it be by the brilliant light of the noonday sun in the cloudless azure sky, giving a brightness to every glittering particle that clothes the trees or surface of the ground, or hangs in heavy masses on the evergreens, converting their fanshaped boughs into foliage of feather whiteness and most fantastic forms—or by the light of a full moon and frosty stars looking down through the snowy tops of the forest trees—sometimes shining through a veil of haze, which the frost converts into a sparkling rime that encases every spray and twig with crystals. The silent fall of the light particles of snow, which the gentlest motion of the air shakes down, is the only motion the still scene affords—with the merry jingle of our sleighbells.

6. Rush (Zhu Ziqing)

Swallows may have gone, but there is a time of return; willow trees may have died back, but there is a time of regreening; peach blossoms may have fallen, but they will bloom again. Now, you the wise, tell me, why should our days leave us, never to return? If they had been stolen by someone, who could it be? Where could he hide them? If they had made the escape themselves, then where could they stay at the moment?

I don't know how many days I have been given to spend, but I do feel my hands are getting empty. Taking stock silently, I find that more than eight thousand days have already slid away from me. Like a drop of water from the point of a needle disappearing into the ocean, my days are dripping into the stream of time, soundless, traceless. Already sweat is starting on my forehead, and tears welling up in my eyes.

Those that have gone have gone for good, those to come keep coming; yet in between, how swift is the shift, in such a rush? When I get up in the morning, the slanting sun marks its presence in my small room in two or three oblongs. The sun has feet, look, he is treading on, lightly and furtively; and I am caught, blankly, in his revolution. Thus—the day flows away through the sink when I wash my hands, wears off in the bowl when I eat my meal, and passes away before my day-dreaming gaze as reflect in silence. I can feel his haste now, so I reach out my hands to hold him back, but he keeps flowing past my withholding hands. In the evening, as I lie in bed, he strides over my body, glides past my feet, in his agile way. The moment I open my eyes and meet the sun again, one whole day has gone. I bury my face in my hands and heave a sigh. But the new day begins to flash past in the sigh.

What can I do, in this bustling world, with my days flying in their escape? Nothing but to hesitate, to rush. What have I been doing in that eight-thousand-day rush, apart from hesitating? Those bygone days have been dispersed as smoke by a light wind, or evaporated as mist by the morning sun. What traces have I left behind me? Have I ever left behind any gossamer traces at all? I have come to the world, stark naked; am I to go back, in a blink, in the same stark nakedness? It is not fair though: why should I have made such a trip for nothing!

You the wise, tell me, why should our days leave us, never to return?

7. This Is a Beautiful Place

On the immense Taihu Lake of 36,000 square hectares, dotted with numerous fishing boat sails and green hills, there is a fairyland named Dongshan Town, a part of Suzhou Wuzhong District. Well known as the original producer of Bi-Luo-Chun quality tea, or the Green-Snail-Spring Tea, it is acclaimed as "the Paradise within the Paradise".

Dongshan, famous across the country for its natural environment, historical sites and cultural heritage, is marked out by the central government as a key spot of Taihu Lake Scenery Zone. It is situated in the southwest of Suzhou City on the great lake as a byland of 96.6 square kilometers, with a population of 53 thousand. With a highly developed transportation network linking a series of quality roads here, you can drive onto the Round-the-City Expressway in 10 minutes and get to Suzhou City proper, Shanghai Nanjing Expressway or Suzhou-Jiaxing-Hangzhou Expressway in 20 minutes. The Town is respectively 120 and 170 kilometers from Shanghai Hong-Qiao International Airport and Pudong International Airport.

Dongshan's civilized history can be traced back to the Old Stone Age. In the early years of the South Song Dynasty, when rich and powerful people including some loyal family members moved southward in a chain to escape the war in the central part of the country, they brought to this place the refreshing civilization of the central plain. For generations since then, Dongshan has always been a cradle of outstanding talents. In the Ming and Qing Dynasties, the town produced 43 top scholars through the Imperial Examination System, and as many as 149 government officials. Among them, Wang Ao served the Ming Court as the Prime Minister. Besides, a great number of successful businessmen of the country during the Ming-Qing Period were also from this land. In the contemporary time, this place has produced even more talents for the country, who hold important positions in various sectors of the society. Among them are 18 provincial and state government leaders, and over 600 leading figures on the municipal level of different places, including 316 specialists, professors and senior researcher professionals.

All these talents through history have won for Dongshan the reputation of "a land of ancient scholars and a town of contemporary professors".

As a famous tourist resort, Dongshan is attractive not only for its beautiful landscape of waters and mountains, but also for its 22 historical sites listed as key cultural heritage items under the provincial and municipal governments' protection. These include the ancient Zi-Jin-An Temple, the Carved Building, the Xi's Garden, and the ancient village of Luxiang. As for San-Shan-Dao, or the Three-Hills-Islets, it is now the No. 1 choice to tourists because of its remote antiquity and wonderful ecological environment.

In recent years, with the local government's intensive efforts to make the best use of Dongshan's advantageous geographic position, many new sites of tourist attractions are developed, including Sha-Tan-Shan and Gu-Shang-Jin Tea Houses, Dai-Hu Mountain Villa, Jin-Long Ecological Farm, and the Scenic Spots of Lingyuan, Bi-Luo and Yu-Hua. The protection of cultural heritages is also given great emphasis, with the renovation of such ancient village as Luxiang going on a grand scale. The homeland of talents is now rejuvenated with a new vigor.

When you are roaming along a time-worn alley here, you may find yourself at a house of long standing and many stories, while the owner is away somewhere for a visit, a sun-bath, a reading over a cup of tea, or a piece of field job.

Dongshan is not only known as the reserve area of Kangxi Emperor's favorite Bi-Luo-Chun Tea, but also as a mountainous land with ever-blooming flowers, fruits of all seasons and a great variety of aquatic products, such as the silver fish, white fish, white shrimps, Dazhaxie Crabs and Chun-Cai water leaves. With its abundant local produce and their great variety, Dongshan has a considerable quarter of its total land listed as key natural conserve areas in Jiangsu Province; and its advantageous ecological environment also serve as many ideal production bases for government-certified pollution-free agricultural products, such as the quality green tea, loquat, waxberry, tomato, cucumber, Chun-Cai water leaves, crabs, etc. Of these local specialties, an increasing quantity is being exported to industrial countries and well received by international consumers after export and import quarantine.

Today's Dongshan is more than a tourist attraction with its remarkable history and culture. It is also an important modernized town of advanced science and technology. There is a 10-square-km Dongshan High-Tech Industrial Park, with its infrastructure following the mode of Suzhou Industrial Park. Presently 5 square km of it has been developed with nearly 100 enterprises from home and abroad. Industrial business lines cover a wide range, including electronics, machinery, plastics, printing materials, medical equipment, biological engineering. With this development, Dongshan is becoming a new highlight spot in the southwestern industrial belt of Suzhou.

In the mean time of the scientific management of the infrastructures, the local government has also laid a good foundation of "soft" facilities, including a comprehensive network of finance, healthcare and education. And, within close vicinity are such quality hotel and recreational establishments as Dongshan Hotel and Mountain-Water Resort, complemented with an edible water supply station and sewage disposal system. The local government has also worked out a series of policies favorable for attracting domestic and international businesses to invest here, including the one-stop service center for going through business launching affairs concerning application, registration and taxation.

In the year 1996, Lee Kuangyu, former Premier of Singapore, visited Dongshan and left such an inscription in praise of the intoxicating landscape: "This is a beautiful place."

If Molifeng Peak of the mountain here is compared to a man of wisdom who has written the history, then the waters of Taihu Lake may be said to resemble a Guqin zither, playing out all the changes of the area from time immemorial. Then the long-stretching ancient alleys of Dongshan Town may be compared to a flute, playing its cultural splendor and prosperity. And the town itself, like a beautiful fairy, will enter your dream with her beautiful songs in unhurried steps.

8. Colorful Stories—the Bridges and Cultural Relics

The bridges of Suzhou stand not only in the alleys but also in history. They span waters as well as time. They are the very things that help to pass down the ancient civilization from the very ancient times.

As we read the bridges, we are reading history; we cross the bridges as we turn over the leaves of history. These bridges have linked the past with the present through time and space with all the changes of dynasties. The bridge we cross today might also be the one the King of the ancient Wu State crossed in pride, the one that was crossed by his Prime Minister Wu Zixu with a sigh. It may also be the very bridge that greatest men of literature and art and all the intelligentsia of the ancient times crossed in different moods.

The bridges crossed by the ancients are now under our feet, but the path that they have never taken is now also taken by us. For generation after generation, the wind that passes through the arches of the bridges has brought mental exchanges between people of different times. And now as we mount the tops of the bridges we are meeting the ancient nobles and saints. Thus, the bridges are of reality, history, and of our heart.

9. Introduction: Chinese Vernacular Dwelling

In the year 2000, Xidi and Hongcun, the ancient villages in Anhui Province of China were inscribed on the 24th session of UNESCO's World Heritage List. In early spring of that year, the Japanese Expert Dr. Naomi Okawa, assigned by UNESCO's World Heritage Committee, highly valued the villages after his field investigation by saying that "it's really an unrivalled village scene such as Hongcun". "The village Xidi still preserved its beautiful ancient streets and alleys, which is seldom in the world". In 1997, old town of Li Jiang in Yunnan Province and ancient city of Pingyao in Shanxi Province were inscribed into the World

Heritage List; nowadays, the famous river town Zhouzhuang in Jiangsu Province is on application for the list. At the turn of the century, the traditional Chinese vernacular dwelling is unveiling itself to the world, becoming a big stage for China's access to the world and for the world to have a better understanding of China.

China is a country with vast territory, varied topography and diversified climate, together with its different kinds of nationalities and cultures, which creates a rich variety of settlements and buildings of traditional vernacular dwelling. The residential houses can generally be divided into three patterns: courtyard, storied and caved (or clay dwelling built with clay materials) dwelling.

二、英汉互译原理在小说中的应用

（一）英译中

1.《福尔赛世家》（第一章节选）（周煦良 译）

（1）碰到福尔赛家有喜庆的事情，那些有资格去参加的人都曾见过那中上层人家的华装盛服，不但看了开心，也增长见识。可是，在这些荣幸的人里面，如果哪一个具有心理分析能力的话（这种能力毫无金钱价值，因而照理不受到福尔赛家人的重视），就会看出这些场面不但只是好看，也说明一个没有被人注意到的社会问题。再说得清楚一点，他可以从这家人的集会里找到使家族成为社会的有力组成部分的证据；很显然这就是社会的一个缩影；这一家人这一房和那一房之间都没有好感，没有三个人中间存在着什么同情，然而在这里他却可以找到那种神秘然而极其牢固的韧性。从这里开始，他可以隐约看出社会进化的来龙去脉，从而对宗法社会、野蛮部队的蜂集、国家的兴亡是怎么一回事，稍稍有所了解。他就像一个人亲眼看见一棵树从栽种到生长的过程——卓绝地表现了那种坚韧不拔、孤军作战的成功过程，这里面也包括无数其他不够顽强和根气虚弱的植物的死亡——将会有一天看见它变得欣欣向荣，长着芬香而肥大的叶子，开着繁花，旺盛得简直引人反感。

（2）一八八六年六月十五日那一天，约在下午四时左右，在老乔里·福尔赛住的斯丹奴普门家里，一个旁观者如果碰巧在场的话，就会看到福尔赛家的全盛时代。

今天这个茶会是为了庆祝老乔里恩的孙女琼·福尔赛和菲利浦·波辛尼先生订婚而举行的。各房的人都来了，满眼都是白手套、黄背心、羽饰和长裙，说不尽的豪华。连安姑太也来了。她住在兄弟悌摩西家里，平日绝少出门；成天坐在那间绿客厅的角落里看书做针线；屋角上面放的一只淡青花瓶，插着染色的潘巴草，就像是她的盾牌，客厅四壁挂着福尔赛三代的画像。可是今天安姑太也来了；腰杆笔直，一张安详衰老的脸显得非常有尊严——十足地代表了家族观念中的牢固占有意识。

（3）当一个福尔赛家的人订婚，或者结婚，或者诞生的时候，福尔赛各房的人都要到场；当一个福尔赛家的人死掉——可是到现在为止，福尔赛家的人还没有一个死掉；他们是不死的，死是和他们的主张抵触的，因此他们都小心提防着死；这些人精力高度充沛，这可以说是天性，因为不论什么事情，只要侵犯到他们的财产，都使他们深恶痛绝。

这一天，在那些和外客周旋的福尔赛家人的身上，都有一种比平时特别整洁的派头，神色自若，然而带有警惕和好奇，兴高采烈，然而保持着身份，就像许多扎抹停当、严阵以待的战士一样。索米斯·福尔赛脸上那种习见的傲慢神气今天已经遍及全军；他们全在戒备着。

2.《俄亥俄，温斯堡》（杜争鸣 译）

作品类型：短篇小说集　　　　　　故事时间：19 世纪末
作者：谢伍德·安德森（1876—1941 年）　地点：俄亥俄，温斯堡
故事类型：心理现实主义　　　　　　出版时间：1919 年

● 评介：

《俄亥俄，温斯堡》是一部现代经典小说集，既优美又悲壮，既现实又超脱。作品虽然并非一般意义上的"长篇小说"，但其中故事篇篇相关，不乏长篇小说所具有的广阔视野和感人魅力。简而言之，谢伍德·安德森用娴熟、动人的语言讲述了一个小城的故事，一个住在那里的人们在孤独、失意中生活的故事。尽管故事背景和其中的人物都生活在这小城里，但这部作品本身具有浓烈的美国风味。自安德森以后，还没有一个人能够把美国民族心灵深处的欲念冲动和孤独感解释得如此透彻、如此感人。

● 故事：

年轻的乔治·维拉德是伊丽莎白和汤姆·维拉德的独子，父亲是本地旅店的老板，生性死板，墨守成规，又迟钝又麻木；母亲早年是谁见谁爱的美人，她对汤姆·维拉德并非真有爱意，只是看见别的姑娘们结婚后个个显得更加欢快，似乎无人不满，于是就嫁给了他，希望从此时来运转，生活真的好起来。可是婚后不久她就感到自己在温斯堡的生活十分乏味，过去的美梦在与维拉德的夫妻生活中变成了毫无意义的生活琐事，没有一点色彩。

只有一个人真正理解伊丽莎白，这就是里非医生，伊丽莎白只有在他那狭小、杂乱的诊室里的时候才感到自由自在，才能真正找到发泄感情的机会。他们的关系从一开始就注定要结出苦果，但这种关系异常甜美，是两个孤独、敏感的人难得的相会。里非医生自己也有一番苦涩的经历：多年前的一天，一个未婚先孕的姑娘来到他的诊室，不久后他就娶了她。第二年春天，姑娘死了，里非医生从此四处奔走，制作纸袋药丸，把口袋塞得满满的。在那一片片小纸上，他胡写乱画，记下了自己对生活中奇妙之处的感受。

伊丽莎白希望通过儿子乔治来显示自己，而且已经看到自己的希望和追求在儿子身上变成了现实。她最害怕的就是儿子会一直在温斯堡待下来，所以听说他想当作家就感到高兴。她已经背着丈夫给儿子攒了一笔钱，至少可以为他的以后先开个头。可是，她壮志未酬就离开了人世。当她安详地躺在床上的时候，在乔治和里非医生两人眼中她似乎并没有

死,倒是显得格外美丽动人。对乔治来说,她似乎一点也不像个母亲;对里非医生来说,她是他所爱恋过的女人,现在就是幻灭的象征。

小城里很多人都来找乔治,对他讲述他们的生活经历,讲述他们心里难以遏止的欲望和冲动,讲述他们想做而又未能做成的事情。奥尔德·温·比德保是个采果工,多年前曾当过教师,他爱自己班上的男孩子们,而且确实比谁都更能理解这些年轻人。可是,班上有个男孩对他迷恋不已,指责他搞同性恋,温·比德保虽然清白无辜,却被人们赶出了城。在温斯堡,他成了当地最能干的采果工,但他那双能够谋生的手却始终让自己感到诧异和恐惧。当乔治在浆果地里碰到他时,温的手自然地伸了出去,似乎要抚摸这个小伙子。可是一股恐惧感突然笼罩过来,他赶快又把双手插进了口袋。对乔治来说,温的手也确实有些奇怪,难以理解。

凯特·斯威夫特当过乔治的老师,她发现乔治有潜力,将来可能成为一名作家,于是尽量教给他有关写作的知识,说明写作的意义。乔治并不能完全听懂,但他懂得凯特并没有以她的教师身份对他讲话,而是以一个女人的身份在对他讲话。一天晚上,凯特在她自己的房间里拥抱了乔治,因为乔治已经成人,是她钟爱的对象。另一天晚上,当小城温斯堡已经沉浸在睡梦之中的时候,她又来到了乔治的房间,可是就在她不由自主地想为乔治献身的时候,却打了他一记耳光,径直跑了出去,弄得乔治一个人待在那里懊恼万分。

凯特住在基督教长老会教堂的街道对面。教堂里的神父,可敬的柯蒂斯·哈特曼偶然发现,从自己钟楼顶的书房里可以看到凯特的卧室。他一夜接一夜地从窗口看躺在床上的凯特,开始时是想证实自己的信念。但他情欲难熬,就在这一天晚上,当凯特从乔治那里跑回来以后,他一直看着她。只见她一丝不挂地猛然倒在床上,疯狂地捶着自己的枕头。后来,又从床上爬起来,跪在地上祈祷。哈特曼神父失声一叫,把圣经拨到地上,举手打碎了窗户上的玻璃,然后冲出教堂跑进那漆黑的街道。他在报纸发售处撞上了乔治,眼睛睁得圆圆的,手上滴着血对惊愕不已的乔治说,上帝以一个裸体女人的形象在他面前显灵了,说凯特就是全能的上帝派来的,说他自己的灵魂已经得救了。

除了凯特以外,乔治的生活中也曾有过别的女人。其中有银行家的女儿海伦·怀特。有一天晚上他们在外面约会,开始时大笑,互相接吻,可是后来一种莫名其妙的感觉控制了他们,把他们分开了。农家女儿路易斯·特鲁宁给乔治写了一封信,信中说只要他需要,自己就是他的人了。天黑以后,乔治就到农场找她,和她一起去散步。就在他们散步走到浆果地的时候,乔治享受了海伦·怀特拒绝给他的那种爱。

和路易斯·特鲁宁一样,路易斯·本特丽也需要爱。在来到温斯堡以前,她住在一个农场,她那贪婪、迷信的父亲对她一点也不疼爱,心里简直就没有她,因为父亲本来只想要男孩,不想要女孩。路易斯·本特丽来到温斯堡以后,就和哈代一家住在一起,平时到学校去上学。她学习好,常受老师表扬,可是却因此受到了哈代家两个女儿的妒忌,她们觉得她总是在显摆自己。这样一来,本特丽就更想有人爱她了。有一天,她给约翰·哈代送了一张纸条,几个星期以后就委身于他了。当本特丽显然已经怀孕后,两个人就结了婚。约翰责怪本特丽对自己的小孩大卫太无情,不给小孩喂奶,有时很长时间连他也不管。本特丽从来就没有爱过自己的丈夫,丈夫也没有爱过她,这种婚姻确实不美满。最后,两个人分手了。不久后本特丽的父亲接走了小小的大卫,把他带到农场和自己一起住。

奥尔德·杰西·本特利确信上帝的存在已经通过自己的孙子表现了出来,认为小大卫就像是圣经中所说的上帝,必将成为救世主,征服那些市侩,那些市侩拥有他自己也想要的土地。一天,老杰西把大卫带到田里,让大卫牵着一只羊,准备作为供奉上帝的牺牲品。小大卫吓得不知如何是好,打了爷爷一拳后逃之夭夭,再也没有回温斯堡。

光阴如水,转眼间乔治到了必须做出最后抉择的时候——是继续在温斯堡待下去呢,还是离家出走开始自己的写作生涯?在母亲死后不久的一天,他一大早就起身向火车站走去。在火车站,女邮政局长祝他一切如愿,他毅然登上火车离温斯堡而去。

3.《名誉领事》节选(一)(杜争鸣 译)

本书中绝无一人以现实生活所见为原型,从英国大使到老人何塞均不在例外。故事的主要背景是阿根廷的某地某城,所以很像那里实际存在的某个地方,对此我不予提名,这是因为我希望能随意发挥,不至囿于特定城市的街区或特定地域的地理情况而难以自拔。

献给维克托莉娅·奥甘波

以此寄怀爱心

纪念我在圣·伊西德罗和马德普拉塔度过的美好的日日夜夜

在阿根廷巴拉那一座小小的码头,周围铁轨纵横交错,黄色的起重机随处可见,爱德华多·普拉尔医生伫立在其间久久地观望:一缕浓烟横着扩散开来,笼罩在查科城的上空,悬浮在落日时分的红霞之间,有如一面国旗上印着的条纹。此时此刻,普拉尔自觉形影相吊,只是河边上那幢楼房外还有个水手在站岗而已。在这样的傍晚,不知是由于什么神秘的原因,渐渐昏暗下去的暮色中掺和着无名草木的气味,它使有些人重新感到了童年的稚气,唤起了他们对未来的希望;而对另一些人来说,却是让他们重温那些早就一去不复返的几乎被忘却了的往事。

周围的那些铁轨,那些黄色的起重机,还有那幢坐落在河边的楼房——所有这些都是普拉尔一到这里就看到的景象。此后年复一年,岁月的流逝并没有改变什么,只是在这里添上了一道黑烟。当初他头一次踏上这片土地时,辽阔的天地之间还没有悬起这道烟雾,此地在巴拉那算是远在一隅。二十多年前,他开始和母亲从北方的共和国南下,每星期一次从巴拉圭到这里来行医,那家冒烟的工厂当时还没有建设起来。

4.《名誉领事》(节选二)(杜争鸣 译)

他想起了他的父亲,还记得他当时在亚松森码头上一艘小船边的样子:身材高大,庄重老成,挺着胸脯,以一种不在话下的语气向他们母子俩许诺,他用不了多久就会回到他们身边。一个月后,不,也许是三个月后,他口气里虽然仍旧流露着希望,但说得支支吾吾,就像是机器中的零件已经生锈,机器运转起来喳喳作响。

对一个14岁的男孩来说,事情似乎不值得大惊小怪,但毕竟有些不寻常:爸爸吻妈妈时是带着一种敬意去吻她的额头,好像吻的是母亲而不是同床共枕的妻子。在那段时间里,普拉尔认为自己很像西班牙人,跟母亲一样,而不像父亲那样明显可以看出是英国出身。父亲理所当然——不是由于护照的缘故——属于狄更斯和柯南道尔笔下那个传奇式的岛国,属于那片雪天雾气笼罩下的土地。虽然他10岁就出海来到国外,本国也许并没有给他留下多少记忆,但这仍然是他的归属。父亲有一本画册,一本爷爷奶奶在他离开英国前最后一刻给他买的书,一直保存到了现在。画册的名字是"伦敦万象",过去亨利·普拉尔常给儿子翻开让他看里面的照片:白金汉宫、伦敦塔、牛津林荫道以及道路上的英式高座马车和各种出租马车,还有那些捏着长裙的窈窕淑女。后来,过了很久以后,普拉尔医生才知道,父亲原来是被流放的,而且这里大片的土地整个是流放区。被流放者中有意大利人、捷克人、波兰人、威尔士人和英格兰本族人。普拉尔少年时读狄更斯的小说,就像是外国人那样读它:由于没有更多的事实作依据,也许只能认为书中的一切当今还依然如故。比如,俄国人就以为英国的郡长和棺材店老板的行当还是老样子,认为在这个世界中,雾都孤儿之类的人仍然被迫住在伦敦的某个地窖里,仍然在无休无止地乞讨更多的东西。

在14岁的年龄,普拉尔还不懂得究竟是什么迫使父亲踏上了这河畔古都的码头。在布伊诺斯艾里斯住了好几年后他才开始明白,被流放者的生活并不那么简单——父亲要写很多文件,要经常去政府机关办事。简单的生活属于那些合法出生在英国的人们,属于那些无论遇到什么情况都能心平气和地接受的人们。西班牙语与罗马语同出一源,而罗马人的生活就很简单。西班牙语中的"马西莫斯"——男子汉的骄傲——相当于罗马语的"维尔图",与英国人所说的勇气几乎毫不相干,也不要绷着上嘴唇发音。父亲之所以选择到巴拉圭那边去,独自一人直面日夜增多的种种危险,也许正是因为他在以这种外国式行为尽量模仿"马西斯莫精神",只不过在码头上他的上嘴唇显得绷得稍微紧了点儿。

青年普拉尔和母亲当时到达河边这个码头时,几乎恰好是现在这样的傍晚时分。那是在他们去共和国南面那个嘈杂的大都会的路上(他们动身的时间由于发生了政治示威而被迫耽搁了几个钟头),当时看到的景象依旧历历在目——殖民地早期的老房子、街上的水池和池边上用拉毛灰泥装饰的旧房子,在那里的长凳上拥抱在一起的一对情人,月光下一个女人的裸体全身塑像和一个姓名平平的爱尔兰族大将军的半身塑像,一个卖饮料的摊子和摊子上面一只大大的电灯泡——就像是熟透了的大苹果……所有这些都已经作为平和宁静而又不同寻常的象征深深地埋在青年普拉尔的记忆中。所以,到了最后,当他感到迫切需要摆脱那一幢幢摩天大楼,摆脱道路上的重重关卡和警车、救护车的尖叫,当他想要逃到什么地方去的时候,他选择的自然是回到北方这座小城来工作——因为他有资本,是来自布伊诺斯艾里斯的有名望的资深医师。对于他的动机,首都的朋友几乎没有一个人能多少予以理解,都说他肯定会感到中美洲北方的天气湿热难熬,对身体不利,而且说那是个死气沉沉的无事城连暴力事件也不会发生。

"也许那里对身体不利正对我医道兴隆有好处,"他总是笑着对朋友这样回答,但他的笑并不能说明什么——也许是违心地笑,就像他父亲表达自己的希望时那样不真实。

在布伊诺斯艾里斯,在一家人分居两地的岁月里,他们只收到过父亲一封信,信封上写的收信人是他们母子俩,太太和公子。然而,这封信并没有经过邮局,是他们在住宅的门缝底下发现的。那是到这里大约四年以后的一个星期天的傍晚,当时母子二人刚看完电影从影院回来,看的影片是《乱世佳人》。这部片子他们已经看了三遍,每逢重映母亲都必看无疑,也许因为它是部老片子,而且主演都是老明星,让人在短暂的几个小时里觉得美国南北战争好像一幅静物画,没有什么危险可言。影片中的男女主角时隔多年后再次登台亮相,多年的硝烟弹雨也没能把他们阻挡。

父亲的来信信封又脏又皱,上面写着"直接传送"字样,但究竟是谁直接传送过来的,他们母子俩自始至终都不得而知。这封信与以前不一样,没有写在用精美的西班牙语花体字印着庄园名的信纸上,而是写在廉价软皮抄的横格纸上。信中充满了虚假的希望——就像他离开前在码头上说的那样,他说"各种事情"都会很快解决。但由于没有注明写信日期,所以也许信还没传到,他所说的"希望"就早已消磨掉了。此后,普拉尔和母亲就一直没有再得到过他的消息;他究竟是被关在监狱里,还是已经命归黄泉,对此母子俩连一点点说法和风声都没有得到。他在信的结尾用的是西班牙式的套话:"使我感到安慰的是,我在这个世界上最爱恋的两个人现在都安然无恙……热爱你们的丈夫和父亲——亨利·普拉尔。"

5.《摩若博士岛》(节选一)(杜争鸣 译)

1887年2月1日,"维因妇人"号在行驶到南纬1度西经107度一带的海域时遭遇碰撞后弃船沉没。

1888年1月5日,也就是11个月4天后,我叔叔爱德华·普兰迪克——一个深居简出的人,一个无疑在卡亚俄登上"维因妇人"号并被认为已经淹死的人——在南纬5度3分西经101度的地方被人从一条小小的敞篷船上救起。小船的名字已经辨认不清,但据推测它原是已经失踪的纵帆船"吐根"号上的救生艇。我叔叔所讲的亲身经历如此离奇,以至于人们都认为他发疯了。于是他干脆说他自从逃离"维因妇人"号那一刻起脑子里就一片空白。心理医生当时讨论了他的情况,认为这是一例奇怪的失忆症,起因于身心高度紧张。以下叙述是笔者本人——他的侄子和唯一继承人在他的文件中发现的,但并没有同时发现任何明确要求出版的声明。

在我叔叔被救起的海域,人们知道只有一座岛屿,即贵人岛。这是一座小小的火山岛,荒无人烟。1891年英国皇家船只"蝎子号"曾到过这里,当时一帮水手也曾登岸,但在岛上并没有发现什么精灵,只见到了一些奇怪的白蛾、野猪和很特别的老鼠。他们也没有弄到这些动物的标本。所以我所讲述的事情并没有什么东西来证实其最关键性的细节。理解了这一点,似乎把这个离奇的故事公之于众也没有什么坏处,我认为这也符合我叔叔的意愿。至少有如下情况可以说明确实如此:我叔叔失踪是在南纬5度西经105度,重新出现在同一海域时已经过了11个月。无论如何他在此其间一定生活着。而且情况似乎如此:一艘名叫"吐根"的纵帆船,在一个醉鬼船长——约翰·戴维斯——的指挥下,于1887年从非洲启航。船上载着一只美洲山豹和其他一些动物;这只船在南太平洋几个港口还颇有名气,而它最后却从这些海域消失了(船上载着大量的干椰肉)。它从班尼亚驶向它吉凶未卜前程时正是1887年12月,与我叔叔讲述的完全吻合。

6.《摩若博士岛》(节选二)(杜争鸣 译)

傍晚,我划动小船出海,驾着轻柔的西南风缓慢而又平稳地行进。小岛变得越来越小,岛上那股稀疏的、盘旋上升的烟雾在火热的夕阳映照下缩小成了一条越来越细的丝线。无边的海水在我四周涌起,从我眼前遮住了那片昏暗的低地。白天的光亮——落日的余晖拖着万缕金光驶出天际,像是从一边拉上了一幅闪光的帷幕。最后,我注视着那因阳光照射而看不到的无边无际的蓝色天穹,只见繁星成群,如漂如流。沉静的大海,沉静的天空,孤独的我伴着黑夜和沉寂。

就这样,我漂泊了三天,一直省吃省喝,同时对发生在我身上的一切苦思冥想,倒也不十分想再见到人。我身上围着一块肮脏的布片,头发纠结成了黑色的一团,发现我的人肯定会以为我是个疯子。说起来也奇怪,可我真觉得没有那种重返人间的欲望,而只是庆幸自己离开了那些丑恶至极的兽魔。在我出海的第三天,一艘从阿皮亚驶往旧金山的横帆双桅船救起了我。船长和他的副手都不相信我讲的故事,他们断定我是由于孤独和危险而变疯了。我估计他们的看法可能正好代表了其他人的看法,于是就控制着自己,不再进一步讲我的历险经过了,而是宣称自己一点也不记得从"维茵夫人"号轮船失事到我又被救起这段时间——整整一年时间里发生的任何事情。

我不得不十分谨慎地行事,以免自己被怀疑为精神失常。我还记得那套法律,记得那两个死去的水手,记得那黑暗中的埋伏,记得那藤林中的死尸,这些记忆都像鬼魂一样地纠缠着我。另外,虽然这显得不正常,可我确实在重返人间以后没有像我曾期望的那样获得信任和同情,而是增强了我居留小岛期间所体验过的那种担心和恐惧。没有人相信我,人们把我看得那样古怪,几乎就像过去兽人看待我那样。也许是我已经染上了我的野生同伴身上的某些东西吧。

人们常说恐惧是一种病症,无论如何我是可以证明这一点的。在从那时起到现在的几年里,一种让人心神不定的恐惧始终驻扎在我心头,类似这样的恐惧也许一只半驯服幼狮同样会感到。我的恐惧病呈现着最奇特的症状:我怎么也不能相信,我所遇到的男男女女不是另一帮有着还算说得过去的人性的兽人,不是被部分地塑造成外观形象是人的动物。我总是感到他们马上就要开始蜕变,开始一点一点地表现出种种兽性的标记。我把我的情况吐露给一个奇怪而又能干的人,他认识摩若,是一位精神病专家,对我的故事似乎半信半疑——就是他极大地帮助了我。虽然我不敢说那座小岛上的恐惧将会完全彻底地从我心里消失,但在绝大多数情况下它都深藏在我心灵深处,只是一团遥远的烟云,一种记忆中的东西和模模糊糊的疑惑。不过,有些时候这团小小的烟云也会扩张开来,以至于整个天空布满乌云。这时我便会环顾四周,看看我的人类同伴,心里又恐惧起来。我看到的面孔有些热情焕发,充满光彩;有些则呆滞麻木或阴森吓人;另一些面孔喜怒无常,缺乏诚意;没有一张面孔显示出一个理性灵魂所具有的静穆的威严。我感到动物性似乎正在他们身上涌起,遍布全身,那些小岛上的兽人的退化会马上在更大的范围内重演。我知道这只是幻觉,我周围这些看上去像人的男男女女确实是人,而且永远是人,是完全有理性的动物,心里充满了人的欲望和温情柔意,摆脱了本能的约束,不再是任何奇异的法律的奴隶——是与兽人全然不同的生灵。虽然如此,我还是畏缩缩地躲避着他们,躲避着他们好奇、刺探的目光,躲避着他们的询问和帮助,总是十分渴望离开他们,独处一地。

　　由于这个缘故,我就住在宽阔舒适的南部丘陵地旁边,一旦那种阴影笼罩我的灵魂的时候就可以逃到那里。这时,那空旷的丘陵在风扫残云的天空下是多么的美好!

　　而当我住在伦敦时,恐惧几乎不堪忍受。我总摆脱不了周围的人;他们的声音穿过窗户传来,锁着的门这种保障也是不堪一击。我常常走上大街和自己的错觉做斗争,轻手轻脚的女人会跟在我身后像猫一样地喵喵叫;心怀鬼胎的男人会向我投来嫉妒的目光;脸色苍白、倦怠的工人们咳嗽着从我身边走过,就像受伤的鹿一样眼光疲惫,步履匆匆;老年人弯腰弓背,神情呆滞地喃喃自语着走过我身边,丝毫也没有注意到身后跟着一串衣衫褴褛的顽童正在把他们嘲弄。这时,我会转身走进一个教堂。可是即使在这里,我精神仍然是那样错乱,以至于在我看来牧师似乎在像猿猴兽人那样喋喋不休地重复这"大思想";不然的话我就会走进某个图书馆,而在这里那些正在看书的紧绷的面孔看来只不过像正在等待猎食对象的野兽。尤其让我感到恶心的是火车和公共马车上那些茫然失色、毫无表情的面孔,他们与其说是我的同类,倒不如说是死尸。所以,我如果不能保证单独一人就不敢外出旅行。而且,甚至连我自己都不像一个合情合理的人,却像一个大脑异常错乱、被病态折磨的动物,失魂落魄地只身游荡,犹如一头得了旋回病的绵羊。

　　不过,谢天谢地,现在这种心绪不太经常出现了。我已经退步抽身,离开了混乱的城市和种种纷扰,让自己生活中的时日沉浸在睿智的书籍中,因为书籍是我们生活中明亮的窗口,映照着真人智慧的光辉。我深居简出,只有一个小小的家。我把我的时光都专注于读书和做化学实验,而且把一个个夜晚都花在研究天文上。虽然我不知其然也不知其所以然,但在那光芒闪耀的日月星辰中显然有一种无限平和与安全的感觉。我想,在那浩瀚无边、亘古无垠的物质定律中,而不是在人们日常的担忧、罪恶与烦恼中,我们身上任何超越动物性的东西才能找到慰藉与希望。我怀抱着希望,否则将无法生存。

　　那么就这样吧,让我在希望与孤独中结束我的故事。

（二）中译英

1. *The Sesame Oil Mill* (Excerpts) (Paul White 译)

- Excerpt 1

Making sesame oil and brewing beer are very similar, insofar as the main thing is the water.

It's the Laoshan mineral water that makes Qingdao beer world-famous. Likewise, it's the water from the Fragrant Spirit Pond that enables Gao Ersao's sesame oil business to captivate so many customers.

And the pond water certainly is unusual!

The Fragrant Spirit Pond is situated south of the village where the Gao family lives. Square in shape, the pond is some one hundred meters across. Its deepest point is no more than 3.3 meters, yet even during severe droughts there is no drop at all in the water level. This is said to be because the pond is fed by some hidden spring. In the summer the surface of the pond is covered with lotus leaves, and when then flowers bloom the whole village is suffused with their fragrance. The water is surprisingly cold, so not many people like going in to pluck lotus roots. Those who do, soon find themselves scrambling out again with chattering teeth and purple lips. The greenish water is home to no fish, shrimps, turtles or suchlike, and it has a bitter taste, as if some kind of herbal medicine had been added to it. The village livestock won't drink it no matter how thirsty they are. But it is this very water that makes such specially good sesame oil; it gives it a brown color, with a slightly reddish tinge, and a smooth, mellow taste. Used for frying or dressing cold dishes, it takes away the taste of rawness and replaces it with a mouth-watering flavor. Used in the preparation of traditional Chinese medicine, it compensates for the lack of yin, cools internal heat and clears poisons, strengthens the marrow and stimulates the appetite. Used for preparing poultices, it has the function of cooling the blood, killing pain and healing flesh wounds.

Gao Ersao's sesame oil mill stands on the north bank of the Fragrant Spirit Pond, with the front gate some fifty paces from it.

- Excerpt 2

It had been going on now for longer than Ersao could remember. For many years it had only been this love affair that had kept hope alive in her breast, that had allowed her to maintain any interest in running the mill. She had known Ren almost since she had entered the Gao household. He used to carry a peddler's pole around the neighboring villages. Dangling on the pole were all kinds of things she liked, such as candies, ribbons, thimbles, etc. But, of course, she had no money to buy anything, and all she could do was to follow him around.

Ren Shizhong noticed her, and sometimes, when nobody was looking, he would throw a piece of candy or a ribbon to the poor little girl who had been sold as a future daughter-in-law. His attitude was one of compassion, and hers, one of admiration, gradually they became firm friends. And this friendship grew until, after a number of years, it became something more than friendship; it was love, but a love which could have no happy ending. She was not the sort of girl who could abandon all sense of propriety, and he could not afford to look after her. So their love existed only in conditions of the strictest secrecy. They used every stratagem they could think of to keep their love hidden from others. In fact, in order to get a moment together they even had to put on a show of disliking each other.

During the hot autumn that year they had been together many nights, but in order not to arouse suspicion they had first devised an elaborate plot. One afternoon Ren Shizhong had deliberately stolen two radishes from the Gao family garden. She saw him, of course, and raised a hue and cry. She then told her husband, and the two of them went and caused a commotion outside Ren's front door, calling him a shameless thief, among many other undesirable things. And while her husband flailed at Ren with his crutch, Ersao scratched his arms. The result was that the villagers were completely fooled into thinking that there was a feud between the two families. A few nights after this incident, Ersao was once lying wrapped in Ren Shizhong's arms, and this time she was tenderly caressing the scratch marks on them.

When she became pregnant with Ren's daughter, Iris, she was at a loss as to how she was going to pass her off as Gao Erdong's because she knew that the child would not have a hereditary disease. To prepare the way for the birth she spread all sorts of stories around the house and around the village. First, she said that a fortune-teller had told her that conception in the first month of the lunar calendar pleased the Lord of Heaven and he would ensure the birth of a healthy baby. Again, she said that a doctor in the town had told her that hereditary diseases don't necessarily afflict every descendant, and it was quite possible that her child could be born perfectly normal. Not content with this, she also told people that she had had a dream, in which a goddess had told her that since she already had child who suffered from epilepsy her next child would possess exceptional intelligence.

This public relations ploy paid off, and when Iris was born perfectly normal it didn't rouse the slightest suspicion among the villagers, nor indeed in Gao Erdong himself. In fact, people even said that this was her reward for being an exemplary wife!

2. Crescent Moon (Excerpt)(Lao She)(Sydney Shapiro 译)

Yes, I've seen the crescent moon again—a chill sickle of pale gold how many times have seen crescent moons just like this one, how many times …

It stirred many different emotions, and brought back many different scenes. As I sat and stared at it, I recalled each time I had seen it hanging in the blue firmament it awakened my memories like an evening breeze blowing open the petals of a flower that is craving for sleep.

The first time, the chill crescent moon really brought a chill. My first recollection of it is a better one. I remember its feeble pale gold beams shining through my tears. I was only seven then—a little girl in a read padded jacket. I wore a blue cloth hat Mama had made for me. There were small flowers printed on it. I remember. I stood leaning against the doorway of our small room, gazing at the crescent moon. The room was filled with the smell of medicine and smoke, with Mama's tears, with Papa's illness. I stood alone on the steps looking at the moon. No one bothered about me, no one cooked my supper. I knew there was tragedy in that room, for everyone said Papa's illness was … but I felt much more sorry for myself. I was cold, hungry, neglected.

I stood there until the moon had set. I had nothing; I couldn't restrain my tears. But the sound of Mama's weeping drowned out my own. Papa was silent; a white cloth covered his face. I wanted to raise the cloth and look at him, but I didn't dare. There was so little space in our room, and Papa occupied it all.

Mama put on white mourning clothes. A white robe without stitched hems was placed over my red jacket. I remember because I kept breaking off the loose white threads along the edges. There was a lot of noise and grief-stricken crying, everyone was very busy; but actually there wasn't much to be done. It hardly seemed worth so much fuss. Papa was placed in a coffin made of four thin boards; the coffin was full of cracks. Then five or six men carried him out. Mama and I followed behind, weeping. I remember papa; I remember his wooden box. That box meant the end of him. I knew unless I could break it open I'd never see him again. But they buried it deep in the ground in a cemetery outside the city wall. Although I knew exactly where it was, I was afraid it would be hard to find that box again the earth seemed to swallow it like a drop of rain.

3. *This Life of Mine* (Excerpt) (Lao She) (W. J. F. Jenner 译)

I studied a bit when I was a boy. Not much, mind you, but enough to read Seven Knights and Five Heroes, the Three Kingdoms, and things like that. I know quite a lot of the stories in Liao Zhai, by heart—I could tell them with all the details if you liked. They make good listening. Not that I can read the originals—that classic language is too hard for me. The bits I know I learned from "Liao Zhai Stories Retold" columns in the papers. They are terrific. They turn the classic stuff into ordinary Chinese, and put jokes in too!

My handwriting is not bad either. It is as good as anything in the official documents they used to write in the government offices in the old days. I'd have made a first-rate clerk. My writing has a good balance to it. I lay the ink on thick and glossy, and my lines are very neat. Of course, I know my limits. I wouldn't say I'd have been good enough to write memorials to the emperor, but I'd guarantee to do a good job of copying out any of the official documents you see these days.

Considering how good I am at reading and writing I ought to have got a job in a government office. It wouldn't have brought much glory on my family, but it'd have been a sight more respectable than any other job. Besides, however low you start you're bound to get some promotion. I've seen more than one top official whose writing's not up to mine, and who can't even sting a sentence together when he's talking. If men like that can get to the top as officials, there's no reason why I shouldn't have done.

But when I was fifteen the family made me start an apprenticeship. There's nothing degrading about learning a trade—it's just that it's a bit less satisfying than having a government job. Learn a trade and you're stuck with it for the rest of your days. Even if you make a pile you're nothing compared with a high official. But I didn't make a fuss about it with my parents. I just went off and served my apprenticeship. I was only fifteen, and you don't make your own choices at that age. Besides, my parents told me that they'd find me a wife when I'd finished my apprenticeship and started earning. In those days I thought getting married would be fun. Stick it out for two or three years, I thought, then earn my living at my trade and have a nice young bride too. I reckoned that would be really living.

4. *K'ung I-chi*(杨宪益、戴乃迭 译)

K'ung was the only long-gowned customer to drink his wine standing. He was a big man, with a pale complexion and scars that often showed among the wrinkles of his face. He had a large, unkempt beard, streaked with white. Although he wore a long gown, it was dirty and tattered, and looked as if it had not been washed or mended for over ten years. He used so many archaisms in his speech, it was impossible to understand half of what he said. As his surname was K'ung, he was nicknamed "K'ung I-chi", the first three characters in a children's copybook. Whenever he came into the shop, everyone would look at him and chuckle. And someone would call out:

"K'ung I-chi! There are some fresh scars on your face!"

Ignoring this remark, K'ung would come to the counter to order two bowls of heated wine and a dish of peas flavored with aniseed. For this he produced nine coppers. Someone else would call out, in deliberately loud tones:

"You must have been steeling again!"

"How can you ruin a man's good name so groundlessly?" he would ask, opening his eyes wide.

"What good name! The day before yesterday I saw you with my own eyes being hung up and beaten for stealing books from the Ho family!"

Then K'ung would flush, the veins on his forehead standing out as he remonstrated: "Taking a book can't be considered stealing … Taking a book! … Can the business of a scholar be considered stealing?!" Then followed sayings that were hard to understand, like "A gentleman keeps his integrity even in poverty," and a jumble of archaic expressions until everybody was roaring with laughter and the whole tavern was filled with merriment.

From the gossip I heard behind his back, K'ung I-chi had studied the classics but had never passed the official examination. With no way of making a living, he grew poorer and poorer, until he was practically reduced to begging. Luckily, he was a good calligrapher, and could do copy word in exchange for a bowl of rice to eat. Unfortunately he had a bad disposition: he liked drinking and was lazy. So after a few days he would invariably disappear, taking books, paper, brushes, and ink-stone with him. After this had happened several times, nobody wanted to employ him as a copyist again. Then there was no alternative for him but occasional pilfering. In our tavern his behavior outshone everyone else's. He never failed to pay up, although sometimes, when he had no ready money, his name would appear on the chalk board where we listed debtors. However, in less than a month he would always settle his account, and his name would be wiped off the board again.

After drinking half a howl of wine, K'ung would regain his composure. But then someone would ask:

"K'ung I-chi, do you really know how to read?"

When K'ung looked as if such a question were beneath contempt, they would continue: "How is it you never passed even the lowest official examination?"

At that K'ung would look disconsolate and ill at ease. His face would turn pale and his lips move, but only to utter those unintelligible classical expressions. Then everybody would laugh heartily again, and the whole tavern would be merry.

5. Care (Mini story) (杜争鸣 译)

Professor Zhuang has always been aloof and proud, but even such a one as him is now feeling angry, because the loneliness is really too much for him to bear. As a well-known professor in an equally well-known prestigious university in China, he has never been treated with such neglect, not even when he was ill in bed in a foreign country on a lecture visit. It is said that intellectuals enjoy the same treatment of high-rank cadres, but how could he—

certainly ranked among the intellectuals—match with the high-rank cadre lying on the sickbed opposite him? All the time, that one has by his bed cadres like division directors and section heads to care for him. In addition, there are even smart young ladies coming to see him and give him some heart-warming words. On his bed stand and window-still are piles of De Lux foodstuff. There are about half a dozen young men on three shifts taking care of him around the clock. Doctors and nurses who come for checks will also first check that guy, that is Manager Wang, who is lacking neither money nor power, and then come to himself—although as a professor of Chemistry he himself is no less well-known. Besides, if Manager Wang's checkup is to take half an hour, his will probably take no more than a quarter. At his bedside is always a cheerless, deserted air, with his son thousands of miles away on the missile project, and his daughter abroad at school. There is only his other half to come each day to bring him a meal and fill his thermos bottle. As for his department, there is even less that he can count on, for it could at best send someone to visit him every other week. For anyone who has fallen into such a situation, what is of least use is nothing else but learning, reputation and putting on airs. However, Prof. Zhuang is just such a one who will not give in regarding his image. So every day he just lies facing the wall, not paying the least attention to whatever is going on at Manager Wang's bedside. God knows what sort of manager this one is! For this is an age of companies everywhere. As organizations of thousands of people may be called a company, one or two persons may hold up a company sign as well.

Then day comes when Manager Wang's conditions suddenly get worse, and the doctor announces that his funeral affairs should be arranged. Naturally, more people have gathered around his bedside, including even Mr. Liu, the always self-assuming vice manager. In stead of lying with some meaningless sweet words to comfort a dying man, Mr. Liu first kept silent for a little while, and then said something very factual, such as asking if he has any demands to make, or if there is anything that he still worries about. To whatever demand the dying man has made, the vice manager gives a satisfactory answer without any hesitation. After all is said, Mr. Liu gets up to take his leave, for he has to arrange the funeral. Then, suddenly, those people attending Manager Wang all rise at once, leaving the patient behind, to win their chance to help Mr. Liu on his way, some go to the front to open the door, others walk on his side, all smiling to please him. Such a crowd! And what a scene! Mr. Liu flies off his handle and shouts: "It is not me who is dying! What is the point of helping me?"

As an exception, Prof. Zhuang turns over, and sees that Manager Wang lies there all by himself, waiting for his last moment, two lines of tears from his face trickling down to the pillow ... The professor feels it fortunate that he himself is an "intellectual", not a "high official", and that his pen will never betray him, not even on his last day.

三、英汉互译原理在诗歌中的应用

（一）英译中

1. 此情可待（杜争鸣 译）

海角天涯，日夜等待
等得我疑幻疑真
你的声音，远方传来
也不能把我安慰
如果今生还能相聚
怎能说分别永久
天下任你走
万事任你行
我都在耐心把你等待
无论对不对
哪怕心已碎
我都在这里把你等待
我从不怀疑
到底不改
这缘分没有完了
听到你笑声
尝到泪滋味
却不能到你身旁
你不明白吗？宝贝
你让我如痴如醉
天下任你走
万事任你行
我都在耐心把你等待
无论对不对
哪怕心已碎
我都在耐心把你等待
我不知道如何继续

这罗曼司
如果最终还能相聚
我绝不放弃
你不明白吗？宝贝
你让我如痴如醉
天下任你走
万事任你行
我都在耐心把你等待
无论对不对
哪怕心已碎
我都在耐心把你等待

译者解读

"Right Here Waiting"是深受世界众多歌迷喜爱的一首英语经典歌曲，其原作原唱是曾在1994年美国世界杯开幕式上以无音乐伴奏形式对数万观众高唱美国国歌的理查德·马克思（Richard Marx）。该歌虽在海内外广泛传唱多年，但迄今为止没有听到中文版本的演唱。在互联网常用搜索引擎搜索，虽然也可以找到零散的译文，但这些译文基本上只是歌词大意的解释而已，显然都不适合歌唱。为了弥补这一缺憾，同时出于对这首歌的喜爱和对翻译的迷恋，我在业余闲暇时间一边反复欣赏，一边试图把它翻译成中文，希望这种翻译同样能够演唱并获得至少类似原唱的审美效果。这自然是一个巨大的挑战，但是经过反复琢磨，我认为这首歌还是可以翻译成中文演唱的。不过，为了达到目的，翻译就必须有所变化，变而不失其本。这种翻译，正如我们翻译教学研究界所常说的那样，就是"译可译，非常译"。

在此，我首先将译文与原文按行编号，然后对其中的翻译变化予以解释。

（1）第1行中，"oceans apart"其实直接译为"远隔重洋"字面上会显得比现在的翻译更加贴近原文，但我没有考虑这样翻译，而是选择了"海角天涯"，原因主要是后者不仅能表达"距离遥远"的意思，而且从歌唱的角度来看声音更清楚易懂。仔细体会、分析，我们可以发现，"海角天涯"字面上虽然没有说出"远隔"二字，但其意思已在不言之中，这是汉语语言理解需要人的主动参与的"意合"特征造成的。另外，英语原文中只有一个音是鼻音，包含在"oceans"中，而"远隔重洋"中的"远""重""洋"这三个字都有鼻音，而且"洋"字还是后鼻音，这样唱起来就会显得声音混浊，不够清亮。选择"海角天涯"大大减少了鼻音，可以唱出清亮的感觉，更容易理解，效果也更接近原声，这一点在尾音"天涯"的"涯"字上体现得尤其明显。

第1行中，"day after day"翻译为"日夜等待"当然也是出于歌唱效果的考虑，即"等待"中的"待"与原文中的"day"发音十分接近，近乎原唱。不过，我的考虑不仅如此，从翻译的角度来看还出于一个更加重要的原因，即汉语是所谓"主题突出"的语言，主题与语境对于汉语的理解具有举足轻重的作用，这里不按照原文字面拘谨地翻译为"日日夜夜"或

"日复一日",而是直接点破"等待"这个主题,实际上对于习惯于根据主题理解文本含义的中国人来说是很有必要的。

（2）第2行"And I slowly go insane"在英文原文中通过"and"与上文衔接,这是英语注重所谓的"形合"结构决定的。由于中文思维更加注重"意合"的话语语义的结构,强调动态衔接,因此根据上句已经说出"等待",用"等得我"引出句子,从而达到上下紧密连贯的目的。中文省去"slowly"一词不译,原因是"等待"本来就是一个缓慢的过程,而"等得我"已经体现了这个缓慢过程,即使不译,中文读者或歌曲听众也可以理解。如果译出这个词而占用了歌词音节,那么后面更加重要的"insane"一词就不能从容地用"疑幻疑真"这四个字表达了。用"疑幻疑真"来翻译"insane",是抓住这个英文词的本意,对其做具体化的、解释性处理:"精神错乱"的主要特征就是由于把现实与幻觉混淆造成的,分不清二者区别就是"精神错乱"的表现。与此同时,使用"疑幻疑真"也正好和原文带鼻音的"insane"的尾音吻合,有利于唱出原唱的感觉。

（3）第3行中,"I hear your voice"在翻译中省略了主语是出于音节数的考虑,因为英文实际上只有四个音节,而照字面翻译为"我听到你的声音"就是七个音节,根本无法配原曲歌唱。汉语思维在可以理解的情况下省略主语是一个普遍的现象,这就为减少音节提供了方便。另外,"听到"两个字在这里暂时省略后"你的声音"也就自然变成了主题,而"听到"则作为述题部分放在后半句补充出来。从整体上看,这种翻译是从英语的"主—谓—宾"三元结构向汉语的"主—述"二元结构的思维模式转换:"你的声音"是主题部分,"远方传来"是述题部分,这种汉语结构不是直接运用英语语法可以说明的。汉语这样翻译后不仅从思维模式上符合中国人的习惯,而且从歌唱的效果上来看也更能表现原唱的感觉,因为"远方传来"虽然没有"on the line"中的鼻音尾音,但是原因一致,听上去感觉基本相同。

（4）第4行"But it doesn't stop the pain"如果直接译为"但这也不能止住我的痛苦"声音就不好听,而且由于音节太多也无法演唱。"pain"是带有一个较响亮的前元音的单词,译成"痛苦"声音的性质也就发生了变化,唱起来太低沉。"安慰"的尾音虽然不带鼻音,但元音性质基本相同,歌唱效果基本一致。整句英文原文实际上并不是说消除或止住身体的伤痛,而是说消除心里的痛楚的感觉,换个说法就是使人得到安慰。所以,表面上的词语虽然似乎发生了改变,而实际意义则没有变。翻译的灵活性必须有一个基础,即把握本意和语言的话语功能（或目的）,如果变化达到了同样的目的或发挥了同样的功能,无论怎么灵活都应该是可以接受的。

（5）第5行"If I see you next to never"很有意味,不少英语语感不够好的学生还不能体会出来。其实"next to never"意味深长之处正在于它对是否还能相见（或相聚）似乎不做明确的肯定或否定,可以理解成"难以见面"或"难得相聚",字面上看就是"几乎永远不能相见",但是仍然不是肯定的"不能相见",这样的表达法对整个歌曲的主题"等待"来说至关重要。本来也可以从相反的角度译为"只要还有任何一丝希望相见",但是这样显然音节不允许。所以,我在这里添加了"今生",省去了其他汉字。整句"如果今生还能相见"

不但和原文音节数相配,而且其中的"还"字与原文中的"next"元音相近,可以使用同一个较高音符唱出,获得与原唱更加接近的效果。

(6) 第 6 行"How can we say forever"紧接着上一行的话似乎很难理解:究竟"say forever"是说什么事情"永远"? 仅仅这几个单词从字面上看是看不出答案的,要理解必须关照主题和语境。根据主题,"forever"是和"等待"有关的,而从语境来看,上一行既然是说"只要还有一丝希望相见"或"只要今生还能相见",那么下面的意思应该是和"等待"的理由有关。由于本行没有明确说明,但是主题和语境都比较明确,我们只能把"forever"理解为"永远这样等待""永远这样远在天涯"。所以,中文翻译成"怎能说分到永久"是把字面上没有但是可以推知的意思表达了出来,如果结合下面的句子,意思就更加肯定了。

(7) 第 7-8 行"Wherever you go"和"Whatever you do"分别翻译为"天下任你走,万事任你行",与原文音节数目相等,从用字表面看似变化大了一点儿,但这种变化背后的道理实际上并不难说清楚:英语既然意思是"无论哪里""无论何事",那么用汉语"天下""万事"就可以表示,原因在于英文注重从个别具体的客体出发思维,而汉语则倾向于首先从总体上把握。如果直接翻译为"无论你走到哪里""无论你做什么",音节就多出来了。当然,为了照顾音节,也可以翻译成"无论你到哪""无论你做啥",但这显然使文体风格发生了变化,变得太口语化,丧失了歌词的优美、文雅色彩,所以是不可取的。"天下任你走,万事任你行"中的"天下"和"万事"虽然都只有两个音节,但意思完全表达了出来;其中重复使用的一个"任"字在意义上就是"无论"的更书面化的表现形式,而且更加充分地体现了汉语注重动态语言思维的特征。由此可见,追求语言简洁和精练是翻译中的一个重要目标。

(8) 第 9 行"I will be right here waiting for you"比较简单,可以有两种比较直接的翻译,都可以与原文音节一致:一是"我都在这里把你等待",二是"我都在这里等待着你"。二者之间我选择了前者,原因还比较微妙:虽然差别很小,但是确实有差别,即把"等待"二字放到末尾更显得主题突出,而把"你"放在末尾则没有太大必要性,因为"等待"谁是毋庸置疑的,关键还是"等待"本身。

(9) 第 10-11 行"Whatever it takes"和"Or how my heart breaks"中,前者变化比较大,翻译成"无论对不对"看似与原文不符,实际交际功能却是相同的:"Whatever it takes"直译就是"无论需要什么代价",由此可以推论,就是"什么都不顾"或"无所顾忌",既然"无所顾忌",那就是不从理性上考虑,本质上完全可以理解为"无论对不对"的意思。由此可见,翻译中灵活性的原则是语言表现的功能和目的,在由于语言思维差异而难以直译的情况下,只要翻译出原文的功能和目的,译者的责任也就算完成了。后面的一行原文中有"or"一个连接词,这是英语形合结构的表现,而汉语是以意合为主的语言,所以可以省去。原文直译应该是"无论如何心碎",翻译"如何"二字没有必要,因为都"心碎"了,再谈如何意义就不大了。汉语添加"哪怕"二字,是语气衔接,与上一行连起来更加体现了"等待"到底的决心。

(10) 第 12 行英文重复,中文照样重复,歌词中更不能随意改变。

（11）第 13 行"I took for granted"在英文中是肯定形式，汉语则从反面否定，译为"我从不怀疑"。肯定与否定是相对而言的，英汉对比研究证明，中文中使用否定的形式比英文比例高一些，这在文学作品和商业应用文体中表现得更加明显，在各种标语、公示语中也是很常见的。汉语常说"不许""请勿""不要""不可"等，而类似的情况英语中则倾向于直接从正面说。

（12）第 14 行"all the times"在最初翻译时首先想到的是"自始至终""始终如一"，但是在把英语原歌词与这种翻译比较、试唱时，发现原文的"all"和"times"这两个音与歌曲音符十分相配，而汉语中与原曲音符相对的"自""始""如一"都无法唱出同样的效果，发音上不适合。于是，经过反复琢磨，最后决定采取现在的"到底不改"，其中"到"与英文"all"元音性质相似，"改"与"times"元音也基本相同，可以演唱出同样的感觉。另外，从意义上来看，最后决定这样翻译还因为"all the times"在英文中作为语法上的状语体现了英语语言结构的静态特征，而"到底不改"则表现了汉语语言结构的"动态"特征，在由英译汉的过程中将静态结构转换为汉语的动态结构是一条基本的规律。仅从词语层面出发把英语中表示状态的名词、形容词转换为汉语的动词和谓语性表达法只是由静到动的一个方面，而从句法上把英语的普通肯定性陈述形式改为汉语的否定形式（甚至改成反问句）是另一个重要方面。此处翻译的"不改"采取了汉语的否定式，也进一步增加了表达的动感。

（13）第 15 行"That I thought would last somehow"分析起来并不简单："that"究竟是不是仅仅作为一个关系词，引导上面的"I take for granted"的主语呢？看来并非如此，因为如果是这样的话，后面的"I thought would last somehow"就没有了逻辑主语，这显然对于注重句法结构的严谨性的英语来说是个问题。因此，"that"即使有连接词的感觉，但是对后面来说它仍然是主语。那么它究竟指什么？这只能根据语境进行分析了。前面唱的是"我都在这里把你等待"，整个歌曲的主题也是"等待"，因此"that"的理解也只能从这里出发。无论如何都要等下去，这是一种情分。把"that"理解、翻译成"缘分"就是出于这样的考虑。整句译为"这缘分没有完了"，也与上句一样，是通过否定词的使用增强汉语动态感的翻译转换，在这一转换中，"完了"的尾音与"somehow"的尾音一致，演唱时可以接近原唱的感觉。

（14）第 16 - 17 行"I hear your laughter, I taste the tears"翻译为"听到你笑声，尝到泪滋味"，其中省略了主语，这当然是为了音节的一致。汉语在意义明确的情况下可以省略主语，这个特点为此提供了方便。

（15）第 18 行"But I can't get near you now"译为"却不能到你身旁"没有什么特别变化，只是放弃了全文中的一个"now"，这根据语境显然是可以理解的。其中的一个"到"字，和上两行中连续出现的同一个字呼应，也增加了这三行的流畅感。

（16）第 19 行"Oh, can't you see it baby"的翻译删去了感叹词"Oh"，在意义没有什么改变的情况下使中文与英文音节数一致，这是可以接受的。原文的"baby"实际上是恋人之间的一种爱称，中文正好有"宝贝"与其相对。这两种不同语言的表达法不仅在意义上吻合，而且在声音上相似，尾音基本十分接近，也是一种难得的巧合。

(17) 第 20 行"You've got me goin' crazy"翻译为"你让我如痴如醉",变化最大的就是"crazy"一词。虽然按照词典注释直接翻译只能是"疯狂""狂热""愚蠢"等,但这些词表面上都是贬义,而原文中却不是贬义,歌颂为爱到痴迷程度,所以必须根据具体的语境考虑使用更确切的表达法。"如痴如醉"是从不含贬义的角度表达同样的意思,而且与原文尾音相符,应该说是一种比较贴切的译法。

(18) 第 21 - 26 行是重复歌词,目的是强调全歌的主题,这里不宜改变翻译方法。

(19) 第 27 - 28 行"I wonder how we can survive / This romance"中的"survive"一词在汉语中没有对应的字或词,词典注释为"经历……之后还活着""幸免于……",但是按照词典释义显然难以理解,也无法翻译。总结该词的实际用法,从中可以知道它有"挺过……""经历……(不幸)"的意思。结合这里的语境,我们可以得出其实际意思就是指爱情经过漫长等待的考验后仍然能够继续下去的意思。"This romance"虽然本意是所谓的"罗曼司"(爱情传奇),但是这里是苦苦的等待的爱,挺过这个"罗曼司"就是指经历"等待"的考验。因此,翻译为"继续",从而达到文字精简、与原文音节相符的目的。

(20) 第 29 行"But in the end if I'm with you"中的"but"是英语型合结构的连接性单词,汉语注重意合,因此没有必要翻译。"with you"翻译成"相聚"只是改变了观察角度,意思也没有变化。中间用较高音符唱出的"I'm"与汉语的"还能"中的"还"相对,声音效果完全相同,有利于唱出原歌的感觉。

(21) 第 30 行"I'll take the chance"翻译为"我绝不放弃",其原理与第 14 行的翻译相同,即使用否定词语从反面着手翻译英文中用肯定形式表现的内容,可以体现英汉语言思维中"静态"与"动态"表现的差异,中文会显得更具表现力。所以,英语的意思是"一定抓住机会",汉语则从反面译为"绝不放弃(机会)",其中的"机会"省略了也不影响表达原意。

(22) 第 31 - 38 行,主题行的重复翻译,即使有其他译法也不再考虑,应该保留重复。

2. 你的眼睛(杜争鸣 译)

你的眼睛,是深邃的天穹,
占据着我,自始至终;
大海般的幽思,浪涛翻滚,
冲击着我的心胸。

(二) 中译英

1. Ten Years(杜争鸣 译)

If those two words did not quiver so
I would not find myself in woe
However uttered, they just mean part and go

Should we have no desire for tomorrow,

Love would seem a tour to follow,

At thousands of open gates, someone is to be first to go.

Now the arms will no longer hold

Why not take the time before we go

To enjoy it in tears and sorrow?

Ten years ago

I didn't know you and you were not my love

We were still in each other's company like strangers who rove

Round street corners we now better know.

The years gone, though

We are still friends to greet by a "hello"

But the tender feeling is no longer fit for our arms to hold,

Lovers at last fall as friends as they go.

Not until we've spent years as friends—just so,

Do I realize that all my tears

Must have been shed, for you, or any third fellow

译者解读

陈奕迅的《十年》是一首当代流行歌曲，从 2004 年以来在中国大陆和世界华人歌坛广为流传，受到了众多青年歌迷很高的评价。2005 年三四月间，歌手曾通过其代理人在国际互联网上征集该歌歌词的英文翻译，但至今没有听到有歌手公开用英文演唱，这足以说明将其翻译成适合演唱的英文并非容易的事。在这里，我们提供英文译文，同时对翻译中的难点加以解释，希望能够得到歌手陈奕迅及其广大歌迷的喜爱。需要特别说明的是，这里的英文版本在 2005 年年底前完成后，曾经由苏州大学外国语学院的四名研究生在全院研究生元旦晚会上演唱。她们通过短暂的熟悉、练习后演唱非常成功，博得了全院师生的热烈掌声。从这一点看，该歌词确实达到了翻译目的。

我们认为，译文歌词有一个原则，就是必须能够像原文歌词那样与乐曲相配，便于歌唱。为了便于歌唱，翻译应该有很大的灵活性，不同的译者可以有不同的译法，但是从总体上讲，它必然受到一般散文翻译所没有的限制。这种限制具体说来主要有两点：原歌词的音节数在翻译中不能随意改变；某些词的声音总体特点不能随意改变，开口音不宜变为闭口音，一句的尾音必须尽可能押韵或类似。在翻译《十年》的过程中，译者认为，要让音节数相等，通过反复思考是可以做到的，要让所有重要的音都相似几乎是不可能的，但在重要的尾音上押韵，使译文便于演唱还是可以做到的。

下面对译者在翻译《十年》中遇到的具体问题和翻译处理的思考进行解释。

（1）首先是该歌名称的翻译。我们知道，"十年"在英文中既可以逐字直接翻译为"ten

years",也可以概括翻译为"a decade"。那么译文为什么选择前者而不是后者呢?译者的考虑是:在有多种翻译可能性的情况下,应该首先选择在语言形式和意思两方面能够同时贴近原文的译法。"ten years"和"a decade"虽然意思基本相同,但是语言形式有所差别,前者是两个音节,后者却是三个音节,与原文不一致;如果为了音节一致而不使用冠词"a"又不符合英文的习惯。而且,这两种表达法的意思基本相同,但并不意味着完全一致:"ten years"更加具体,体现了"十年"的时间一年一年地流逝的感觉,而"decade"则是对这段时间的整体概括,丧失了"一年一年"或"年复一年"的意味。二者相比之下,前者更能符合歌曲主人公表达十年情感经历的需要。

(2) 我们知道,英文的"word"与汉语的"字"实际上并不等同,因为汉语中虽然有"word"所指的"词",英文中却没有汉语中的"字"。然而,正因为英文中没有"字",汉语中的"字"包括在"词"里面,所以就可以不考虑它的翻译了。当然,如果死板地翻译,那就只能用"character"(甚至需要用"Chinese character")来译,那样做的话,句子的音节数必然超过原文,结果就无法演唱了。这说明文学翻译不能像数学那样做到"科学"与"精确"。

"shake"虽然翻译出了"颤抖"的意思,但其音无法唱出"颤抖"的效果,原因主要是它的第二个音节和"抖"发音时开口大小与舌位高低及与前后位置都有所不同。英文加入一个"as they go",与原文中的"抖"尾音完全一致,演唱效果相同。对它的理解是"在被说出口的时候"(或"就其本身的意思而言"),意思也没有损失,反而更有深度。所以,这里的添加是十分必要的。

(3) "难受"在词典上的注释一般是"suffer",可以指身体、心理上承受的痛苦,但这里应该是强调心理上的痛苦或悲伤。所以,笔者认为更具体、准确的英文词实际上不是词典上的释义词,而是"sorrow"、"woe"(甚至是"grief")。如果选用"sorrow",意思虽然适合,押韵也没有问题,但音节数会多出一个,对于歌手的演唱来说就可能增加了难度。"woe"不仅有"痛苦,苦恼"之义,能够体现"难受"的感觉,而且尾音与原句一致,体现了原文的声音效果。

(4) "part"虽有分手之义,但它的发音与"手"相差太大,显得突兀、不协调;而选择添加一个"go",不仅可以使译文押韵,而且更在内容上对"part"这个词的意义做了补充,体现了原歌词中"分手"一词的深层含义,意味着恋人的转身而去,美好的感情像泼出去的水那样一去不复返,留下的只有上句所唱到的"woe"。

(5) "牵牵手就像旅游"一句的翻译关键在于"love"一词的选择。"牵牵手"实际上只是一个形象、具体的表达方式,这是由汉语思维注重形象性的特点所决定的,而英文更注重直接性的表达,因此应该考虑将其意义进行抽象概括,提取实质性内容。因此,选用"love"就是翻译实质,而且这样不仅丰富了"牵牵手"的意义,也避免了将其就字面转换译成英文的烦琐,而"love"则简洁明确,意义也并不缺失。"follow"的添加体现了原文的韵尾,也使译文的意义更加生动、完整。

(6) "怀抱既然不能逗留"一句的翻译转换了一个角度:改变视角观察、理解原文,我们可以推出其真正的意图就等于说"爱的拥抱"不能持久。"持久"的意思隐含在"逗留"中，与"永久相爱，白头到老"的意思融为一体。碰巧的是，英文"hold"意思覆盖面较广，既能体现恋人之间的拥抱，又有"持久"的意思和"始终如一"的感觉。选择这个英文单词使这句话表达精确，仅仅通过一个音节便表达了原文所蕴含的复杂意义。而且我们都知道，演唱英语歌曲时，歌手通常都是将最后一词的辅音部分进行弱化处理甚至完全省略，所以即使在一般的朗诵中不押韵，在演唱中听起来就押韵了。仔细品味"hold"的声音效果，我们会感到它很柔和，有很强的可以延续性，丝毫没有生硬别扭的感觉，这就给歌手留下了发挥个性的余地。

（7）第7行与下行在原文中是相连的两个部分，第7行给出时间，下行说出主句内容。"在离开的时候"实际上也就是"在还没有离开的时候"或"将要离开的时候"，所以英文翻译就是"before we go"。把这个时间状语按照英语的惯常做法放在两行中间，不仅是押韵的需要，而且也符合原文的语序。后者甚至比前者更加重要，原因是唱歌与说话的不同之处也在于唱歌总是比说话慢，而且可以慢很多。如果颠倒了语序就使译文与原文接连两行无法对应，造成较大混乱。因此，尽量按照原文顺序翻译，这也可以说是歌词翻译的一个重要原则。

原文第9行"一边享受一边泪流"翻译为"enjoy it in tears and sorrow"，添加了"sorrow"一词，是将中文形象具体的描述表现为英文概括的描述，符合英汉双语思维的不同倾向，同时也照顾到了押韵。"tears"虽然可以表现"sorrow"，但是我们知道人激动、高兴也会有流泪的情况。这里的"泪"应该包括此时还能"享受"的"泪"和不得不分手的遗憾、后悔的"泪"。因此，如果只是死板地翻译"in tears"，不敢添加"sorrow"，就很难获得同样的效果。

（8）在考虑使这句话原文与译文音节数相匹配的同时，把"你不属于我"翻译为"you were not my girl"，似乎音节仍然多了一个，但实际上"you were"可以连起来唱，在歌词中可以看作一个音节。而且比直译为"you didn't belong to me"更符合英文注重使用简单名词或名词词组表意的语言思维习惯。另外，从押韵上来说，虽然这按照一般的诗歌不算押韵，但在歌词中能获得如同押韵的效果，因为它和韵脚在发音部位上十分相近，唱起来感觉基本不变。这也反映了一般诗词押韵与歌词押韵的不同规律。

（9）第12句翻译时添加了"rove"，这既是为了弥补中文音节数，使之与原文的音节数相等，又是为了押韵。实际上，根据上面所谈的歌词翻译应该尽量贴近原文语序的原则，这似乎并不是理想的翻译，因为"走过"在原文中属于下一行，而这里却提前了。不过，仔细考虑一番，我们也可以认为，"陪在一个陌生人左右"完全可以，而且应该理解为"陪着走"的意思，这里直接翻译为"rove"，同时解决了音节数、押韵和本句与下句衔接三个问题，也不失为一种较好的办法。另外，与前面的解释一样，使用"rove"在一般诗词翻译中不算押韵，但在歌词里具有押韵的效果。

（10）从字面出发，对"街头"的理解可以有三种情况：一是十字交叉路口，二是丁字路口，三是一条街的转弯处。"走过"可以转弯，也可以不转弯。译者的理解是，如果不转弯而直接"走过"，那这个"街头"也未必就是"街头"。更重要的是，这里是用"街头"表示人生道路上比较重要的点，即我们通常所说的人生"转折点"，所以"走过"就是"转过"，英文应该翻译成"round street corners"，而不是"pass the intersection"。

（11）第14句的翻译添加一个"though"，照顾音节、押韵，同时使语篇衔接、语气自然。

（12）"再也找不到拥抱的理由"翻译为"no longer fit for our arms to hold"表面上似乎变化很大，实际上意思没有改变。"找不到"是汉语注重动态和感性语言思维的表现形式，"fit for"是英文强调静态（未必一定是名词）和理性语言思维的表现形式。中文的"理由"在英文中隐含在"fit for"之中，是否有"理由"也就是还是否"fit"，所以这样翻译完全可以表示原文的整体意义和联想：时过境迁之后，恋人之间的隔膜与生疏造成原来的"拥抱"不再"适宜"。所以，"fit"远比"reason"更适合。

另外，这里的"hold"一词与笔者在上文(6)中所解释的有所不同，它只是指互相"拥抱"，借以表现"温柔之情"，而没有"天长地久"的含义。由于语境、搭配不同，意义大小有异，这在文学翻译中是很普遍的现象。

（13）"fall"一词体现了一个"沦"字中所包含的无奈、落寞以及后悔的心情。最后一个"go"既押韵，又体现了恋人之间随着十年的流逝，感情也愈加流逝，事态发展虽不如人意甚至出乎意料却自然而然的情况，同时进一步表现主人公那种难以挽回的落寞的心情。

（14）"friends"一词并不能将原句的韵味唱出来，而且音节与原文也有差距，故在"friends"之后添加"just so"，可译为"也仅仅如此而已"，不仅沿用了上句的韵脚，而且在内容上也是对上句意味的延伸或两句中重复使用"friends"的总结，体现了歌者心里一种淡淡的遗憾。

（15）原文最后一句需要仔细体会其中的含义：为情而流泪，是人成长过程中必然发生的事，至于泪为谁流则很难说。爱的意义在于真情付出，而不取决于泪为谁流。在叙事者的情感旅程中，任何一个与他同行的人都会给他带来同样的无奈。理解了这层含义，才能在译文中得以准确传达。笔者在翻译中选择使用"or"和"any other"，就是为了达到这个目的。至于选择"girl"这个词，从感觉上来说原因与注释(8)相近，都是为了在歌唱中获得近似于押韵的效果。

总结：歌词翻译与一般的诗词翻译有明显的不同，具体主要体现在三个方面：其一是译文与原文的音节数必须相同；其二是押韵不是一般诗词的死板押韵，而是除了普通的押韵还可以压发音效果类似的韵；其三是语序不能随意颠倒，尤其不能串行翻译，使歌词的词序发生混乱。这三个方面实际上对歌词翻译提出了更高的要求，是文学翻译中颇具挑战性的一类文体。我们希望，《十年》翻译的体验能够对以后的流行歌曲翻译提供可资借鉴的方法。

2. Poems in Praise of Suzhou Gardens（杜争鸣 译）

（1）In Praise of Suzhou（1）

Zheng Xiaoxie

White walls enclose quietness within the busy town,

And garden life of bounty in the fairy land.

The rockery peaks, ranges and streams contain much;

All old-style buildings far from the world noises stand.

As every plant and flower play with their shadows,

The seasons change, without extremes at either end.

Out of broken silence sound the tunes of pipe n' string

Finding all over the world fans if not a band.

（2）In Praise of Suzhou（2）

Zheng Xiaoxie

As all arts are valued in both form and substance,

Suzhou's best scenes are in her classic gardens.

Made as if by the Nature's hand in smaller size,

They find roots in the nation's spiritual essence.

（3）Reminiscenes of the Ancient Guan-Wa Palace（to the Tune of Yumeiren）

Luo Zhewen

About Lingyan Mountain Temple the grass is green;

Time passes through streaming sunlight and drizzling rain,

That blurs the Wu's Mount when the day is to clear and be plain.

Cloudy woods look fuzzy; people live away;

And the day drawing to evening.

The ancient Guan-Wa Palace is now lost,

And its traces never the same all times.

But all times, the ancient love is not forgot,

With the wood-sole shoes' steps still echoing about.

Notes：Guan-Wa Palace, over two millennia ago, was one of the earliest royal palaces and a famous garden.

(4) **In Praise of Suzhou Scenic Gardens**

Meng Zhaozhen

Nature and Man are the Chinese dragon in one,

Making the Wu styles by hills 'n dales under the sun.

The gardens are built and masterpieces all done,

And the town ever thrives in nature, peered by none.

(5) **The Corridor of Resounding Wood Sandals**

Meng Zhaozhen

Mount Lingyan has a corridor o'er rocks,

With earthen jars under to serve as sound box

Structured with tenons and light wooden board,

Carrying dancers tick tacking for the king and lord.

(6) **In Praise of the Mountain Villa with Embracing Beauty**

Meng Zhaozhen

A small landscape of water and a hill looks great,

Leading streams under peaks 'n vales mutually relate.

In close vicinity the cliffs stand steep and high;

The maze of caves has beams that naturally over fly.

3. Translation Collection of Tang Poems

(1) **Hoeing for Rice Shoots**（杜争鸣 译）

Li Shen

Hoeing under the sun at the midday,

The farmer's sweating to wet the topsoil.

Now we should know that the rice in the tray

Has in every grain the hardest toil.

(2) **A Retrospect**（Herbert A. Giles 译）

Cui Hu

On this day last year what a party were we!

Pink cheeks and pink peach-blossoms smiled

  Upon me;

But alas the pink cheeks are now far far away,

Though the peach-blossoms smile as they smiled

  On that day.

（3）**The Heights**（W. J. B. Fletcher 译）

Du Fu

The wind so fresh, the sky so high

Awake the gibbons' wailing cry.

The isles clear-cut, the sand so white,

Arrest the wheeling sea-gulls' flight.

Through endless Space with rustling sound

The falling leaves are whirled around.

Beyond my ken a yeasty sea

The Yangtze's waves are rolling free.

From far away, in Autumn drear,

I find my self a stranger here.

With dragging years and illness wage

Lone war upon this lofty stage.

With troubles vexed and trials sore

My locks are daily growing hoar；

Till Time, before whose steps I pine,

Set down this failing cup of wine.

（4）a. **At Dawn**（Herbert A. Giles 译）

Jin Changxu

Drive the young orioles away,

Nor let them on the branches play；

Their chirping breaks my slumber through

And keep me from my dreams of you.

b. **A Complaint in Spring**（许渊冲 译）

Jin Changxu

Drive orioles from the tree；

Their songs awake poor me

From dreaming of my dear

Far off on the frontier.

4. Suzhou People Are Bosom Friends of People from the Whole World (Children Dance)(杜争鸣 译)

(1)

It is the same moon in the same sky;
It is the same sun that gives the same light;
On the same world live us all;
And this same world we make so small.
Suzhou is so close to your own native land;
Our friends from all countries go hand in hand.
Ah, our friends from all countries go hand in hand.

(2)

Colorful clouds fly in the same blue sky,
Like fresh flowers on the same land nearby.
On the same world we all live side by side,
To say we are in the same family is all right.
Suzhou is so close to your own native land;
Our siblings from all countries go hand in hand.
Ah, our siblings from all countries go hand in hand.

5. Suzhou, the City of My Heart(杜争鸣 译)

I'm coming, coming, once again to the Chilly Hill Temple,
To the Grand Canal flowing down from Beijing.
Here are the tender willows, the Maple Bridge at dusk
And the resounding bell,
With which Suzhou greets another evening.
Here, and just here, lies my beloved land, land of my heart.
I'm coming, coming, once again to the beautiful water city,
To the Grand Canal flowing to the city of Hangzhou.
Here in the shade of phoenix trees, life is good in the green,
The dwelling boats passing apace, and moving about,
To embrace the tender night of the lovely city.
I'm coming, coming, once again to the North Temple Pagoda,
By the torrential water of the Grand Canal relating a long story.
In today's prosperity are also remains of the Sui-Tang Dynasties,
Here the moonlight on the water is waiting
For you and me to enjoy the sweet, serene evening.

四、英汉互译原理在应用文中的应用

1. 便笺（Notepaper）

（1）请假条（Request for Leave）

To Department Office
    Secretary Zhang   Nov. 2, 2007
Dear Sir,
    I beg to apply for one week's leave of absence from the 2nd to the 8th instant, both days inclusive, in order to return home to see my grandfather, who is now dangerously ill.
    To support my application, I herewith submit a telegram to that effect received from my father.
    I should be very much obliged if you will grant me my application. As regards the lessons to be missed during my absence, I will do my best to make them up as soon as I get back from leave.

                                                                     Yours respectfully,
                                                                     Xi Zaochi

（2）Forms of IOU（借条）

October 12, 2007
To the Finance Office of the Corporation
I. O. U. one hundred yuan only.

                                                                                                XXX

2. 邀请函（Letter of Invitation）

（1）朋友赴宴邀请（Inviting a Friend to Dinner）

亲爱的洛娜：
    请您和韦斯特先生于五月五日（星期二）晚上七时与我们共进晚餐，不知能来否？自上次欢晤以来，又有很长时间了，我们非常希望你们能够光临。

                                                                     您真挚的
                                                               伊丽莎白·K.本顿

（2） 应邀（Acceptance）

亲爱的本顿夫人：

　　韦斯特和我将在五月五日（星期二）晚上七时愉快地与你们共进晚餐，承你们邀请，非常高兴！

　　我们以极其愉快的心情，盼望着再一次和您以及本顿医生晤面。

　　　　　　　　　　　　　　　　　　　　　你们非常真挚的
　　　　　　　　　　　　　　　　　　　　　洛娜

（3） 谢却（Regret）

亲爱的本顿夫人：

　　我一直盼望着韦斯特能从南京及时赶回来参加你们的宴会，以致迟迟未复。现悉，在五日（星期二）以前，他不能返回本市，因此我们不能接受您在那一天的宴请了。特此奉告，深为抱歉。

　　感谢你们的盛情邀请。我们不能同您及本顿医生共度那一个夜晚，我想韦斯特一定和我一样会感到遗憾，因为在你们家中度过这样的夜晚总是令人十分愉快的。

　　　　　　　　　　　　　　　　　　　　　您真挚的
　　　　　　　　　　　　　　　　　　　　　洛娜

（4） 婚礼邀请信（Wedding Invitation）

亲爱的贝蒂：

　　戴维和我已经决定了婚期，我们让您首先知道，婚礼定于六月十二日（星期四）正午在区公共教堂举行。邀请的客人不多，只有几位近亲和密友。

　　贝蒂，望您十一时到我家，然后一起去教堂，礼毕一同回家，参加妈妈为我们举办的一次小型便宴。

　　希望十二日那天是一个明朗的晴天！

　　　　　　　　　　　　　　　　　　　　　美好的祝愿
　　　　　　　　　　　　　　　　　　　　　海伦

3. 信息咨询(Asking for Information)

Dear Sir,

    I graduated from Dongnan (Southeast China) University in August, 1989, majoring in engineering. Now I am an assistant lecturer and lab technician of Soochow University. To further my studies, I wish to enter the Graduate School of Engineering of the Massachusetts Institute of Technology for the degree of Master of Science. Your institute has a long history and a fine tradition of scholarship. It is well staffed and equipped, enjoying worldwide fame. To find a place in such an ideal school of higher education is indeed a matter of the greatest honor. It is my long-cherished hope that I will be fortunate enough to be admitted into MIT.

    I would be grateful to know the conditions under which the applicants are accepted. Would you please send me an application form and some related information?

    I am looking forward to hearing from you soon.

                                                    Respectfully yours,

                                                        Li Feng

4. 商业合同(Business Contract)

CONTRACT

    This Contract made on this 8th December, 1988, by and between Victory Electronic Trading Co., Ltd. (hereinafter called "the sellers"), a corporation duly organized and existing under the laws of China's Hong Kong, with its head office at _____, Hong Kong and Pan-African Trading Co., Ltd. (hereinafter called "the Buyers"), a corporation duly organized and existing under the laws of Nigeria, with its head office at _____, Nigeria.

    WHEREAS, the Sellers are desirous of exporting the undermentioned products to the territory stipulated below; _____ and

    WHEREAS, the Buyers are desirous of importing the said goods for sale in the said territory;

    NOW, THEREFORE, it is hereby agreed and understood as follows:

Description of Goods: "Victory" Brand Portable Radio Cassette Tape Recorders Model VEC-886.

    Quantity: 5,000 sets with the packing as per Manufacturer's standard.

    Price: Total Amount HK $1,000,000 with the unit price of HK $200 per set FOB Hong Kong Net.

    Shipment: August 1989 subject to receipt of L/C by the end of May.

    Terms of Payment: By Confirmed Irrevocable L/C to be opened by Buyers.

    Remarks: Subject to the procurement of the necessary permits in China's Hong Kong and Nigeria. Insurance covers FPA and WA only if the Buyers require it to be added. Shipping particulars including marks and port of entry must be advised to the Sellers before the 20th July, 1989. The goods can only be sold in Nigeria and other parts of West Africa.

    Accepted and Signed by Buyers   Sellers
    Pan-African Trading Co., Ltd.   Victory Electronic
                                                 Trading Co., Ltd.

5. 通知、公告(Notice and Announcement)

(1) 报告会通知(Notice about a Report Meeting)

All are welcome

Under the Auspices of Foreign Language Department

a report will be given

on impression of visiting America

by Prof. xxx

in Room 101 of the Department

on Wednesday, October 21, 2007, at 3:30 p. m.

The Department Office

October 20,1991

(2) 停水通知(Notice of Water Supply Suspension)

Notice is hereby given that the water supply is not available from 7:00 a. m. to 11:00 p. m. tomorrow, owing to the repairs of the water pipes.

General Affairs Service

Nov. 2, 2007

(3) 公告(Announcement)

It is hereby informed that the Ministry of Environmental Protection of the People's Republic of China (hereinafter referred to as MEP) has been set up to replace the State Environmental Protection Administration of China (SEPA) in accordance with the Government Reshuffle Plan of the State Council approved by the First Session of the 11th National People's Congress (NPC). Hence, the official website of SEPA shall also be changed into the website of MEP with the new domain name of WWW. MEP. GOV. CN on March 18, 2008 in due form.

The new domain name shall be put into service on March 25, 2008.

Ministry of Environmental Protection of the People's Republic of China

March 18, 2008

6. 证书 (Certificate)

(1) 学位证书 (Certificate of Degree)

爱丁堡大学

学士学位证书

兹证明戴维·史密斯于1988年12月18日正式取得爱丁堡大学文学学士学位。

校长 ×××

注册主任 ×××

(2) 公证书 (Notarial Certificate)

Certificate No. 011023 (2007)

This is to certify that Liao Azhen (female, born on March 9, 1966) and Cheng Anzhong (male, born on November 1, 1963) registered a marriage in Wenzhou City, Zhejiang Province on March 20, 1989, and were mediated to divorce by Wenzhou City Lucheng District People's Court on October 28, 2004. In accordance with (2004) LY. MC. Zi. No. 121 Civil Mediation by Wenzhou City Lucheng District People's Court, the legitimate daughter of Liao Azhen and Cheng Azhong, Cheng Lin (female, born on June 10, 1989) will be fostered by Liao Azhen.

Wenzhou City Zhongxin Notary Public Office

Zhejiang Province

The People's Republic of China

(Seal)

Notary:

(Signature)

March 30, 2007

7. 合作倡议(Proposal for Cooperation)

(1) 出版社合作倡议(A Publisher's Proposal for Cooperation)

Modern Education Press is a large-scale education oriented publishing organizatition established lately by the Chinese government as an effort to accelerate China's publishing enterprise for conformity with the international regulations of the trade. It has 10 publishing centers under its organization, respectively managing a wide range of publishing businesses, including school course books, auxiliary education materials, dictionaries and tool books, books of world education, outstanding international readings and translations, etc. With the aim of forming up China's special base of education oriented publication, Modern Education Press has presently organized a strong staff of editors, specialized translators, and has built up a wide circulating network. It has already started its vigorous drive to introduce a great amount of books in relation to world education.

Modern Education Press sincerely hope to establish a friendly relation of cooperation with your organization, a specialized publishing organization with wide international influence. The fields of our proposed cooperation may include the following:

1. Mutual exchange of publishing information, including regular exchange of catalogues of the latest publications and, if necessary, catalogues of published books.

2. Establishing copyright cooperation channels, so that each side of us will enjoy the other's prior permission to translate and publish its books under friendly negotiation and contracts.

3. Establishing a mutual visit system which will ensure convenience of necessary visits to each other, though the expense of such visits will still be on the visiting party.

4. Other means of cooperation, which may satisfy our sincere wish to keep a lasting, friendly, and close cooperating relation with you for promoting our publishing enterprise, cultural exchange and mutual benefit.

Dr. Song Yifu
President of Modern Education Press

(2) 公司合作倡议 (A Company's Proposal for Cooperation)

> The Shanghai Group Company of SISU, established by the Shanghai International Studies University (SISU), is the first comprehensive group company among all the colleges and universities in Shanghai registered on the book of the Shanghai Municipal Industrial and Commercial Administration with the approval of the Shanghai Municipal Education and Public Health Office. With a comprehensive advantage in the talents and information in SISU, the group company works in accordance with the standardization of the modern enterprise system. Abiding by the enterprise principle of "lawful management, high prestige, first class service, and benefits to the people and the country", the authorities of the group company strive to build it into a strong foreign-languages-oriented economic entity of science and technology.
>
> With a total capital fund of 50 million *yuan* and 8 sub-companies, the Shanghai Group Company of SISU mainly provides foreign languages audio-visual products, foreign languages textbooks, periodicals and magazines, translation service, the training of the personnel to be working abroad, and tours both inside and outside China. To fit in with the intense competition of the market economy, the group company will continuously extend and strengthen its power, and strive for better conditions in order to have a multiplicity of management as in the development of science and technology projects, domestic and foreign trade, international tours, and the development of real estate; and the group company wishes to work in extensive cooperation with all circles in the society in an effort to make investment for the establishment of some joint ventures and cooperative ventures both inside and outside the Chinese borders as soon as possible.
>
> The Shanghai Group Company of SISU awaits with great enthusiasm people from all walks of life both at home and abroad coming for talks over business and long-term cooperation in an effort to become pioneers in a great joint undertaking.

8. 学生守则 (Rules for the Students)

(1) Love the motherland and the people, support the Communist Party of China, study diligently and be ready to contribute your bit to socialist modernization.

(2) Come to school punctually, do not be late for class, do not leave before a period ends and do not be absent from class without permission.

(3) Listen to the teachers' lectures attentively, be good at thinking independently about what you learn, and try to complete your homework earnestly.

(4) Persist in physical training so as to keep fit and take an active part in recreational activities.

(5) Pay attention to hygiene, do not smoke or drink alcohol and do not spit anywhere you like.

(6) Take an active part in physical labour, and be thrifty and simple in daily life.

(7) Observe school discipline, public order and laws and decrees of the State.

(8) Respect the teachers and elders, maintain close relations with your schoolmates, be polite to others and do not swear at or start a fight with others.

(9) Love the collective, protect state property and do not do anything harmful to the collective or others.

(10) Be modest and honest and try to correct any mistakes you make.

9. 年度工作总结(Annual Summing-Up Report)

Annual Summing-Up Report of Foreign Language Association for Middle and Primary Schools

The year of 2007 has passed. In order to overcome the shortcomings, add to the achievements and do still better in the future we sum up here what we have done in the past year. As all the members are united and co-operative, we have accomplished the following work successfully:

(1) New members have been recruited and the membership has been enlarged from 105 to 198.

(2) Eight open classes have been given this year so that teachers can learn from each other and improve their teaching methods.

(3) Meetings have been held once a month. All the participants are enthusiastic in exchanging their teaching experience and technique, and in the discussion of the questions they have met with in their teaching reform.

(4) A short-term training class has been set up in order to raise the quality of new teachers.

(5) "English Corner" has been set up in Workers' Cultural Palace. Teachers and students can practise their oral English together with foreign tourists.

(6) Scholars and specialists at home and abroad have been invited to give academic lectures so as to stimulate the influx of teaching experience and get the latest information about foreign language teaching.

(7) Two collections of research papers on English teaching have been published. It has won the favourable comments from English teachers both in middle schools and in primary schools.

10. 序、后记、摘要（Foreword, Afterword and Abstract）（杜争鸣 译）

(1)

Foreword to *Discover Zhujiajiao in Shanghai*
Jiang Yao (Governor of Qingpu District, Shanghai)

Zhujiajiao, a well-known outskirt town of Shanghai, is situated in the west of the city in its Qingpu District on the beautiful water land by Dianshan Lake, bordering Zhejiang and Jiangsu Provinces. To the pride of the sober mannered local people, it is historically renowned as a typical Yangtze Delta water town of abundant natural produce and fine scene.

A birthplace of Shanghai area's earlier civilization, Zhujiajiao began to have agriculture as early as 6,000 years ago. It was part of the ancient Wu State's territory during the period of the Three Kindoms, became prosperous during the Tang and Song Dynasties, and evolved as a trading center later in the Song and Yuan period (when it was called Zhujiacun, namely the Zhu's Village). The town formed on the basis of this village during Wanli Emperor's reign of the Ming Dynasty. It kept developing later through the Ming and Qing Dynasties and eventually became a well-known trading center of all daily necessities.

Currently, with the further development of Shanghai as a metropolitan city, the protection and inheritance of Zhujiajiao's cultural heritage has drawn greater attention from the public. The town is officially accredited as one of the top four representative towns of Shanghai area. In 2006, after winning the gold medal for being one of the 50 places of the greatest international tourist attraction, it is being considered for applying for the status of historically and culturally renowned town of China. The local people are determined to further widen their vision and enhance their ambition in the process of its protection, appropriately handle the contradictions among protection, inheritance, utilization and development, with considerate planning and greater financial backing, so as to keep the original appearance of the water town in the course of improving its environment. The government will gradually utilize its resources in the mean time of protecting its cultural heritage.

Now with the approaching season of osmanthus, this picture book is out before you. And you will find in it original thoughts, unique perspectives and profound appreciation of Zhujiajiao's history, cultural development, general appearance and the people's customs. In it you will also experience the local people's respect for learning and morality, their open mind and containing spirit. Ultimately you will understand how they have made such great achievements.

As we present this book before you, we wish to welcome you to Zhujiajiao on behalf of the ingenuous and enthusiastic local people, who also believe that exchanges of experiences and ideas is to the benefit of us all.

August 2006

(2) **Preface to** *Glimpses Abroad* (Album)

This world lacks not in beauty, but discovery. —F. A. Rodin

To be honest, I really didn't believe—not at the moment if I do now—that such a stack of pictures could all be out of his own camera when Jianye handed them over to me for appreciation!

Born in the watery country of this lower reaches of the great Yangtz River, Jianye had been brought up with all that this inspiring land had to offer, and mostly the beauty that is reflected in everything. He made a good start from the very beginning of his career, first in the government office for about a dozen years, based on his profound learning and rich experience. So in my impression, he has been always busy, keeping himself on the run for lacking time. With his strong sense of responsibility, together with his desire to make everything perfect, it should not be hard to understand why he has made such great achievements in his career.

However, it is indeed hard for me to figure out how such a busy person like him could have spared the time for taking such a great quantity of pictures. With this question in mind, I studied his pictures as closely as possible. And then something dawned upon me: the fact that his work involved himself in frequent travel to places in all the major continents of the world, and that he has made full use of this advantage to take pictures of the changing world and its beautiful sights with his simple automatic camera. From city sights and buildings to natural views, environmental art objects, gardens, sculptures, views of folkways, nothing of special flavor escaped his shutter. Although an amateur in photography, Jianye could borrow the specialist point of view and find a unique structure, finely arranged light throw for his rich, implicative pictures, which have thoroughly represented the exotic beauty. His camera doesn't lie, nor does he lie with his camera. The result is the most natural freshness, fully reflecting the force of the artist's cultural background and deep insight. Or, to use the artist's own word, he has taken those pictures not for their own sake, but for the message of the time, and the pulse of civilization. It is for use as reference to us. We may say, for the same reason, that there is no doubt as to the contribution of the pictures to his own career.

As Denis Diderot said, "Wherever is affection, there is beauty." So in appreciating Jianye's works, I have felt the beauty embodied in the affection, another side of the artist as a man. Now that the carefully selected pictures in this album will be appreciated by more friends, it is indeed something worth congratulating. And it also remains my hope that Jianye's camera will know no bounds, and thus more and better pictures are yet to come out in the future.

Written on the Mid-Autumn Day, in Jian-Bo Study, South Quarter of Suzhou City.

(3)
Summary of the Contents in *My 5-Year-Experience in CPPCC*

Contained in the book are the author's rich personal experiences of participating in government affairs as a personage outside the Communist Party and a member of the 10th Chinese People's Political Consultative Conference, as well as his feelings and reflections about making contributions to the country with this given capacity.

The author has also explained his part in the function of the government by playing the integrated role combining that of a Non-CPC member, member of CPPCC, educator and government official, as well as his unique style formed on such an integration in dealing with government affairs.

The book falls into five sections, with each composed of six parts that are highly academic as well as enjoyable. Altogether, it contains 81 initiatives the author proposed to the government in the recent five years, with the government's replies attached. They are included under four subtitles: Feelings of Participating in Government, Discussions of Government Affairs on the Internet, Attentions of the Media, and Notes of the Two Congresses.

The value of this book lies in that it aims to mirror the process of the political democratization of China in a personal extent of the author, besides providing references for CPPCC members in participation of the government.

(4)
Preface to *The Return of Xu Beihong to the South: Special Exhibition of Xu Beihong's Classic Paintings in Suzhou*

Talking about Suzhou, a beautiful city located in East China, people would mention the old saying: "Paradise in Heaven, Suzhou and Hangzhou on earth." In spite of the change of outlook in every other Chinese city, with incessantly appearing high-rises in the economic boom, this city has nevertheless preserved its classicality as its architectural feature, fitting in harmoniously with its surrounding green hills and clear waters, and manifesting the profundity of Chinese culture.

Beihong was born in Yixing, Jiangsu Province, a place close to Suzhou. He had an unbreakable bond with Suzhou and regarded Suzhou as his hometown. During the eight years' War of Resistance against Japanese invasion, he resided in the mountain area of Chongqing and would often make hasty trips abroad, arranging exhibitions of paintings to raise donations for helping the refugees and the martyrs' families during the war. Then, after the war, he was sent to Beiping (today's Beijing) to take over the state-run Beiping Art College. Though he was busy with teaching there, his obsession for his hometown and the east never faded. After liberation of the country and the establishment of the People's Republic of China, he took the post of dean of the Central Academy of Fine Arts. In the year 1953, when the second National

Congress of Literary and Art Workers convened, he planed to go to the east to revisit the place and old friends he yearned for. However, unexpectedly, on the first day of the meeting, as executive president, he had meetings to attend all day; and in the evening, he had to accompany the delegate from Poland for dinner. Being excessively tired, he had a sudden attack of cerebaral haemorrhage. In spite of all rescue measures, he passed away.

Our memorial museum for Xu Beinghong attached great importance to this art exhibition in Suzhou, not only because Suzhou is famous throughout the country and abroad, but also because of the fact that Beihong has had a deep affection towards this city. He was a bosom friend of Yan Wenliang, a famous oil painter of Suzhou, who helped to teach for him in School of Art in Central University when Beihong was in Europe for exhibition of paintings in 1933. The two held the same view in art and they both had studied in the same state-run Art University of Paris. Besides, Beihong had given lectures at Art College of Suzhou, during which time, he gave a grand-sized Chinese painting as a present to Mr. Yan Wenliang. In that painting, he solemnly wrote four characters:"中流砥柱"(means "tower of strength"), with a line of additional small characters on the side:"素描者艺之操也"(means "the virtue of art lies in the reflection of the truth"). The deep friendship he experienced in Suzhou was a heat-warming comfort for Beihong in the 1930s, when he had a lot of suffering. We especially named this Exhibition of Paintings in Suzhou "Return of Beihong" to realize Beihong's dream which he was unable to fulfill in his life time. Bearing this purpose in mind, and with the generous help of Beijing Administration of Cultural Heritage, we have made ample preparation for this exhibition. We have brought with us the huge-sized oil painting "Tian Heng Wu Zhuang Shi"(Tian Heng and His Five Hundred Men), which was the first huge-sized oil painting he produced after Xu's return to China from his study in Europe.

It is certainly my pleasure and honor now that I can personally escort Beihong's original works to Suzhou for exhibition in spite of my age of eighty-five years. The forty-eight original works we brought here are all among Beihong's masterpieces, including oil and Chinese paintings, lineal drawings, sketches, watercolor paintings and pictures in crayons, all of which exhibit Beihong's adept and refined artistry, perfect organization, luxuriant use of color and the unique combination of Chinese and Western styles. They portray and mirror the reality and are treasures of his times.

Though born into a poor family, Beihong nevertheless made himself an international figure with his never yielding perseverance and incomparable diligence, which sets a fine example for the young people of today.

I wish this exhibition a complete success and would like to extend my heartfelt thanks to the leaders of Suzhou government and all the people who have helped to implement this exhibition.

主要参考文献

Austen, J. *Pride and Prejudice*. New York: Dover Publications, 1997.

Bronte, E. *Wuthering Heights*. London: Penguin English Library, 1985.

Galsworthy, J. *The Forsyte Saga*. London: Penguin Books, 1981.

Hardy, T. *Tess of the d'Urberbilles*. London: Macmillan London Ltd., 1975.

Joseph, S. M., et al. *Modern Chinese Stories and Novellas (1919–1949)*. New York: Columbia University Press, 1981.

Kelly, Jeanne & Mao, Nathan K. *Fortress Besieged*. Bloomington: Indiana University Press, 1979.

Lao, She. *Crescent Moon and Other Stories*. Beijing: Chinese Literature Press, 1997.

Scollon, R., et al. *Contrastive Discourse in Chinese and English*. Beijing: Foreign Language Teaching and Research Press, 2000.

Wells, H. G. *Four Comp Novels: Time Machine / The Island of Dr. M / Invisible Man / War of the Worlds*. Fall River: Fall River Press, 1994.

Yang, Hsien-yi & Yang, Gladys. *A Dream of Red Mansions*. Beijing: Foreign Language Teaching and Research Press, 1994.

(英)艾米莉·勃朗特. 呼啸山庄[M]. 杨苡,译. 南京:江苏人民出版社,1980.

蔡基刚. 英汉·汉英段落翻译与实践[M]. 上海:复旦大学出版社,2001.

蔡基刚. 英汉写作对比研究[M]. 上海:复旦大学出版,2001.

曹雪芹,高鹗. 红楼梦[M]. 北京:人民文学出版社,1982.

陈宏薇. 汉英翻译基础[M]. 上海:上海外语教育出版社,1998.

程镇球. 翻译问题探索——毛选英译研究[M]. 北京:商务印书馆,1980.

崔永禄,李静滢. 翻译本质与译者任务的一些思考[J]. 外语与外语教学,2004(3):39-42.

杜争鸣. "一国两制"原译切不可轻率改动[J]. 中国翻译,1997(2):55.

杜争鸣. 中国英语问题及其他[J]. 外语教学,1998(3):6-14.

杜争鸣. 英汉同声传译中的"断点"浅议[J]. 上海科技翻译,1998(4):14-15.

杜争鸣. 世界英语语境与中国英语中的语言与文化[J]. 外语与外语教学,1998(8):

14-16.

杜争鸣.《翻译与创作》:钩沉百年文学翻译的启示[J].中国翻译,2000(6):47-48.

杜争鸣.连贯与文体:关于英汉语篇翻译中的交际力度问题[J].外语研究,2002(1):57-61.

杜争鸣.一部学术精华,几个翻译问题——《结构功能语言学》(序)翻译中的可改进之处[J].中国翻译,2002(3):75-77.

杜争鸣."瓜子"英译质疑及其它[J].上海科技翻译,2004(4):26-27.

杜争鸣.是谁准备了这盛大的晚宴?——"隐形的译者"与"中国化"的美国前总统尼克松[J].中国翻译,2004(6):53-57.

杜争鸣.外语·翻译·文化[M].南京:东南大学出版社,2006.

杜争鸣.从苏州大学校训中管窥中英互译原理[J].苏州大学学报,2007(2):111-112.

杜争鸣,孟祥春.Workload Studies:一项以人为本的口译工作调研——国际会议口译协会(AIIC)译员"工作负荷研究"述评[J].中国翻译,2005(5):76-79.

杜争鸣,孟祥春.同声传译中的"等待"——一个值得商榷的问题[J].解放军外国语学院学报,2006(5):69-73.

杜争鸣,杨姗."红木"的中国文化内涵及其英译[J].中国科技翻译,2006(4):18-19.

冯朝雄,范贻光.苏州古典园林[M].杜争鸣,(美)篮雅安,译.北京:新世界出版社;中国对外翻译出版公司,2007.

冯庆华.实用翻译教程[M].上海:上海外语教育出版社,2002.

(英)格林.名誉领事[M].杜争鸣,译.南京:译林出版社,1999.

郭建中.文化与翻译[M].北京:中国对外翻译出版公司,2000.

何善芬.英汉语言对比研究[M].上海:上海外语教育出版社,2002.

胡适.中国的文艺复兴[M].邹小站,尹飞舟,等译.北京:外语教学与研究出版社,2000.

贾文波.汉英时文翻译[M].北京:中国对外翻译出版公司,1999.

康娟.英语专业八级考试翻译指南[M].青岛:中国海洋大学出版社,2007.

连淑能.英汉对比研究[M].北京:高等教育出版社,1993.

林语堂.吾国与吾民.北京:外语教学与研究出版社,2002.

刘传珠.翻译的本质:间接认识,易语表达[J].湛江师范学院学报,2004(5):91-95.

陆章一,蒋晓红.走进上海朱家角[M].杜争鸣,译.北京:中国对外翻译出版公司,2006.

鲁迅.鲁迅全集[C].北京:人民文学出版社,1981.

鲁迅.关于翻译的通信[C]//鲁迅全集(第4卷).北京:人民文学出版社,2005.

吕叔湘.中诗英译比录[M].上海:上海外语教育出版社,1980.

马祖毅.英译汉技巧浅谈[M].南京:江苏人民出版社,1980.

茅风华.英语专业八级全真题详解[M].上海:世界图书出版公司,2004.

米·居·奎维古尔.何为美国人[J].杜争鸣,译.中国翻译,2003(6):86-87.
南木.翻译理论与翻译技巧论文集[M].北京:中国对外翻译出版公司,1983.
潘文国.英汉对比纲要[M].北京:北京语言文化大学出版社,1997.
钱钟书.围城[M].北京:人民文学出版社,2001.
邱文生.文体与翻译层次[J].漳州师范学院学报(哲学社会科学版),1999(2):91-97.
汪榕培,尤志明,杜争鸣,编译.评弹精华:弹词开篇选[M].苏州:苏州大学出版社,2004.
王大伟.现代汉英翻译技巧[M].上海:世界图书出版公司,1999.
王宏.对当前翻译研究几个热点问题的思考[J].上海翻译,2007(2):4-8.
王寅.英汉语言区别特征研究[M].北京:新华出版社,1994.
王志远,主编译.世界名著鉴赏大辞典[Z].北京:中国书籍出版社,1991.
夏征农.辞海[Z].上海:上海辞书出版社,1999.
熊文华.汉英应用对比概论[M].北京:北京语言学院出版社,1997.
徐刚生.走进苏州平江[M].杜争鸣,译.北京:中国对外翻译出版公司,2006.
许渊冲,译.唐诗三百首(汉英对照)[M].北京:高等教育出版社,2000
杨莉藜.英汉互译教程[M].开封:河南大学出版社,1993.
杨自伍.英国散文名篇欣赏[M].上海:上海外语教育出版社,1995.
英帆,编译.外国领导人访华讲话选集(英汉对照)[M].北京:中国对外翻译出版公司,1988.
余高峰.英语专业八级历年全真试题解析[M].上海:华东理工大学出版社,2004.
喻云根.英美名著翻译比较[M].武汉:湖北教育出版社,1996.
翟玉章.罗素论人生[M].北京:世界知识出版社,2000.
张今,刘光耀.英语抽象名词研究[M].开封:河南大学出版社,1996.
张立民,阎兴朋,孙泰霖,等.英汉对照应用文大全[M].南京:江苏科学技术出版社,1994.
张培基,喻云根,等.英汉翻译教程[M].上海:上海外语教育出版社,1980.
张培基,译注.英译中国现代散文选[M].上海:上海外语教育出版社,2007.
张英霖.苏州古城地图集[M].苏州:古吴轩出版社,2004.
周大新.香魂女[M].北京:人民文学出版社,2016.
周向群.走进苏州[M].杜争鸣,译.北京:文化艺术出版社,2004.
朱建胜.苏州桥[M].苏州:古吴轩出版社,2005.
朱永新.吴文化读本[M].苏州:苏州大学出版社,2003.
庄绎传.英汉翻译练习集[M].北京:中国对外翻译出版公司,1984.
邹申.新编高等学校英语专业八级考试指南[M].上海:上海外语教育出版社,2005.
(英)伯特兰·罗素.罗素自传(第一卷)[M].胡作玄,赵慧琪,译.北京:商务印书馆,2002.

(英)简·奥斯汀.傲慢与偏见[M].孙致礼,译.南京:译林出版社,1990.

(英)简·奥斯汀.傲慢与偏见[M].方华文,译.南京:译林出版社,2011.

(英)简·奥斯汀.傲慢与偏见[M].王科一,译.上海:上海译文出版社,2013.

(英)托马斯·哈代.德伯家的苔丝[M].张谷若,译.北京:人民文学出版社,2020.

(英)威尔斯.摩若博士岛[M].杜争鸣,译.石家庄:河北科学技术出版社,1998.

(英)威廉·福克纳.美国,没有童年[M].贾文山,杜争鸣,译.北京:工人出版社,1988.

(英)夏洛蒂·勃朗特.简·爱[M].李霁野,译.西安:陕西人民出版社,1990.

(英)夏洛蒂·勃朗特.简·爱[M].祝庆英,译.上海:上海译文出版社,1990.

(英)夏洛蒂·勃朗特.简·爱[M].黄源深,译.南京:译林出版社,1994.

(英)伊迪思·内斯比特.追踪护身符[M].昌慧,杜争鸣,译.杭州:浙江文艺出版社,2006.

(英)约翰·高尔斯华绥.福尔赛世家[M].周煦良,译.上海:上海译文出版社,1993.

(加)罗森鲍姆.回荡的沉默:布鲁姆斯伯里文化圈侧影[M].杜争鸣,王杨,译.南京:江苏教育出版社,2006.